EYEWITNESS TRAVEL
SOUTHWEST USA
& LAS VEGAS

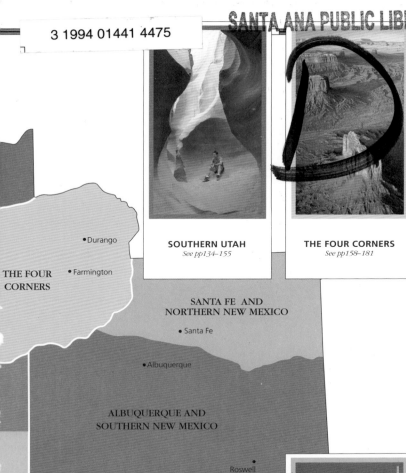

•Durango

THE FOUR
CORNERS

• Farmington

SOUTHERN UTAH
See pp134–155

THE FOUR CORNERS
See pp158–181

SANTA FE AND
NORTHERN NEW MEXICO

• Santa Fe

•Albuquerque

ALBUQUERQUE AND
SOUTHERN NEW MEXICO

Roswell
•

0 km   100

0 miles   100

**ALBUQUERQUE AND
SOUTHERN NEW
MEXICO**
See pp208–227

**SANTA FE AND
NORTHERN NEW
MEXICO**
See pp190–207

EYEWITNESS TRAVEL

SOUTHWEST USA
& LAS VEGAS

LONDON, NEW YORK,
MELBOURNE, MUNICH AND DELHI
www.dk.com

Produced by Duncan Baird Publishers, London, England
MANAGING EDITORS Michelle de Larrabeiti, Rebecca Miles
MANAGING ART EDITOR Vanessa Sayers
EDITORS Liz Atherton, Georgina Harris, Judith Ledger
DESIGNER Dawn Davies-Cook
DESIGN AND EDITORIAL ASSISTANCE Kelly Cody, Jessica Hughes
VISUALIZER Gary Cross
PICTURE RESEARCH Ellen Root
DTP DESIGNER Sarah Williams

CONTRIBUTORS
Randa Bishop, Donna Dailey, Paul Franklin,
Michelle de Larrabeiti, Philip Lee

PHOTOGRAPHERS
Demetrio Carrasco, Alan Keohane, Francesca Yorke

ILLUSTRATORS
Gary Cross, Eugene Fleurey, Claire Littlejohn,
Chris Orr & Associates, Mel Pickering, Robbie Polley,
John Woodcock

Reproduced by Colourscan (Singapore)
Printed and bound by South China Printing Co. Ltd., China

First American Edition, 2001

11 12 13 10 9 8 7 6 5 4 3 2

Published in the United States by
DK Publishing, 375 Hudson Street,
New York, New York 10014

Reprinted with revisions 2002, 2003, 2004, 2006, 2008, 2010

Copyright © 2001, 2010 Dorling Kindersley Limited, London
A Penguin Company

ISSN 1542-1554
ISBN 978 0 75666 195 3

FLOORS ARE REFERRED TO THROUGHOUT IN
ACCORDANCE WITH AMERICAN USAGE; IE THE "FIRST FLOOR"
IS AT GROUND LEVEL.

*Front cover main image: Mount Holmes, Lake Powell area,
Little Rockies, Utah*

MIX
Paper from
responsible sources
FSC
www.fsc.org FSC™ C018179

**The information in this
DK Eyewitness Travel Guide is checked regularly.**
Every effort has been made to ensure that this book is as up-to-date
as possible at the time of going to press. Some details, however,
such as telephone numbers, opening hours, prices, gallery hanging
arrangements and travel information are liable to change. The
publishers cannot accept responsibility for any consequences arising
from the use of this book, nor for any material on third party
websites, and cannot guarantee that any website address in this
book will be a suitable source of travel information. We value the
views and suggestions of our readers very highly. Please write to:
Publisher, DK Eyewitness Travel Guides,
Dorling Kindersley, 80 Strand, London WC2R 0RL, Great Britain.

◁ Tall saguaro cacti in the Sonoran Desert, southern Arizona

CONTENTS

View over Grand Canyon's
North Rim in northern Arizona

ARIZONA

Flute players petroglyph from
Walnut Canyon, Arizona

Mesa Arch overlooking Canyonlands National Park in southern Utah

Half-size replica of the Eiffel
Tower at Paris Hotel, Las Vegas

Hispanic pottery

Visitors enjoying a trail ride at a
dude ranch in southern Arizona

San Xavier del Bac Mission
in Tucson, southern Arizona
(see pp88–9)

HOW TO USE THIS GUIDE

This travel guide helps you to get the most from your visit to the Southwest US. *Introducing the Southwest* maps the region, and sets it in its historical and cultural context. The region includes the two states of New Mexico and Arizona, the city of Las Vegas, and sizeable chunks of Colorado and Utah. Each chapter describes important sights, using maps, photographs, and illustrations. Recommended restaurants and hotels are listed in *Travelers' Needs*, as is advice on accommodations and food. The *Survival Guide* has tips on such issues as transportation and tipping.

THE SOUTHWEST REGION BY REGION

The Southwest has been divided into five regions, each of which has its own chapter. Two of these regions are further divided into areas. All major towns and attractions have been numbered on an Area Map at the start of each chapter.

A locator map shows where you are in relation to the rest of the region.

Sights at a Glance lists the chapter's sights by category: Historic Towns and Cities, Areas of Natural Beauty, etc.

2 Area Map
An overview of the landscape and history is followed by a map that numbers and locates all sights.

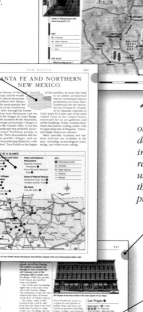

1 Regional Map
This gives an illustrated overview of the whole region, detailing the main places of interest. It shows the road and rail network and also provides useful hints on getting around the area both by car and by public transportation.

Each area of the Southwest can be identified by its color coding.

3 Detailed Information
All the important towns, important buildings in towns and cities, and other places to visit are described individually. They are listed in order, following the numbering on the Area Map. A map reference refers the reader to the road map inside the back cover.

LAS VEGAS

This unique city has its own chapter, which is introduced by a historical feature. The main sights are numbered and plotted on the *City Map*, as are points of interest in the Greater Las Vegas area. The information for all the sights is easy to locate within the chapter as it follows the numerical order on the map. The city has its own *Practical Information* section, which offers useful advice on shopping, entertainment, and gambling.

1 Introduction
The landscape, history, and character of Las Vegas are described here, showing how the city was developed and what it offers the visitor today.

2 City Map
For easy reference, sights are numbered and located on a map.

3 Street-by-Street Map
This provides a bird's-eye view of the heart of a sightseeing area.

A suggested route for a walk is shown in red.

Stars indicate the sights that no visitor should miss.

For all top sights, a Visitors' Checklist provides all the practical information you need to plan your visit.

4 Top Sights in the Southwest
These are given two or more full pages. Historic buildings are dissected to reveal their interiors; interesting districts are given street-by-street maps; national parks and forests have maps showing facilities and trails.

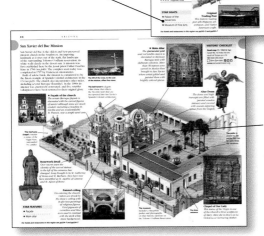

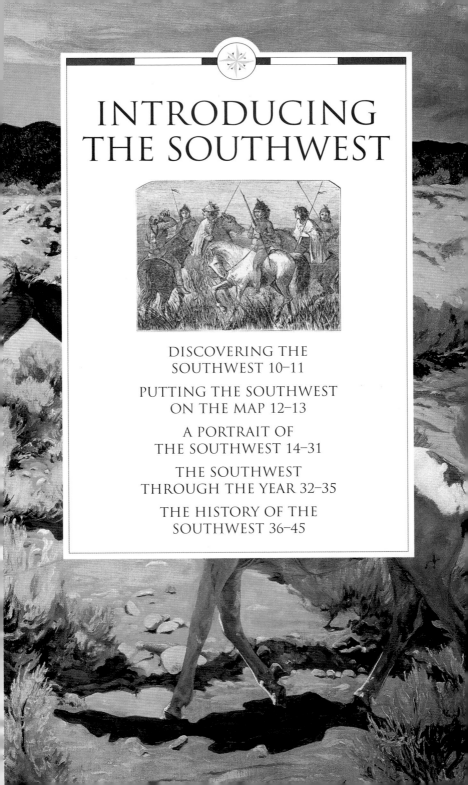

INTRODUCING
THE SOUTHWEST

DISCOVERING THE SOUTHWEST

The Southwest is the USA's most colorful region – from the red-rock monoliths of Utah, to Arizona's Grand Canyon, to the snow-white sand dunes of southern New Mexico. The stunning landscape is reason enough to come, but visitors will also discover ancient ruins and Native American pueblos, a vibrant Hispanic culture, stunning artworks, and fascinating wildlife. You can enjoy outdoor adventures in the mountains and canyons, or rest at an impressive range of top spas and golf courses. Las Vegas brings a different kind of color – its bright, brash neon lights make it a beacon of entertainment in the desert. These pages offer a brief overview of the highlights of each area.

Tall saguaro cactus, Arizona

GRAND CANYON AND NORTHERN ARIZONA

- Grand Canyon
- Petrified Forest National Park and Painted Desert
- Historic mining towns

Arizona's varied terrain ranges from mountains to grasslands and vast tracts of forest. The **Grand Canyon** *(see pp58–63)* is the region's biggest draw, offering hiking, river rafting, and other activities, in addition to the breathtaking scenery. Minerals created the amazing landscapes of the **Petrified Forest National Park** *(see p73)*, crossed by the famous **Painted Desert**, while a volcano formed **Sunset Crater** *(see p69)* and its lava field. **Sedona** *(see p73)* is surrounded by stunning red-rock country. Cool, shady **Oak Creek Canyon** *(see p69)* has hiking trails and swimming holes. **Flagstaff** *(see pp66–8)* is a pleasant base for exploring the region's historic mining towns and ancient Native American ruins.

PHOENIX AND SOUTHERN ARIZONA

- Top spas and golf courses
- Towering saguaro cacti
- Wild West towns

Phoenix *(see pp76–9)* boasts the Heard Museum and several attractions in its metropolitan area, such as the golf courses and spas of **Scottsdale** *(see p80)*. Tall

An aerial view of the magnificent Grand Canyon

saguaro cacti grow in abundance at **Saguaro National Park** *(see p86)*, near **Tucson** *(see pp84–5)*. Nearby is the **Arizona-Sonora Desert Museum** *(see p86)*, with its wealth of desert plants and wildlife, and the splendid **San Xavier del Bac Mission** *(see pp88–9)*. **Bisbee** and **Tombstone** *(see p92)* are historic Wild West towns, and there are desert landscapes to explore at **Organ Pipe Cactus** *(see p90)* and **Chiricahua** *(see p93)* national monuments.

The replica Manhattan skyline at the New York New York in Las Vegas

LAS VEGAS

- Fantastic theme hotels
- Glittering casinos
- World-class entertainment
- The Hoover Dam

The neon-lit boulevard known as the Strip is home to Las Vegas's extravagant hotels and glitzy casinos. Among the most lavish are the **Luxor** *(see p106)*, **New York New York** *(see p107)*, and **Mirage** *(see pp114–15)*, with its erupting volcano. Top international stars perform nightly, while the **Liberace Museum** *(see p109)* honors the city's greatest showman. All the bright lights are powered by the **Hoover Dam** *(see p120)*, and the adjacent reservoir provides fishing, boating, and watersports in the **Lake Mead National Recreation Area** *(see p120)*. The scenic beauty of **Valley of Fire State Park** *(see pp120–21)* and **Red Rock Canyon** *(see p121)* provide more escapes from the city.

◁ *The Southwest* (oil on canvas) by Walter Ufer (1876–1936)

SOUTHERN UTAH

- **Beautiful national parks**
- **Amazing red-rock formations**
- **Outdoor recreation**

The natural beauty of Southern Utah is preserved in its magnificent national parks. **Arches** *(see pp140–41)* and **Bryce Canyon** *(see pp152–3)* feature stunning red-rock formations; **Zion** *(see pp154–5)* has numerous hiking trails through its leafy canyon; and **Canyonlands** *(see p142)* is a vast rocky wilderness carved by the Colorado River. There are dramatic views of this mighty river from **Dead Horse Point State Park** *(see p143)*. The **Lake Powell and Glen Canyon National Recreation Area** *(see pp150–51)* offers outdoor recreation such as biking, boating, and watersports. **Moab** *(see p141)*, **Cedar City** *(see pp148–9)*, and other historic towns serve the region's many visitors.

An impressive rock arch at the Arches National Park, Utah

THE FOUR CORNERS

- **Stunning Rocky Mountain scenery**
- **Fascinating ancient ruins**
- **Monument Valley**
- **Native American reservations**

Ancient ruins left by the Ancestral Puebloan peoples dominate this region where the four Southwestern states meet. Some of the largest and

Remains of ancient Puebloan dwellings at Mesa Verde

best-preserved ruins are those at **Mesa Verde National Park** *(see pp180–81)*, **Chaco Culture National Historical Park** *(see pp174–5)*, and **Canyon de Chelly National Monument** *(see pp168–9)*. There is dramatic natural beauty, too, in the towering monoliths of **Monument Valley** *(see pp164–5)* and the grandeur of the Rocky Mountains. The **San Juan Skyway Tour** *(see p178)* features some of the most impressive scenery in the Rockies. The region is still home to Native peoples, and the **Hopi Indian Reservation** *(see p166)* and the **Hubbell Trading Post** *(see p167)* are well worth a visit.

SANTA FE AND NORTHERN NEW MEXICO

- **Superb history and art museums of Santa Fe**
- **Native American pueblos**
- **Historic mission churches**
- **Beautiful pottery, art, and architecture**

Striking architecture, historic sites, and a wealth of impressive museums make **Santa Fe** *(see pp192–9)* a favourite destination. From the **Georgia O'Keeffe Museum** *(see p194)* to the galleries on Canyon Road, Santa Fe is truly an artists' town. There are lovely historic mission churches here and at **Chimayo** *(see p203)*. A tour of the

Northern Pueblos *(see p202)* is a chance to visit Native American communities and perhaps purchase a piece of the region's famous pottery direct from the artist. **Taos** *(see pp204–5)* is another historic arts center with good museums. At **Taos Pueblo** *(see p206)*, the Indian community lives as their ancestors did in communal adobe houses. **Bandelier National Monument** *(see pp200–1)* has impressive ancient cliff dwellings.

ALBUQUERQUE AND SOUTHERN NEW MEXICO

- **Intriguing Indian petroglyphs**
- **Billy the Kid's outlaw trail**
- **White Sands National Monument**
- **Carlsbad Caverns**

Among the highlights of **Albuquerque** *(see pp210–15)* are fine museums and a picturesque Old Town. The Indian Pueblo Cultural Center and the **Petroglyph National Monument** *(see p215)* offer fascinating glimpses of early Native Americans, along with the **Acoma Pueblo** *(see p217)* and the **Gila Cliff Dwellings** *(see pp218–19)*. The trail of Billy the Kid passes through the Wild West towns of **Silver City** *(see p219)*, **Mesilla** *(see p222)*, and **Lincoln** *(see p225)*. Discover Space Age wonders at **Alamogordo** *(see p224)* and UFO mysteries at **Roswell** *(see p227)*. The snow-white sand dunes of **White Sands National Monument** *(see p223)* and the stunning cave formations in **Carlsbad Caverns** *(see pp226–7)* are natural marvels.

Petroglyphs on a basalt boulder in Petroglyph National Monument

Putting the Southwest on the map

For the purposes of this guide the Southwest
includes Arizona, New Mexico, the Four Corners
area, which takes in southwestern Colorado and
southern Utah, and the city of Las Vegas. The region
is contained by borders with Mexico in the south,
California in the west, and Texas in the east, and
covers around 326,000 sq miles (835,000 sq km). The
region is sparsely populated since 60 percent of its
population of around 10 million live in the cities.

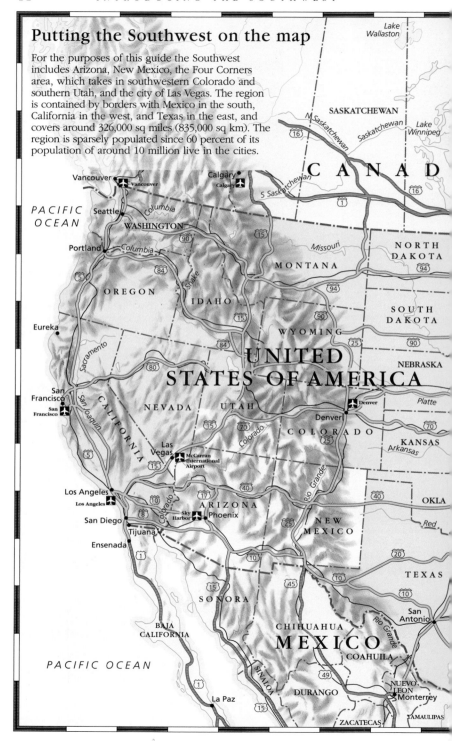

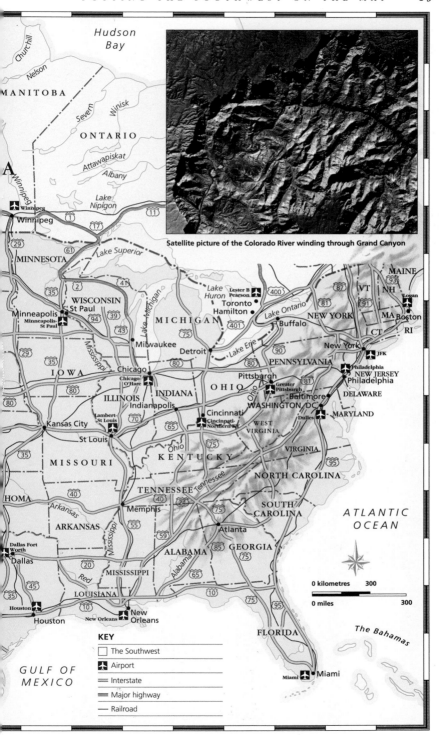

Satellite picture of the Colorado River winding through Grand Canyon

Hudson Bay

MANITOBA

ONTARIO

A

Lake Nipigon

Winnipeg

MINNESOTA

Lake Superior

WISCONSIN
St Paul

Minneapolis
Minneapolis-St Paul

MICHIGAN

Lake Huron

Lester B Pearson
Toronto
Hamilton

Lake Ontario

Buffalo

NEW YORK

MAINE

VT NH

MA Boston
Logan

CT RI

Milwaukee

Detroit

Lake Erie

New York

JFK

IOWA

Mississippi

Chicago
Chicago-O'Hare

ILLINOIS

INDIANA

Indianapolis

OHIO

Pittsburgh

PENNSYLVANIA

Greater Pittsburgh

WASHINGTON, DC

Baltimore

Philadelphia
NEW JERSEY
Philadelphia

DELAWARE

Kansas City

Lambert-St Louis

St Louis

Cincinnati
Cincinnati-Northern KY

WEST VIRGINIA

Dulles

MARYLAND

MISSOURI

Ohio

KENTUCKY

VIRGINIA

NORTH CAROLINA

HOMA

Arkansas

TENNESSEE

Tennessee

Memphis

SOUTH CAROLINA

ATLANTIC OCEAN

ARKANSAS

Mississippi

Atlanta

Dallas Fort Worth
Dallas

GEORGIA

ALABAMA

MISSISSIPPI

Alabama

Red

LOUISIANA

Houston
Houston

New Orleans
New Orleans

FLORIDA

The Bahamas

GULF OF MEXICO

0 kilometres   300

0 miles   300

Miami

KEY

☐	The Southwest
✈	Airport
═	Interstate
▬	Major highway
—	Railroad

A PORTRAIT OF THE SOUTHWEST

Distinguished by its dramatic landscape, the Southwest is a land of twisting canyons, cactus-studded desert, and rugged mountains. For more than 15,000 years, the region was inhabited by Native Americans, but by the 20th century Anglo-American traditions had mingled with those of the Hispanic and Native populations to create the Southwest's multicultural heritage.

America's Southwest includes the states of Arizona and New Mexico, southwestern Colorado and southern Utah, and the city of Las Vegas, Nevada. Perceptions of this region are influenced by the landscape: the red sandstone mesas of Monument Valley, the tall saguaro cacti in Arizona's Sonoran Desert, the staggering scale of Grand Canyon, and the adobe architecture of New Mexico. At the heart of the region is its defining geological feature – the Colorado Plateau – a rock tableland rising more than 12,000 ft (3,660 m) above sea level and covering a vast area

Skull of a buffalo

of around 130,000 sq miles (336,700 sq km). The plateau was created by the same geological upheavals that formed the Rocky Mountains. Subsequent erosion by wind, water, and sand molded both hard and soft rock to form the plateau's canyons, mesas, and mountains.

Many of these natural wonders are now protected by national parks, such as the Grand Canyon and Zion. The region's underground attractions are no less beautiful, with the cave formations of Carlsbad Caverns in New Mexico and the Kartchner Caverns in southern Arizona.

Cacti and dried chiles adorn this flower shop in Tucson's historic El Presidio district

◁ **Spring flowers, sand verbena, and dune primrose cover the desert landscape**

SOCIETY

The Southwest is a crossroads of the three great cultures that shaped America: Native American, Hispanic, and Anglo-American. The Spanish language is prominent, and everyday English is peppered with a range of Spanish phrases, reflecting a heritage stretching back to the 16th century: Spanish explorers were in the Southwest in 1540, 80 years before the Pilgrims landed at Plymouth Rock.

A host of Native American languages are also spoken across the Southwest, reflecting the history of the region's native inhabitants. The Hopi and other Pueblo peoples trace their ancestry back to the ancient peoples who built the cliff dwellings at Mesa Verde, Canyon de Chelly, and Chaco Canyon. The Navajo occupy the largest reservation in the US, stretching across the northern ends of both Arizona and New Mexico. The Apache and several other tribes also occupy land here. Today's Native populations have a hand in the government of their own lands and use a variety of ways to support their economies – through casinos, tourism, the production of coal, and crafts such as pottery, baskets, and Hopi *kachina* dolls. Some Native festivals and dances are open to visitors, although, for spiritual reasons, some are private affairs.

Hopi
kachina **doll**

A trinity of religions is dominant in the Southwest. Native American spiritual beliefs are complex, as each tribe has different practices often tied to ancestors and the land. The Roman Catholicism brought here by the conquering Spanish is the main religion in much of the region, although some Protestant denominations are also prominent. Utah's residents, however, are predominantly Mormon.

POLITICS

When Arizona and New Mexico gained statehood in 1912, they became part of the democratic republic of the United States of America. Today, they are the nation's fifth- and sixth-largest states. Although Phoenix is the fifth most populated city in the US, the region still remains one of the least populated.

The cities of Phoenix, Tucson, Santa Fe, Albuquerque, and Las Cruces account for around 60 percent of the

Looking out from Mummy Cave Overlook in Canyon de Chelly's Canyon de Muerto

Mountains rise behind the towering walls of Hoover Dam across the Colorado River bordering Nevada and Arizona

performers visit such cities as Phoenix and Las Vegas, which is world-renowned for its dazzling casinos.

One of the region's most famous attributes is the quality of light found in the hills of northern New Mexico. Georgia O'Keeffe's paintings of the local landscape in the 1940s helped to make the area around Santa Fe a mecca for all kinds of artists. Today, the city has the second-largest art trade in the US. Native artisans also produce fine artifacts: the pottery of Maria Martínez (1881–1980) of San Idelfonso Pueblo is highly regarded, as are the paintings of Navajo R. C. Gorman (1931–2005), and the work of Pueblo potter Nancy Youngblood Lugo.

Southwest's population. Such intense urbanization has put pressure on the region's resources, particularly water. In the 1930s, dam-building projects were initiated in the western states, starting with the Hoover Dam. By the 1960s, however, it was clear that in order to generate electricity, irrigate farms, and supply cities, more dams were needed. The controversial Glen Canyon Dam, opened in 1963, flooded a vast area of natural beauty, as well as Native ruins and sacred sites. Today, many local tribes have asserted ownership of the water on their lands.

CULTURE AND THE ARTS

Vast wilderness and a warm climate make outdoor leisure popular in the Southwest. There are miles of hiking trails, rivers for white-water rafting, lakes for watersports, ski resorts, and some of the US's finest golf courses. One of the best ways to experience the landscape is on a trail ride, while armchair cowboys can attend that great Southwestern event – the rodeo.

Phoenix, Tucson, Santa Fe, and Albuquerque are home to symphony orchestras, theater, opera, and dance companies. A flourishing Hispanic music scene and Native American traditional dances meet in the fusion sound of Carlos R. Nakai, a Navajo flautist who performs classical music and jazz. International star

Hikers on the Bright Angel Trail in Grand Canyon

The Southwest is as much a state of mind as it is a geographical region. The attractions of the landscape and a romantic sense of the past combine to conjure up the idealized legends of the "Wild West." For many visitors, the Southwest offers the opportunity to indulge that bit of cowboy in their souls.

Landscapes of the Southwest

The colorful, beautiful, and varied landscape of the Southwest has been shaped by volcanic eruption, uplift, and wind and water erosion. For much of the Paleozoic Era (between about 570 to 225 million years ago) the region was mostly covered by a vast inland sea that deposited over 10,000 ft (3,048 m) of sediment, which eventually hardened into rock. Following the formation of the Rocky Mountains, some 80 million years ago, rivers and rainfall eroded the rock layers and formed the deep canyons and arches that distinguish the landscape of the Southwest.

The central geological feature of the region is the Colorado Plateau, which covers some 130,000 sq miles (336,700 sq km). The plateau is cut through by many canyons, including Grand Canyon *(see pp58–63).*

Coral Pink Sand Dunes State Park's *shimmering pink sand dunes cover more than 50 percent of this 3,700-acre (1,497-ha) park* (see p149).

The butte formations of Monument Valley *(see pp164–5)* are the result of erosion and their tops mark the level of an ancient plain.

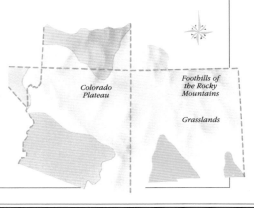

The mountains *of the Southwest are part of the Rockies and were formed during volcanic activity and continental plate movement some 65 million years ago. Snow-covered peaks, forests of pine and juniper, spruce and fir, streams and small lakes fed by snow melt, as well as alpine meadows are all found in this area.*

GEOGRAPHICAL REGIONS

Despite the great variations in the landscape, more than 70 percent of the land is classified as desert, with four distinct areas: the Great Basin, Chihuahuan, Sonoran, and Mojave deserts *(see pp20–21).* Each area supports flora and fauna uniquely adapted to their harsh environment.

KEY

- Great Basin Desert
- Chihuahuan Desert
- Sonoran Desert
- Mojave Desert

Colorado Plateau

Foothills of the Rocky Mountains

Grasslands

Large areas of grassland *once covered the broad river basins of New Mexico and Arizona. However, little of this landscape remains as it was largely turned to desert through overgrazing by Anglo-American ranchers in the 1880s.*

Canyons *such as this one at Zion National Park (see pp154–55) started life when a stream began to cut a relentless path into the rock. As the cut grew deeper, erosion by wind, rain, and ice began widening it, and the stream carried away the debris.*

The orange sand of Monument Valley's desert floor is dotted with sagebrush.

MESAS, BUTTES, AND SPIRES

Like canyons, mesas come in many sizes. Some very large ones measure over 100 miles (161 km) across and are often the result of land being forced up by geological forces. Other mesas, buttes, and spires are hard-rock remains left behind as a large plain cracked, and then eroded away.

The Colorado Plateau *is crossed by river-forged canyons. Elevations here range from 2,000 ft (600 m) above sea level to around 13,000 ft (3,900 m). Dramatic variations in the landscape include desert, verdant river valleys, thickly forested peaks, and eroded bizarre sandstone formations.*

Desert Flora and Fauna

Despite the fact that around 70 percent of the Southwest region is occupied by desert, it is not an arid, lifeless wasteland. There are four distinct deserts: the Sonoran, the Chihuahuan, the Great Basin, and the Mojave. The Sonoran Desert has one of the richest arrays of flora and fauna in the country. The Chihuahuan Desert supports hardy yuccas and agaves, and its hills and plains are covered with a dry, wheat-colored grass. The Great Basin is a cooler desert and home to a variety of grasses and desert animals. Spring rains and run-off from the mountains can transform even the driest deserts. At such times some 250 species of flower bloom in the Mojave.

All living things in these southwestern desert regions adapt remarkably well to their harsh environment; the plants in particular are capable of storing water when it is available and using it sparingly during dry periods.

Bighorn sheep *are shy, elusive creatures and are not easily spotted. Now a protected species, they are being gradually reintroduced throughout the desert areas.*

THE SONORAN
Found in southern Arizona, the Sonoran's summer "monsoons" and winter storms make it the greenest of the deserts. It is famous for the tall saguaro cactus *(see p86)*, some of which attain heights of 50 ft (15 m) and provide a home for such desert animals as the Gila woodpecker and the elf owl.

THE CHIHUAHUAN
Mainly found in Mexico, the Chihuahuan also reaches north to Albuquerque, New Mexico, and into parts of southeastern Arizona. Cacti, agaves, and yuccas, and lizards, rattlesnakes, and coyotes survive in conditions that include snowfall in winter and high temperatures and thunderstorms in summer.

The desert tortoise *can live for more than 50 years. It is now a protected species and is increasingly difficult to spot.*

The javelina *is a strange piglike mammal that wanders the Chihuahuan and Sonoran deserts in small packs.*

Prickly pear cacti *flower in spring and are among the largest of the many types of cacti that flourish in the Sonoran Desert.*

Yucca plants *have been gathered for centuries and have many uses: their fruit can be eaten, and the roots make shampoo.*

DANGERS IN THE DESERT

The danger of poisonous desert creatures has often been exaggerated. Although some desert creatures do, on rare occasions, bite or sting people, the bites are seldom fatal unless the victims are small children or have serious health problems. To avoid being hurt, never reach into dark spaces or up onto overhead ledges where you can't see. Watch where you place your feet, and shake out clothes and shoes before putting them on. Never harass or handle a poisonous creature. If you are bitten, stay calm and seek medical help immediately.

The desert scorpion *is golden in color. Its bite is venomous so anyone who has been bitten should go to a hospital for an antidote.*

The Gila monster *is the only venomous lizard in the US. It is a slow-moving but rarely seen inhabitant of the desert regions, and will only bite if it feels threatened.*

THE GREAT BASIN

With its canyons, cliffs, mesas, and buttes, the landscape of the Great Basin Desert appears most characteristic of the region. It extends from the far northwest corner of Arizona into eastern Utah and Oregon, and its scattering of cacti, sage, and mesquite is home to the bighorn sheep and various types of rattlesnake.

THE MOJAVE

This vast desert extends into central and northern Arizona. The Mojave is dry for most of the year, but a small amount of winter rain results in a display of wildflowers in spring. Other flora and fauna found here include creosote bush, cacti, yucca, jackrabbits, desert tortoises, and bighorn sheep.

Sagebrush *is a pervasive sub-shrub that covers vast areas of the cooler Great Basin Desert. It smells of sage.*

The blacktailed jackrabbit *is born with a full coat of muted fur to camouflage it from predators such as the coyote.*

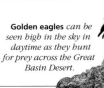

Golden eagles *can be seen high in the sky in daytime as they hunt for prey across the Great Basin Desert.*

The Joshua tree *was named by Mormons who pictured the up-raised arms of Joshua in its branches.*

Architecture of the Southwest

The history of architecture in the Southwest reaches back to the Ancestral Puebloan or Anasazi builders of such cities as Mesa Verde *(see pp180–81)*, demonstrating skilled craftsmanship. Across the region, historic architecture can be seen in many towns and cities, with the adobes of their old-town districts arranged around a central plaza. But there are also other architectural styles, from the Spanish Colonial of the 18th century to those of the 19th and early 20th century. Wooden storefronts, Victorian mansions, and miners' cottages all lend a rustic charm to many mountain towns, and one of the 20th century's most famous architects, Frank Lloyd Wright, set up an architectural school in Scottsdale *(see p81)*.

San Felipe de Neri Church, Albuquerque Old Town

TRADITIONAL ADOBE

Adobe ovens *(hornos)* at El Rancho de las Golondrinas

The traditional building material of the southwestern desert is adobe, a mixture of mud or clay and sand, with straw or grass as a binder. This is formed into bricks, which harden in the sun, then built into walls, cemented with a similar material, and plastered over with more mud. Adobe deteriorates quickly and must be replastered every few years. Modern adobe-style buildings are often made of cement and covered with lime cement stucco painted to look like adobe. Original dwellings had dirt floors and wooden beams *(vigas)* as ceiling supports. Roofs were flat, with pipes *(canales)* for water run-off.

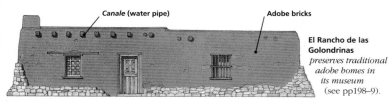

Canale (water pipe)

Adobe bricks

El Rancho de las Golondrinas *preserves traditional adobe homes in its museum* (see pp198–9).

SPANISH COLONIAL

In the 17th and 18th centuries, Spanish Colonial missions combined the Baroque style of Mexican and European religious architecture with native design, using local materials and craftsmen. This style underwent a resurgence in the 20th century as Spanish Colonial Revival, from 1915 to the 1930s, being incorporated into private homes and public buildings. Red-tiled roofs, ornamental terracotta, and stone or iron grille work were combined with white stucco walls. A fine example is Tucson's Pima County Courthouse *(see p84)*, with its dome adorned with colored tiles.

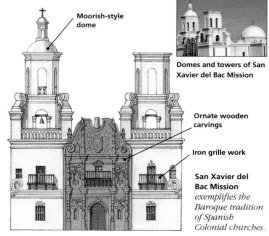

Moorish-style dome

Domes and towers of San Xavier del Bac Mission

Ornate wooden carvings

Iron grille work

San Xavier del Bac Mission *exemplifies the Baroque tradition of Spanish Colonial churches.*

MISSION REVIVAL

Similar in spirit to Spanish Colonial trends, the early 20th-century Mission Revival style is characterized by stucco walls made of white lime cement, often with graceful arches, flat roofs, and courtyards, but with less ornamentation. A fine example of a Mission Revival-style bungalow is the J. Knox Corbett House in Tucson's Historic District *(see p84)*. Built of brick but plastered over in white to simulate adobe, it has a red-tile roof and a big screen porch at the back.

Façade of the J. Knox Corbett House

Red-tiled roof   **White plaster**

J. Knox Corbett House *in Tucson was designed in the popular Mission Revival style by the Chicago architect David Holmes in 1906.*

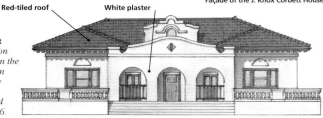

PUEBLO REVIVAL

Santa Fe Museum of Fine Arts

Pueblo Revival was another southwestern style that became particularly fashionable in the first three decades of the 20th century. It featured adobe or simulated adobe walls, with projecting *vigas*, and flat roofs with *canales*. The second and third stories were usually set back to resemble multistory pueblo dwellings, such as Taos Pueblo *(see p206)*, hence the name. Features include rounded parapets, framed portal windows, and wood columns. This style has been used frequently in public buildings; the Museum of Fine Arts in Santa Fe *(see p194)* is an outstanding example.

Framed portal window   **Flat roof**   **Rounded parapet**

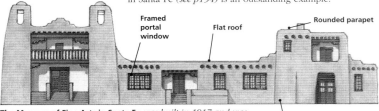

The Museum of Fine Arts in Santa Fe *was built in 1917 and was the first building in Pueblo Revival style in the city. A central courtyard providing shade from the sun is one of its features.*

Adobe wall

CONTEMPORARY ARCHITECTURE

Two of America's most prominent architects, Frank Lloyd Wright (1867–1959) and Paolo Soleri (*b.* 1919), practiced in the Southwest. Wright's "organic architecture" advocated the use of local materials and the importance of the setting. His architectural complex at Taliesin West *(see p81)* included a school, offices, and his home. It was built from desert stones and sand, and the expansive proportions reflect the Arizona desert. In the 1940s, Italian Soleri studied at Taliesin. In 1956 he established the Cosanti Foundation *(see p81)* devoted to "arcology," a synthesis of architecture and ecology that minimizes the waste of energy endemic in modern towns.

Interior of Taliesin West, designed by Frank Lloyd Wright

Colonizers of the Southwest

The remote wilderness areas of the Southwest were among the last regions of the US to be colonized by Anglo-Americans, in the mid- to late 19th century. The Spanish were the first Europeans to reach this area in the 1500s, led by soldier and explorer Francisco Vasquez de Coronado (1510–54), and Santa Fe was established in 1610. In 1752, the Spanish established the first European settlement in Arizona at Tubac. Kit Carson and fellow fur trappers explored east–west routes in the mid-19th century, while the Mormons founded Salt Lake City in the 1840s. In the later 19th century, explorers and prospectors, most notably US national hero John Wesley Powell, traveled across the region.

Inscription Rock *rises over a natural spring in New Mexico (see p217), and was a resting place for travelers over centuries. The rock features Zuni petroglyphs and graffiti, including Oñate's carved name.*

The Butterfield Stage route *was established in 1858. Sanctioned by Congress to provide a twice-weekly service for isolated Westerners, it aided the establishing of settlements in remote areas.*

ROUTES OF THE COLONIZERS

The promise of gold brought the first Spanish travelers to the Southwest in the 1500s. Various groups of colonizers and traders soon followed, forging many new routes across this rugged region.

KEY

▬	Coronado Trail
▬	Oñate Trail
▬	Santa Fe Trail
▬	Butterfield Stage route
▬	Old Spanish Trail
▬	Powell Expedition
▬	Anza Trail
▬	Camino Real
--	State boundaries

UTAH

NEVADA

CALIFORNIA

ARIZONA

Los Angeles

Fort McDowell

San Diego

Fort Yuma

Tucson

Colorado River

MEXICO

Juan Bautista de Anza, *Spanish commander of the Tubac settlement (see p90), explored the Anza Trail from 1774 to 1776. Reaching the Pacific Coast, Anza went on to found San Francisco.*

JOHN WESLEY POWELL (1834–1902)

Raised in Illinois, John Wesley Powell was by any standards a remarkable man. An early interest in natural history led him to embark on long, solitary expeditions into the outback to collect geological and botanical samples. In 1860, he enlisted in the Union army and became a major in the Civil War. He lost an arm at the Battle of Shiloh, and the pain was with him for the rest of his life. He led two expeditions down the Colorado River, in 1869 and 1871, and went on to run the new US Geological Service and the Bureau of American Ethnology. He was a staunch campaigner for Native American rights.

John Wesley Powell with Ute Native *(see p27)*

The Powell Expedition was launched in 1869 when John Wesley Powell and nine companions pushed four wooden boats out into the Green River of Wyoming bound for the Colorado River. Several weeks later, Powell's party emerged at the western end of Grand Canyon *(see p143)*.

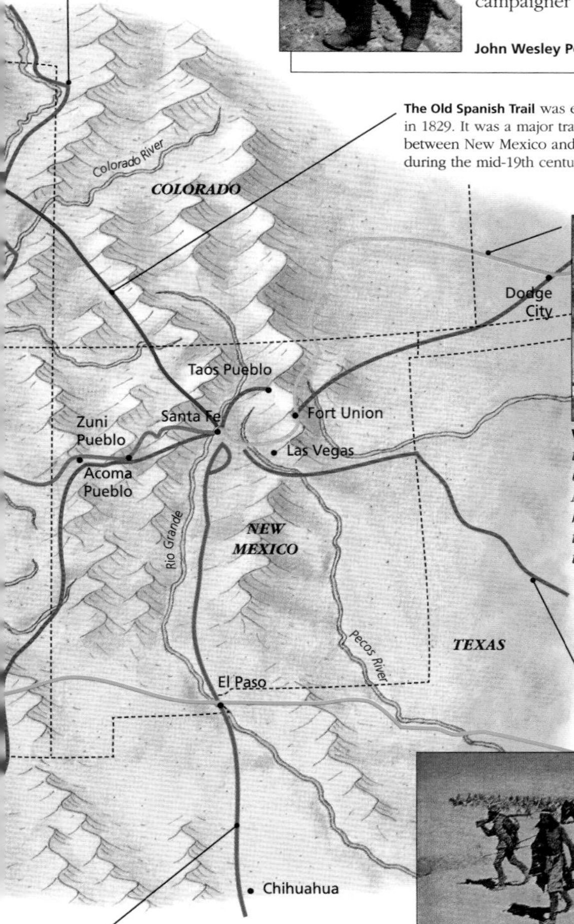

The Old Spanish Trail was established in 1829. It was a major trading route between New Mexico and California, during the mid-19th century.

William Becknell *first traveled the Santa Fe Trail in 1821, bringing goods by wagon from Missouri. Spanish soldiers bought his wares, and then the wagon trains followed, bringing welcome trade to the region* (see p42).

COLORADO

Colorado River

Dodge City

Taos Pueblo

Zuni Pueblo

Santa Fe

Fort Union

Las Vegas

Acoma Pueblo

Rio Grande

NEW MEXICO

Pecos River

TEXAS

El Paso

| 0 km | 100 |
| 0 miles | 100 |

Chihuahua

Juan de Oñate, a Spanish fortune-seeker, first traveled the Camino Real in 1598. He named part of this harsh, desert path "Journey of the Dead" but safely reached the Rio Grande *(see p39)*.

Francisco Vasquez de Coronado (1510–1554) *headed north from Mexico in 1540 with 336 soldiers and 1,000 Native Americans to spend two years exploring the region. His route became the Coronado Trail.*

Native Cultures of the Southwest

Hopi wicker plaque

The Native peoples of the Southwest have maintained many of their distinct ways of life, in spite of more than 400 years of hardship since the arrival of the Spanish in 1539. Disease, armed conflict, and brutal attempts at cultural assimilation have forged the determination of Native groups to retain their cultural identity. Since the mid-20th century they have led political campaigns for the restoration of homelands and compensation for past losses.

Today, there are more than 50 Native reservations in the Southwest, the Navajo Reservation being the largest. Native peoples are found across the region, working in cities and running modern farms. In most tribes, a growing economy based on tourism and gambling has brought much-needed revenue, but battles over land rights and environmental issues are ongoing.

Rodeo at a Mescalero Apache reservation near Ruidoso, New Mexico

THE APACHE

Despite their reputation as fierce warriors, reinforced by their legendary leaders Cochise and Geronimo *(see p42)*, the Apache were mainly hunter-gatherers thought to have roamed south from their Athabaskan-speaking homelands in northern Canada during the 15th century. Just as, historically, the Apache lived in bands, so today they are divided into three main groups: the Jicarilla, Mescalero-Chiricahua, and Western Apaches.

Successful management of their natural resources has ensured a degree of economic stability. The Jicarilla Reservation in northern New Mexico is noted for its excellent hunting and fishing programs, and the Mescalero Reservation in southern New Mexico, near the city of Ruidoso *(see p224)* boasts a ski area and a casino.

Visitors are welcome at the Apache reservations, to watch rituals such as the Nah'ih'es or Sunrise Ceremony which marks a girl's transition to womanhood. Dances, festivals, and rodeos are also held on reservations *(see pp32–5)*.

THE NAVAJO

With a population of more than 200,000, the Navajo Nation is the largest reservation in the Southwest, covering more than 25,000 square miles (64,750 sq km) in Arizona, New Mexico, and southern Utah. The spiritual center of the Navajo Nation is Canyon de Chelly *(see pp168–71)*, where Navajo

farmers still live, tending the sheep that were introduced by the Spanish and using their wool to make rugs.

The Navajo are generally welcoming to visitors and act as guides in Monument Valley and other sites on their land *(see pp164–5)*. Until 2008 when they opened Fire Rock Casino in New Mexico, they resisted building casinos to raise money, basing their economy on tourism and the sale of natural resources such as oil, coal, and uranium. Additional casinos are now planned, reducing their dependence on industrial practices such as strip-mining.

While many Navajo now live off the reservation in cities and towns, the traditional dwelling, the hogan, remains an important focus of their cultural life. Today's hogan is an octagonal wood cabin, often fitted with electricity and other modern amenities, where family gatherings take place.

Navajo religious beliefs are still bound up with daily life, with farmers singing corngrowing songs and weavers incorporating a spirit thread into their rugs. Colorful sand paintings play a part in healing ceremonies, which aim to restore *hozho*, or harmony, to ill or troubled individuals.

Navajo Indian woman shearing the wool from a sheep

THE PUEBLO PEOPLE

Comprising 20 tribes in New Mexico, including the Zuni, and the Hopi in Arizona, the Pueblo people share religious and cultural beliefs. However, there are

HOPI SPIRITUALITY

Religion is a fundamental element of the Hopi lifestyle. Their religious ceremonies focus on *kachina* (or *katsina*), spirit figures which symbolize nature in all its forms. Familiar to visitors as the painted, carved wooden dolls available in many gift stores, the *kachina* lie at the heart of Hopi spirituality. During the growing season (December to July), these spirit figures are represented by *kachina* dancers who visit Hopi villages. During the rest of the year, the spirits are believed to reside in a shrine in the high San Francisco Peaks, north of Flagstaff. Hopi religious ceremonies are often held in the *kiva*, a round underground chamber, usually closed to visitors *(see p161)*. Other Pueblo tribes also use kivas for ceremonial events, a practice thought to date from the days of the Ancestral Puebloans.

Young Hopi Rainbow Dancer

linguistic differences, with five languages spoken in different pueblos. Most Pueblo tribes trace their ancestry to the Ancestral Puebloan people *(see pp160–61)*, who spread across the area from around 300–200 BC. Acoma Pueblo, also known as "Sky City" because of its high position on a sandstone mesa, is thought to be among the oldest inhabited pueblos in the country. Nineteen of the pueblos are strung out along the fertile valley of the Rio Grande River Valley. Their history and varied culture is traced at Albuquerque's impressive Indian Pueblo Cultural Center *(see pp214–15)*.

Today, most pueblos produce distinctive arts and crafts, such as the artistic pottery of the Hopi or the fine jewelry of Zuni. The colorful ceremonies of the Rio Grande Pueblos vary from village to village, with the Corn Dance being the most common. Held on various dates from late spring to summer *(see p33)*, the dance is meant to insure a successful harvest. Visitors should behave respectfully, remembering that despite the festive atmosphere, these dances are religious rituals. Much Pueblo ceremony is carried out in private, away from the eyes of tourists.

Tohono O'odham painters restore frescoes at San Xavier del Bac

THE TOHONO O'ODHAM

Along with their close relatives, the Pima people, the Tohono O'odham live in southern Arizona's Sonoran Desert. Due to the harsh nature of the environment here, neither tribe has ever been moved off its ancestral lands. However, both tribes are among the most anglicized in the region. The Pima were guides to the US Army during the Indian Wars of the 1860s. Today's Tohono O'odam are mainly Christian, the mission church of San Xavier del Bac is on Tohono O'odham land south of Tucson *(see pp88–9)*, but still hold some of their traditional ceremonies, such as the Nawait or Saguaro Wine Festival and the Tcirkwena Dance. They are also known for their fine basketwork.

THE UTE

This tribe once reigned over a vast territory. As late as the 1850s their lands covered 85 percent of Colorado. Steady encroachment by settlers and mining interests eventually forced them to resettle. Today, the Ute welcome visitors to their two reservations along the southern Colorado border. The Ute Mountain Reservation is home to the little known but spectacular Ancestral Puebloan ruins of Ute Mountain Tribal Park *(see p172–3)*, and the southern Ute Reservation attracts thousands of visitors each year to the popular Sky Ute Casino, Lodge, and Museum. The southern Utes also hold a colorful Bear Dance on Memorial Day weekend that is open to the public.

Ute woman sewing moccasins with Mount Ute in the background

Native Art of the Southwest

Hopi-made coiled basket

The Native peoples of the American Southwest have a proud artistic heritage. They produced painted pottery, basketwork, and jewelry of distinction for centuries, often using stylized images of animals and plants to express their spiritual relationship with nature. As the region's tourist trade developed, in the 19th century, such products became sought after by visitors. In the 20th century a Native fine art movement began with watercolors, which initially depicted Native ceremonies. Such works proved popular with collectors and marked the beginning of an interest in and market for southwestwern Native art. Today, artists work in all media, including sculpture, video, and installations, and in all styles such as abstract expressionism or realism.

Basketwork *is a tradition associated with all Native peoples of the Southwest. Braided, twined, or coiled from willow or yucca leaves, the baskets are decorated differently according to the tribe.*

Rugmaking *traditions in the Southwest belong to the Navajo and Pueblo, with Puebloan examples dating from prehistoric times. Navajo weaving is best known; these rugs were sought after by tourists as early as the mid-1800s, and by the late 19th century colorful regional distinctions emerged.*

NATIVE AMERICAN PAINTING

The Apache developed the art of animal-skin painting in which warriors celebrated their deeds in pictographs. Designs, often scenes of men and horses in battle or hunting, were scratched on the surface and color added with bone or brush. After 1900 a fine art movement developed, including fine impressionistic and abstract works such as *Red Tailed Hawk* (1986) by Hopi/Tewa artist Dan Namingha.

Pottery *originated around 200 BC with the coiled pots of the Mimbres people. These mid-20th-century pots are a polished blackware jar from San Ildefonso Pueblo (left) and a patterned jar from Acoma (above).*

Contemporary sculpture *by Native American artists can be seen in galleries across the Southwest. They include this piece called* Dineh *(1981) by famous American sculptor Allan Houser. Dineh is the word the Navajo use to describe themselves. This is a modernist work, cast in bronze, whose smooth planes and clean lines appear to represent the dignity and strength of this couple.*

EARLY NATIVE AMERICAN ART

Outstanding examples of early Southwestern pottery, basketwork, and hide paintings have been marvelously preserved because of the area's dry climate, in spite of the fact that they are made from perishable organic materials such as clay, yucca fiber, and painted animal skins. As a result, more is known about early indigenous art here than in any other part of North America. The earliest pieces date back to around 200 BC, with textiles a later development. By AD 600, the styles of the three main groups: the Hohokam, Mogollon, and Ancestral Puebloan peoples had begun to merge and to absorb outside influences, seen in the Mexican designs on some ancient pots.

Ancient pottery bowl

Silverwork *has been produced by the Navajo, Zuni, and Hopi peoples for centuries. Since the mid-19th century, Navajo jewelers have incorporated Spanish styles. Zuni and Hopi silver is made in a different way. They adopted an intricate overlay process in the 1930s, distinguished by raised silver patterns against a dark background.*

Carving *focuses mainly on wooden dolls, or* kachinas, *whittled mostly from pine or cottonwood. The Pueblo peoples, especially the Hopi, are noted for their masked figurines, which depict* kachina *spirits.*

The Southwest: Backdrop for the Movies

The panoramic desert landscape of the Southwest is familiar the world over thanks to the countless movies that have been filmed here. As legendary actor John Wayne once said: "TV you can do on the back lot; for the real outdoor dramas, you have to do them where God put the West." Monument Valley *(see pp164–5)* is famous for its association with John Ford's Westerns, while the stark beauty of southern Utah, particularly around the Moab and Kanab areas, has appeared in several films. The popular idea of the "Wild West" *(see pp54–5)* has been formed more through film than by any other medium, and visitors to the Southwest may find much of its scenery strangely familiar. Many TV series and commercials have also been shot here.

Old Tucson Studio *was built for the 1940 motion picture* Arizona. *The studio is still a popular movie location and is now also home to a family-oriented, Wild West theme park (see pp86–7).*

Johnson Canyon, *near Kanab* (see p148), *was the location of the 1962 film* How the West was Won. *It is a western town set that was built for the 1952 movie* Westward the Women. *Today, the set is open to visitors.*

JOHN FORD AND MONUMENT VALLEY

John Ford was not the first director to shoot a movie using Monument Valley's spectacular buttes as a backdrop. That honor goes to George B. Seitz, who filmed *The Vanishing American* there in 1924. But it was John Ford's genius that captured the spectacle of the West as people had never seen it before. His first movie there, *Stagecoach* (1939), so enthralled audiences that it brought the Western back into vogue and made the young John Wayne into a star. Ford set a new standard for movies, bringing the grandeur of the West to the big screen, and setting off a "studio stampede" of directors wanting to utilize the beauty of the region. In all, over 60 movies and countless TV shows, commercials, and videos have used Monument Valley as a spectacular panoramic backdrop.

Moab's *snow-capped mountains, red rock formations, and deep river canyons* (see p141) *have been the backdrop for over 100 major motion pictures, including* Thelma and Louise *in 1991.*

Director John Ford on the set of *Stagecoach*

Robert Zemeckis *used Monument Valley in 1990 as the backdrop for the third installment of his* Back to the Future *series of films, starring Michael J. Fox and Christopher Lloyd.*

THE SUNDANCE FILM FESTIVAL

Actor and director Robert Redford owns the Sundance Resort, which combines an environmentally responsible mountain vacation development with an institute for the promotion of the cinematic arts. Founded by Redford in 1981, the Sundance Film Festival takes place annually in the second half of January. The majority of screenings, which showcase independent film- and documentary-makers, are not held at the Sundance Resort (about 75 miles (121 km) northwest of Moab), but in Park City and at the Tower Theater in Salt Lake City. The festival has become America's foremost venue for innovative cinema and attracts the big Hollywood names. Tickets sell out quickly, so make ticket and lodging reservations ahead.

Robert Redford at the Sundance Film Festival in 1998

Monument Valley *was favored by John Ford, who directed nine movies using the area dubbed "Ford Country" and other southern Utah sites as backdrops. Many, like the 1956 epic* The Searchers, *are considered classics.*

Dead Horse Point State Park (see p143) *has long been used by directors who want a spectacular setting. It was seen in the 1991 film* Thelma and Louise *and, in 2000, actor Tom Cruise free-climbed up the sheer cliff-face in the thrilling opening sequence of* Mission Impossible: 2.

Tombstone *was the setting for the 1993 film of the same name (see p92). Starring Val Kilmer, Sam Elliott, Bill Paxton, and Kurt Russell, it is a modern interpretation of the Western genre.*

Lake Powell *is the most spectacular artificial lake in the US (see pp150–51). Its stark and otherworldly beauty has been used as a set for such diverse movies as the 1967 Dean Martin Western* Rough Night in Jericho, *the 1965 biblical epic* The Greatest Story Ever Told *(pictured here), with Charlton Heston, and the 1968 science fiction classic* Planet of the Apes.

THE SOUTHWEST THROUGH THE YEAR

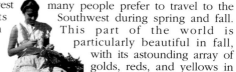

The weather in the Southwest is well known for its extremes, ranging from the heat of the desert to the ice and snow of the mountains – temperatures vary according to altitude, so the higher the elevation of the land, the cooler the area will be. Because the climate can be unbearably hot during the summer, particularly in Arizona, southern Utah, and New Mexico,

Stringing ristras of hot chile peppers

many people prefer to travel to the Southwest during spring and fall. This part of the world is particularly beautiful in fall, with its astounding array of golds, reds, and yellows in the forests and national parks. The area's diverse mix of Native, Hispanic, and European (Anglo) cultures gives visitors the opportunity to experience many different kinds of festivals and celebrations.

SPRING

Although the weather can be unpredictable in the spring, many festivals and celebrations are held at this time throughout the Southwest. Around Easter, prayers for a good harvest inspire several of the festivals and rituals held in the pueblos.

MARCH

Guild Indian Fair and Market *(first weekend)* Phoenix. Held at the Heard Museum, the fair features Indian dancing, arts, crafts, and Native American food.
Rio Grande Arts and Crafts Festival *(mid-Mar)* Albuquerque. This popular festival features handcrafted items from more than 200 artists and craftsmen.

Native dancer at the Guild Indian Fair and Market, Phoenix

Hispanic musicians or *mariachis* play at a Cinco de Mayo celebration

APRIL

American Indian Week *(mid-Apr)* Albuquerque. Arts and dancing at the Indian Pueblo Cultural Center.
Tucson International Mariachi Conference *(mid–late Apr)* Tucson. Annual celebration of Mexican *mariachi* music and dancing.
Gathering of Nations Pow Wow *(late Apr)* Albuquerque. Native American performers and traders from 300 tribes.
T or C Fiesta *(late Apr)* Truth or Consequences. A rodeo and old-time fiddlers' competition.

SUMMER

The warm summer weather is the time for many open-air events, from boat racing and rodeos to cultural events as diverse as country music and

opera. The weather in July and August, however, can be extreme, especially in southern Arizona, which sees very high temperatures and violent summer storms.

MAY

El Cinco de Mayo *(5 May)* Celebrated across many southwestern towns. Festivities to mark the 1862 Mexican victory over the French include parades, dancing, and Mexican food.
Santa Cruz Feast Day *(early May)* Taos and Cochiti pueblos. Celebrations include blessing the fields and a colorful corn dance.
Tucson Folk Music Festival *(early May)* Tucson. A wide selection of folk music at various venues in Tucson.
Taste of Durango *(mid-May)* Durango. Food, music, and

family fun fill the streets as the town's restaurants stage a cook-off contest.

La Vuelta de Bisbee *(late Apr or early May)* Bisbee. A professional, 80-mile (129-km) bicycle race in the Bisbee area.

Helldorado Days and Rodeo *(mid-May)* Las Vegas. A four-day festival of rodeo events and concerts.

Phippen Western Art Show & Sale *(Memorial Day weekend)* Prescott. Western art and sculpture buyers, sellers, and admirers come for the juried fine art show.

JUNE

San Antonio Feast Day *(13 June)* Sandia Pueblo. This festival welcomes visitors and features tribal dancing.

Albuquerque Pride *(mid-Jun)* Albuquerque. A three-day celebration of music, comedy, hosted by the gay and lesbian community.

The Annual Bluegrass and Country Music Festival *(mid-Jun)* Telluride. One of the West's biggest music events is held outdoors here.

Utah Summer Games *(mid-late June)* Cedar City. The games include a marathon, cycling, tennis, and swimming.

New Mexico Arts and Crafts Fair *(late Jun)* Albuquerque. Traditional arts and crafts, plus food and entertainments.

Utah Shakespeare Festival *(late Jun–Oct)* Cedar City. Plays are produced in two of the town's theaters.

Taos Summer Chamber Music Festival *(Jun–Aug)* Taos and Angel Fire. This festival takes the form of a series of outdoor concerts.

JULY

UFO Encounter *(early Jul)* Roswell. A series of lectures on UFOs, also featuring concerts and entertainment.

An exhibit at Roswell's UFO Encounter event

Nambe Falls Celebration *(early Jul)* Nambe Pueblo. Traditional dancing, food, and arts and crafts in a beautiful hillside setting.

Fourth of July *(4 July)* Most Southwestern towns. Celebrations include parades, fireworks, rodeos, sports, music festivals, and ceremonial Indian dances.

Hopi Festival of Arts and Culture *(early Jul)* Flagstaff. Music, dance, and over 70 award-winning Hopi carvers, painters, jewelers, potters, quilters, and weavers.

Frontier Days *(first week)* Prescott. The oldest professional rodeo in the world, featuring calf roping and wild horse racing.

Rainbow Dancers at Nambe Falls Celebration

Taos Pueblo Pow Wow *(second week)* Taos Pueblo. Traditional ceremonies and dances at the Taos Pueblo.

Shakespeare Sedona *(early–mid-Jul)* Sedona. Theatrical productions of Shakespearean selections are performed throughout the whole month of July.

Bat-Flight Breakfast *(mid-Jul)* Carlsbad Caverns. Participants can enjoy an outdoor breakfast, while watching thousands of bats as they return to the caves.

Spanish Market *(last weekend)* Santa Fe. A lively celebration featuring arts and crafts by contemporary Hispanic artists.

Arizona Cardinals Training Camp *(late Jul–mid-Aug)* Flagstaff. Most practice sessions of this NFL team are open to the public.

Santa Fe Opera *(Jul–Aug)* Santa Fe. The company performs a variety of operas in an open-air arena.

Chamber Music Festival *(Jul–Aug)* Santa Fe. One of the finest chamber music festivals in America is held at venues throughout the city.

AUGUST

Old Lincoln Days *(first weekend)* Lincoln. A festival featuring a re-enactment of the death of Billy the Kid, including the *Last Escape of Billy the Kid* pageant.

Inter-Tribal Indian Ceremonial *(mid-Aug)* Red Rock State Park, near Gallup. Fifty tribes take part in dances, pow wows, parades, rodeos, and races. Includes arts and crafts.

Indian Market *(third weekend)* Santa Fe. Held since 1922, the market is an opportunity to buy a wide selection of high-quality Native arts and crafts.

Great American Duck Race *(fourth weekend)* Deming. Includes live duck racing, a tortilla toss, a best dressed duck contest, concerts, food, and Deming's biggest parade.

Annual Bluegrass and Country Music Festival in Telluride

FALL

The autumnal forests and mountains of the Southwest are striking, ablaze with brilliant yellows, reds, and golds. Fall is one of the best seasons for touring and sightseeing because the temperatures become cooler and more comfortable.

SEPTEMBER

Navajo Nation Fair and Rodeo *(early Sep)* Window Rock. The largest Indian fair in the US features a parade, a rodeo, traditional song and dance, and arts and crafts.
Hatch Chile Festival *(early Sep/Labor Day weekend)* Hatch. Cooking, music, and arts and crafts in the center of the chile-growing industry.
Rendezvous of the Gunfighters *(Labor Day weekend)* Tombstone. Includes a parade, stage-coach rides, chili cook-offs, and mock shootouts.

The All-American Futurity *(early Sep/Labor Day)* Ruidoso Downs Racetrack. Quarter horse race with prize money in excess of $2 million.
New Mexico State Fair *(mid-Sep)* Albuquerque. One of the largest state fairs in the nation, with rodeos, carnivals, exhibits, and music.
Grand Canyon Music Festival *(mid-Sep)* Grand Canyon Village. Fine chamber music, from baroque to classical, jazz, fusion, and crossover.
Flagstaff Festival of Science *(late Sep)* Flagstaff. Ten days of events, including field trips and interactive exhibits, at museums and observatories.
The Whole Enchilada Festival *(late Sep)* Las Cruces. Featuring the world's largest enchilada *(see p250)*, as well as arts and crafts.

OCTOBER

Albuquerque International Balloon Fiesta *(early Oct)* Albuquerque. More than 850 balloons take part in this stunning event *(see p280)*, which is the largest of its kind in the world.
Lincoln County Cowboy Symposium *(second weekend)* Ruidoso. A celebration of life in the Old West, with cowboy poets, storytellers, and musicians as well as country dancing.
Geronimo Days *(mid-Oct)* Truth or Consequences. Celebrations with Native American, Hispanic, and cowboy entertainers.

Calf roping at Lincoln County Cowboy Symposium

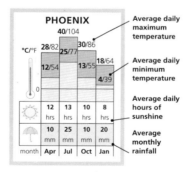

LAS VEGAS			
	39/102		
°C/°F	27/81	29/81	
	20/68		16/61
7/45		8/46	
0			-2/28
11 hrs	12 hrs	10 hrs	8 hrs
8 mm	13 mm	8 mm	18 mm
month	Apr	Jul	Oct	Jan

PHOENIX			
	40/104		
°C/°F	28/82	30/86	
	25/77		18/64
12/54		13/55	
			4/39
0			
12 hrs	13 hrs	10 hrs	8 hrs
10 mm	25 mm	10 mm	20 mm
month	Apr	Jul	Oct	Jan

Average daily maximum temperature

Average daily minimum temperature

Average daily hours of sunshine

Average monthly rainfall

Climate
The climate varies across the region. Phoenix and the southern areas have hot and dry summers and mild, sunny winters, whereas such northern areas as Southern Utah, Arizona, and New Mexico have snowy winters that are colder due to their higher elevation.

GRAND CANYON (SOUTH RIM)			
	29/84		
°C/°F	16/61	18/64	
	12/54		5/41
		3/37	
	-1/30		-7/19
0			
11 hrs	11 hrs	9 hrs	8 hrs
26 mm	45 mm	27 mm	33 mm
month	Apr	Jul	Oct	Jan

SANTA FE			
	27/81		
°C/°F	15/59	17/63	
	14		4/39
	2	3	
0			-8/18
10 hrs	10 hrs	9 hrs	7 hrs
27 mm	61 mm	31 mm	18 mm
month	Apr	Jul	Oct	Jan

MOAB (UTAH)			
	37/99		
°C/°F	22/72	23/73	
		18/64	
5/41		5/41	4/39
0			-8
10 hrs	10 hrs	9 hrs	6 hrs
19 mm	20 mm	30 mm	17 mm
month	Apr	Jul	Oct	Jan

Helldorado Days *(third weekend)* Tombstone. The festival features re-enactments, parades, a carnival, music, and street entertainment.
Moab Ho-Down Bike Festival *(last week)* Moab. Mountain bike guided tours, workshops, and a hill climb.

WINTER

Christmas in the Southwest is celebrated in traditional American style, with lights decorating almost every building and tree. The ski season stretches from mid-November to early April in the region's many resorts. Skiing, snow-boarding, and ice-skating are all popular.

NOVEMBER

Festival of the Cranes *(mid-Nov)* Socorro. Festival held during the November migration of whooping cranes to the Bosque del Apache Wildlife Refuge *(see p218)*.

DECEMBER

La Fiesta de Tumacacori *(first weekend)* Tumacacori. Festival held on mission grounds to celebrate the Native American heritage of the upper Santa Cruz Valley.
Santa Fe Film Festival *(first week)* Santa Fe. Screening of films from around the world, including the best in contemporary cinema and tributes to veteran stars.

A skier descending the Ridge in Taos Ski Valley

Old Town Stroll *(first Friday)* Albuquerque. The town's Christmas festivities begin in the Old Town with a parade, lighting of the tree, live music, and food stalls.
Canyon Road Farolito Walk *(Dec 24)* Santa Fe. Candle-lit tour of Canyon Road with carol singing and bonfires.

JANUARY

Fiesta Bowl Festival and Parade *(Dec 31/New Year's Day)* Phoenix. College football at ASU Sun Devil Stadium.
San Ildefonso Pueblo Feast Day *(late Jan)* San Ildefonso Pueblo. Ceremonial dances commemorate this feast day.
Tucson Area Square Dance Festival *(mid-Jan)* Tucson. The festival attracts thousands of dancers.
PGA Phoenix Golf FBR Open *(late Jan or Feb)* Phoenix. PGA's annual golf championship in Phoenix.

PUBLIC HOLIDAYS

New Year (Jan 1)
Martin Luther King Jr Day (3rd Mon in Jan)
Presidents' Day (3rd Mon in Feb)
Easter Sunday (variable)
El Cinco de Mayo (May 5)
Memorial Day (last Mon in May)
Independence Day (July 4)
Pioneer Day (July 24 – Utah)
Labor Day (1st Mon in Sept)
Columbus Day (2nd Mon in Oct)
Veterans Day (Nov 11)
Thanksgiving (4th Thu in Nov)
Christmas Day (Dec 25)

Saguaro Cactus illuminated by Christmas lights

FEBRUARY

Tubac Festival of the Arts *(early Feb)* Tubac. A highlight of the town's calendar, and one of the most important arts and crafts festivals in southern Arizona.
Silver Spur Rodeo *(mid-Feb)* Yuma. Along with the rodeo, this festival features arts and crafts and Yuma's biggest parade.
Tucson Gem and Mineral Show *(mid-Feb)* Tucson. Open to visitors, this is one of the biggest gem and mineral shows in the US.
La Fiesta de los Vaqueros *(late Feb)* Tucson. Come to this fiesta to enjoy a rodeo and other cowboy events, plus the world's largest non-motorized parade.

Player at PGA/FBR Open golf championship in Phoenix

THE HISTORY OF
THE SOUTHWEST

*T**he Southwest is known for its landscape, dominated by desert, deep canyons, and high mesas. Despite the arid conditions native civilizations have lived here for thousands of years, adjusting to the arrival of other cultures – the Hispanic colonizers of the 17th and 18th centuries and the Anglo-Americans of the 19th and 20th. Its rich history has created a fascinating multicultural heritage.***

Long before the appearance of the first Spanish explorers in the 1500s, the Southwest was inhabited by a variety of native populations. Groups of hunters walked here across the Bering Straits over a land bridge that once joined Asia with North America around 25,000–35,000 years ago. Descendants of these primitive hunter-gatherers, sometimes called Paleo-Indians, gradually fanned out across the American continent as far south as present-day Argentina. The early inhabitants of the Southwest endured centuries of hardship and adaptation to develop the technology and skills required to survive the rigors of life in this arid landscape.

Kachina doll

THE FIRST INHABITANTS

The first Native American peoples in the Southwest region have been called the Clovis, named for the site in New Mexico where stone spearheads were found embedded in mammoth bones. This hunter society roamed the area in small groups between 10,000 and 8,000 BC. Gradually, however, their prey of large Pleistocene mammals died out, and tribal people turned to roots and berries to supplement their diets. Anthropologists believe settled farming societies appeared gradually as the population grew, and that new crops and farming techniques were introduced by migrants and traders from Mexico in around 800 BC, when corn first began to be cultivated in the region.

Among the early farmers of the Southwest were the Basketmakers, named for their finely wrought baskets. Part of the Early Ancestral Puebloan, or Anasazi, culture, these people are thought to have lived in extended family groups, in pithouse dwellings. These were holes dug out of the earth up to 6 ft (2 m) deep, with roofs above ground. The Basketmakers were efficient hunters, using spears and domesticated dogs. They kept turkeys, whose feathers were highly valued as decoration.

By around AD 500, agrarian society was well established in the Southwest and large villages, or pueblos, began to develop. These usually centered around a large

TIMELINE

			800 BC Corn brought to the Southwest from Mexico. Start of agriculture, although the semi-nomadic quest for food still predominates
Stone spear point	10,000–8,000 BC Nomadic Clovis culture hunted in New Mexico. They made tools out of mammoth ivory and stone		
30,000 BC	**20,000 BC**	**10,000 BC**	
30,000–25,000 BC First nomadic people cross Bering Strait land bridge from Asia to North America	10,000 BC Man reaches the tip of South America		5,000–500 BC Cochise people arrive in southeastern Arizona. Also known as people of the "Desert Culture"

◁ **Papago Indian woman from Pima County, Arizona, 1903**

pithouse that was used for communal or religious use – the forerunner of the ceremonial kiva, which is still very much in use today *(see p161)*.

ANCIENT CULTURES

By AD 700 there were three main cultures in the Southwest: the Hohokam, the Mogollon, and the Ancestral Puebloan. They had slowly developed, from around 200 and 300 BC, into societies based on settled communities and cultivated crops.

Hohokam pot

Ancestral Puebloan people began to build more elaborate dwellings that grew into cities such as Chaco Canyon *(see pp174–5)* in AD 800 and Mesa Verde *(see pp180–81)* in AD 1000. These settlements were mysteriously abandoned in the 12th and 13th centuries *(see p161)*. It is thought the people migrated to the Pueblo Indian settlements along the Rio Grande valley and northwest New Mexico, and to Hopi mesa and Acoma, where their descendants live today.

The Hohokam farmed the deserts of central and southern Arizona between 300 BC and AD 1350. Their irrigation systems enabled them to grow two crops a year. It is thought that today's Tohono O'odham (Papago) and the Pima Indians of southern Arizona are descendants of the Hohokam *(see pp26–7)*.

The Mogollon were known for their pottery and adjusted to an agrarian lifestyle when agricultural crops arrived from Mexico. They are thought to have become assimilated into Ancestral Puebloan groups and their descendants living in the north of the region.

THE NAVAJO AND THE APACHE

The Navajo and Apache peoples originated in the Athabascan culture of the north of the American continent, in Canada and Alaska. The Navajo moved south between 1200 and 1400, while the Apache are thought to have arrived in the Southwest some time in the late 15th century.

The Navajo were hunters who took to herding sheep brought by the Spanish. There were four Apache groups: the Jicarilla, the Mescalero, the Chiricahua, and the Western Apache, who continued their nomadic lifestyle. The Apache were known as skillful warriors, especially the Chiricahua Apache of southern Arizona, whose leaders Cochise and Geronimo fought Hispanic and Anglo settlers in an attempt to deter them from colonizing the area in the late 19th century.

Navajo cornfield near Holbrook, Arizona, in 1889

THE ARRIVAL OF THE SPANISH

In 1539, the Franciscan priest, Fray Marcos de Niza, led the first Spanish expedition into the Southwest region. He was inspired by hopes of finding wealthy Indian cities, such as those the Spanish had conquered in South America, and the desire to convert native populations to Christianity. His

TIMELINE

300 BC Hohokam civilization in central and southern Arizona

200 BC Pre-Ancestral Puebloan Basketmakers culture in Four Corners region

Ancient bracelet

700 First ancestors settle on the Hopi mesas. Villages of pit houses well established

AD 1	200	400	600	800

200 BC Mogollon culture in southwestern New Mexico and southeastern Arizona. Mimbres people develop hand-coiled pottery

500 BC Beans and squash are grown. Agriculture develops

Mimbres coiled pot

600 Earliest date for settlement of Acoma and Hopi Mesas

800 Large pueblos such as Chaco Canyon under construction

HOPI MESA AND ACOMA PUEBLO

The Hopi villages of Old Oraibi and Walpi, and the Acoma Pueblo perch on high mesas in northeastern Arizona and northern New Mexico. Dated to AD 1150, they are believed to be America's oldest continually occupied settlements. The Ancestral Puebloan forebears of the Hopi and Acoma peoples arrived between AD 1100 and 1300, a period known as the "Gathering of the Clans." The first to arrive was the Bear Clan, from Mesa Verde. Others came from Canyon de Chelly, Chaco Canyon, the cliff dwellings of Keet Seel, and Betatakin in the Navajo National Monument.

Acoma pueblo, New Mexico *(see p217)*

expedition sent an advance party into Zuni tribal lands. Messages came back describing villages that Marcos identified as the fabled kingdom of gold, or Cibola. The priest never got there, but the myth of riches persisted.

A year later, Francisco Vasquez de Coronado *(see p216)* returned with 330 soldiers, 1,000 Indian allies, and more than 1,000 head of livestock. He conquered the trading center of Zuni Pueblo and spent two years traversing Arizona, New Mexico, Texas, and Kansas in search of Cibola. Coronado's brutal treatment of the Pueblo people, sacking homes and burning villages, sowed the seeds for the Pueblo Revolt 140 years later.

THE COLONY OF NEW MEXICO

Without gold, the Spanish lost interest until Juan de Oñate's 1598 expedition. Oñate established the city of Santa Fe and the colony of New Mexico, which included the present-day states of New Mexico and Arizona and parts of Colorado, Utah, Nevada, and California.

Spanish attempts to conquer the Indian pueblos led to bloody battles. Governor Oñate's cruelty, the harsh conditions, and bad harvests caused many settlers to flee the colony. A new governor, Don Pedro de Peralta, was instated in 1610, and Santa Fe became the capital.

Engraving by Norman Price of Coronado setting out to discover a legendary kingdom of gold in 1540

	1100–1300 "Gathering of the Clans" on the Hopi mesas	**1400** The Navajo and Apache migrate from Canada to the Southwest **1300** Mesa Verde deserted	**1540–42** Francisco Vasquez de Coronado leads a search for gold in New Mexico	**1610** Don Pedro de Peralta founds the capital of Santa Fe
1000		**1200**	**1400**	**1600**
1020 Chaco Canyon is at its height as a trading and cultural center	**c.1250** Ancient sites are mysteriously abandoned; new pueblos established along Rio Grande		**1539** Fray Marcos de Niza heads first Spanish expedition to Southwest **1598** Juan de Oñate founds permanent colony in New Mexico	**1680** The Pueblo Revolt

Juan de Oñate

Despite the harsh conditions, more settlers, priests, and soldiers began to return to the area, determined to subdue the native people and to suppress their religious practices.

Illustration of the 1680 Pueblo Indian Revolt

THE PUEBLO REVOLT

As the colonists spread out, they seized Pueblo farmlands and created huge ranches for themselves. The Pueblo people refused to work for them and continued to resist the new religion. When, in 1675, three native religious leaders were hanged in Santa Fe and more than 40 others publicly whipped, Popé, a Pueblo leader, started a resistance movement. The uprising on August 9, 1680, resulted in the deaths of 375 colonists and 21 priests, with the remaining 2,000 settlers driven south across the Rio Grande.

The Pueblo people did not manage to rid the region of the Spanish. In 1692, Don Diego de Vargas reclaimed Santa Fe. There were signs, however, of a relatively more tolerant relationship between Indian and colonizer.

THE END OF THE SPANISH ERA

By the late 18th century, the Spanish wanted to extend their power to California and secure the Pacific coast against the English and the Russians. Their first Arizona settlement was at Tubac, near Tucson in 1752. In 1775, Juan Bautista de Anza reached the Pacific Coast and founded San Francisco in Alta California *(see p24).*

As the Southwest opened up, Anglo-Americans were presented with new trading opportunities. In the Louisiana Purchase of 1803, Napoleon sold Louisiana, an enormous area of about 828,000 sq miles (2.2 million sq km) of land, to the recently formed United States. The US and New Mexico now shared a border, but the Anglos proved the stronger power.

The fight for Mexico's independence from Spain began on September 16, 1810, but it was not until 1821 that independence was finally declared.

THE MISSIONS

In the late 17th century, Jesuit missionary Father Eusebio Kino lived alongside and established a rapport with the Pima people of southern Arizona. He initiated the Jesuit practice of bringing gifts of livestock and seeds for new crops, including wheat. Those natives involved in the missionary program escaped forced labor. Kino inspired the natives living south of Tucson, at a place called Bac, to begin work on what was to become the Southwest's most beautiful mission church, San Xavier del Bac *(see pp88–9).* When Kino died in 1711, there were around 20 missions across the area.

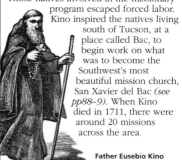

Father Eusebio Kino

TIMELINE

1692 Diego de Vargas retakes Santa Fe	**1706** Settlement established at Albuquerque		**1730s** First European settlement in Arizona established at Tubac	*Anza*	**1775** City of Tucson founded. Juan Batista de Anza forges trail to San Francisco
	1711 Death of Father Kino; 20 missions in southern Arizona				

1700	**1720**	**1740**	**1760**

1691 Jesuit missionary Father Eusebio Kino, establishes first mission at Tumacacori, Arizona	*Mission at Tumacacori*	**1752** Presidio (fortress) built at Tubac, near Tucson, Arizona	**1776** Franciscan priests, Escalante and Dominguez, first travel the Old Spanish Trail

The Republic of Mexico was founded in 1824. Newly independent Mexicans were glad to do business with their Anglo-American neighbors, who brought much-needed trade after the Spanish block on goods going west.

ANGLO-AMERICAN SETTLEMENT

Conflicts over land rights marked the period following the 1803 Louisiana Purchase. While the Hispanic and Native inhabitants of the region were happy to trade with the Anglos, they were angered by the new settlers who built ranches and even towns on lands to which they had no legal right. By the 1840s the United States had embarked on a vigorous expansion westward, with settlers accompanied by United States' soldiers. In 1845 the US acquired Texas and, when Mexico resisted further moves, the president sent an army to take control of New Mexico, starting the Mexican War. The Treaty of Guadalupe-Hidalgo ended the conflict in 1848, and gave the US the Mexican Cesion (comprising California, Utah, including Nevada and parts of Wyoming and Colorado, and New Mexico, which included northern Arizona) for $18.25 million. In 1854 the United States bought southern Arizona through the Gadsden Purchase for $10 million. While each region had its own territorial capital for administering law, they were not able to elect national representatives to Congress.

The Louisiana Purchase of 1803

THE IMPACT OF THE AMERICAN CIVIL WAR

When the Civil War broke out in 1861, many Southwesterners had Confederate sympathies, siding with the southern states against the north, or Union. They tried to declare Arizona a Confederate territory but in 1862, Union forces repelled Confederates at Glorieta Pass, near Santa Fe. In 1863, the federal government recognized Arizona as a separate territory, and drew the state line that exists between it and New Mexico today. After the Civil War, reports of land and mineral wealth in the West filtered back east, and Anglo settlement of the West rapidly increased. Rich lodes of gold, silver, and copper were discovered in Arizona, and mining camps such as Tombstone, Jerome, and Bisbee in Arizona *(see pp92–3)*, and Silver City in New Mexico became boomtowns. In Colorado, Silverton, Ouray, and Telluride *(see pp178–9)* also grew up around the mining industry in the late 19th century.

Engraving depicting an Apache attack on Anglo settlers (c.1886)

The Arrival of the Anglo-Americans

The first non-Spanish people of European descent, or Anglo-Americans, to arrive in the Southwest were "mountain men" or fur trappers in the early 1800s. They learned survival skills from Native tribes, married Native women, and usually spoke more than one Native language, and Spanish.

The opening of the Old Spanish Trail in 1776, and the forerunner to the Santa Fe Trail from St. Louis in the East in 1792, made the region accessible to traders and settlers *(see pp24–5)*. Yet it was only after Mexican independence was declared in 1821 that the territory opened up to Anglo traders who brought luxury goods such as oranges, silk handkerchiefs, and whisky. American soldiers arrived in 1846, and by the 1850s the US government had taken the region from the Mexicans. The Anglos, determined to subdue both Native and Hispanic populations, wrested away their lands to make way for vast ranches and towns such as Tombstone, which grew around the discovery of silver in 1877.

Mountain Man
Jim Bridger was one of many rugged individuals to open up trade routes to the west in the 1820s.

The Mexican War
This lithograph shows a battle in the 1846–8 war between the US and Mexico. After capturing Mexico City, the Americans agreed to pay $18.25 million in exchange for possession of New Mexico and California.

APACHE WARRIORS

The nomadic Apache lived in small communities in southeastern Arizona, and southern and northwestern New Mexico. Seen as a threat to the settlement of these territories, the US military was determined to wipe them out. The hanging of one of Chief Cochise's relatives in 1861 instigated a war which lasted more than a decade until Apache reservations were established in 1872. In 1877, a new leader, Victorio, launched a three-year guerrilla war against settlers that ended only with his death. The most famous Apache leader, Geronimo, led a campaign against the Mexicans and Anglos from 1851 until he surrendered in 1886 and was sent to a reservation in Florida.

Apache leader Geronimo, in a fierce pose in this picture from 1886

Mining Boom Prospector

In the second half of the 1800s, the region was a magnet for miners seeking their fortune. In reality, few individuals profited as large companies swiftly gained control of the mining areas.

The Coming of the Railroad

In 1869, the transcontinental railroad brought an influx of miners, adventurers, and tourists to the Southwest, and saw new industries emerge.

The Long Walk

Portrait of Navajo leader, Manuelito (1818–94) taken after the Long Walk. More than 8,000 Navajo were sent to New Mexico in 1864. Many died on the way.

WAGON TRAINS ON THE SANTA FE TRAIL

Charles Ferdinand's *The Attack on the Emigrant Train* (1856) depicts the conflicts between the Apache and traders and settlers who poured into the Southwest after the establishment of the Santa Fe Trail *(see pp24–5).*

Apache were often depicted attacking wagon trains. The Apache, who had a fierce reputation, felt justifiably threatened by Anglo settlers.

Anglo-American Influence

John Gast's American Progress *(1872) shows Indians pursued by a woman in a white robe – a symbol of American culture. The schoolbook represents education; trains, ships, and settlers are all signs of "civilization."*

A group of cowboys roping a steer, painted by C. M. Russell (1897)

LAND DISPUTES

After the Civil War, the US government set about clearing more land for settlers. In 1864, more than 8,000 Navajo people were forced from their lands and made to march "The Long Walk" of 400 miles (644 km) east to a reservation at Bosque Redondo in New Mexico. Some died en route as a result of the harsh weather and many more from disease at the reservation. In 1868, the Navajo were given 20,000 square miles (51,800 sq km) of land across Arizona, New Mexico, and southern Utah. The Chiricahua Apache continued to fight against forced settlement for most of the 19th century until their defeat and the surrender of their leader, Geronimo, in 1886.

In the 1870s, vast areas of the Southwest became huge cattle and sheep ranches. Battles between farmers, smallholders, and ranchers were common. Frequent "Range Wars"

Engraving showing Billy the Kid shooting a man in a bar

included the Lincoln County War, known for its famous protagonist, Billy the Kid *(see p54)*. As Anglo ranchers seized land, the New Mexicans' tradition of communal land use was overturned and many indigenous farmers lost their livelihoods.

By the 1880s four major railroads crossed the region bringing new Anglo settlers in search of prosperity. They came fully believing in their right to exploit the resources of this new land, and the railroad became a catalyst for new industries in the region, such as lumberjacking, cattle farming, and mineral mining. Luxury goods brought from the East by rail also made life a little easier.

New Mexico and Arizona were granted statehood in 1912. In the years leading up to and following World War I, Arizona, in particular, experienced an economic boom because of its rich mineral resources.

TIMELINE

1860	1880	1900	1920

1877 Copper found at Bisbee, Arizona. Silver discovered at Tombstone, Arizona.

Geronimo (1829–1909)

1886 Indian Wars end with the surrender of Geronimo

1912 New Mexico and Arizona become 47th and 48th states of the Union

1917 The US enters World War I

1931–36 Hoover Dam constructed in Arizona

1868 Navajo Reservation established in the Four Corners region

1878 The Lincoln County War begins in Lincoln, New Mexico

1881 Gunfight at OK Corral. Billy the Kid shot in New Mexico

1889 Phoenix becomes the territorial capital of Arizona

1901 Grand Canyon railroad opens, bringing tourists to the region

Grand Canyon steam train

THE DEMAND FOR WATER

As the region's population expanded, water supply became a pressing issue, and a series of enormous, federally funded dams were built to channel precious water for the burgeoning population of such cities as Phoenix. Dam- and road-building projects aided the region's economy and attracted even more settlers.

The Hoover Dam was constructed between 1931 and 1936, but by the 1960s even that proved inadequate. Glen Canyon Dam was completed in 1963, flooding forever an area of great beauty. The dam created the huge reservoir of Lake Powell, destroying a number of ancient Native ruins.

The issue of water continues to be a serious problem in the Southwest as the population keeps on rising. Projects to harness water from any available source are under debate.

WORLD WAR II

The legacy of the war years changed the economic course of the Southwest. New Mexico's sparsely populated and remote desert areas provided secret research, development, and testing sites for the first atomic bomb, starting with Los Alamos and the Manhattan Project in 1945 (see p186). Military installations such as the Titan Missile Base in southern Arizona and New Mexico's White Sands Missile Range were of national importance during the Cold War period of the 1950s.

Military research, computer technology, and other industrial off-shoots led to urbanization and a post-war population boom. Today, Phoenix and Albuquerque are among the fastest-growing cities in the US.

Patriot missile test at White Sands, New Mexico

The Southwest continues to be a major center for national defense research and development, as well as for research into space travel.

THE SOUTHWEST TODAY

The Southwest's economy continues to prosper, and its population is still growing, augmented by numbers of winter residents or "snowbirds." Ever-increasing numbers of tourists visit the region's scenic and historic wonders, preserved in the area's national parks. Established in the early 20th century, the parks have encouraged a heightened awareness of both conservation issues and Native cultures and their legacies, all of which will help guard the Southwest's precious heritage for generations to come.

Return of an early 19th-century Ancestral Puebloan artifact

1945 First atomic bomb tested at the Trinity site in southern New Mexico	**1958** Joint Use Area established in Arizona to settle Hopi and Navajo land disputes	**1963** Opening of the Glen Canyon Dam	**1982** Space Shuttle *Columbia* lands at White Sands Space Harbor	*Columbia*

1940	1960	1980	2000	2020

1943 Scientists begin the top-secret Manhattan Project to build an atomic bomb at Los Alamos, New Mexico *Fat Man atomic bomb*	**1974** Start of the Central Arizona Project to extract water from the Colorado River	**1996** Bill Clinton signs Navajo-Hopi Land Dispute Settlement Act	**2007** Opening of the Skywalk at Grand Canyon West in March	

An awe-inspiring view of Grand Canyon ▷

ARIZONA

Introducing Arizona

This large expanse of land is a region of stunning natural beauty. In Arizona's southwest corner lies the hostile, but eerily beautiful, Sonoran desert. Its boundaries are occupied by the cities of Tucson and Phoenix, the state's biggest city and its economic center. To the north, the landscape changes, rising through high desert plateaus toward forests, canyons, and mountains. Here, the city of Flagstaff and the picturesque mountain towns of Sedona and Jerome attract thousands of visitors. The state's most famous sight is Grand Canyon (see pp58–63), which draws millions of tourists to Arizona every year.

The distinctive buttes of Cathedral Rock overlooking a fishing lake at Red Rock crossing near Sedona

GETTING AROUND

Phoenix is a major hub for international and domestic flights. Driving, however, is the preferred option and Arizona has a good network of well-maintained highways. Northern Arizona is bisected by I-40 and I-10 cuts across the south; I-17 is the main north-south artery. Amtrak operates two train services that cross Arizona, and Greyhound buses run regular services to Arizona from major cities across the US.

KEY

▬	Interstate
▬	Major highway
═	Highway
═	River

SEE ALSO

Skyscrapers dominate the skyline of Downtown Phoenix

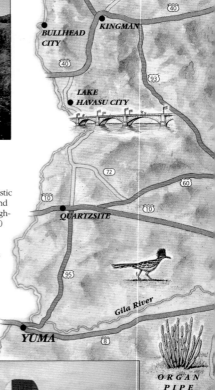

GRAND CANYON NATIONAL PARK

93

66

40

BULLHEAD CITY

KINGMAN

40

93

LAKE HAVASU CITY

72

60

10

QUARTZSITE

10

95

Gila River

YUMA

8

ORGAN PIPE CACTUS NAT. MON.

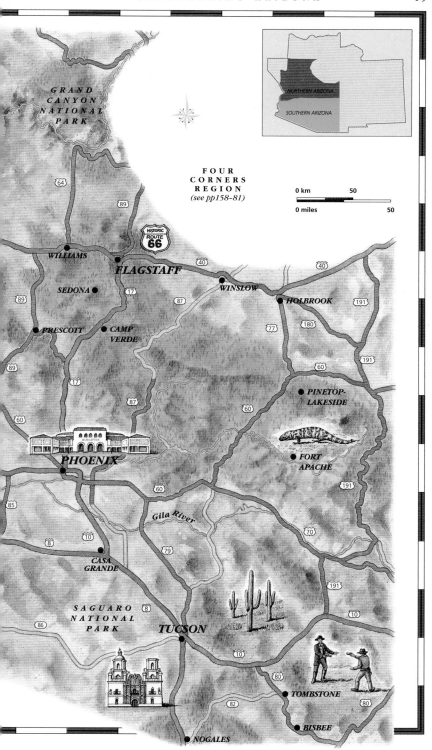

GRAND
CANYON
NATIONAL
PARK

NORTHERN ARIZONA

SOUTHERN ARIZONA

FOUR
CORNERS
REGION
(see pp158–81)

0 km   50

0 miles   50

HISTORIC
ROUTE
66

WILLIAMS

FLAGSTAFF

WINSLOW

HOLBROOK

SEDONA

PRESCOTT

CAMP
VERDE

PINETOP-
LAKESIDE

PHOENIX

FORT
APACHE

Gila River

CASA
GRANDE

SAGUARO
NATIONAL
PARK

TUCSON

TOMBSTONE

BISBEE

NOGALES

Route 66 in Arizona

**Route 66
Flagstaff sign**

Route 66 is America's most famous road. Stretching for 2,448 miles (3,941 km), from Chicago to Los Angeles, it is part of the country's folklore, symbolizing the freedom of the open road and inextricably linked to the growth of automobile travel. Known also as "The Mother Road" and "America's Main Street," Route 66 was officially opened in 1926 after a 12-year construction process linked the main streets of hundreds of small towns that had been previously isolated. In the 1930s, a prolonged drought in Oklahoma deprived more than 200,000 farmers of their livelihoods and prompted their trek to California along Route 66. This was movingly depicted in John Steinbeck's novel *The Grapes of Wrath* (1939).

Seligman *features several Route 66 stores and diners. Set among Arizona's Upland mountains, the road here passes through scenery that evokes the days of the westward pioneers.*

Route 66 *in Arizona passes through long stretches of wilderness bearing none of the trappings of the modern world. The state has the longest remaining stretch of the original road.*

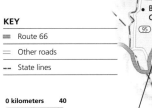

KEY

▬▬ Route 66

═══ Other roads

-- State lines

0 kilometers   40

0 miles   40

Oatman *is a former gold-mining boomtown. Today, its historic main street is lined with 19th-century buildings and boardwalks. Gunfights are regularly staged here.*

The Grand Canyon Caverns, *discovered in 1927, are around 0.75 miles (1.2 km) below ground level. On a 45-minute guided tour visitors are led through football field-sized caverns adorned with stalagmites and seams of sparkling crystals.*

ROUTE 66 IN POPULAR CULTURE

In the 1940s and 1950s, as America's love affair with the car grew and more people moved west than ever before, hundreds of motels, restaurants, and tourist attractions appeared along Route 66, sporting a vibrant new style of architecture. The road's end as a major thoroughfare came in the 1970s with the building of a national network of multilane highways. Today, the road is a popular tourist destination in itself, and along the Arizona section, enthusiasts and conservationists have helped to ensure the preservation of many of its most evocative buildings and signs.

LOCATOR MAP

— *Route 66*

☐ *Map area*

**Bobby Troup, composer of the popular song,
Route 66, in a 1948 Buick convertible**

Holbrook was founded in 1882 and is another Route 66 landmark. It is famous for Wigwam Village, a restored 1950s motel, where visitors can stay in rooms that are designed to resemble Indian teepees.

Flagstaff *is home to the famous Museum Club roadhouse, a large log cabin, built in 1931. It became a nightclub nicknamed "The Zoo," which was favored by country musicians traveling the road, including such stars as Willie Nelson.*

Williams *is known for its many nostalgic diners and motels. Twisters café (see p254), also known as the Route 66 Place, is crammed with road memorabilia, including the original 1950s soda fountain and bar stools.*

The Geology of Grand Canyon

Grand Canyon's multicolored layers of rock
provide the best record of the Earth's formation
of anywhere in the world. Each stratum of rock
reveals a different period in the Earth's geological
history beginning with the earliest, the Precambrian
Era, which covers geological time up to 570 million
years ago. Almost two billion years of history have
been recorded in the canyon, although the most
dramatic changes took place relatively recently, five
to six million years ago, when the Colorado River
began to carve its path through the canyon walls.
The sloping nature of the Kaibab Plateau has led to
increased erosion in some parts of the canyon.

A view of Grand Canyon's plateau and South Rim

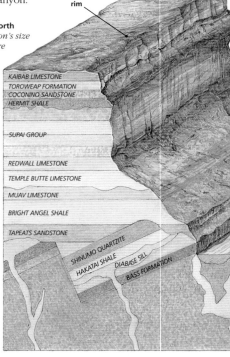

Canyon rim

KAIBAB LIMESTONE
TOROWEAP FORMATION
COCONINO SANDSTONE
HERMIT SHALE

SUPAI GROUP

REDWALL LIMESTONE

TEMPLE BUTTE LIMESTONE

MUAV LIMESTONE

BRIGHT ANGEL SHALE

TAPEATS SANDSTONE

SHINUMO QUARTZITE
HAKATAI SHALE
DIABASE SILL
BASS FORMATION

View of the North Rim *The canyon's size and beauty are what make it one of the most visited sights in the US (see pp58–63).*

RECORD OF LIFE

The fossils found in each layer tell the
story of the development of life on
Earth. The oldest layer, the Vishnu
Schist, was formed in the Proterozoic
era, when the first bacteria and algae
were just emerging. Later layers were
created by billions of small marine
creatures whose hard shells eventually
built up into thick layers of limestone.

The Asymmetrical Canyon
The North Rim of Grand Canyon is more eroded than the South Rim. The entire Kaibab Plateau slopes to the south, so rain falling at the North Rim flows toward the canyon and over the rim, creating deep side canyons and a wide space between the rim and the river.

The Surprise Canyon Formation
Classified by geologists in 1985, this new strata can be seen only in remote parts of the canyon. It was formed 335 million years ago.

The Colorado River
About 5 million years ago the Colorado River changed its course. It is thought that it was encompassed by another, smaller river that flowed through the Kaibab Plateau. The force of the combined waters carved out the deep Grand Canyon.

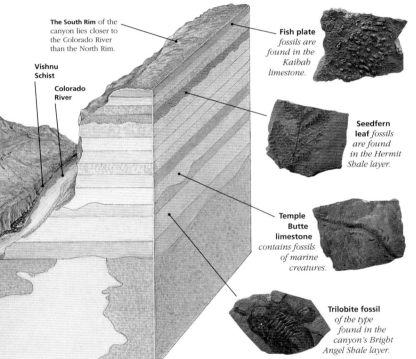

The South Rim of the canyon lies closer to the Colorado River than the North Rim.

Vishnu Schist

Colorado River

Fish plate *fossils are found in the Kaibab limestone.*

Seedfern leaf *fossils are found in the Hermit Shale layer.*

Temple Butte limestone *contains fossils of marine creatures.*

Trilobite fossil *of the type found in the canyon's Bright Angel Shale layer.*

HOW THE CANYON WAS FORMED

While the Colorado River accounts for the canyon's depth, its width and formations are the work of even greater forces. Wind rushing through the canyon erodes the limestone and sandstone a few grains at a time. Rain pouring over the canyon rim cuts deep side canyons through the softer rock. Perhaps the greatest canyon-building force is ice. Water from rain and snowmelt works into cracks in the rock. When frozen, it expands, forcing the rock away from the canyon walls. The layers vary in hardness. Soft layers erode quickly into sloped faces. Harder rock resists erosion, leaving sheer vertical faces.

Crack formed by ice and water erosion

The Wild West

Romanticized in a thousand cowboy movies, the "Wild West" conjures up images of tough men herding cattle across the country before living it up in a saloon. But frontier life was far from romantic. Settlers arriving in this wilderness were caught up in a first-come-first-serve battle for land and wealth, fighting Native Americans and each other for land.

The rugged life of the mining prospectors and ranch cowboys helped to create the idea of the American West. Today, visitors can still see mining ghost towns such as Jerome *(see p72)* or enjoy re-enacted gunfights on the streets of Tombstone. In the late 19th century, however, such survival skills as good shooting often co-existed with a kill-or-be-killed ethos.

Old mining cottages, *such as this one, may be seen in the Southwest's many former mining towns. The region's mining past can be traced in towns such as Oatman* (see p70) *and Bisbee* (see p92).

A reward poster *for William Bonney (better known as Billy the Kid), who was one of the Wild West's most notorious outlaws. He was eventually tracked and killed by Sheriff Pat Garrett at Fort Sumner on July 14, 1881* (see p225).

REWARD

($5,000.00)

Reward for the capture, dead or alive, of one Wm. Wright, better known as

"BILLY THE KID"

Age, 18. Height, 5 feet, 3 inches. Weight, 125 lbs. Light hair, blue eyes and even features. He is the leader of the worst band of desperadoes the Territory has ever had to deal with. The above reward will be paid for his capture or positive proof of his death.

JIM DALTON, Sheriff.

DEAD OR ALIVE!
BILLY THE KID

Deadwood Dick *was the nickname of cowboy Nat Love – earned because of his cattle-roping skills. Although there were around 5,000 black cowboys, there are no sights or museums commemorating them in the Southwest today.*

Cowboys were famous for their horsemanship and sense of camaraderie. The painting shows two friends attempting to save another.

The Questionable Companionship (1902) *by Frederic Remington highlights the tensions between Native Americans and the US army, who had played a central role in removing tribes from their ancestral lands.*

all over the west they wear

LEVI STRAUSS & CO'S
COPPER RIVETED
Overalls.

Cowboy fashion *began to appear in advertisements in around 1900. The ever popular Levi Strauss denim clothing can be bought across the region* (see p272).

Guided trail rides *are a great way to explore the Wild West and are part of the package of activities available at dude ranches* (see p279). *These ranches offer visitors the opportunity to experience the contemporary cowboy lifestyle.*

Horses were vividly depicted in Remington's dramatic action scenes. They were painted with astonishing realism, revealing a profound knowledge of their behaviour and physique.

SOUTHWESTERN COWBOYS

New York-born artist Frederic Sackrider Remington (1861–1909) became well known for his epic portraits of cowboys, horses, soldiers, and Native Americans in the late 19th century. One such example of his work is the oil painting *Aiding a Comrade* (1890), which celebrates the bravery and loyalty of the cowboy, at a time when they and small-scale ranchers were being super-ceded by powerful mining companies and ranching corporations. Remington lamented the passing of these heroes: "Cowboys! There are no cowboys anymore!"

THE GUNFIGHT AT THE OK CORRAL

One of the most famous tales of the Wild West is the Gunfight at the OK Corral, in Tombstone, Arizona *(see p92)*. This struggle pitted two clans against each other, the Clantons and the Earps. The usual, often disputed, version features the Clantons as no-good outlaws and the Earps as the forces of law and order. In 1881 Virgil Earp was the town marshal, and his brothers Morgan and Wyatt were temporary deputies. The showdown on October 26 had the Earps and their ally Doc Holliday on one side and Billy Clanton and the McLaury brothers, Tom and Frank, on the other. Of the seven combatants, only Wyatt Earp emerged untouched by a bullet. Billy, Tom and Frank were all killed. Wyatt Earp moved to Los Angeles, where he died in 1929.

Scene from the 1957 film, *Gunfight at the OK Corral,* **with Burt Lancaster and Kirk Douglas**

GRAND CANYON AND NORTHERN ARIZONA

For most people, northern Arizona is famous as the location of Grand Canyon, a gorge of breathtaking proportions carved out of rock by the Colorado River as it crosses the state on its way west to California. Northern Arizona's other attractions include the high desert landscape of the Colorado Plateau, with its sagebrush and yucca, punctuated by the forested foothills of the San Francisco Peaks. The Kaibab, Prescott, and Coconino National Forests cover large areas, and provide the setting for the lively city of Flagstaff as well as for the charming towns of Sedona and Jerome. This region is also dotted with fascinating mining ghost towns such as Chloride and Oatman, a reminder that Arizona won its nickname, the Copper State, from the mineral mining boom that took place in the first half of the 20th century.

More than 25 percent of Arizona is Native American reservation land. The state is also home to several centuries-old Puebloan ruins, most notably the hilltop village of Tuzigoot and the hillside remains of Montezuma Castle.

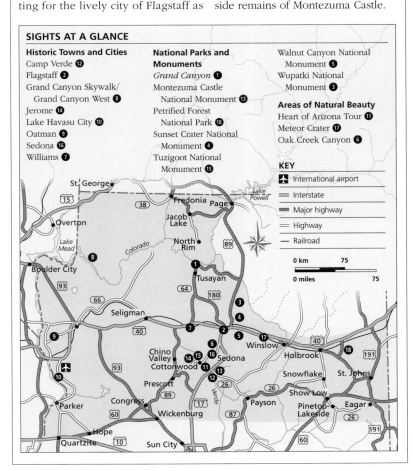

SIGHTS AT A GLANCE

Historic Towns and Cities
Camp Verde ⑫
Flagstaff ②
Grand Canyon Skywalk/
  Grand Canyon West ⑧
Jerome ⑭
Lake Havasu City ⑩
Oatman ⑨
Sedona ⑯
Williams ⑦

National Parks and Monuments
Grand Canyon ①
Montezuma Castle
  National Monument ⑬
Petrified Forest
  National Park ⑱
Sunset Crater National
  Monument ④
Tuzigoot National
  Monument ⑮

Walnut Canyon National
  Monument ⑤
Wupatki National
  Monument ③

Areas of Natural Beauty
Heart of Arizona Tour ⑪
Meteor Crater ⑰
Oak Creek Canyon ⑥

KEY
✈ International airport
═ Interstate
▬ Major highway
═ Highway
— Railroad

0 km   75

0 miles   75

◁ **Route 66 memorabilia decorating a shop on the Arizona section of the famous road** *(see pp50–51)*

Grand Canyon ●

Grand Canyon is one of the world's great natural wonders and an instantly recognizable symbol of the Southwest. The canyon runs through Grand Canyon National Park *(see pp60–63)*, and is 277 miles (446 km) long, an average of 10 miles (16 km) wide, and around 5,000 ft (1,500 m) deep. It was formed over a period of six million years by the Colorado River, whose fast-flowing waters sliced their way through the Colorado Plateau *(see pp18–19)* which includes the gorge and most of northern Arizona and the Four Corners region. The plateau's geological vagaries have defined the river's twisted course and exposed vast cliffs and pinnacles that are ringed by rocks of different color, variegated hues of limestone, sandstone, and shale *(see pp52–3)*. By any standard, the canyon is spectacular, but its special beauty is in the ever-shifting patterns of light and shadow and the colors of the rock, bleached white at midday, but bathed in red and ocher at sunset.

Mule trip convoy
A mule ride is a popular method of exploring the canyon's narrow trails.

Havasu Canyon
Since 1300 Havasu Canyon has been home to the Havasupai Indians. Now a population of around 500 Indians lives on the Havasupai Reservation, making a living from the tourist trade.

Grandview Point
At 7,400 ft (2,250 m), Grandview Point is one of the highest places on the South Rim, the canyon's southern edge. It is one of the stops along Desert View Drive (see p61). The point is thought to be the spot from where the Spanish had their first glimpse of the canyon in 1540.

North Rim

The North Rim receives roughly one tenth the number of visitors of the South Rim. While less accessible, it is a more peaceful destination offering a sense of unexplored wilderness. It has a range of hikes, such as the North Kaibab Trail, a steep descent down to Phantom Ranch on the canyon floor (see p60).

View from Hopi Point

Projecting far into the canyon, the tip of Hopi Point offers one of the best sunset-watching spots along Hermit Road. As the sun sets, it highlights four of the canyon's beautiful sculpted peaks.

YAVAPAI POINT AT THE SOUTH RIM

Situated 5 miles (8 km) north of the canyon's South Entrance, along a stretch of the Rim Trail, is Yavapai Point. Its observation station offers spectacular views of the canyon, and a viewing panel identifies several of the central canyon's landmarks.

Bright Angel Trail

Used by both Native Americans and early settlers, the Bright Angel Trail follows a natural route along one of the canyon's enormous fault lines. It is an appealing option for day-hikers because unlike some other trails in the area, it offers some shade and several seasonal water sources.

Grand Canyon National Park

Grand Canyon National Park is a World Heritage Site located entirely within the state of Arizona. The park covers 1,904 sq miles (4,930 sq km), and is made up of the canyon itself, which starts where the Paria river empties into the Colorado, and stretches from Lees Ferry to Lake Mead *(see p120)*, and adjoining lands. The area won protective status as a National Monument in 1908 after Theodore Roosevelt visited in 1903, observing that it should be kept intact for future generations as "… the one great sight which every American … should see." The National Park was created in 1919.

    The park has two main entrances, on the North and South rims of the canyon, However, the southern section of the park receives the most visitors and can become very congested during the summer season *(see pp62–3)*.

North Kaibab Trail follows Bright Angel Creek bed, past Roaring Springs, and descends to Phantom Ranch.

North Rim Entrance Station

67

Point Sublime

Crystal Creek

Bright Angel Point

Grand Canyon Lodge
Perched above the canyon at Bright Angel Point, the Grand Canyon Lodge has rooms and a number of dining options (see p63).

Shiva Temple

Colorado River

Isis Temple

HAVASU CANYON

Diana Temple

BRIGHT ANGEL CANYON

Bright Angel Creek

Bright Angel Trail starts from the South Rim. It is well maintained but demanding. It descends into the canyon and connects with the North Kaibab Trail up on the North Rim.

Hopi Point

Yavapai Point

Grand Canyon Village

Yaki Point

Hermits Rest

64

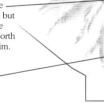

Phantom Ranch *(see p232)* is the only lodge on the canyon floor, and is accessible by mule, raft, or on foot.

FLAGSTAFF WILLIAMS

Tusayan

Hermit Road
A free shuttle bus runs along this route to the Hermes Rest viewpoint during the summer. It is closed to private vehicles March to November.

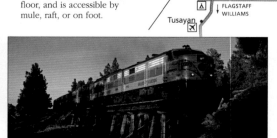

Grand Canyon Railway
Restored steam trains make the 64-mile (103-km) trip from the town of Williams to Grand Canyon Village.

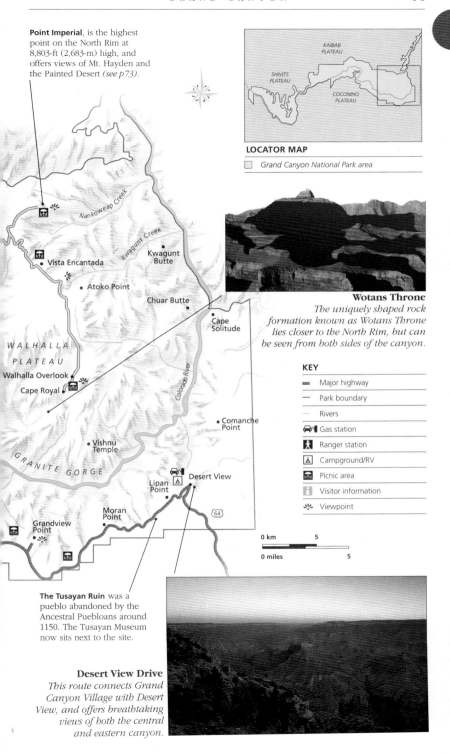

Point Imperial, is the highest point on the North Rim at 8,803-ft (2,683-m) high, and offers views of Mt. Hayden and the Painted Desert (*see p73*).

LOCATOR MAP

Grand Canyon National Park area

KAIBAB PLATEAU

SHIVITS PLATEAU

COCONINO PLATEAU

Nankoweap Creek

Kwagunt Creek

Kwagunt Butte

• Vista Encantada

• Atoko Point

Chuar Butte

Cape Solitude

WALHALLA PLATEAU

Walhalla Overlook

Cape Royal

Colorado River

GRANITE GORGE

• Vishnu Temple

• Comanche Point

Lipan Point

• Desert View

Moran Point

Grandview Point

64

Wotans Throne

The uniquely shaped rock formation known as Wotans Throne lies closer to the North Rim, but can be seen from both sides of the canyon.

KEY

▬	Major highway
—	Park boundary
—	Rivers
🚗	Gas station
🚶	Ranger station
🅰	Campground/RV
	Picnic area
ℹ	Visitor information
☼	Viewpoint

0 km   5

0 miles   5

The Tusayan Ruin was a pueblo abandoned by the Ancestral Puebloans around 1150. The Tusayan Museum now sits next to the site.

Desert View Drive

This route connects Grand Canyon Village with Desert View, and offers breathtaking views of both the central and eastern canyon.

Exploring Grand Canyon National Park

Grand Canyon offers awe-inspiring beauty on a vast scale. The magnificent rock formations with towers, cliffs, steep walls, and buttes recede as far as the eye can see, their bands of colored rock varying in shade as light

Bell near Hermits Rest

changes through the day. The park's main roads, Hermit Road and Desert View Drive, both accessible from the south entrance, overlook the canyon. Grand Canyon Village is located on the South Rim and offers a full range of facilities. Visitors can also enter the park from the north, although this route (Hwy 67) is closed during winter. Walking trails along the North and South rims offer staggering views, but to experience the canyon at its most fascinating the trails that head down toward the canyon floor should be explored. The Bright Angel Trail on the South Rim, and the North Kaibab Trail on the North Rim, descend to the canyon floor, and are tough hikes involving an overnight stop.

is not only the starting point for most of the mule trips through the canyon, but also the terminus for the Grand Canyon Railway.

The South Rim

Most of the Grand Canyon's 4.3 million annual visitors come to the South Rim, since, unlike the North Rim, it is open year-round and is easily accessible along Highway 180/64 from Flagstaff or Williams. **Hermit Road** is closed to private vehicles from March to November each year, but there are free shuttle buses. **Desert View Drive** (Hwy 64) is open all year. Both roads start at Grand Canyon Village and encompass a selection of the choicest views of the gorge. From Grand Canyon Village, Hermit Road extends 8 miles (13 km) to Hermits Rest and, in the opposite direction, Desert View Drive covers 26 miles (42 km) and passes the stunning overlook of Desert View.

Beginning at Grand Canyon Village, Hermit Road meanders along the South Rim, its first viewpoint being **Trailview Overlook**, which provides an overview of the canyon and the winding course of the Bright Angel Trail. Moving on, **Maricopa Point** offers especially panoramic views of the canyon but not of the Colorado River, which is more apparent from nearby **Hopi Point**. At the end of Hermit Road lies **Hermits Rest**, where a gift shop, decorated in rustic style, is located in yet another Mary Colter-designed building. Just east of Grand Canyon Village is **Yavapai Point** from where it is possible to see Phantom

Adobe, Pueblo-style architecture of Hopi House, Grand Canyon Village

⛩ Grand Canyon Village

Grand Canyon National Park.
Tel *(928) 638-7888.* ♿ *partial.*
Grand Canyon Village has its roots in the late 19th century. The extensive building of visitor accommodations started after the Santa Fe Railroad opened a branch line here from Williams in 1901, though some hotels had been built in the late 1890s. The Fred Harvey Company constructed a clutch of well-designed, attractive buildings. The most prominent is El Tovar Hotel *(see p233).* Opened in 1905, it is named after Spanish explorers who reached the gorge in 1540. The Hopi House also opened in 1905 – a rendition of a traditional Hopi dwelling, where locals could sell their craftwork as souvenirs. It was built by Hopi craftsmen and designed

by Mary E. J. Colter. An ex-schoolteacher and trained architect, Colter drew on Southwestern influences, mixing both Native American and Hispanic styles *(see pp22–3).* She is responsible for many of the historic structures that now grace the South Rim, including the 1914 Lookout Studio and Hermits Rest, and the rustic 1922 Phantom Ranch on the canyon floor.

Today, Grand Canyon Village has a wide range of hotels, restaurants, and stores. It can be surprisingly easy to get lost here since the buildings are spread out and discreetly placed among wooded areas. The Village

The interior of the Hermits Rest gift store with crafts for sale lining the walls

For hotels and restaurants in this region see pp232–4 and pp252–4

Desert View's stone watchtower on Desert View Drive

CALIFORNIA CONDORS

The California Condor is America's largest bird, with a wingspan of over 9 ft (2.7 m). The species was almost extinct in the 1980s, when the last 22 condors were captured for breeding in captivity. In 1996 the first captive-bred birds were released in Northern Arizona. Today, about 60 condors fly the skies over Northern Arizona. They are frequent visitors to the South Rim, though visitors should not approach or feed them.

A pair of California condors

Ranch *(see p232)*. This is the only roofed accommodation available on the canyon floor, across the Colorado River.

The longer Desert View Drive winds for 12 miles (20 km) to **Grandview Point**, where the Spaniards may have had their first glimpse of the canyon in 1540. Ten miles (16 km) farther on lie the pueblo remains of Tusayan Ruin, where there is a small museum featuring exhibits on Ancestral Puebloan life. After a few miles, the road leads to **Desert View** where the Watchtower was Colter's most fanciful creation, its upper floor decorated with early 20th-century Hopi murals.

The North Rim

Standing at about 8,000 ft (2,400 m), the North Rim is higher, cooler, and greener than the South Rim, with dense forests of ponderosa pine, aspen, and Douglas fir. Visitors are most likely to spot wildlife on the North Rim. Mule deer, Kaibab squirrel, and wild turkey are among the most common sights. The North Rim is reached via Highway 67, off Highway 89A, ending at **Grand Canyon Lodge** *(see pp233 and 252)* where there are visitor services, a camp-ground, gas station, restaurant, and a general store. Nearby, there is a National Park Service information center, which offers maps of the area. The North Rim and its facilities are closed mid-October–mid-May, when it is often snowed in.

The North Rim is twice as far from the river as the South Rim, and the canyon really stretches out from the over-looks giving a sense of its 10-mile (16-km) width. There are about 30 miles (45 km) of scenic roads along the North Rim as well as hiking trails to high viewpoints or down to the canyon floor, (particularly the North Kaibab Trail that links to the South Rim's Bright Angel Trail.) The picturesque **Cape Royal Drive** starts north of Grand Canyon Lodge and travels 23 miles (37 km) to Cape Royal on the Walhalla Plateau. From here, several famous buttes and peaks can be seen, including Wotans Throne and Vishnu Temple. There are also several short, easy walking trails around Cape Royal, both along the top. A 3-mile (5-km) detour leads to **Point Imperial**, the highest point on the canyon rim, while along the way the **Vista Encantada** has delightful views and picnic tables overlooking the gorge.

Mule deer on the canyon's North Rim

The Bright Angel Trail

This is the most popular of all Grand Canyon hiking trails. The Bright Angel trailhead is at Canyon Village on the South Rim. The trail begins near the Kolb Studio at the western end of Grand Canyon Village. It then switches dramatically down the side of the canyon for 9 miles (13 km). The trail crosses the river over a suspension bridge, ending a little further on at Phantom Ranch. There are two resthouses and a fully equipped campground along the way. It is not advisable to attempt the whole trip in one day. Many walk from the South Rim to one of the rest stops and then return up to the rim. Temperatures at the bottom of the canyon can reach 110°F (43°C) or higher during the summer. Day hikers should therefore carry a quart (just over a liter) of water per person per hour for summer hiking. Carrying a first-aid kit is also recommended.

Hikers taking a break on the South Rim's Bright Angel Trail

Breathtaking view of Grand Canyon at dusk ▷

Flagstaff ❷

**Colorful Lowell
Observatory sign**

Nestling among the pine forests of Northern Arizona's San Francisco Peaks, Flagstaff is one of the region's most attractive towns. It is a lively, easy-going place with a good selection of bars and restaurants among the maze of old red-brick buildings that make up its compact downtown. Flagstaff's first Anglo settlers were sheep ranchers who arrived in 1876. The railroad came in 1882, and the town developed as a lumber center.

Flagstaff is the home of Northern Arizona University, which has two appealing art galleries, and is a good base for visiting Grand Canyon's South Rim, which is just under two hours' drive away. The surrounding mountains attract hikers in summer and skiers in winter.

The town of Flagstaff with the San Francisco Peaks as a backdrop

Exploring Flagstaff

Flagstaff's center is narrow and slender, channeling north toward the Museum of Northern Arizona and south to the University. At its heart is a pocket-sized historic district, an attractive ensemble of red-brick buildings, which houses the best restaurants and bars. Lowell Observatory is located on Mars Hill, a short distance from downtown, and the popular Arizona Snowbowl ski resort is an enjoyable ten-minute drive to the north of the town.

🏛 The Lowell Observatory

1400 West Mars Hill Road. *Tel (928) 774-3358.* ⏱ Mar–Oct: 9am–5pm daily; Nov–Feb: noon–5pm daily; evening hours all year, call for details. 🌑 public hols. 📷 ♿ 🎫 www.lowell.edu

Tucked away on a hill about a mile northwest of the town center, the Lowell Observatory was founded in 1894 and named for its benefactor,

Percival Lowell, a member of one of Boston's wealthiest families. He financed the observatory to look for life on Mars and chose the town because of its high altitude and clear mountain air.

The Lowell Observatory went on to establish an international reputation with its documented evidence of

**1930 Pluto dome at Flagstaff's
Lowell Observatory**

an expanding universe, data that was disclosed to the public in 1912. One of the observatory's famous astronomers, Clyde Tombaugh, discovered the planet Pluto on February 18, 1930.

Visitors have access to the main rotunda, exhibit halls, and the John Vickers McAllister Space Theater, which shows presentations on the night sky and current research at Lowell. Campus tours are available daily, and telescope viewings nightly.

🏛 Historic Downtown

Just ten minutes' walk from end to end, Flagstaff's historic downtown dates mainly from the 1890s. Many buildings sport decorative stone and stucco friezes and are now occupied by cafés, bars, and stores. Architecturally, several buildings stand out, particularly the restored Babbitt Building and the 1926 train station that today houses the visitor center. Perhaps the most attractive building is the Weatherford Hotel, which was opened on January 1, 1900. It was named after its owner, Texan entrepreneur John W. Weatherford, and was much admired for its grand two-story wraparound veranda and its sunroom.

🏛 Northern Arizona University

624 S. Knoles Dr. Flagstaff. *Tel (928) 523-9011.* ⏱ *Times vary, so call in advance.* www.nau.edu

Flagstaff's lively café society owes much to the 16,000 students of Northern Arizona University (NAU). The main entrance point to the campus is located on Knoles Drive. Green lawns, stately trees, and several historic buildings make for a pleasant visit. Of particular note are two campus art galleries: the Beasley Gallery in the Fine Art Building, which features temporary exhibitions and student work, and the Old Main Art Museum and Gallery housed in Old Main Building – the university's oldest. This features the permanent Weiss collection, which includes works by the famous Mexican artist Diego Rivera.

Arts and Crafts swinging settee at Riordan Mansion

🏛 Riordan Mansion State Historic Park

409 Riordan Road. *Tel (928) 779-4395.* ⬜ *May–Oct: 8:30am–5pm daily; Nov–Apr: 10:30am–5pm daily.* ⬤ *Dec 25.* 📷 ♿ www.azstateparks.com

In the mid-1880s, Michael and Timothy Riordan established a lumber company that quickly made them a fortune. The brothers then built a house of grandiose proportions, a 40-room log mansion with two wings, one for each of them. Completed in 1904 and now preserved as a State Historic Park, the house has a rustic, timber-clad exterior, and Arts and Crafts furniture inside.

🏛 Pioneer Museum

2340 N. Fort Valley Rd. *Tel (928) 774-6272.* ⬜ *9am–5pm Mon–Sat.* ⬤ *Sun, public hols.* 📷 www. arizonahistoricalsociety.org

Flagstaff's Pioneer Museum occupies an elegant stone building that was originally built as a hospital in 1908. The museum opened in 1960 and incorporates the Ben Doney homestead cabin. On display in the grounds are a steam locomotive of 1929 and a Santa Fe Railroad caboose. Inside, a particular highlight is a selection of Grand Canyon photographs taken in the early 1900s by photographers Ellsworth and Emery Kolb.

Arizona Snowbowl

Snowbowl Road, off Hwy 180. *Tel (928) 779-1951.* 📠 *Flagstaff Snow Report: (928) 779-4577.* ⬜ *Dec–mid-Apr.* www.arizonasnowbowl.com

Downhill skiing is available at the Arizona Snowbowl just 7 miles (11 km) north of town. The mountains here are the San Francisco Peaks, which receive an average of 260 in (660 cm) of snow every year,

enough to supply the various ski runs that pattern the lower slopes of the 12,356-ft- (3,707-m-) high Agassiz Peak. Facilities include four chairlifts, and a ski school for beginners.

In summer, there is a hiking trail up to the peak, while for those less inclined to walk the Arizona Scenic Skyride is a cable car trip that offers spectacular views of the scenery.

🏛 Museum of Northern Arizona

(see pp68–9)

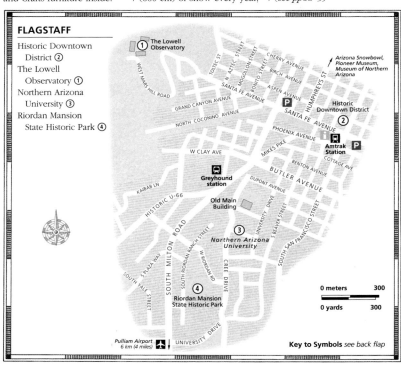

FLAGSTAFF

Historic Downtown District ②
The Lowell Observatory ①
Northern Arizona University ③
Riordan Mansion State Historic Park ④

The Lowell Observatory ①

Arizona Snowbowl, Pioneer Museum, Museum of Northern Arizona

Historic Downtown District ②

Amtrak Station

Greyhound station

Old Main Building

Northern Arizona University ③

Riordan Mansion State Historic Park ④

Pulliam Airport 6 km (4 miles)

| 0 meters | 300 |
| 0 yards | 300 |

Key to Symbols *see back flap*

Museum of Northern Arizona, Flagstaff

The Museum of Northern Arizona holds one of the Southwest's most comprehensive collections of Southwestern archaeological artifacts, as well as fine art and natural science exhibits. The collections are arranged in a series of galleries around a central courtyard. Beside the main entrance is the Archaeology Gallery, with a fine introduction to the region's historic cultures. The Ethnology Gallery documents 12,000 years of Hopi, Zuni, Navajo, and Pai tribal cultures on the Colorado Plateau. The museum shop sells contemporary native fine arts and the bookstore specializes in native arts and crafts.

VISITORS' CHECKLIST

3101 North Fort Valley Rd.
Tel (928) 774-5213. ◯ 9am–
5pm daily. ⬤ public hols. 📷
♿ 📷 www.musnaz.org

★ Ethnology Gallery
This gallery highlights the living cultures of the region; that of the Hopi, Navajo, Pai, and Zuni people.

The inner courtyard has exhibits that focus on the variety of plants and animals found on the Colorado Plateau through the ages.

The Kiva Gallery replicates the inside of a kiva *(see p161).*

Babbitt gallery

KEY

☐	Archaeology Gallery
▨	Ethnology Gallery
☐	Babbitt Gallery
☐	Geology Gallery
☐	Historic courtyard
☐	Exhibition Gallery
▨	Non-exhibition space

Entrance

Archaeology Gallery

Geology Gallery
A lifesize skeletal model of a Dilophosaurus is ringed by dioramas of ancient Arizona desert scenes.

Museum Façade
Built in 1935, the museum has a stone façade and is listed on the National Register of Historic Places.

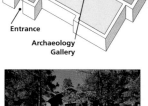

STAR SIGHTS

★ Ethnology Gallery

Wupatki National Monument **❸**

Road map C3. Forest Service Road 545, Sunset Crater/Wupatki Loop Rd. *Tel* (928) 679-2365. 🚌 *Flagstaff.* 🚌 *Flagstaff.* ⭘ *9am–5pm daily.* ● *Dec 25.* 📷 ♿ *partial.* 📷 **www**.nps.gov/wupa

Covering more than 35,000 acres (14,000 ha) of sun-scorched wilderness to the north of Flagstaff, the Wupatki National Monument incorporates about 2,700 historic sites once inhabited by the ancestors of the Hopi people. The area was first settled after the eruption of Sunset Crater in 1064. The Sinagua people and their Ancestral Puebloan cousins realized that the volcanic ash had made the soil more fertile and consequently favourable for farming. The power of the volcanic eruption may also have appealed to their spirituality. They left the region in the early 13th century, but no one really knows why *(see pp160–61).*

The largest site here is the Wupatki Pueblo, built in the 12th century and once a four-story pueblo complex of 100 rooms, housing more than 100 Sinagua. The structures rise from their rocky outcrop overlooking the desert. A trail explores the remains, the most unusual feature of which is a ballcourt. Here the Sinagua may have played at dropping a ball through a stone ring without using hands or feet.

Sunset Crater Volcano National Monument **❹**

Road map C3. Hwy 545 off Hwy 89, Sunset Crater/Wupatki Loop Rd. *Tel* (928) 526-0502. 🚌 *Flagstaff.* 🚌 *Flagstaff.* ⭘ *daily.* ● *Dec 25.* 📷 ♿ **www**.nps.gov/sucr

In 1064, a mighty volcanic eruption formed the 400-ft (120-m) deep Sunset Crater, leaving a cinder cone that rises 1,000 ft (300 m) above the surrounding lava field. Aptly named, the cone is black at the base and tinged with reds and oranges farther up. The one-mile (1.6-km) self-guided Lava Trail offers an easy stroll around the ashy landscape with its lava tubes, bubbles, and vents.

Walnut Canyon National Monument **❺**

Road map C3. Hwy 40 exit 204. *Tel* (928) 526-3367. 🚌 *Flagstaff.* 🚌 *Flagstaff.* ⭘ *9am–5pm daily* (8am–5pm May–Oct). ● *Dec 25.* 📷 ♿ *partial.* 📷 **www**.nps.gov/waca

Located about ten miles (16 km) east of Flagstaff, off Interstate Hwy 40, Walnut Canyon houses an intriguing collection of cliff dwellings. These were inhabited by the Sinagua, ancestors of the Hopi, in the 12th and 13th centuries. The Sinagua were attracted to the canyon by its fertile soil and plentiful water from nearby Walnut Creek.

Today, visitors can tour 25 cliff dwellings huddled underneath the natural overhangs of the canyon's eroded sandstone and limestone walls.

The Sinagua left the canyon abruptly around the middle of the 13th century, possibly as a result of war, drought, or disease *(see pp160–61).* Sinagua artifacts are on display in the Walnut Canyon Visitor Center.

Petroglyph from Walnut Canyon

Oak Creek Canyon **❻**

Road map C3. ℹ️ (800) 228-7336.

Just south of Flagstaff, Highway 89A weaves a charming route which makes for a very pleasant drive through Oak Creek Canyon on the way to Sedona *(see p73).* In the canyon, dense woods shadow the road, and the steep cliffs are colored in bands of red and yellow sandstone, pale limestone, and black basalt. This is a popular summer vacation area with many day-hiking trails, such as the East Pocket Trail, a steep wooded climb to the canyon rim. At nearby Slide Rock State Park, swimmers enjoy sliding over the rocks that form a natural water chute.

The Wupatki National Monument with ruins of a 12th-century pueblo building and San Francisco Peaks behind

Williams ❼

Road map B3. 🏔 *2,700.* 🚊
ℹ *200 W. Railroad Ave. (928) 635-4061.* **www.**williamschamber.com

This distinctive little town was named in 1851 for Bill Williams (1787–1849), a legendary mountain man and trapper who lived for a time with the Osage Indians in Missouri. The town grew up around the railroad that arrived in the 1880s, and when this was followed by a spur track to Grand Canyon's South Rim in 1901, Williams became established as a tourist center. By the late 1920s, it was also a popular rest stop on Route 66 *(see pp50–51)*.

Today, the town retains its frontier atmosphere, complete with Stetson-wearing locals. Most of its hotels and diners are arranged around a loop that follows Route 66 on one side and its replacement, Interstate Highway 40, on the other. Diners evoke the 1950s and are filled with Route 66 memorabilia, including original soda fountains and posters.

Twisters, a retro-style diner off Route 66 in Williams *(see p254)*

Grand Canyon Skywalk/Grand Canyon West ❽

Road map B3. ℹ *Grand Canyon West: reservations (877) 716-9378.* 🖥 **www.**destinationgrandcanyon.com

The Grand Canyon Skywalk – a dramatic 70-ft (21-m) glass walkway cantilevered beyond the rim and 4,000 ft (1220 m) above the floor of the Grand Canyon – is a project of the Hualapai tribe. Located near their modest resort, the Hualapai Ranch, the Skywalk and Grand Canyon West are situated much closer to Las Vegas than to the

The Skywalk, suspended high above the Colorado River

famous South Rim of the canyon which is nearly 250 miles (402 km) away.

All-inclusive package tours can be booked from Las Vegas and on site. These include demonstrations of cowboy skills, horseback riding, and helicopter or boat tours, in addition to the Skywalk itself. An Indian Village features recreated dwellings of the Hualapai tribe and three other Arizona tribes. Native American cultural performances and presentations are put on daily in the village's authentically constructed amphitheater. A shuttle bus operates within the Grand Canyon West area as no private vehicles are permitted.

Oatman ❾

Road map A3. 🏔 *100.* ℹ *P.O. Box 423, Oatman (928) 768-6222.* **www.**oatmangoldroad.org

In 1904, prospectors struck gold in the Black Mountains and Oatman became their main supply center. Today, it is popular with visitors wanting a taste of its boomtown past, such as the 1920s hotel where

Carole Lombard and Clark Gable honeymooned in 1939. Gunfights are staged daily.

Lake Havasu City ❿

Road map A4. 🏔 *45,000.* ✈ 🚊
ℹ *314 London Bridge Road (928) 453-3444.* **www.**golakehavasu.com

California businessman Robert McCulloch founded Lake Havasu City in 1964. The resort city he built on the Colorado River was popular with the landlocked citizens of Arizona, however, came four years later when he bought London Bridge and transported it from England to Lake Havasu. Some mocked McCulloch, suggesting that he had thought he was buying London's Gothic Tower Bridge, not this much more ordinary one. There was more hilarity when it appeared that there was nothing in Havasu City for the bridge to span. Undaunted, McCulloch simply created the waterway he needed. Today the area is one of Arizona's most popular for outdoor recreation, with visitors enjoying the shops and restaurants here.

London Bridge spans a man-made waterway in Lake Havasu City

For hotels and restaurants in this region see pp232–4 and pp252–4

Heart of Arizona Tour **⑪**

The Verde River passes through the wooded hills and fertile meadows of central Arizona, before opening into a wide, green valley between Flagstaff and Phoenix. The heart of Arizona is full of charming towns such as Sedona, hidden away among stunning scenery, and the former mining town of Jerome. Over the hills lies Prescott, once state capital and now a busy, likable little town with a center full of dignified Victorian buildings. The area's ancient history can be seen in its two beautiful pueblo ruins, Montezuma Castle and Tuzigoot.

TIPS FOR DRIVERS

Recommended route: From Sedona, take Hwy 89A to Tuzigoot, Jerome, and Prescott. Hwy 69 runs east from Prescott to the Interstate Highway 17, which connects to Camp Verde, Fort Verde, and Montezuma Castle.
Tour length: 85 miles (137 km).
When to go: Spring and fall are delightful; summer is very hot.

Sedona ①
Set among dramatic red rock hills, Sedona is a popular resort, known for its New Age stores and galleries as well as for its friendly ambience.

KEY

▬ Tour route
═ Other roads

↑ FLAGSTAFF

Tuzigoot National Monument ②
Stunning views of the Verde River Valley are seen at this ruined hilltop pueblo, occupied until 1425.

Cottonwood

Verde River

Prescott Valley

Sedona

179

260

6

5

Jerome ③
A popular relic of Arizona's mining boom, Jerome is known for its 1900s brick buildings that cling to the slopes of Cleopatra Hill.

4

Prescott

69

17

0 km   10

0 miles   10

↓ PHOENIX

Montezuma Castle National Monument ⑥
The Ancestral Puebloan ruins here date from the 1100s and occupy one of the loveliest sites in the Southwest.

Prescott ④
This cool hilltop town is set among the rugged peaks and lush woods of Prescott National Forest, making it a popular center for many outdoor activities.

Camp Verde ⑤
A highlight of this little town is Fort Verde. Built by the US Army in 1865, this stone fort is manned by costumed guides.

Pueblo remains of Montezuma Castle, built into limestone cliffs

Camp Verde ⑫

Road map B4. 🏠 6,000. ℹ️ 385
South Main St. (928) 567-9294. 🄰
www.visitcampverde.com

Farmers founded the small
settlement of Camp Verde in
the heart of the Verde River
Valley in the 1860s. It was a
risky enterprise as the Apache
lived nearby, but the US Army
quickly moved in to protect
the settlers, building **Fort
Verde** in 1865.
Today, Camp Verde
remains at the
center of a large and
prosperous farming
and ranching com-
munity. It was from
Fort Verde that the
army orchestrated
a series of brutal
campaigns against
the Apache, which
ended with the
Battle of the Big
Dry Wash in 1882.
Once the Apache
had been sent to reservations,
Fort Verde was no longer
needed and it was decom-
missioned in 1891. Four of its
original buildings have survived. The former army admin-
istration building contains a
collection of exhibits on army
life. The interiors of the other
three houses, on Officers' Row,
have been restored. On weekends from spring to fall, volun-
teers in period costume act as
guides and reenact scenes
from the fort's daily life.

Costumed guides at
Fort Verde State
Historic Park

🏛 **Fort Verde at Camp Verde
State Historic Park**
Off Hwy I-17. **Tel** (928) 567-3275.
🄾 9am–5pm daily. ⚫ Dec 25. 🈳

Montezuma Castle National Monument ⑬

Road map C4. Hwy I-17 exit 289.
Tel (928) 567-3322. 🄾 early
Sep–end May: 8am–5pm daily;
end May–early Sep: 8am–6pm daily.
🈳 **www**.nps.gov/moca

Dating from the 1100s, the
pueblo remains that make up
Montezuma Castle occupy an
idyllic location, built
into the limestone
cliffs high above
Beaver Creek, a
couple of miles to
the east of Interstate
Highway 17. Once
home to the
Sinagua people,
this cliff dwelling
originally contained
20 rooms spread
over five floors.
Montezuma Castle
was declared a Nat-
ional Monument in
1906 to preserve its excellent
condition. The visitor center
has a display on Sinaguan life
and is found at the start of an
easy trail along Beaver Creek,
with its views of the ruins.
The National Monument
also incorporates Montezuma
Well, situated about 11 miles
(18 km) away to the northeast. This natural sinkhole,
50 ft (15 m) deep and
470 ft (140 m) in
diameter, had relig-
ious significance for
Native Americans,
with several tribes
believing it was the
site of the Creation.
Over 1,000 gallons
(3,790 liters) of water flow
through the sinkhole every
minute, an inexhaustible supply that has long been used to
irrigate the surrounding land.
A narrow trail leads around
the rim before twisting its way
down to the water's edge.

Jerome ⑭

Road map B4. 🏠 500. ℹ️ Box K,
Jerome. 🅖 partial. **www**.jerome
chamber.com & **www**.azjerome.com

Approached from the east
along Highway 89A, Jerome is
easy to spot in the distance,
its tangle of old brick
buildings perched high above
the valley, clinging to the
steep slopes of Cleopatra Hill.
Silver mining began here in
the 1870s, but the town's big
break came in 1912 when
prospectors hit a vein of copper no less than 5 ft (1.5 m)
thick. Just two years later,
World War I sent the price of
copper sky high and Jerome
boomed. In the Wall Street
Crash of 1929, however,
copper prices tumbled and,
although the mines survived
until 1953, the boom times
were over. To make matters
worse, underground dynamit-
ing had made Cleopatra Hill
unstable, and the town began
to slide downhill at a rate
of 4 in (10 cm) a year. By the
early 1960s, Jerome was virtually a ghost town, but its fortunes were revived by an influx of artists and artisans,
whose galleries and stores
attracted tourists. Today Jerome
is often busy with day-trippers
who come to see the late 19th-
and early 20th-century brick
buildings that make up the
town's historic center.

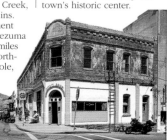
Façade of an early 20th-century store
on Jerome's historic Main Street

The ford across picturesque Oak Creek at Red Rock Crossing, Sedona

Tuzigoot National Monument ⑮

Road map B4. *Follow signs from Hwy 89A.* **Tel** *(928) 634-5564.* ☐ *end May–early Sep: 8am–6pm daily; early Sep–end May: 8am–5pm daily.* ● *Dec 25.* 🏷 **www.**nps.gov/tuzi

Perched on a solitary and slender limestone ridge, the ruins of Tuzigoot National Monument offer splendid views of the Verde River Valley. The pueblo was built by the Sinagua people between the 12th and 15th centuries and, at its peak, had a population of around 300. It was abandoned in the early 15th century, when it is believed the Sinagua migrated north to join the Ancestral Puebloans.

Tuzigoot was partly rebuilt by a local and federally funded program during the Depression in the 1930s. This emphasized one of the most unusual features of pueblo building, the lack of doorways. The normal pueblo room was entered by ladder through a hatchway in the roof. Sinaguan artifacts and art are on display at the visitor center.

Sedona ⑯

Road map C3. 🏙 *16,000.* ✈ 🚌 🛈 *331 Forest Rd. (800) 288-7336.* **www.**visitsedona.com

The little town of Sedona sits among the wooded hills and canyons south of Flagstaff. In 1981, the psychic and writer Page Bryant identified seven vortexes in the area, which she believed emanated electromagnetic energies that invigorated the soul. The subsequent influx of "New Agers" was followed by a burgeoning tourist industry that is reflected in the range of restaurants, hotels, stores, and art galleries here.

Sedona is a good base from which to explore the area. Accessed from Red Rock Loop Road, Crescent Moon Ranch is a US Forest Service Recreation Area with a ford across Oak Creek. Farther along Red Rock Loop Road is Red Rock State Park, where a gentle, wooded stretch of Oak Creek offers hikes and lovely picnic spots.

Meteor Crater ⑰

Road map C3. *Off Hwy 40 exit 233.* **Tel** *(928) 289-2362.* ☐ *Jun–Aug: 7am–7pm daily; Sep–May: 8am–5pm daily.* ● *Dec 25.* 🏷

The Barringer Meteor Crater, a meteorite impact crater, was formed nearly 50,000 years ago. The crater is 550 ft (167 m) deep and 2.4 miles (4 km) in circumference, and so closely resembles a moon crater that NASA astronauts trained here in the 1960s. Guided rim tours are available and the visitor center tells the story of the crater through exhibits and a film.

Petrified Forest National Park ⑱

Road map D3. *Off Hwy I-40.* **Tel** *(928) 524-6228.* ☐ *winter: 8am–5pm daily; summer: 7am–7pm daily.* ● *Dec 25.* 🏷

This national park is one of Arizona's most unusual attractions. Millions of years ago rivers swept trees downstream into a vast swamp that once covered this area. Groundwater transported silica dioxide into downed timber, eventually turning it into the quartz stone logs seen today, with colored crystals preserving the trees' shape and structure.

Running the length of the forest is the Painted Desert, an area of colored bands of sand and rock that change from blues to reds as the light catches the mineral deposits. From the Painted Desert Visitor Center, a scenic road travels the length of the park. There are nine overlooks on the route, including Kachina Point, where the Painted Desert Wilderness trailhead is located.

Cross section of petrified log

Near the south end of the road is the **Rainbow Forest Museum**.

🏛 **Rainbow Forest Museum**
Off Hwy 180 (south entrance). **Tel** *(928) 524-6822.* ☐ *winter: 8am–5pm daily; summer: 7am–7pm daily.* ● *Dec 25.* 🏷

PHOENIX AND SOUTHERN ARIZONA

Mountain ranges and sun-bleached plateaus ripple the wide landscapes of southern Arizona, a staggeringly beautiful region dominated by pristine tracts of desert, parts of which are protected within the Saguaro National Park and the Organ Pipe Cactus National Monument. This land was first farmed around 400 BC by the Hohokam people *(see p38)* who carefully used the meager water supplies to irrigate their crops. When the Spanish arrived in the 16th century they built forts and established settlements across the region. This Hispanic heritage is recalled by the beautiful mission churches of San Xavier del Bac and Tumacacori and in the popular historic city of Tucson that grew up around the 1776 Spanish fort. When silver was discovered nearby in the 1870s, the scene was set for a decade of rowdy frontier life. Today, towns such as Tombstone, famous for the "Gunfight at the OK Corral", re-create this wild west era. The influx of miners also spurred the growth of Phoenix, a farming town established on the banks of the Salt River in the 1860s. Phoenix is now the largest city in the Southwest, known for its warm winter climate and recreational facilities.

SIGHTS AT A GLANCE

Historic Towns and Cities
Bisbee ❿
Globe ❸
Nogales ❾
Phoenix ❶
Tombstone ⓫
Tubac ❽
Tucson ❺
Yuma ❻

Parks, Museums, and National Monuments
Amerind Foundation Museum ⓭
Casa Grande Ruins National Monument ❹
Chiricahua National Monument ⓮
Kartchner Caverns State Park ⓬

Organ Pipe Cactus National Monument ❼

Areas of Natural Beauty
The Apache Trail ❷

KEY

✈	International airport
═══	Interstate
▬▬▬	Major highway
══	Highway
──	Railroad

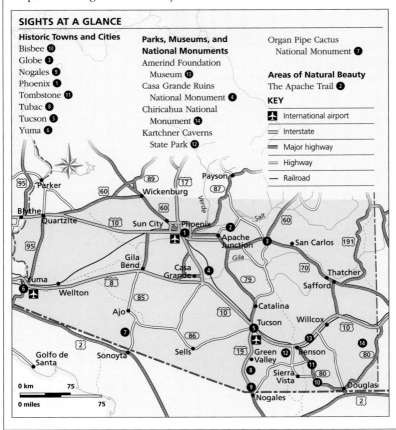

Phoenix ❶

Cash register at the Museum of History

Phoenix is a huge metropolis, stretching across the Salt River Valley. Farmers and ranchers settled here in the 1860s. By 1912, the city had developed into the political and economic focus of Arizona and was the state capital. As it grew, it absorbed surrounding towns, although each district still maintains its identity. Downtown Phoenix is now being reinvigorated. It is home to many historic attractions, including restored Victorian houses in Heritage Square, the Phoenix Art Museum, and the Heard Museum (see pp78–9) with its excellent collection of Native American artifacts.

The 1900 façade of the Arizona State Capitol Building

Exploring Downtown Phoenix

Downtown Phoenix, where the city began in the 19th century, is centered on Washington and Jefferson Streets, which run east to west between 7th Street and 19th Avenue. Central Avenue is the main north-south axis: to its east, parallel roads are labeled as "Streets," while roads to the west are "Avenues." City sights are mostly too far apart to see on foot, and driving is the best option. A DASH bus runs from Downtown to the State Capitol regularly on weekdays.

🏛 Arizona State Capitol Museum

1700 West Washington St.
Tel (602) 542-4675.
⬜ 9am–4pm Mon–Fri.
⬤ public hols.
📷 10am & 2pm. ♿
www.lib.az.us/museum
Completed in 1900, the Arizona State Capitol housed the state legislature until they moved into nearby new premises in 1960. The handsome building

is topped by a copper dome. The interior is now a museum; guided tours include both original legislative chambers, which have been carefully restored, and a series of sepia photographs that document the history of Phoenix.

🏛 Arizona Mining and Mineral Museum

1502 West Washington St. **Tel** (602) 771-1611. ⬜ 8am–5pm Mon–Fri; 11am–4pm Sat. ⬤ public hols. ♿ 📷 **www**.admmr.state.az.us
The search for precious stones and metals brought waves of prospectors to the Southwest in the years following the Civil War (1861–65). The riches they unearthed in Arizona's sun-seared hills were fabulous. A mountain of silver was discovered in the Dragoon Mountains near Tucson, while quantities of gold, silver, copper, and turquoise were found farther north in the Cerbat Mountains outside Kingman. As word

Azurite and malachite rock

spread, thousands of prospectors converged on the Superstition Mountains to the east of Phoenix. However, many ended up destitute, never discovering the large deposits of gold rumored to be hidden in the hills.

This museum traces the colorful history of Arizona mining through photographs and displays of historic tools. There are also glittering examples of the various rocks the miners quarried, the most striking of which are the copper-bearing ores such as malachite and azurite, in vivid greens and blues.

🏛 Heritage Square

115 N. 6th St. ♿ partial.
Phoenix is a thoroughly modern city, which grew rapidly after World War II. Many of its older buildings did not survive this expansion. However, a few late 19th- and early 20th-century buildings remain, and the most interesting of these are found on Heritage Square. Rosson House is a handsome wooden mansion on Monroe Street dating from 1895. It has a wraparound veranda and distinctive hexagonal turret. Visitors may tour the house, which is furnished in period style (call 602 262-5070). Next door is the Burgess Carriage House, constructed in an expansive colonial style rare in the Southwest. The 1900 Silva House also features exhibits detailing Arizona's history. The tree-lined square with its cafés is pleasant for a stroll.

2 Arizona Mining and Mineral Museum
1 Arizona State Capitol Museum

| 0 meters | 500 |
| 0 yards | 500 |

Key to Symbols see back flap

🏛 Arizona Science Center

600 E. Washington St. **Tel** (602)
716-2000. ⬤ 10am–5pm daily.
⬤ Thanksgiving, Dec 25. 📷 ♿
www.azscience.org

This ultra-modern facility has
over 300 interactive science
exhibits, covering everything
from physics and energy to
the human body, spread over

three levels. The popular "All
About You" gallery on Level
One focuses on human biol-
ogy. Here, visitors can take a
virtual reality trip through the
body. Level Three has "The
World Around You," where
visitors explore a 90-ft- (27-m-)
long rock wall, as well as testing the surface temperature of
different substances. The center
also has a large-screen cinema
on Level One. It is popular
with children, but there is
something here for everyone.

range of unusual artifacts,
including 19th-century land
surveying equipment, a steam-
powered bicycle, Phoenix's
first printing press, and
reconstructions of a general
store and the first jail.

🏛 Phoenix Art Museum

1625 N. Central Ave. **Tel** (602)
257-1222. ⬤ 10am–5pm
Wed–Sun; 10am–9pm Tue.
⬤ Mon, public hols. 📷 🖥 🛍
♿ www.phxart.org

Housed in an austere
modern building, the highly
acclaimed Phoenix Art
Museum has an enviable
reputation for the quality
of its temporary exhibitions.
These usually share the
lower of the museum's two
floors with a permanent
collection of contemporary
European and US art. The
second floor features 18th-
and 19th-century American
artists, with a focus on
painters connected to the
Southwest. The exhibit here
includes first-rate work from
the Taos art colony of the
1900s and Georgia O'Keeffe
(1887–1986) (see p203), the
most distinguished member
of the group. Among other
featured artists are Gilbert
Stewart (1755–1828), whose
celebrated Portrait of George
Washington (1796) is seen
on every dollar bill.

🏛 Phoenix Museum of History

105 N. 5th St. **Tel** (602) 253-2734.
⬤ 10am–5pm Tue–Sat.
⬤ Sun, Mon, public hols. 📷 ♿
www.pmoh.org

This inventive museum
concentrates on the early
years of the city's history.
There is a fascinating

SIGHTS AT A GLANCE

Arizona Mining and Mineral
Museum ②
Arizona Science Center ④
Arizona State Capitol Museum ①
Heard Museum ⑦
Heritage Square ③
Phoenix Art Museum ⑥
Phoenix Museum of History ⑤

Heard Museum ⑦
MONTE VISTA ROAD
THIRD STREET
ALVARADO STREET
NORTH
Phoenix Art Museum ⑥
MC DOWELL ROAD
CENTRAL AVENUE
WILLETTA STREET
⑩
MORELAND STREET
PORTLAND STREET
SEVENTH STREET
SECOND STREET
GARFIELD ST
FIFTH STREET
SIXTH STREET
MC KINLEY ST
⑩
PIERCE ST
FIRST STREET
THIRD STREET
FILMORE ST
Sky Harbor
International Airport ✈
8 km (5 miles)
Greyhound station 🚌
6 km (4 miles)
TAYLOR ST
ROOSEVELT STREET
MC KINLEY STREET
SECOND AVENUE
FIRST AVENUE
FILMORE STREET
P
Phoenix
Museum of History ⑤ ③ Heritage Square
ℹ ④ Arizona Science Center
SEVENTH AVENUE
SIXTH AVE
FIFTH AVE
THIRD AVE
FOURTH AVE
BUREN STREET
P
DOWNTOWN
GRAND AVE
VAN
MONROE STREET
P
WOODLAND AVE
ADAMS STREET
WEST WASHINGTON STREET
JEFFERSON STREET
MADISON

Façade of the Phoenix Museum of History

Heard Museum

The Heard Museum was founded in 1929 by Dwight Heard, a wealthy rancher and businessman who, with his wife, Maie, assembled an extraordinary collection of Native Southwestern American art in the 1920s. Several benefactors later added to the collection, including Senator Barry Goldwater of Arizona and the Fred Harvey Company, who donated their *kachina* dolls. The museum's wide-ranging collection contains more than 40,000 works, but the star attraction is its display of more than 500 dolls. Additionally, the museum showcases baskets, pottery, textiles, and fine art, as well as sumptuous silverwork by the Navajo, Zuni, and Hopi peoples.

Entrance to the Heard Museum, which occupies a Spanish Colonial Revival-style building

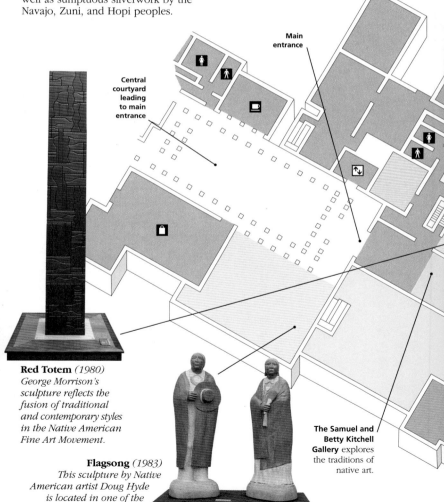

Main entrance

Central courtyard leading to main entrance

Red Totem *(1980)*
George Morrison's sculpture reflects the fusion of traditional and contemporary styles in the Native American Fine Art Movement.

Flagsong *(1983)*
This sculpture by Native American artist Doug Hyde is located in one of the Heard's tranquil courtyards.

The Samuel and Betty Kitchell Gallery explores the traditions of native art.

Red Tailed Hawk
Painted in 1986 by Dan Namingha, this is an impressionistic view of a Hopi Kachina in hawk form. It is displayed as part of the Heard's fine art collection.

VISITORS' CHECKLIST

2301 North Central Ave, Phoenix, AZ 85004. **Tel** *(602) 252-8840;* (602) 252-8848. *Phoenix Greyhound Station.* 9:30am–5pm Mon–Sat, 11am–5pm Sun. public hols. **www.**heard.org

KEY

☐	Samuel and Betty Kitchell Gallery
☐	Crossroads Gallery
☐	Sandra Day O'Connor Gallery
☐	Ullman Learning Center
☐	Freeman Gallery
☐	Home: Native People in the Southwest Gallery
☐	Lincoln Hall
☐	Pritzlaff Courtyard
☐	Edward Jacobson Gallery of Indian Art
▨	Maureen and Dean Nichols Garden
☐	Temporary exhibition space
▨	Non-exhibition space

Navajo Child's Blanket
Woven in the 1870s, this richly colored, traditional blanket is one of the highlights of the Sandra Day O'Connor Gallery, which documents the history of the Museum, and showcases the Heard family's early collection of Native American artifacts.

Ullman Learning Center features interactive exhibits related to Native American life in Arizona.

Every Picture Tells a Story
An interactive hands-on display shows how artists interpret their environments through art.

The South Courtyard offers additional space for the museum's fine sculptures.

★ Home: Native Peoples in the Southwest
This award-winning gallery spans 14 centuries, encompassing a superb collection of kachina *dolls as well as jewelry, pottery, basketry, and textiles.*

STAR COLLECTION

★ Home: Native Peoples in the Southwest

Exploring Metropolitan Phoenix

Phoenix is one of North America's largest cities. In addition to its city population of more than one million, Phoenix has a burgeoning number of residents in its metropolitan area, totaling more than three million. The city fills the Salt River Valley, occupying more than 2,000 sq miles (5,200 sq km) of the Sonoran Desert. It is famous for its winter temperatures of 60–70°F (16–21°C) and around 300 days of sunshine a year. This makes Phoenix a popular destination with both tourists and "snow birds," visitors who spend their winters here.

Metropolitan Phoenix includes the former town of Scottsdale, 12 miles (19 km) northeast of Downtown. Replete with air-conditioned malls, designer stores, hotels and restaurants, it is also a good base for visiting Taliesin West and Papago Park and is famous for its world-class golf courses *(see p276)*. Tempe, 6 miles (10 km) east of Downtown, is home to Arizona State University and the Pueblo Grande Museum, while finally Mesa has the Arizona Temple, a large Mormon church built in 1927.

buildings, which house many of the city's most fashionable restaurants as well as bars, antique stores, and art galleries. In addition to the Renaissance-style Borgata shopping mall, there is the El Pedregal Festival Marketplace, and Scottsdale Downtown with its arts shopping district around Main Street, Marshall Way, Old Town, and Fifth Avenue. Scottsdale is also the location for Phoenix's most popular shopping mall – Fashion Square – offering an array of designer stores and excellent restaurants *(see p272–3)*.

SIGHTS AT A GLANCE

Camelback Mountain ④
Cosanti Foundation ③
Mystery Castle ⑦
Papago Park ⑥
Pueblo Grande Museum and
    Archaeological Park ⑤
Scottsdale ②
Taliesin West ①

KEY

- ▦ Downtown Phoenix
- ▢ Metropolitan Phoenix
- ✈ International airport
- ═ Interstate
- ▬ Major highway
- ═ Highway
- — Railroad

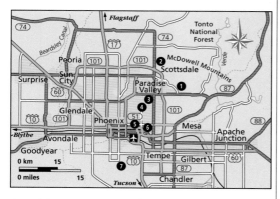

Scottsdale's elegant shopping mall, Fashion Square

🐫 Camelback Mountain

Scottsdale.
Named for its humped shape, Camelback Mountain rises high above its suburban surroundings just 7 miles (11 km) northeast of Downtown Phoenix. One of the city's most distinctive landmarks, the mountain is a granite and sandstone outcrop formed by prehistoric volcanic forces. Camelback Mountain is best approached from the north via the marked turn off McDonald Drive near the junction of Tatum Boulevard. From the parking lot, a well-marked path leads to the summit, a steep climb that covers 1,300 ft (390 m) in the space of a mile.

Camelback Mountain adjoins the Echo Canyon Recreation Area, a lovely wooded enclave with a choice of shady picnic sites.

Scottsdale

Founded in the late 19th century, Scottsdale was named after its developer, army chaplain Winfield Scott (1837–1910), whose religious scruples helped keep the early settlement free from saloons and gambling. Scottsdale's quiet, tree-lined streets and desert setting attracted the famous architect Frank Lloyd Wright,

who established Taliesin West here in 1937. The area still attracts artists and designers, but it is best known for its many golf courses – there are 175 in and around Scottsdale.

At the center of the district, to either side of Scottsdale Road between 2nd Street and Indian School Road, the streets are lined with low, brightly painted adobe

Innovative design of the Cosanti Foundation gift shop

🏛 **The Cosanti Foundation**

6433 Doubletree Ranch Rd., Paradise Valley. *Tel (480) 948-6145.* ⬜ *9am–5pm Mon–Sat; 11am–5pm Sun.* ⬤ *public hols.* 🖼 *donation requested.* ♿ **www**.arcosanti.org

In 1947, Italian architect Paolo Soleri (*b*. 1919) came to study at Taliesin West. Nine years later, he set up the Cosanti Foundation in Scottsdale to further his investigations into what he termed "arcology": a combination of architecture and ecology to create new urban habitats (*see p23*).

Today, the Cosanti site consists of simple, low structures housing studios, a gallery, and workshops. This is where Soleri and his workers make and sell their trademark wind-bells. Guided tours can be arranged with advance notice.

Visitors can also tour Soleri's main project, which lies 60 miles (100 km) north of Phoenix on Interstate Highway 17. Arcosanti is an educational housing project that began in 1970 to test the "arcology concept" as a way to reduce human impact on the environment while improving quality of life. Residents live and work in structures that combine work and leisure space. Workshops, tours, and accommodations are available.

🏛 **Taliesin West**

Cactus Rd. at Frank Lloyd Wright Blvd., Scottsdale. *Tel (480) 860-8810.* ⬜ *9am–4pm daily.* ⬤ *Jan 1, Thanksgiving, Dec 25.* 🖼 ♿ 🎦 **www**.franklloydwright.org

Generally regarded as the greatest American architect of all time, Frank Lloyd Wright (1869–1959) established the 600-acre (240-ha) Taliesin West complex as a winter school for his students in 1937. Wright had come to prominence in Chicago during the 1890s with a series of strikingly original houses that featured an elegant open-plan style. Although noted for his use of local materials such as desert rocks and earth, he also pioneered the use of pre-cast concrete (*see p23*).

Today, Taliesin West is home to the Frank Lloyd Wright School of Architecture, where students live and work. There are a variety of tours, from one to three hours. One-hour tours begin every half hour from 10am to 4pm.

Taliesin West is approached along a winding desert road. The muted tones of the low-lying buildings reflect Wright's enthusiasm for the desert setting. He was careful to enhance, rather than dominate, the landscape.

🏛 **Pueblo Grande Museum and Archaeological Park**

4619 E. Washington St. *Tel (602) 495-0900.* ⬜ *9am–4:45pm Mon–Sat; 1–4:45pm Sun.* ⬤ *public hols.* 🖼 ♿ **http://**phoenix.gov/parks/pueblo.html

Located 5 miles (8 km) east of Downtown Phoenix, this museum displays an ancient Hohokam ruin, as well as many of their artifacts, including cooking utensils and pottery. Many of these pieces come from the adjacent Archaeological Park, the site of a Hohokam settlement from the 8th to the 14th centuries. The site, originally excavated in 1887, has a path through the ruins and signs pointing out the many irrigation canals once used by the Hohokam to water their crops.

Taliesin West façade, designed to blend with the desert landscape

Cacti in the Desert Botanical Garden at Papago Park

❀ Papago Park

Galvin Parkway & Van Buren Street. **Tel** *(602) 261-8318.* **www**.phoenix. gov/parks/hikepapa

Papago Park is located 6 miles (10 km) east of Phoenix's Downtown and is a popular place to unwind, with several hiking and cycling trails, picnic areas, and fishing lakes. Within the park, the **Desert Botanical Garden** is a 145-acre (59-ha) area devoted to more than 20,000 cacti and protected desert flora from around the world. The gardens are prettiest in spring, when many species flower. Guided tours explain the extraordinary life cycles of the desert plants.

The rolling hills and lakes of the **Phoenix Zoo** also occupy a large area of the Papago Park. The zoo reproduces a series of habitats including the Arizona-Sonora Desert and a tropical rainforest. Each zone provides a home for

Trail's End sign at Phoenix Zoo

more than 1,300 animals, their movement controlled by banks and canals rather than fences. A Safari Train provides a narrated tour of the zoo.

❀ Desert Botanical Garden
1201 N. Galvin Parkway. **Tel** *(480) 941-1225.* ○ *May–Sep: 7am–8pm daily; Oct–April: 8am–8pm daily.* ● *major public holidays.* 🎫 🚻 🖼 **www**.dbg.org

🦒 Phoenix Zoo
455 North Galvin Parkway. **Tel** *(602) 273-1341.* ○ *Jan 8–May: 8am–5pm daily; Jun–Sep: 7am–2pm daily (to 4pm Sat–Sun); Oct–Nov 6: 9am–5pm daily; Nov 7–Jan 7: 9am–4pm daily.* ● *Dec 25.* 🎫 🚻 **www**.phoenixzoo.org

♣ Mystery Castle
800 East Mineral Road. **Tel** *(602) 268-1581.* ○ *Oct–Jun: 11am–4pm Thu–Sun.* 🎫 🖼

Mystery Castle is possibly Phoenix's most eccentric attraction. In 1927, Boyce Luther Gulley came to Phoenix hoping that the warm climate would improve his ailing health. His daughter had loved building sandcastles on the beach, and since Phoenix was so far away from the ocean, Gulley set about creating a real-life fairy-tale sandcastle for her. He started work in 1930 and continued until his death in 1945. Discarded bricks and an assortment of scrapyard junk, including old car parts, have been used to build the structure. The 18-room interior can be seen on a guided tour, which explores the quirky building and its eclectic collection of antiques and furniture from around the world.

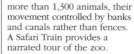

Façade of Phoenix's unusual Mystery Castle

The Apache Trail ❷

Road map C4. 🚗 ℹ️ *Globe Chamber of Commerce, 1360 N. Broad St., Globe (928) 425-4495 or Greater Phoenix Convention & Visitors Bureau, 50 N. 2nd St. (602) 254-6500.* **www**.visitphoenix.com

Heading east from Phoenix, Hwy 60 cuts straight across the desert to the suburb of Apache Junction at the start of Hwy 88. This road then begins its winding trail up into the Superstition Mountains. It is called the Apache Trail after the Native Americans who once lived here. The road is a wonderfully scenic mountain route that runs for 45 miles (72 km) up to Theodore Roosevelt Lake, which was created by the damming of the Salt River in 1911. Hwy 88 begins by climbing up into the hills and after 5 miles (8 km) reaches the Lost Dutchman State Park, named after the gold mine quarried here by Jacob Waltz and Jacob Weiser in the 1870s. These two miners cashed in a series of huge gold nuggets but kept the location of the mine to themselves. After their deaths, hundreds of prospectors worked these mountains in search of the famed gold mine but without success.

Beyond the state park, the highway passes by several campsites and through rugged terrain before reaching the tiny hamlet of Tortilla Flat, 17 miles (27 km) farther on, where there is an excellent café. This settlement is at the east end of slender Canyon Lake, the first of several Salt River reservoirs created to provide Phoenix with water. The lake has a marina, and 90-minute cruises are offered on *Dolly's Steamboat.* As the road climbs higher into the Superstition Mountains it becomes more difficult to negotiate, before it reaches the 280-ft- (84-m-) high Theodore Roosevelt Dam, where there is good fishing and a variety of watersports.

Three miles (5 km) east of the dam lies the **Tonto National Monument**, which comprises two large sets of

View of a section of the winding Apache Trail from Fish Creek Hill

ruined cliff dwellings. The Salado people, who created some of the superb pottery on display at the Heard Museum (see pp78–9) built these pueblos of rock and mud in the early 14th century. A steep, short trail leads up to the 19-room Lower Cliff Dwelling, but the 40-room Upper Cliff Dwelling can be visited only with a ranger.

Mining artifacts at the Gila County Historical Museum

🏛 Tonto National Monument

Hwy 188. *Tel* (928) 467-2241.
🕙 8am–5pm daily. 🚫 Dec 25. 🏷
🅿 Nov–Apr: Sat, Sun & Mon.

Globe ❸

Road map C4. 🏔 6,000. 🚌 🅷
Globe Chamber of Commerce, 1360 N. Broad St. (928) 425 4495. 🅰

The mining town of Globe lies about 100 miles (160 km) east of Phoenix in the wooded Dripping Spring and Pinal Mountains. In 1875, prospectors struck silver near here in what was then part of an Apache Reservation. The reservation was divested of its silver-bearing hills, and Globe was founded as a mining town and supply center. It was named for a massive nugget

of silver, shaped like a globe, which was unearthed in the hills nearby. The silver was quickly exhausted, but copper mining continued to thrive until 1931. Today, Globe has an attractive historic district with several notable late 19th- and early 20th-century buildings. The **Gila County Historical Museum** outlines Globe's history, with displays of a wide range of mining paraphernalia. On the south side of town are the Besh-Ba-Gowah Ruins, home of the Salado people in the 13th and 14th centuries.

🏛 Gila County Historical Museum

1330 N. Broad St. *Tel* (928) 425-7385. 🕙 10am–4pm Mon–Fri; 11am–3pm Sat. 🚫 Jan 1, Dec 25.
🏷 Donation requested.

Casa Grande Ruins National Monument ❹

Road map C4. *Tel* (520) 723-3172.
🕙 9am–5pm daily. 🚫 Dec 25. 🏷
♿ **www**.nps.gov/cagr

From around 200 BC until the middle of the 15th century, the Hohokam people farmed the Gila River Valley to the southeast of Phoenix. Among

the few Hohokam sites that remain, the fortresslike structure that makes up the Casa Grande National Monument is one of the most distinctive. Built in the early decades of the 14th century and named the "Big House" by a passing Jesuit missionary in 1694, this sturdy four-story structure has walls up to 4-ft (1.2-m) thick and is made from locally quarried caliche, a hard-setting subsoil. Experts believe that the holes cut in three of the walls were used for astronomical observations, but this is conjecture. The interior is out of bounds, but visitors can stroll round the exterior. The visitor center has a small museum with some interesting exhibits on Hohokam history and culture.

Casa Grande is located 15 miles (24 km) east of Interstate Highway 10 (I-10) on the outskirts of the town of Coolidge. It should not be confused with the town of Casa Grande found to the west of I-10.

The fortresslike Casa Grande Ruins National Monument

Tucson ❺

Despite being Arizona's second-largest city, Tucson has a friendly, welcoming atmosphere and a variety of interesting attractions to entertain the increasing number of visitors it receives each year. The city is located on the northern boundary of the Sonoran Desert in Southern Arizona, in a basin surrounded by five mountain ranges. When the Spanish colonizers arrived in the early 18th century they were determined to seize land from the local Tohono O'odham and Pima native tribes, who put up strong resistance *(see p40)*. This led the Spanish to move their regional fortress, or presidio, from Tubac to Tucson in the 1770s. The city was officially founded by Irish explorer Hugh O'Connor in 1775. Tucson's pride in its history is reflected in the careful preservation of 19th-century downtown buildings in the Barrio Historic District.

Exhibit at Arizona University

Contemporary glass skyscrapers in downtown Tucson

Exploring Tucson

Tucson's major art galleries and museums are clustered around two central areas: the University of Arizona campus (lying between Speedway Blvd., E. Sixth Street, Park, and Campbell Avenues) and the downtown area, which includes the Barrio and El Presidio historic districts. The latter contains many of the city's oldest buildings and is best explored on foot, as is the Barrio Historic District, south of Cushing Street.

🏛 Tucson Museum of Art and Historic Block

140 N. Main Ave. **Tel** (520) 624-2333.
⬜ 10am–4pm Tue–Sat, noon–4pm Sun. ⬤ public hols.
🆓 (free 1st Sun of month). ♿ 📷
www.tucsonarts.com
The Tucson Museum of Art opened in 1975 and is located on the Historic Block, which also contains five of the

Presidio's oldest dwellings – most of which are at least a hundred years old. These historic buildings form part of the art museum and house different parts of its extensive collection. The Museum's sculpture gardens and courtyards also form part of the Historic Block complex.

The art museum itself displays contemporary and 20th-century European and American works. In the adobe Stevens House (1866), the museum has its collection of Pre-Columbian tribal artifacts, some of which are 2,000 years old. There is the Spanish Colonial collection with some stunning pieces of religious art. The 1850s Casa Cordova houses *El Nacimiento*, a

Nativity scene with more than 300 earthenware figurines, on display from December to March. The J. Knox Corbett House, built in 1907, has Arts and Crafts Movement pieces such as a Morris chair.

Both guided and self-guided walking tours of this district are available from the Tucson Museum of Art.

🏛 Pima County Courthouse

115 N. Church Ave.
The Courthouse's pretty tiled dome is a downtown landmark. It was built in 1927, replacing its predecessor, a one-story adobe building dating from 1869. The position of the original presidio wall is marked out in the courtyard, and a section of the wall, 3-ft- (1-m-) thick and 12-ft- (4-m-) high, can still be seen inside the building.

🏚 El Presidio Historic District

The El Presidio Historic District occupies the area where the original Spanish fortress (presidio), San Agustin del Tucson, was built in 1775. More than 70 of the houses here were constructed during the Territorial period, before Arizona became a state in 1912. Today, these historic buildings are largely occupied by shops, restaurants, and offices, although archaeological excavations in the area have found artifacts from much earlier residents, the Hohokam Indians.

⛪ St. Augustine Cathedral

192 S. Stone Ave. **Tel** (520) 623-6351. ⬜ Services only; call for times.

Stained-glass window in the cathedral

St. Augustine Cathedral was begun in 1896 and modeled after the Spanish Colonial style of the Cathedral of Querétaro in central Mexico. This gleaming white building features an imposing sandstone façade with intricate carvings of the yucca, the saguaro, and the horned toad – three symbols of the Sonoran Desert – while a bronze statue of St. Augustine, the city's patron saint, stands above the main door.

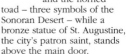

One of many 19th-century adobe houses in the Barrio Historic District

VISITORS' CHECKLIST

Road map C5. 👥 *750,000.*
✈ *Tucson International, 10 miles
(16 km) south of downtown.*
🚆 *Amtrak Station, 400 E. Toole
Ave.* 🚌 *Greyhound Lines, 471
W. Congress.* ℹ️ *Metropolitan
Tucson Convention & Visitors
Bureau, 110 S. Church Ave.
(520) 624-1817; (800) 638-
8350.* 🎭 *La Fiesta de los
Vaqueros (late Feb).*
www.visittucson.org

🏛 Barrio Historic District

This area was Tucson's business district in the late 19th century. Today, its streets are quiet and lined with original adobe houses painted in bright colors. On nearby Main Street is the "wishing shrine" of **El Tiradito**, which marks the spot where a young man was killed as a result of a lovers' triangle. Local people lit candles here for his soul and still believe that if their candles burn for a whole night, their wishes will come true.

🏛 The University of Arizona

Visitors' Center, 845 E. University Blvd, Suite 145. ***Tel** (520) 621-5130.*
Several museums are located on or near the UA campus, about a mile (1.6 km) east of downtown. The **Arizona Historical Society Museum** traces Arizona's history from the arrival of the Spanish in 1540, to modern times. The **University of Arizona Museum of Art** focuses on European and American fine art from the Renaissance to the 20th century. Opposite the

Museum of Art is the **Center for Creative Photography**, which contains the work of many of the 20th century's greatest American photographers. Visitors can view the extensive archives by advance reservations. The **Flandrau Science Center** features a range of child-friendly interactive exhibits.

One of the most renowned collections of artifacts, covering 2,000 years of native history, is displayed by the **Arizona State Museum**, which was founded in 1893.

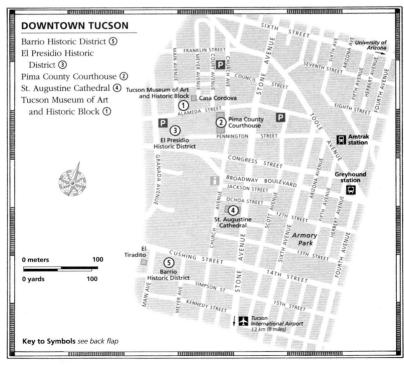

DOWNTOWN TUCSON

Barrio Historic District ⑤
El Presidio Historic
    District ③
Pima County Courthouse ②
St. Augustine Cathedral ④
Tucson Museum of Art
    and Historic Block ①

Key to Symbols *see back flap*

Exploring Around Tucson

Beyond the city center, metropolitan Tucson extends north to the Santa Catalina Mountains, the foothills of which are the start of a scenic drive to the top of Mount Lemmon. To the west are the Tucson Mountains, which frame Saguaro National Park West. This park has a sister park to the east of the city. To the south lies the beautiful mission church of San Xavier del Bac (*see pp88–9*), which stands out from the flat, desert landscape of the Tohono O'odham Indian Reservation.

SIGHTS AT A GLANCE

Arizona-Sonora Desert
  Museum ②
Mission San Xavier del Bac
  See pp88–9 ④
Mount Lemmon ⑥
Old Tucson Studios ③
Pima Air and Space Museum ⑤
Saguaro National Park
  (East and West) ①

KEY

🔲 Downtown Tucson

⬜ Greater Tucson

✈ International airport

══ Interstate

━━ Major highway

══ Highway

── Railroad

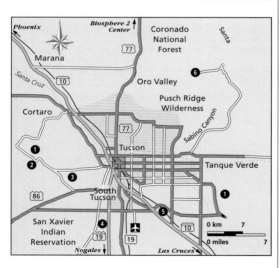

Vistas of tall saguaro cacti in Saguaro National Park

are also more than 100 miles (160 km) of hiking trails here. Both sections of the park offer ranger-guided walks during the winter season.

🏛 Arizona-Sonora Desert Museum

2021 N. Kinney Rd. **Tel** (520) 883-2702. ⬜ Mar–Sep: 7:30am–5pm daily (Jun–Aug: to 3pm Mon–Fri, 10pm Sat); Oct–Feb: 8:30am–5pm daily. 📷 ♿ www.desertmuseum.org
This fascinating natural history park covers more than 21 desert acres (8.5 ha), and includes a botanical garden, zoo, and natural history museum. At the museum, displays describe the history, geology, and flora and fauna of the Sonoran Desert region. Outside, a 2-mile (3-km) walkway passes more than 1,200 varieties of plants, the setting for hummingbirds, wildcats, and Mexican wolves.

🌵 Saguaro National Park

3693 S. Old Spanish Trail. **Tel** (520) 733-5153. ⬜ 9am–5pm daily. ● Dec 25. 📷 (Loop Drive only). ♿ www.nps.gov/sagu
Perhaps the most famous symbol of the American Southwest, the saguaro (pronounced sa-wah-ro) cactus is unique to the Sonoran desert. The largest species of cactus in the United States, the saguaro has a life span of up to 200 years. Those that survive into old age may reach heights of up to 50 ft (16.5 m) and weigh more than 8 tons (7.3 kg).

Set up in 1994, the park comprises two tracts of land on the eastern and western flanks of Tucson, which together cover more than 91,000 acres (36,800 ha). The 9-mile (14.5-km) Bajada Loop Drive runs deep into the park on a dirt road, past hiking trails and picnic areas. One of these trails leads to ancient Hohokam petroglyphs carved into the volcanic rock. The eastern park has the oldest saguaros, which can be seen along the 8-mile (13-km) Cactus Forest Drive. There

One of many flowering cacti from the Arizona-Sonora Desert Museum

🎬 Old Tucson Studios

201 S. Kinney Rd. **Tel** (520) 883-0100. ⬜ 10am–4pm daily (to 6pm mid-Feb– mid-Apr). ● Thanksgiving, Dec 24 & 25. 📷 ♿ www.oldtucson.com
Modeled on an old Western town of the 1860s, this Wild West theme park was built as

a set for a Western movie in 1939. Since then, Old Tucson Studios has formed the backdrop for some of Hollywood's most famous Westerns, such as *Gunfight at the OK Corral* (1957) starring Burt Lancaster and Kirk Douglas, and *Rio Bravo* (1958) starring John Wayne. The popular 1970s TV series *Little House on the Prairie* was also filmed here. More recently, movies such as *The Three Amigos* (1986) and *Tombstone* (1993) were partly shot here.

Main Street's 1860s frontier atmosphere provides an authentic setting for performers in period costume, who entertain visitors with stunt shows, gunfights, and stagecoach rides. Visitors can also try panning for gold.

Gunfight staged outside the mission at Old Tucson Studios

🏠 San Xavier del Bac Mission
See pp88–9.

🏛 Pima Air and Space Museum
6000 E. Valencia Rd. **Tel** *(520) 574-0462.* 🕘 *9am–5pm daily.* 🕘 *Thanksgiving, Dec 25.* 🎦 📷 *call for times.* **www**.pimaair.org

Some 9 miles (14.5 km) southeast of downtown Tucson, the Pima Air and Space Museum contains one of the largest collections of aircraft in the world. Visitors are met with the astonishing sight of more than 275 vintage aircraft set out in ranks across the desert.

Three presidential aircraft are displayed here – Kennedy's, Nixon's, and Johnson's – as well as a replica of the Wright brothers' famous 1903 aircraft, and some advanced jet fighters. Exhibits in four aircraft hangars show military and aviation memorabilia, including a replica World War II barracks. The adjacent **Davis-Monthan Air Force Base** displays more than 2,000 planes, including

B-29s and supersonic bombers. The museum also runs the **Titan Missile Museum** (open daily all year) located 20 minutes south of the city at Sahuarita, which is a ballistic missile silo.

✈ Mount Lemmon
📱 *(520) 749-8700.*

Mount Lemmon is the highest peak in the Santa Catalina Mountains, standing at 9,157 ft (2,790 m). During the hot summers the cooler air of the mountains' higher elevations attracts many visitors. A one-hour scenic drive, beginning in the Tucson city limits and connecting to the Mount Lemmon Highway, takes you to the summit. There are around 150 miles (240 km) of hiking trails here, while a side road leads to the quaint resort village of Summerhaven, with shops and restaurants. At the top, the Sky Valley lift operates for a small fee most of the year.

🏛 Biosphere 2 Center
5 miles N.E. of jct. of Hwys 77 & 79. **Tel** *(520) 838-6200.* 🕘 *9am–4pm daily.* 🕘 *Thanksgiving, Dec 25.* 🎦 ♿ 📷 **www**.b2science.org

Biosphere 2 is a unique research facility that was set up in 1991. Eight people were sealed within a futuristic structure of glass and white steel furnished with five of the Earth's habitats: rainforest, desert, savanna, marsh, and an ocean with a living coral reef. Over a period of two years the effect of the people on the environment as well as the effect on them of isolation in this "world," were studied, with varying results.

Today, there are no people living in the Biosphere, which is currently being used to study the effect of increased carbon dioxide in the atmosphere. Visitors can take a two-hour guided tour of the facility. There are two tours of the inside, one of which incurs an additional charge.

BIRDWATCHING IN THE CANYONS OF SOUTHERN ARIZONA

The landscape of southern Arizona may seem dry at first glance, but this high desert environment gets about 11 in (280 mm) of rain annually. This enables a surprising range of vegetation to flourish, from cacti to brightly colored wildflowers in spring. In turn, this attracts an amazing variety of birds, and the area is one of the top five birdwatching locations in the US.

The verdant canyons between Tucson and the Mexican border offer the best birdwatching. Just off I-19, near Green Valley, Madera Canyon plays host to some 400 bird species. As well as more common varieties of hummingbirds, flycatchers, and warblers, many rare species such as the brown-crested flycatcher and the black-and-white warbler are often sighted here. Further afield, Ramsey Canyon in the Huachuca Mountains is the country's hummingbird capital with 14 varieties of these tiny delicate creatures.

Broad-billed hummingbird

Space age buildings of the Biosphere 2 Center, north of Tucson

San Xavier del Bac Mission

San Xavier del Bac is the oldest and best-preserved mission church in the Southwest. An imposing landmark as it rises out of the stark, flat landscape of the surrounding Tohono O'odham reservation, its white walls dazzle in the desert sun. A mission was first established here by the Jesuit priest Father Eusebio Kino in 1700 *(see p40)*. The complex seen today was completed in 1797 by Franciscan missionaries.

Built of adobe brick, the mission is considered to be the finest example of Spanish Colonial architecture in the US *(see p22)*. The church also incorporates other styles, including several Baroque flourishes. In the 1990s its interior was extensively renovated, and five *retablos* (altarpieces) have been restored to their original glory.

The Hill of the Cross, to the east of the mission, offers fine views

The bell tower's elegant, white dome that reflects the Moorish styles that are incorporated into San Xavier's Spanish Colonial architecture.

★ Façade of the church
The ornate Baroque façade is decorated with the carved figures of saints (although some are much eroded) including a headless St. Cecilia and an unidentifiable St. Francis, now a simple sand cone.

The mortuary chapel contains a statue of the Virgin Mary, surrounded by candles.

Stonework detail
Over recent years the identity of the carved statues to the left of the entrance has changed. Long thought to be St. Catherine of Siena and St. Barbara, they have now been identified as St. Agatha of Catania and St. Agnes of Rome.

Painted ceiling
On entering the church, visitors are struck by the dome's ceiling with its glorious paintings of religious figures. Vivid pigments of vermilion and blue were used to contrast with the stark white stone background.

STAR FEATURES

★ Façade

★ Main altar

★ Main Altar
The spectacular gold and red retablo mayor is decorated in Mexican Baroque style with elaborate columns. More than 50 statues were carved in Mexico then brought to San Xavier where artists gilded and painted them with brightly colored glazes.

VISITORS' CHECKLIST

Road map C5. 1950 W. San Xavier Rd, 10 miles (16 km) south of Tucson on I-19.
Tel (520) 294-2624.
🕐 *8am–5pm daily.* ♿ 🖼 🛍
www.sanxaviermission.org

Altar Dome
The dome and high transepts are filled with painted wooden statuary and covered with murals depicting scenes from the Gospels.

The patio is closed to the public but can be seen from the museum.

Chapel of Our Lady
This statue of the Virgin is one of the Church's three sculptures of Mary. Here she is shown as La Dolorosa *or* Sorrowing Mother.

The museum includes a sheepskin psalter and photographs of other historic missions on the Tohono O'odham Reservation.

The shop entrance

Boats and watersports in the picturesque setting of Lake Yuma

Yuma ❻

Road map A4. 🏛 *65,000.*
🚊 *Amtrak, 281 S. Gila St.*
🚌 *Greyhound, 170 E. 17th Place.*
ℹ️ *Yuma Convention and Visitors'*
Bureau, 139 S. 4th Ave. (800) 293-
0071. 🅰 *www.visityuma.com*

Yuma occupies a strategic
position at the confluence of
the Colorado and Gila rivers.
Though noted by Spanish
explorers in the 16th century,
it was not until the 1850s that
the town rose to prominence,
when the river crossing
became the gateway to
California for tens of
thousands of gold seekers.
Fort Yuma, built in 1849, also
boosted steamboat traffic
along the Colorado River.
    Today, Yuma's hot and
sunny winter climate makes it
a popular winter destination
for travelers or "snowbirds,"
escaping colder climes. Two
state historic parks highlight
its rich history: Yuma Crossing,
covering 20 acres (8 ha) along
the Colorado, looks at river
transportation and army life
in the later 1800s, while Yuma
Territorial Prison re-creates
conditions at the state's main
prison facility from 1876–1909.

Organ Pipe Cactus National Monument ❼

Road map B5. *Tel (520) 387-6849.*
⭕ *daily; visitor center 8am–5pm.*
⭕ *public holidays.* 🎫 🦽 📷 🅰
www.nps.gov/orpi

The organ pipe is a Sonoran
desert species of cactus,
which is a cousin to the
saguaro *(see p86)* but with
multiple arms branching up
from the base, as its name
suggests. The organ pipe is
rare in the United States,
growing almost exclusively
in this large and remote area
of land along the Mexican
border in southwest Arizona.
Many other plant and animal
species flourish in this un-
spoiled desert wilderness,
although a lot of animals, such
as snakes, jackrabbits, and
kangaroo rats, emerge only in
the cool of the night. Other
cacti such as the saguaro, the
Engelmann prickly pear, and
the teddybear cholla are best
seen in early summer for their
glorious displays of floral color.
    There are two scenic drives
through the park: the 21-mile
(34-km) Ajo Mountain Drive
and the shorter 5-mile (8-km)
Puerto Blanco Drive. The Ajo
Mountain Drive takes two
hours and winds through
startling desert landscapes in
the foothills of the mountains.
The Puerto Blanco Drive
leads to a half-hour trail into

Red Tanks Tinaja, a natural
water pocket, and the picnic
area near Pinkley Peak. A
variety of hiking trails in the
park range in difficulty from
paved, wheelchair-accessible
paths to wilderness walks. A
visitor center offers exhibits
on the park's flora and fauna,
as well as maps and camping
permits, and there are guided
walks available in winter.
    Be aware that the park is a
good two-and-a-half- to three-
hour drive from Tucson one
way. If you want to explore
this environment in any detail,
plan to camp overnight. Ajo,
34 miles (55 km) to the north,
has motels and services.

Tubac ❽

Road map C5. 🏛 *150.* ℹ️ *Tubac
Chamber of Commerce (520) 398-
2704.* **www**.tubacaz.com

The Royal Presidio (fortress)
of San Ignacio de Tubac was
built in 1752 to protect the
local Spanish-owned ranches
and mines, as well as the
nearby missions of Tumacacori
and San Xavier, from attacks
by local Pima natives. Tubac
was also the first stopover on
the famous overland
expedition to colonize the San
Francisco Bay area in 1776.
The trek was led by the fort's
captain, Juan Bautista de Anza
(see p40). Following his return,
the garrison moved north to
Tucson and for the next
hundred years, Tubac

Rare cacti at the Organ Pipe Cactus National Monument

Mission church at Tumacacori National Historical Park

declined. Today, the town is a small but thriving art colony, with attractive shops, galleries, and restaurants lining the streets around the plaza.

Tubac's historical remains are displayed at the **Tubac Presidio State Historic Park**, which encompasses the foundations of the original presidio in an underground display, as well as several historic buildings, including the delightful Old Tubac Schoolhouse. Also here, the Presidio Museum contains artifacts covering over one hundred years of Tubac's history, including painted altarpieces and colonial furniture.

Environs

Just 3 miles (5 km) south of town lies **Tumacacori National Historical Park** with the beautiful ruined mission. The present church was built in around 1800 upon the ruins of the original 1691 mission established by Jesuit priest, Father Eusebio Kino *(see p40)*. The Mission was abandoned in 1848, and today its weatherbeaten ochre façade together with its brick columns, arched entry, and carved wooden door is an evocative reminder of former times. The cavernous interior is wonderfully atmospheric, with patches of exposed adobe brick and faded murals on the sanctuary walls. A small museum provides an excellent background on the mission builders and native Pima Indians. Weekend craft demonstrations, including tortilla making, basketry, and Mexican pottery, are held September through June. During the first weekend in December, La Fiesta de Tumacacori *(see p35)*, which

celebrates the cultural heritage of the upper Santa Cruz Valley, is held on the mission grounds.

🏛 Tubac Presidio State Historic Park
Burrel St. & Presidio Drive. **Tel** (520) 398-2252. ⏰ 8am–5pm daily. ⏰ Dec 25. 🅿 ♿ 🅿

🏛 Tumacacori National Historical Park
Tel (520) 398-2341. ⏰ 9am–5pm daily. ● Thanksgiving, Dec 25. 🅿 ♿ 🅿 www.nps.gov/tuma

Nogales ❾

Road map C5. 🏔 19,500. ✈ 🚌
ℹ 123 W. Kino Park (520) 287-3685.

Nogales is really two towns that straddle the US border with Mexico, at the end of Mexico's Pacific Highway. This is a busy port of entry, handling huge amounts of freight, including 75 percent of all winter fruit and vegetables sold in North America. The town attracts large numbers of visitors in search of bargains at shopping districts on both sides of the border. Decorative blankets, furniture, and crafts

Mexican pottery found in Nogales

are good value. There is a profound contrast between the US side and the ramshackle houses across the border, and visitors should be aware that the Mexican Nogales can be crowded with continuous hustle from street vendors eager for business. Still, it is a popular day-trip and there are several good restaurants here.

Visitors are advised to leave their cars on the US side, where attendants mind the parking lots, and to walk across the border. Those who drive across the border should check that their car insurance is valid in Mexico. Visas are required only for those traveling farther south than the town and for stays of more than 72 hours. US and Canadian citizens should carry a passport for identification as drivers' licenses are not sufficient proof of citizenship. Foreign nationals should make sure their visa status enables them to re-enter the US; those on the Visa Waiver Scheme *(see p284)* should have no problem. US dollars are accepted everywhere.

ASTRONOMY IN SOUTHERN ARIZONA

Southern Arizona's dry air and dark, clear nights have made it an international center for astronomy. Within a 75-mile (120-km) radius of Tucson, there is a cluster of prestigious observatories located in the mountains, including the Kitt Peak National Observatory, with its large telescopes, and the Fred Lawrence Whipple Observatory, both of which can be toured. Mount Graham International Observatory features some of the world's most advanced telescope technology. Opportunities for star-gazing are exceptional, but even without high-powered equipment, anyone can enjoy the countless constellations in the night skies.

Observatories in the mountains of southern Arizona

Bisbee ⑩

Road map C5. 🏚 6,500. 🚃
🛈 Bisbee Chamber of Commerce,
1 Main St. (520) 432-5421.
www.bisbeearizona.com

This is one of the most atmospheric mining towns in the Southwest. The discovery of copper here in the 1880s sparked a mining rush, and by the turn of the century Bisbee was the largest city between St. Louis and San Francisco. Victorian buildings such as the landmark Copper Queen Hotel still dominate the historic town center, while attractive clusters of houses cling to the sides of the surrounding mountains.

Visitors can tour the mines that once flourished here, such as the deep underground Queen Mine or, a short drive south of town, the Lavender Open Pit Mine. Exhibits at the Bisbee Mining and Historical Museum illustrate the realities of mining and frontier life here.

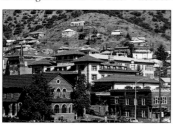

The Victorian mining town of Bisbee clings to the slopes of the surrounding mountains

Tombstone ⑪

Road map C5. 🏚 6,500. 🛈 Visitor
Center, 395 E. Allen St. (520) 457-
3929. **www**.tombstone.org

Tombstone is a living legend, forever known as the site of the 1881 gunfight at the OK Corral between the Earp brothers and the Clanton gang (see p55). The town's historic streets and buildings form one of the most popular attractions in the Southwest.

Tombstone was founded by Ed Schieffelin, who went prospecting on Apache land in 1877 despite a warning that "all you'll find out there is your tombstone." He found a mountain of silver instead,

Re-enactment of the gunfight at the OK Corral, Tombstone

and his sardonically named shanty town boomed with the ensuing silver rush. One of the wildest towns in the West, Tombstone was soon full of prospectors, gamblers, cowboys, and lawmen. In its heyday, the town was larger than San Francisco. More than $37 million worth of silver was extracted from the mines between 1880 and 1887, when miners struck an aquifer and flooded the mine shafts.

In 1962 "the town too tough to die" became a National Historic Landmark, and, with much of its historic downtown immaculately preserved, it attracts many visitors, all eager to sample the unique atmosphere. Allen Street, with its wooden boardwalks, shops, and restaurants, is the town's main thoroughfare. The **OK Corral** is preserved as a museum, and re-enactments of the infamous gunfight between the Earp brothers, Doc Holliday and the Clanton gang are staged daily at 2pm.

Tombstone Courthouse on Toughnut Street was the seat of justice for the county from 1882 to 1929 and is now a state historic site. It contains a museum featuring the restored courtroom and many historical exhibits and artifacts, including photographs of some of the town's famous characters. Toughnut Street used to be known as "Rotten Row" as it was once lined with miners' tents, bordellos, and more than one hundred bars.

Among other buildings worth looking for in the downtown area is the Rose Tree Inn Museum, home of what is reputedly the world's largest rosebush. There is also the Bird Cage Theater, once a bawdy dance hall and bordello, and so-named for the covered "crib" compartments, or cages, hanging from the ceiling, in which ladies of the night plied their trade. Nearby is the once rowdy Crystal Palace Saloon, which is still a bar.

Just north of town, the famous Boothill Cemetery is full of the graves of those who perished in Tombstone, peacefully or otherwise. This evocative place is not without the occasional spot of humor. Look for the marker lamenting the death of George Johnson, hanged by mistake in 1882, which reads: "He was right, we was wrong, but we strung him up, and now he's gone".

🏛 **OK Corral**
Allen St. **Tel** (520) 457-3456.
🕐 9am–5pm daily. 📷 ♿
www.ok-corral.com

🏛 **Tombstone Courthouse**
219 Toughnut St. **Tel** (520) 457-
3311. 🕐 8am–5pm daily. ● Dec
25. 📷 ♿ **www**.azstateparks.com

Tombstone Courthouse in the town center is now a museum

Kartchner Caverns State Park ⑫

Road map C5. **Tel** (520) 586-2283.
⬜ 7am–6pm daily (cave tours 8:30am–4:30pm by reservation).
⬤ Dec 25. 🖼 🚻 🎦 obligatory. 🅿
www.azstateparks.com/parks/kaca

The Kartchner Caverns are one of Arizona's great natural wonders. Located in the Whetstone Mountains, the caves were discovered in 1974 when two cavers crawled through a sinkhole in a hillside into 7 acres (3 ha) of caverns filled with colorful formations. Out of concern to protect the caves, they kept their discovery a secret for 14 years as they explored this wonderland of speleotherms, or cave formations, made of layers of calcite deposited by dripping or flowing water over millions of years. In 1988 the land was purchased by the state, but it took 11 years to complete the development that would allow public access while conserving the special conditions that enable these "wet" caves to continue growing.

Before entering the caves, visitors are introduced to the geology of the formations at the Discovery Center. Once inside, visitors must not touch the features, as skin oils stop their growth. Along with huge stalactites and stalagmites, there is an abundance of other types of formation such as the aptly named 21-ft (132-m) soda straw, the turnip shields, and popcorn.

Orange and white column formations at Kartchner Caverns

Amerind Foundation ⑬

Road map C5. **Tel** (520) 586-3666.
⬜ 10am–4pm Tue–Sun.
⬤ Mon, public holidays. 🖼
www.amerind.org

The Amerind Foundation is one of the most important private archaeological and ethnological museums in the country. The name Amerind is a contraction of "American Indian," and this collection contains tens of thousands of artifacts from different Native American cultures. All aspects of Native American life are shown here, with displays covering Inuit masks, Cree tools, and sculpted effigy figures from Mexico's Casas Grandes.

The adjacent Amerind Art Gallery has a fine collection of western art by such prominent artists as William Leigh

(1866–1955) and Frederic Remington (1861–1909). The delightful pink buildings, designed in the Spanish Colonial Revival style (see p22), are also of interest.

Chiricahua National Monument ⑭

Road map D5. **Tel** (520) 824-3560.
⬜ 8am–4:30pm daily. ⬤ 25 Dec.
🖼 🚻 🎦 🅿 **www**.nps.gov/chir

The Chiricahua Mountains were once the homeland of a band of Apache people and an impenetrable base from which they launched attacks on settlers in the late 1800s. This 12,000-acre (4,800-ha) area now preserves stunning rock formations, which were created by a series of volcanic eruptions around 27 million years ago. Massive rocks balanced on small pedestals, soaring rock spires, and enormous stone columns make up the bizarre landscape, visible from the monument's scenic drive and hiking trails.

The nearby town of Willcox houses the intriguing **Rex Allen Arizona Cowboy Museum**, which is devoted to a native son who became a famous movie cowboy, starring in 19 films in the 1950s.

🏛 **Rex Allen Arizona Cowboy Museum**
155 N. Railroad Ave. **Tel** (520) 384-4583. ⬜ 10am–4pm daily.
⬤ public holidays. 🖼 🚻

Massive rock spires formed by million-year-old volcanic eruptions at Chiricahua National Monument

LAS VEGAS

The Changing Face of Las Vegas

No other city in the US has reinvented itself so often and with such profitable results as Las Vegas. Set in an unpromising landscape, bordering three deserts, artesian waters beneath the land first supported life here. Successive groups, from Native Americans to Mexican traders, Mormons, and railroad workers, all survived the environment. They added to a unique set of factors that gave birth to a Las Vegas they would barely recognize today.

No longer unique in offering casinos, the city still draws the crowds. Associated with some of the biggest names in show business, such as Frank Sinatra and Elvis Presley, with eccentric millionaires like Howard Hughes, with mobsters such as Bugsy Siegel, and above all with glamour, Vegas continues to fire the imagination as the fun city of stretch limos, showgirls, and an "anything goes" ethos for those who can pay for it.

Helen Stewart *was a local ranch owner who sold her land to the railroad, which led to the founding of the city of Las Vegas in 1905.*

DOWNTOWN LAS VEGAS

The city grew up around Fremont Street in Downtown Las Vegas in the early 1900s. By the 1960s *(see right)*, the area had began to suffer from competition from the Strip. Today, the area has been revived as the Fremont Street Experience *(see below right and p118)*.

Roulette *was one of the games offered in Las Vegas once gambling was legalized in Nevada in 1931. The city was a hedonistic escape from the 1930s' Depression.*

Construction of the Hoover Dam, *34 miles (55 km) from Las Vegas on the Colorado River, brought a rise in the city's fortunes (see p121). By the early 1920s Las Vegas had declined, and its population had fallen to 2,300. When construction began in 1931, money and people flowed into town, and by the early 1930s the population had swelled to around 7,500. Tens of thousands of visitors arrived to see the building of the dam and to enjoy the new gambling clubs springing up.*

Benjamin Siegel, *(left) called "Bugsy" behind his back, was a New York City gangster. He moved to Los Angeles in the 1930s and created the luxurious Flamingo hotel and casino in Vegas* (see p111). *He was killed by fellow investors only a year after the casino had opened in 1946, probably because other mobsters disliked his high profile. Although nothing remains of the original Flamingo building, there is still a tropical-themed luxury hotel on this spot.*

HOWARD HUGHES

Billionaire Howard Hughes arrived in Las Vegas in November 1966, moving into a luxurious suite on the ninth floor of the Desert Inn hotel. When the hotel's management tried to move him out a few months later, Hughes bought the place for $13.2 million. Although he never left his room in four years, he spent some $300 million buying Vegas properties. These included the Silver Slipper hotel and casino across the Strip, whose blinking neon slipper disturbed him. As owner he had it switched off.

Hughes is credited with bringing legitimate business and a sanitized image to Vegas, sounding the death knell of mob investment in the city. In the 1960s, family oriented resorts such as Circus Circus opened, and such entertainment corporations as MGM, Hilton, and Holiday Inn began legitimate building programs. However, as recently as the 1970s and 80s mobsters were caught skimming profits from some Vegas hotels.

Billionaire entrepreneur Howard Hughes

THE STRIP

From a few low-rise buildings along a desert road in the 1960s to the glittering neon canyon of today, the transformation of the Strip has been remarkable *(see pp102–105).*

The Rat Pack, *which included Peter Lawford, Sammy Davis Jr., Frank Sinatra, Joey Bishop, and Dean Martin, sealed Las Vegas' reputation as an entertainment mecca in the 1950s with shows at the now-demolished Sands hotel.*

LAS VEGAS

*R*ising like a mirage out of Nevada's beautiful southern desert, Las Vegas is a glittering wonderland that promises fun to all its visitors. The city's unique attraction is its hotels with their fantastic architecture, re-creating such cities as New York and Venice. At the heart of these palaces lie the casinos where the lure of million-dollar jackpots draws almost 37 million visitors each year.

Occupied by the Ancestral Puebloan peoples until around 1150 AD, the Las Vegas area was the home of several Native American tribes, including the Paiute, until Mexican traders arrived in the early 19th century. Mormon pioneers built a fort here in 1855, establishing the beginnings of a settlement in the area, which gradually developed. Officially founded in 1905, the city of Las Vegas expanded in the 1930s with the building of the Hoover Dam across the Colorado River, some 30 miles (45 km) away, and the legalization of gambling here in 1931. The influx of construction workers with money to burn, and the electricity and water provided by the dam, paved the way for the casino-based growth that took place in the 1940s and 1950s.

Since the 1990s, numbers of ever more extravagant resorts have been built in the city, including the impressive Bellagio, Venetian, and Aladdin, and this expansion shows no signs of slowing. For those who can tear themselves away from the city, the surrounding country has much to offer. Lake Mead and the stunning rock formations of the Valley of Fire State Park provide a range of outdoor pleasures from horseback riding to watersports.

In 2006, Las Vegas was the fastest growing city in the US, but the population has since stabilized at just under two million. Tourism and gaming remain the most successful industries – it has 19 of the 25 largest hotels in the world – but it is also known for its wedding chapels and entertainment.

Decorative stained-glass ceiling of the Tropicana Hotel's elegant casino

◁ One of the city's oldest neon signs, "Vegas Vic" located on Fremont Street, downtown Las Vegas

Exploring Las Vegas

Las Vegas has two centers – the wonderland of the
Strip, and the older Downtown area, where the city
began in 1905 *(see pp96–7)*. The Strip is really Las
Vegas Boulevard (Hwy 604), a 4.5-mile- (7.2-km-)
long street that runs northeast through the city. The
Downtown area crosses the Strip around Fremont
Street *(see p118)*. Strictly speaking, the part of the
Strip that lies south of the Sahara Hotel is in Clark
County, while the city proper is centered around
Downtown Vegas. Ringed by mountains, canyons,
and desert, the Las Vegas area also has a wealth
of natural beauty in a variety of parks, some of it
just a short drive from the Strip *(see pp120–21)*.

The dazzling sight of the Las Vegas Strip, illuminated
at night by myriad shimmering neon lights

GETTING AROUND

The Strip is a long road, and driving
is recommended as the best way to
get around. Major hotels have free
parking lots, as well as valet service.
The Deuce bus runs along the Strip
stopping at the major hotels, and the
monorail service operates between
the MGM Grand and the Sahara
Hotel. Taxis are also an option and
are best hailed at hotels.

KEY

▨	The Strip *see pp102–105*
✈	International airport
🚉	Train station
🚌	Bus station
ℹ	Visitor information
═	Interstate
═	Major highway
═	Highway

0 meters   500

0 yards   500

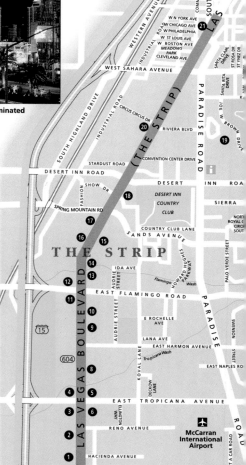

The famous Caesars Palace Forum

SEE ALSO

- **Where to Stay** pp237–40
- **Where to Eat** pp257–61

SIGHTS AT A GLANCE

Hotels and Casinos
Bellagio ⑪
Caesars Palace ⑫
Circus Circus ⑳
Excalibur ③
Flamingo Las Vegas ⑬
Las Vegas Hilton ⑲
Luxor Las Vegas ②
Mandalay Bay ①
MGM Grand ⑤
Mirage ⑯
New York New York ④
Paris ⑩
Planet Hollywood Resort
  & Casino ⑨
Riviera ⑱
Stratosphere ㉑
Treasure Island ⑰
Tropicana Resort & Casino ⑥
Venetian ⑮

Historic Towns and Cities
Boulder City/Hoover
  Dam ㉖

Streets and Malls
Fremont Street
  Experience ㉒
Showcase Mall ⑧

Museums and Galleries
Autocollections at the
  Imperial Palace ⑭
Las Vegas Natural History
  Museum ㉔
Liberace Museum ⑦
Lied Discovery Children's
  Museum ㉓
Old Las Vegas Mormon
  State Historic Park ㉕

Areas of Natural Beauty
Lake Mead National
  Recreation Area ㉗
Mount Charleston ㉙
Red Rock Canyon National
  Conservation Area ㉚
Valley of Fire State Park ㉘

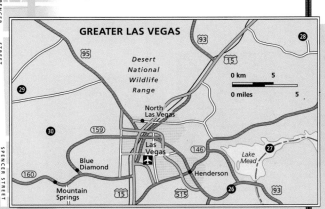

A View of The Strip I

The heart of Las Vegas lies along Las Vegas Boulevard, a sparkling vista of neon known simply as "the Strip." This southern stretch of the Strip is home to a cluster of vast, lavishly-themed hotels, including Luxor, New York New York, and the Bellagio. Aiming to satisfy all a visitor's needs in one location, with restaurants, shops, and casinos, the hotels are best-appreciated at night when the lights come on and these megaresorts become a fantasyland of such riotous design as the sphinx that fronts the Luxor hotel's striking pyramid. Change is constant along the Strip, where hotels get even larger, acclaimed chefs open new restaurants, and long-running shows close to make room for the latest stars.

The glittering Strip by night

Luxor
The re-created Grand Staircase is one of the highlights of the Titanic Artifact Exhibition at the Luxor ❷

New York New York
A replica of the Statue of Liberty forms part of the façade of this hotel, which is composed of a host of Manhattan landmarks such as the Empire State Building ❹

Monte Carlo's Renaissance-style architecture comes to life at this hotel.

Mandalay Bay's interior, with its palm trees and bamboo, re-creates a 19th century tropical paradise.

Excalibur's towers are a kitsch fantasy of medieval England.

TROPICANA AVE

LAS VEGAS BLVD

Showcase Mall is a striking building, with its giant neon Coca-cola bottle. A huge games arcade makes the mall popular with families.

Tropicana
This casino was rebuilt in the late 1970s, with a stunning Art Nouveau-style stained-glass ceiling and glass lamps ❻

MGM Grand Hotel
This famous statue of Leo, symbol of the Hollywood film studio, MGM, rises 45 ft (15 m) above the corner of Tropicana Avenue ❺

For hotels and restaurants in this region see pp237–40 and pp257–61

Caesars Palace

Reproduction Roman statuary adorns the grounds of Caesars Palace. One of the Strip's oldest and most glamorous hotels, Caesars was built in 1966. Inside, the lavish Forum Shops mall features moving statues **12**

Lobby of the Bellagio

Lighting the ceiling of the hotel's elegant lobby, this colorful glass installation was designed by famous glass artist Dale Chihuly **11**

Imperial Palace

A pagoda fronts this Asian-themed hotel, famous for its classic car collection that is open to visitors **14**

Paris resort's half-scale replica of Parisian land-mark, the Eiffel Tower, dominates the Strip.

W. DUNES RD

THE STRIP

FLAMINGO ROAD

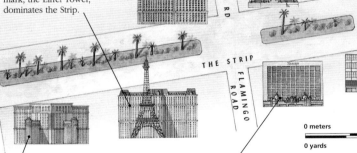

0 meters 300

0 yards 300

Planet Hollywood Resort & Casino

The reputation of this hotel, which opened in 1963, as one of the glitziest on the Strip was sealed when Elvis married Priscilla here in 1967. It retains the old glamor under its new guise, Planet Hollywood **9**

Flamingo Las Vegas

The flaming pink and orange neon flower of the Flamingo hotel's façade is a famous Strip icon. Redesigned in the 1970s and 80s, the original 1946 building was the beloved project of gangster Bugsy Siegel (see p97) **13**

A View of The Strip II

The first casino resort to open on Las Vegas' Strip in 1941 was the El Rancho Vegas Hotel-Casino, which was located on the northern section of the Strip, on the corner of Sahara Avenue. A building boom followed in the 1950s, resulting in a swathe of resorts. The Sands, Desert Inn, Sahara, and Stardust hotels began the process that has transformed the Strip into a high-rise adult theme park. Many of these north Strip resorts remain, but they are now unrecognizable from their earlier incarnations – thanks to million-dollar rebuilding programs.

View of the Venetian and north Strip

Today, resorts such as the Venetian and the Mirage have established the Strip's reputation for upscale quality and almost nothing remains of the spit-and-sawdust atmosphere the city once had.

Treasure Island
The pirate-themed world of Treasure Island lures passers-by to the spectacular Sirens of TI *show, held each evening on the hotel's Strip-side lagoon* ⑰

The Fashion Show Mall is currently the largest shopping destination in Vegas, with more than 200 stores, an entertainment complex, and a food court serving both fast and fresh food.

The Mirage is both stylish and ornate – its beautiful, Strip-facing gardens feature an "erupting" volcano.

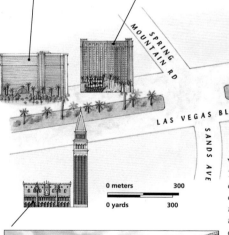

SPRING MOUNTAIN RD

LAS VEGAS BLVD

SANDS AVE

| 0 meters | 300 |
| 0 yards | 300 |

Wynn Las Vegas
This hotel has it all: a casino, an exclusive golf course, oversized luxurious rooms, restaurants with award-winning chefs, nightclubs, and dozens of designer shops.

Guardian Angel Cathedral
Located on Cathedral Way, this chapel has elegant marble floors and imposing buttress support columns.

Venetian
One of the world's most luxurious hotels, this has mock canals flowing through its shopping area ⑮

For hotels and restaurants in this region see pp237–40 and pp257–61

Busy traffic on the Strip at dusk

Stratosphere Tower
An observation deck at the top of this 1,149-ft (350-m) tower offers fine views of the city and the ring of mountains that rise from the desert **㉑**

Circus Circus
Lucky the clown beckons visitors to this resort, which offers circus acts and traditional carnival games on the mezzanine floor above the casino **⑳**

W. SAHARA AVE

W. SAHARA AVE

THE STRIP

Riviera
The colorful, neon-lit, and seemingly jewel-encrusted façade of Riviera highlights the hotel's hit shows, and is one of the most dazzling landmarks along North Strip **⑱**

Neon lights at the Riviera Hotel

LAS VEGAS NEON
The twinkling, flashing neon sign remains the dominant icon of Las Vegas, even though several of the new themed megaresorts here have opted for a more understated look. Neon is a gas discovered by British chemist Sir William Ramsey in 1898. But it was a French inventor, Georges Claude, who, in 1910, discovered that an electric current passed through a glass tube of neon emitted a powerful, shimmering light. In the 1940s and 50s the craft of neon sign-making was elevated to the status of an art form in Las Vegas.

Sahara
This Moroccan-themed hotel opened in 1952 and is one of the city's oldest hotels. It features two of the most popular attractions on the Strip – the fast-paced Cyber Speedway and the thrilling roller-coaster ride Speed.

| 0 meters | 300 |
| 0 yards | 300 |

The neon-lit façade of the Mandalay Bay hotel on the Las Vegas Strip

Mandalay Bay ❶

3950 Las Vegas Blvd. **Tel** (702) 632-7777; (877) 632-7800. ♿ ☑
☐ 24 hours (see p239).
www.mandalaybay.com

The Mandalay Bay resort aims to re-create the tropics of the late 19th century. Located at the south end of the Strip, it opened in 1999 and has 3,300 rooms. Tropical plants and white stucco architectural features such as arches and decorative cornices evoke a colonial atmosphere. Even the vast 135,000-sq-ft (12,550-sq-m) casino manages to suggest elegant 1890s Singapore. One highlight is the 11-acre (4.5-ha) lagoon-style swimming pool with its sandy beach and wave machine, plus a water ride around the pool. More restrained than other Strip resorts, the Mandalay Bay includes over 20 restaurants, nightclubs, and a theater which often hosts Broadway musicals. It is also the only resort on the Strip to feature a non-gaming hotel, the Four Seasons, located on the Mandalay's top four floors.

Luxor ❷

3900 Las Vegas Blvd. **Tel** (702) 262-4000; (877) 386-4658.
☐ 24 hours (see p238). ♿ ☑
www.luxor.com

The Luxor's famous 30-story bronze pyramid opened in 1993 and quickly became a Las Vegas icon. Despite the fact that the resort is modeled on the Eygptian city of Luxor, which has no pyramid, there is impressive attention to detail in the range of Ancient Egyptian architectural features. Painted temple pillars adorn the casino, and a repro-duction Cleopatra's Needle graces the entrance. Visitors enter the pyramid through the legs of a giant sphinx to find themselves inside the casino, where the ranks of ringing slot machines are surrounded by walls decorated with copies of paintings and hieroglyphs from the original Karnak temple in Luxor.

As a tribute to Egypt's ancient religions, a beam of light is projected from the pyramid's apex nightly – so powerful that it can be seen from planes cruising above Los Angeles 250 miles (400 km) away.

Among the hotel's many attractions, a free ride in the guest elevators (named "inclinators") ranks high – they travel along the inclines of the 350-ft (110-m) pyramid at an angle of 39 degrees.

Bodies, The Exhibition showcases whole bodies and hundreds of organs that have been preserved through an innovative process. The specimens provide a unique, three-dimensional view of the human form, with all its skeletal, muscular, and circulatory systems. Also on show are organs that have been damaged by over-eating and lack of exercise.

Titanic: The Artifact Exhibition tells the story of the Titanic, a floating palace that sank on a calm night in 1912 when it struck an iceberg in the North Atlantic. Actual artifacts recovered

Impressive Egyptian-style lobby of the Luxor hotel

For hotels and restaurants in this region see pp237–40 and pp257–61

from the ship are on display, including luggage, the ship's whistles, and an unopened bottle of champagne vintage 1900. Visitors can walk through re-created first- and third-class rooms.

🏛 **Bodies, The Exhibition**
Luxor. ⭕ 10am–10pm daily.

🏛 **Titanic: The Artifact Exhibition**
Luxor. ⭕ 10am–10pm daily.

Excalibur's towers are designed to create a medieval fantasy castle

Excalibur ❸

3850 Las Vegas Blvd. **Tel** (702) 597- 7777; (877) 750-5464.
⭕ 24 hours (see p238).
www.excalibur.com

The Excalibur is a family-friendly theme park resort with a casino attached. The inspiration of the medieval world of King Arthur and his knights is obvious at first sight of the castle-like exterior, with its white towers, turrets, moat, and drawbridge. Suits of armor line the entrance, which leads into the heavily themed casino where even the one-armed bandits have such signposts as "Medieval Slot Fantasy."

The second floor houses the Medieval Village, where quaint alleyways are lined with shops and restaurants, such as the Sherwood Forest Café and Roundtable Buffet and Prime Rib House. The shops and kiosks on Castle Walk offer merchandise

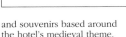
and souvenirs based around the hotel's medieval theme.

The Fantasy Faire Midway features Magic Motion Machine Rides, which are thrilling three-minute sight-and-sound simulation adventures, such as a bobsled run and a runaway train. On the floor below are a variety of carnival-themed video games, including a SpongeBob Squarepants simulator ride.

New York New York ❹

3790 Las Vegas Blvd.
Tel (702) 740-6969; (888) 693-0763.
⭕ 24 hours (see p239).
www.nynyhotelcasino.com

This hotel's re-creation of the Manhattan skyline dominates the Tropicana Avenue corner of the Strip – no mean feat in a street of such impressive façades. Considered to be one of Las Vegas' most appealing sights, New York New York is fronted by a 150-ft (46-m) replica of the Statue of Liberty, behind which are 12 of Manhattan's most famous landmark buildings, including the Empire State, the Chrysler, and Seagram's.

Every interior detail of the hotel is designed to reflect a part of New York City, including the areas around the casino floor, which feature many of the city's most

famous landmarks including Times Square. This fabulous casino is entered from the Strip via a replica of Brooklyn Bridge, which is one-fifth the size of the original.

Roaring around the complex is the thrilling, Coney-Island style Roller Coaster that twists and dives at speeds of 65 mph (105 kph) and passes through the casino itself.

Adding to the Manhattan flavor are versions of many popular New York eateries. Set among Greenwich Village brownstones is a wide selection of cafés, restaurants, and bars offering a choice of live music from swing and jazz to Motown and rock.

The Roller Coaster at New York New York speeding through the air

MGM Grand ⑤

3799 Las Vegas Blvd. *Tel* (702) 891-
1111; (800) 929-9410. 🕐 24 hours
(see p238). ♿🏊
www.mgmgrand.com

The emerald-green MGM
Grand building is fronted
by the famous Leo, a 45-ft-
(15-m-) tall bronze lion used
as the symbol of the MGM
Hollywood film studio. The
original MGM hotel was built
in the 1970s, farther down the
strip on the site of the present
Bally's hotel, and was named
for the 1930s film, Grand
Hotel, starring Greta Garbo.
In 1980 the worst hotel fire in
Las Vegas history destroyed
the building and
killed 84 people.
Although the Grand
did reopen on this site,
it was not until 1993 that
the MGM Grand of today
opened, on the corner of the
Strip and Tropicana Avenue.
It covered a mammoth 114
acres (46 ha) and was
themed on the movie The
Wizard of Oz. A 1999
refurbishment expanded
this theme to include all
MGM movies. Over
$500 million have been
spent on the resort,
which prides itself as Vegas'
"City of Entertainment."

With more than 5,000
rooms, the Grand also boasts
an array of entertainment and
restaurants, and a 171,500-ft-sq
(16,000-sq-m) casino. Its recreation of New York's famous
club, Studio 54, is one of the

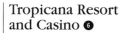

**MGM Grand
figurine**

Strip's most popular
nightspots. Another favorite,
the **MGM Grand Lion Habitat**,
offers the chance to see these
magnificent animals at
close quarters. The
Grand Garden Arena is a
17,000-seat venue famous
for hosting big-name acts,
including Barbra
Streisand, the Rolling
Stones, and Elton John. The
Arena is also a venue for
major sports events and
world championship box-
ing. The more intimate
750-seat Hollywood
Theater attracts many
top entertainers, such
as David Copperfield and
comedians Drew Carey
and Lewis Black. It has
also hosted Jay Leno's "The
Tonight Show".

🍴 **MGM Grand Lion Habitat**
MGM Grand. 🕐 11am–7pm
daily. ♿

Seen from across the Strip at night, the Tropicana hotel building

Tropicana Resort and Casino ⑥

3801 Las Vegas Blvd. *Tel* (702)
739- 2222; (888) 826-8767.
🕐 24 hours (see p240). ♿
www.tropicanalv.com

One of the few 1950s boom
hotels still on the Strip, the
Tropicana was built in 1957.
Las Vegas' famous illusionist
act, Siegfried & Roy, first
appeared here, at its Folies
Bergères in 1973. In 1995 the
resort was restyled, and it now
boasts lush tropical gardens
and a fine Caribbean village
façade. A 5-acre (2-ha) water
park is one of the hotel's most
delightful attractions. Waterfalls and exotic flowers and
foliage provide a habitat for
flamingoes, black swans, and
Brazilian parrots. The huge
main pool with the Coconut
Cove Bar also offers somewhat
unusual casino action with
swim-up blackjack tables
which have a waterproof
surface and money dryers.
The heated indoor pool is
also surrounded by tropical
gardens, and is one of the
few Las Vegas pools open
all year. A third pool, the
beautiful adults-only seasonal
Garden Pool, is a great place
to enjoy a quieter dip, away
from the hustle and bustle
found at the other pools.
The resort also offers several
outdoor spas for the ultimate
in relaxation. Visitors come
here to escape from the bright
lights and full-on action of
the city and enjoy luxurious
spa treatments amongst
the tropical greenery.

Visitors viewing lions through the glass-walled tunnel at the MGM Grand

Liberace Museum ❼

1775 E. Tropicana Ave. **Tel** (702) 798-5595. ◯ 10am–5pm Mon–Sat; noon–4pm Sun. ◐ Jan 1, Thanksgiving, Dec 25. ▦ ♿ www.liberace.org

The serene Spanish-style façade of the Liberace Museum is a vivid contrast to its glittering contents. Founded in 1979, the museum celebrates the life and work of one of Las Vegas's best-loved performers, Liberace (1919–87). The cars, pianos, and famously bejeweled costumes of this flamboyant personality are exhibited in three sections. The main area houses 18 of Liberace's 39 pianos, and the cars include a rare Rolls Royce covered with mirror tiles and etched galloping horses in which Liberace, dressed to match, would arrive at his Las Vegas show. Lavishly rhinestoned costumes and stage jewelry are also on show. The costumes worn at his final 1986 performance took six seamstresses, wearing protective sunglasses against the glare of the stones, several months to make. The world's largest

Liberace in his King Neptune costume

Austrian rhinestone, weighing over 50 lbs (23 kg), is displayed here, near to Liberace's personal memorabilia, which includes several precious jewel-encrusted tiny music boxes.

Showcase Mall ❽

3785 Las Vegas Blvd. **Tel** (702) 597-3122. ◯ varies for each attraction. ♿

This neon-clad building features a 100-ft- (33-m-) high neon Coca-Cola bottle. The Mall is an excellent place to take children but also offers enough to satisfy adults who are badly in need of a break from casinos. There are two main attractions – **GameWorks** (the brainchild of movie mogul Steven Spielberg), and M&M's World. While the latter is hardly more than a promotional exhibit for the company's products, it does offer fun elements and plentiful chocolate samples on the M&M's tour. GameWorks, on the other hand, offers its visitors hands-on entertainment with Indy-car simulator rides, virtual gun battles, and a daunting 75-ft (26-m) climbing wall. There

are also reasonably priced cafés, restaurants, and the Hard Rock Café.

▦ **GameWorks**
Showcase Mall. **Tel** (702) 432-4263. ◯ 10am–midnight Sun–Thu; 10am–1am Fri & Sat. ▦ for climbing wall. ♿ www.gameworks.com

Planet Hollywood Resort & Casino ❾

3667 Las Vegas Blvd. S. **Tel** (702) 785-5555; (866) 919-7472. ◯ 24 hours (see p239). ♿ www.planethollywoodresort.com

Formerly the Aladdin, site of the 1967 wedding of Elvis and Priscilla Presley, Planet Hollywood Resort & Casino opened in 2007. The glamorous, 1930s-style lobby features eight sparkling crystal chandelier columns.
  There are a number of amenities such as a spa and fitness center for the use of guests and non-guests. The hotel's two pools offer *al fresco* poolside cocktails. Entertainment venues showcase *Peepshow*, the sophisticated, full-throttle production show combining sexy striptease, story telling, and celebrity stars. *America's Got Talent* is a live show featuring the most popular performers from the hit NBC TV show. The hotel's Miracle Mile offers 170 shops, 15 restaurants, and three nightclubs.

The neon lights and giant Coca-Cola bottle of Showcase Mall

Paris ⑩

3655 Las Vegas Blvd. *Tel* (877) 603-4386. ⬤ *24 hours* (see p239). ♿
📧 www.parislv.com

Located next to Bally's Hotel *(see p238)* on the Strip, Paris is a $760 million resort that looks like a Hollywood film set of the real French capital. The façade is composed of replicas of such Paris landmark buildings as the Louvre, the Hôtel de Ville, and the Arc de Triomphe. A 50-story, half-scale Eiffel Tower dominates the complex, and visitors can ride an elevator to the observation deck at the top or dine in its gourmet restaurant 100 ft (33 m) above the Strip. The casino contains architectural details that meticulously re-create Parisian streetlife, including cast-iron street lamps, and everything is set beneath a fabulous painted sky.

Cocktail waitress

Cobblestone streets wind along the edge of the casino and are filled with shops selling an array of expensive French goods including clothes, wine, cheese, and chocolate. The resort also boasts five lounges, a spa, and two wedding chapels. There are nine restaurants, including the brasserie-style Mon Ami Gabi

Half-size model of the Eiffel Tower in the Paris hotel complex

(see p260). This restaurant has tables situated outside overlooking the Strip, where diners can enjoy fine French cuisine in true Paris style.

Bellagio ⑪

3600 Las Vegas Blvd. *Tel* (702) 693-7111; (888) 987-6667. ⬤ *24 hours* (see p239). ♿ 📧
www.bellagio.com

This $1.6 billion luxury resort opened in 1998 on the site of a previous hotel called the Dunes. Its design is based on the northern Italian town of Bellagio, with ocher- and terracotta-colored Mediterranean buildings set back from the Strip behind an 8-acre (3-ha) lake modeled on Italy's Lake Como. One of the hotel's many attractions is the sublime fountain display on the lake that springs into action at regular intervals through the day and evening. Crowds gather to watch the free show – a choreographed water dance set to music, accompanied by visual effects including a rolling mist and, at night, stunning light effects.

No expense has been spared on the Bellagio's interior either; beautiful carpets and marble floors line the parade of upscale shops that includes some of the most stylish names in Italian design, such as Armani and Prada. Delicate Carrara marble mosaics adorn all the entrance hall floors, and the main lobby ceiling is hung with Dale Chihuly's sculpted glass flowers of every color. Even the casino manages to be light and airy; powerful air-conditioning helps banish the smoky atmosphere.

Perhaps the most surprising aspect of the Bellagio is its **Gallery of Fine Art**, which features major international shows of collections ranging from the photographs of Ansel Adams to Pablo Picasso's ceramics. Advance reservations are recommended and tickets for the gallery can be booked up to 30 days ahead.

🏛 **Gallery of Fine Art**
Bellagio. *Tel* (702) 693-7871. ⬤ *10am–6pm Sun–Thu, 10am–7pm Fri–Sat.* 📷 ♿ 🔊

The Bellagio's famous dancing fountains shooting high into the air

For hotels and restaurants in this region see pp237–40 and pp257–61

Caesars Palace, seen from its entrance on the Strip at night

Caesars Palace ⑫

3570 Las Vegas Blvd S.
Tel (702) 731-7110; (866) 227-5938.
◯ 24 hours (see p239). ♿
www.caesarspalace.com

Roman statues, Greek columns, and cocktail waitresses in togas could all be found at Caesars Palace when it opened in 1966. The decor and waitresses remain part of the ambience here, but in a less kitsch, more upscale way since more than $600 million was spent refurbishing the resort during the 1990s.

This classic Vegas casino was the first themed hotel on the Strip and quickly established a reputation for attracting top artists, from Andy Williams in the 1960s to the singer Celine Dion and the magician David Copperfield in the 1990s. Since the 1980s Caesars has also hosted international sports events, including championship tennis, featuring stars such as John McEnroe and André Agassi, and boxing, with such names as world champions Muhammad Ali and Mike Tyson.

Today the hotel houses three casinos, four lounges, a health spa, and the 4.5-acre (1.8-ha) Garden of the Gods – a pleasant landscaped area with four swimming pools. Caesars' elegant façade is fronted by fountains and cypress trees. The casinos have all been refurbished and, with their

high ceilings and light decor, create an elegant and upbeat atmosphere.

The entrance to the chic and highly exclusive Forum Shops *(see p124)* continues the ancient Greek and Roman theme and is as impressive as the hotel and casinos. The grand portico features a *trompe l'oeil* sky ceiling and is adorned with statues and relief sculpture.

Replicas of the Trevi and Triton Fountains in Rome adorn a sweeping plaza that is topped by a glass dome ceiling and has a large reflective pool at its center. There is also a majestic spiral escalator leading to the shopping mall itself, which offers more than 150 upscale clothes stores, specialty stores, and 13 different restaurants including Italian, Chinese, and seafood.

Bagel-shaped sign for Bugsy's Deli

Flamingo Las Vegas ⑬

3555 Las Vegas Blvd S. *Tel* (702) 733-3111; (888) 902-9929. ◯ 24 hours (see p238). ♿ www.flamingolv.com

The briliant pink and orange neon plume of the Flamingo hotel's façade is, to many, the archetypal Las Vegas icon. However, nothing remains of the original 1946 casino: the last vestiges of this building, including mobster Bugsy Siegel's private suite, were bulldozed in 1976 *(see p97)*. One of the few remaining signs of this notorious gangster's involvement in the hotel is a display of 1940s and 1950s black-and-white photographs, situated at the east entrance. In the 1990s a $130-million renovation created one of the most elegant pool areas in Vegas. Set among 15 acres (6 ha) of landscaped gardens, two Olympic-sized pools are veiled by tropical plants and palm trees, with islands that provide a home to pink flamingos, swans, turtles, and huge Japanese Koi fish. There is a kids' pool, two Jacuzzis, and a water slide that leads to three additional pools. The hotel's pretty wedding chapel is also set in the pool area. Both guests and visitors may use the renowned tennis club, which has four floodlit night courts, a practice court, and a tennis shop.

Lush palms surround the pool at the Flamingo Las Vegas

The Statue of Liberty dominates New York New York's Manhattan skyline façade ▷

Autocollections at the Imperial Palace ⑭

3535 Las Vegas Blvd. S. *Tel (702) 794-3174.* ◯ *10am–6:30pm daily.* 🅿 ♿ **www.** autocollections.com

Located on the fifth floor of the Imperial Palace Hotel's parking lot, this multi-million-dollar

An example of the celebrity-owned cars on show at the Imperial Palace

collection of classic cars from around the world will impress even the most auto-phobic of visitors. Ralph Engelstad, owner of the Imperial Palace Hotel, began his collection with a 1929 Ford Model A Roadster in 1979. Two years later, the museum was opened with enough space for 200 cars.

As well as vintage Fords, the exhibition includes such classics as Mercedes, Chevys, Cadillacs, and a range of military vehicles. Today, many of the cars are for sale, some with price tags of more than one million dollars.

The collection is constantly changing as cars are sold and new ones replace them. At various times the exhibits

have included a Duesenberg Murphy Roadster owned by Howard Hughes. More recent, but no less stylish, are the Cadillacs, Lincolns, and Chevrolets of the 1950s and 1960s with their elongated tail fins, leather seats, and chrome accessories, such as the 1961 Lincoln Continental used by Jacqueline Kennedy. A 1976 Cadillac that once belonged to Elvis Presley is another former exhibit.

Venetian ⑮

3355 Las Vegas Blvd. S. *Tel (702) 414-1000; (877) 883-6423.* ◯ *24 hours (see p239).* ♿ 🏳 **www.**venetian.com

This astounding piece of architecture re-creates the city of Venice and currently contains more than 4,000 suites. The Venetian Wedding Chapel overlooks the garden, with seating for up to 150 guests. One of the new breed of luxury Vegas megaresorts, the Venetian has been built on the site of the legendary Sands Hotel. The Sands was

the home of the "Rat Pack" *(see p97)*, and a famous swim-up craps table, which was demolished in 1996. Facing the Strip, facsimiles of the Doge's Palace, the Campanile, and the Ca d'Oro overlook the blue waters of the Grand Canal – complete with a gondola park beneath a Rialto Bridge. Craftsmen have made sure that every detail is authentic, even the concrete has been aged to look like 400-year-old stone.

The colonnaded cloister of the Doge's Palace offers visitors one of the best views of the Strip. It is possible to rent a gondola to travel gently through the building along a winding canal to the Grand Canal Shoppes. The Venetian fantasy continues here with high-quality stores and restaurants set among cobble-stone walkways and bridges beneath a blue painted sky that resembles a Renaissance painting. Acres of lavish marble flooring, statues, and replicas of famous

Entertainer at the Venetian

Venetian paintings are found throughout this elegant complex. The stunning front lobby has a dome decorated with scenes from Venetian master paintings while the entrance to the Grand Canal Shoppes boasts a copy of Veronese's 1538 painting, *The Apotheosis of Venice.*

Mirage ⑯

3400 Las Vegas Blvd. S. *Tel (702) 791-7111; (800) 374-9000.* ◯ *24 hours (see p239).* ♿ 🏳 **www.**themirage.com

The Mirage hotel-casino opened in the fall of 1989 at the staggering cost of $620 million. At the time it was the largest hotel in the US, with 3,044 rooms. This new megaresort aimed to cater not only to gamblers but also to vacationers and

The stylish Venetian Hotel, complete with reproduction Campanile

For hotels and restaurants in this region see pp237–40 and pp257–61

An explosive battle scene from the *Sirens of TI* show, TI

conventioneers. Perhaps more than any other hotel, the Mirage revolutionized the Strip, setting out to draw visitors with attractions other than just the casino – a kind of fantasyland for adults.

The Mirage occupies an entire block along Las Vegas Boulevard, between Caesars Palace and Treasure Island, and offers a range of attractions to its own guests and Vegas visitors alike. Its traffic-stopping façade introduces the complex's South Sea island theme, with tropical gardens, waterfalls, and a lagoon. But the star of the show is undoubtedly a volcano that erupts, spewing fire and smoke, every hour from 6pm to midnight.

Inside the complex, an atrium filled with exotic plants (some real, some fake) is kept suitably steamy by computerized misters. Behind the main desk a 20,000-gallon (90,000-liter) aquarium is filled with brightly colored fish and small sharks.

As well as gaming, visitors can shop in designer stores, eat in one of 15 restaurants and bars, or see rare animal breeds, such as the Royal White tiger and white lions, in Siegfried and Roy's Secret Garden. This delightful zoo and research center is set amongst the hotel's lush, landscaped gardens. Adjacent to the zoo is the Dolphin Habitat, home to Atlantic Bottlenose dolphins.

Treasure Island ⓱

3300 Las Vegas Blvd.S. **Tel** (702) 894-7111; (800) 228-7206. ⃝ *24 hours* (see p239). ♿ **www**.treasureisland.com

This hotel resort and casino offers luxurious accommodations and award-winning service. Guests can relax in the hotel spa or sip cocktails by the heated outdoor pool. There are eight restaurants to choose from, as well as several bars and lounges; nightclubs include the Kahunaville Party Bar and the fashionable Christian Audigier The Nightclub, one of the hippest clubs on the Las Vegas Strip.

The pirate-themed hotel boasts a blue-water lagoon that fronts the Strip and is surrounded by high rock cliffs, shrubs, and palm trees. It is the setting for the spectacular *Sirens of TI* show, a free 12-minute musical adventure set in the 17th century. The action features sultry sirens who lure a band of pirates into their clutches with seductive songs, stir up a storm, and transform the area into a party.

The hotel is also host to the stunning contemporary circus *Mystère* by Cirque du Soleil, performed in a specially customized showroom (see p127).

The exotic rainforest atrium in the Mirage

Sparkling neon stars light up the Riviera façade at night

Riviera 🔞

2901 Las Vegas Blvd.
Tel (702) 734-5110; (800) 634-
3420. ◯ 24 hours (see p238).
♿ www.rivierahotel.com

One of the group of Las
Vegas hotels that were built
on the Strip
during the post-
World War II
building boom,
the Riviera
opened in 1955.
Its nine-story
tower made the
hotel the city's
first high-rise.
Some of the key
characters of Las Vegas' past
have featured in the hotel's
history. Liberace was the first
headliner here, appearing
with legendary Hollywood
actress Joan Crawford, who
was the official hostess on
opening night. Liberace
was paid a record-breaking
$50,000 a week. Over the
next ten years the Riviera
consolidated its reputation
for offering glamorous
entertainment, attracting
such Hollywood stars as
Orson Welles, Ginger Rogers,
and Marlene Dietrich.
 Today the Riviera occupies
1,000 ft (300 m) of the north
Strip, and boasts 2,075 rooms.
While its glamor is somewhat

**Bronze sculpture of
showgirls at the Riviera**

faded, the Riviera nevertheless retains an "old Vegas"
atmosphere, symbolized by
its large, brash casino. The
hotel's neutral theme also
makes it a good shooting
location for scenes in feature
films. This is one of the less
expensive big Strip hotels, but
it still offers a
good range
of facilities,
including an
Olympic-sized
pool, tennis
courts, and
a health spa.
There are
several restau-
rants, cafés,
bars, and stores, as well as
six live shows including a
comedy showcase.

Las Vegas Hilton 🔟

3000 Paradise Road. **Tel** (702) 732-
5111; (800) 732-7117. ◯ 24 hours.
♿ www.lvhilton.com

Elvis Presley is the star most
associated with this hotel
(which opened as The International in 1969), appearing
here for a record 837 performances, all of which were
sold out. Today, big-name
singers such as Johnny Mathis
and Barry Manilow perform
here, but visitors can still pay
tribute to the memory of the
King at his lifesize statue just
off the lobby. The hotel's
proximity to the Las Vegas
Convention Center makes it
popular with businesspeople,
but luxurious surroundings,
a monorail station, and a
plush casino draw other
visitors to the resort.
 Contemporary and classic
design elements characterize
this resort, where touches of
class offer relief from the
standard themed Strip resorts.
There are water features
in the lobby, and crystal
chandeliers run the length
of the main casino ceiling.
The casino offers all of the
popular games, from slot
machines to baccarat, with a
high-limit table area, and slots.
The vast Race and Sports
SuperBook betting venue
boasts more than 60 screens
and monitors displaying live
action from arenas around the
world. There are also over 15
restaurants to choose from;
the Benihana offers fine
Japanese cuisine prepared by
talented chefs who display
their culinary skills on the

The luxurious Las Vegas Hilton resort

For hotels and restaurants in this region see pp237–40 and pp257–61

Seen from the south, the brightly lit Circus Circus façade features Lucky the clown

hibachi tables; Casa Nicola offers savory dishes from Italy and the Mediterranean; TJ's Steakhouse serves steak and seafood in an Old World atmosphere. For entertainment, the Hilton Theater hosts comedy shows and concerts; and production shows are held in the Shimmer Showroom.

Circus Circus ⑳

2880 Las Vegas Blvd. *Tel (702) 734-0410; (800) 634-3450.* ◯ *24 hours (see p238).* ⓑ **www**.circuscircus.com

Located at the north end of the Strip, Circus Circus opened in 1968 and is a themed resort offering family entertainment. The hotel has a choice of reasonably priced restaurants and buffets, including a delicious steak house.

This vast property covers over 68 acres (27.5 ha) and has the largest indoor theme park in the country. The huge **Adventuredome** is housed inside a pink dome, with a re-created Southwest landscape of sandstone cliffs, caves, and a waterfall, and is maintained at a temperature of 72°F (21°C) year round. The range of rides here includes the terrifying double loop, double corkscrew roller coaster, a water flume ride that races down a mountain, and the Fun House Express – an Imax™ simulator ride. The three casinos here cover an

incredible 100,000 sq ft (9,500 sq m). Above the main casino is the Big Top with its circular walkway of traditional games where the children are the winners – they can often be seen here carrying lots of stuffed toys. This is also the place to find the seating for the live circus acts that perform half-hourly from 11am to midnight. World-class acrobats can be seen flying high above the heads of the gamblers filling the slot machines below.

Neon sign rising above the Stratosphere

🎬 The Adventuredome
Circus Circus. *Tel (702) 794-3939.* ◯ *daily (times vary).* 🎫 ⓑ

Stratosphere ㉑

2000 Las Vegas Blvd S. *Tel (702) 380-7777.* ◯ *24 hours (see p239).* ⓑ **www**.stratospherehotel.com

Somewhat isolated at the north end of the Strip, away from the main attractions, this resort hotel boasts the 1,149-ft-(350-m-) high Stratosphere Tower – a Vegas landmark and the tallest building west of the Mississippi River. The summit has indoor and outdoor observation decks, which offer unparalleled views of the city and the surrounding desert and mountains, and a popular revolving restaurant *(see p260)*. The tower elevators take just

30 seconds to whisk visitors to the top, where three thrilling rides are located. The **X-Scream** giant teeter-totter propels riders 27 ft (8 m) over the tower edge, and the **Big Shot** shoots visitors 160 ft (49 m) up in the air. At ground level the 100,000 sq ft (9,500 sq m) casino includes a poker room and a keno lounge. The Stratosphere also offers two shows, and several restaurants and stores.

🎬 The X-Scream and the Big Shot
Stratosphere. ◯ *10am–1am Sun–Thu; 10am–2am, Fri, Sat, & holidays.* 🎫 ⓑ *for observation deck only.*

The Stratosphere Tower, landmark of Las Vegas' north Strip

Evening light show at the Fremont Street Experience

Fremont Street Experience ❷

Light shows: hourly 6pm–midnight daily.   **www**.vegasexperience.com

Known as "Glitter Gulch," Fremont Street was in the heart of Las Vegas when it was incorporated in 1905. This is where the first casinos were located, complete with stylish neon signs, and famous illuminated icons such as Vegas Vic and Vickie lit up the night sky. However, during the 1980s and 1990s, Fremont Street suffered in competition with more lavish attractions on the Strip and became a run-down city center avoided by tourists. In 1994 the city's ambitious $70-million project to revitalize the area was initiated.

A vast steel canopy, known as Via Vision, rises 90 ft (27 m) above a 1,500-ft (457-m) long five-block section of Fremont Street. Every night, on the hour, the spectacular Fremont Street Experience sound and light shows are projected onto the canopy. The sound system is comprised of 208 speakers that produce concert quality sound. Visitors experience high-resolution images presented by over 12 million synchronized LED modules.

The street is pedestrianized and visitors can easily stroll from casino to casino, stopping to snack and shop at a variety of stalls along the way. Although some of the famous 1950s and 1960s neon signs gave way to the new show, many of the dazzling neon façades belonging to some of the city's oldest and best-loved casinos remain. In contrast to the Strip, the buildings are closer together here, making casino-hopping an easy option.

For many years the landmark casino in Vegas was Binion's Horseshoe, now known as **Binion's**. Benny Binion is one of the city's legendary characters, who is said to have arrived in town in 1946 wearing a ten-gallon hat and carrying a suitcase filled with $2 million in cash. Binion's is now managed by Harrah's Casinos,

Golden Nugget neon sign at the Fremont Experience

and the legend continues, offering table games, slot machines, and card games. Today, Binion's is famous for its poker heritage. The Binion's Gallery of Champions, Poker Hall of Fame, and the contemporary Binion's Hall of Fame Poker Room, decorated with historic photos, commemorate the many poker competitions held here.

Other historic Las Vegas casinos along Fremont Street include **The Plaza**, built in 1971 on the site of the original Union Pacific Railroad depot, with its atmospheric 1970s style. The friendly **El Cortez**, with its Mexican styling, faces Fremont Street from Las Vegas Boulevard, and is one of the few casinos to retain architectural features from its original 1950s building. The **Four Queens**, named for the owner's four daughters, was built in 1966 and has one of the best arrays of lights on Fremont Street. Inside, gilt mirrors and chandeliers evoke early 19th-century New Orleans and the casino claims to have the largest slot machine in the world. At 9-ft (3-m) high and 20-ft (6-m) wide, it takes six players at a time. Fully renovated in 1976, the **Golden Nugget** is bright and clean. The eponymous golden nugget is the world's largest, weighing an incredible 61 lbs 11 oz (27 kg).

Binion's
128 E. Fremont St. *(see p237).*
Tel (702) 382-1600. ☐ 24 hours.
  www.binions.com

The Plaza
1 Main St. *(see p237).*
Tel (702) 386-2110. ☐ 24 hours.
  www.plazahotelcasino.com

El Cortez
600 E. Fremont St. *(see p237).*
Tel (702) 385-5200. ☐ 24 hours.
  www.elcortezhotelcasino.com

Four Queens
202 E. Fremont St. *(see p237).*
Tel (702) 385-4011. ☐ 24 hours.
  www.fourqueens.com

Golden Nugget
129 E. Fremont St. *(see p237).*
Tel (702) 385-7111. ☐ 24 hours.
  www.goldennugget.com

Binion's, one of Fremont Street's most traditional casinos

The modernist façade of the Lied Discovery Children's Museum

fauna of the Mojave desert. Animatronic dinosaurs include a 35-ft- (10.5-m-) long *Tyrannosaurus rex*, while the marine exhibit has live sharks and eels. In the hands-on discovery room visitors can dig for fossils and explore the five senses.

Lied Discovery Children's Museum ㉓

833 Las Vegas Blvd N. *Tel (702) 382-5437.* ◻ *9am–4pm Tue–Fri (Jun–Labor Day: 10am–5pm); 10am–5pm Sat; noon–5pm Sun.* ◓ *Mon (except school holidays), Jan 1, Thanksgiving, Dec 25.* ▨ ♿ **www.**ldcm.org

A conical, concrete teepee forms part of this striking building, which also houses a branch of the Las Vegas City Library. Opened in 1990, this excellent museum is devoted to interactive exhibits that are fun for both adults and children. The first floor focuses on the arts and is the venue for workshops including mask-making and designing musical instruments. Children can stand inside a gigantic bubble, freeze their shadows on a wall, and hear simple phrases translated into different languages, including Navajo. The second floor features the in-house radio station, which encourages children to explore how radio works. Changing exhibitions cover a range of subjects from world cultures to art and wildlife.

The Las Vegas Natural History Museum ㉔

900 Las Vegas Blvd. *Tel (702) 384-3466.* ◻ *9am–4pm daily.* ◓ *Jan 1, Thanksgiving, Dec 25.* ▨ ♿ **www.**lvnhm.org

A popular choice with the families who need a break from the Strip resorts, this museum has an appealing range of exhibits. Dioramas re-create the African savannah and display a variety of wildlife from leopards and cheetahs to several African antelope species such as nyalas, bush boks, and duikers. The Wild Nevada Room features the flora and

Old Las Vegas Mormon State Historic Park ㉕

500 East Washington Blvd. *Tel (702) 486-3511.* ◻ *8am–4:30pm Mon–Sat.* ◓ *Nov–May: Mon.* **www.**parks.nv.gov/olvmf.htm

Located just opposite the children's museum on Las Vegas Blvd., the small soft-pink adobe building that is the only remains of a Mormon fort is a tranquil spot. The oldest building in Las Vegas, the fort dates back to 1855, when the first group of Mormon settlers arrived in the area. They constructed an adobe fort arranged around a 150-ft- (45-m-) long *placita* (small rectangular plaza) with 14-ft- (4-m-) high walls, but abandoned it three years later. The fort became part of a ranch in the 1880s and was run by Las Vegas pioneer Helen Stewart (see p96). The City of Las Vegas bought the site in 1971.

Today, the Visitor Center is a reconstruction of the original adobe house with its simply furnished interior much as it would have been under Mormon occupation. The building also contains an exhibition that describes the Mormon missions and their impact on Las Vegas.

An animatronic *Tyrannosaurus rex* in roaring form at the Las Vegas Natural History Museum

Neat lawns and houses in the Boulder City suburbs

Boulder City and Hoover Dam ㉖

Road map A3. 🚶 12,500. ✈ 🚌
🛈 *Hoover Dam Visitor Center:*
summer: 9am–5pm daily; winter:
9am–4pm daily. **Tel** *(702) 494-2517.*
🎴 ♿

Just eight miles (13 km) west
of the colossal Hoover Dam,
Boulder City was built as a
model community to house
dam construction workers.
With its neat yards and
suburban streets, it is one of
Nevada's most attractive and
well-ordered towns. Its
Christian founders banned
casinos, and there are none
here today. Several of its
original 1930s buildings remain,
including the restored 1933
Boulder Dam Hotel, which
houses the quaint yet engaging
Hoover Dam Museum.
    The Hoover Dam was built
between 1931 and 1935 across
the Colorado River's Black
Canyon, 30 miles (48 km) east
of Las Vegas. Hailed as an
engineering victory, the dam

gave this desert region a
reliable water supply and
provided inexpensive
electricity. Today, the dam
supplies water and
electricity to the three
states of Nevada,
Arizona, and
California, and has
created Lake Mead
– a popular tourist
center. Visitors to
the dam can take the
Hoover Dam
Powerplant Tour,
which includes a trip to the
observation deck where there
are panoramic views of eight
of the dam's 17 huge
generators. The guided tour
leads through old construction
tunnels and explains how
the dam was built.

🏛 **Hoover Dam Museum**
1305 Arizona St., Boulder City.
Tel *(702) 294-1988.* 🕙 *10am–*
5pm Mon–Sat; noon–5pm Sun.
⚫ *public hols.* 🎴 ♿
www.bcmha.org

Lake Mead National Recreation Area ㉗

Road map A3. **Tel** *(702) 293-8906;*
Alan Bible Visitor Center (702) 293-
8990. 🚌 *Las Vegas.* 🕗 *8:30am–*
4:30pm daily. ⚫ *Jan 1,*
Thanksgiving, Dec 25. 🎴 ♿
limited. 🅰 www.nps.gov/lame

After the completion of the
Hoover Dam, the waters of
the Colorado River filled the
deep canyons that once tower-
ed above the river to create a
huge reservoir. This lake, with
its 700 miles (1,130 km) of
shoreline, is the centerpiece
of Lake Mead National
Recreation Area,
a 1.5-million-acre
(600,000-ha) tract
of land. The focus
is on water sports,
especially sailing,
waterskiing, and
fishing. Striped bass
and rainbow trout
are popular catches.
There are also several campgrounds and marinas.

**Power boating
on Lake Mead**

Valley of Fire State Park ㉘

Road map A3. **Tel** *(702) 397-2088.*
🚌 *Las Vegas.* 🕗 *8:30am–4:30pm*
daily. 🎴 ♿ *partial.* 🅰
www.desertusa.com/nvval/

This spectacularly scenic
state park has a remote,
desert location some 60
miles (97 km) northeast
of Las Vegas. Its name
derives from the red
sandstone formations
that began as
huge, shifting

Extraordinary rock formations in the Valley of Fire State Park

For hotels and restaurants in this region see pp237–40 and pp257–61

sand dunes about 150 million years ago. There are four well-maintained trails across this wilderness, including the Petroglyph Canyon Trail, an easy half-mile (0.8-km) loop, which takes in several fine prehistoric Ancestral Puebloan rock carvings. Here, summer temperatures often reach 112°F (30°C). The best time to visit is in spring or fall.

The nearby town of Overton lies along the Muddy River. Ancestral Puebloan people *(see pp26–7)* settled here in around 300 BC but left some 1,500 years later, perhaps because of a long drought. Archaeologists have unearthed hundreds of prehistoric artifacts in the area since the first digs began in the 1920s. Overton's **Lost City Museum of Archaeology**, just outside the town, has a large collection of pottery, beads, woven baskets, and delicate turquoise jewelry.

Lost City Museum of Archaeology
721 S. Moapa Valley Blvd.,
Overton. *Tel (702) 397-2193.*
☐ 8:30am– 4:30pm daily. ● Jan 1, Thanksgiving, Dec 25. ☒ ☒

Mount Charleston ㉙

Road map A3. *Tel (702) 872-5486; (702) 515-5400 (Forest Service).* ☒ Las Vegas. ☒ **www**.fs.fed.us/htnf

About 45 miles (72 km) north-west of Las Vegas, Mount Charleston rises to 11,918 ft (35,754 m) out of Toiyabe National Forest, clad with pine, mountain mahogany, fir, and aspen. Also known as the Spring Mountain Recreation Area, it offers refuge from the Las Vegas summer heat, with a variety of hiking trails and picnic areas. In the wintertime, skiing and snowboarding are popular *(see p279).*

A range of hikes is available, including two demanding trails that snake up to the summit: the 11-mile (18-km) North Loop Trail, and the 9-mile (14-km) South Loop Trail. Easier walks on the forested slopes are also marked, including a one-hour hike up Cathedral Rock. This walk

Rainbow Mountain in Red Rock Canyon National Conservation Area

starts from a picnic area at the end of Nevada State Hwy 157. This is the more southerly of the two byroads leading to Mount Charleston off Hwy 95; the other is Hwy 156, which runs to the Lee Canyon Ski Area, catering to both skiers and snowboarders.

Red Rock Canyon ㉚

Road map A3. *Tel (702) 515-5350.* ☒ Las Vegas. ☐ 8am–4:30pm daily. ● public hols. ☒ ☒ limited. ☒ **www**.nv.blm.gov/redrockcanyon

From downtown Las Vegas, it is a short, 10-mile (16-km) drive west to the low hills and steep gullies of the Red

Rock Canyon National Conservation Area. A gnarled escarpment rises out of the desert, its gray limestone and red sandstone the geological residue of an ancient ocean and the huge sand dunes that succeeded it. Red Rock Canyon is easily explored on an enjoyable 13-mile (21-km) scenic road that loops off Hwy 159. Beside the road are picnic spots and trailheads for a series of short hikes that cover the area's steep winding canyons. The visitor center at the start of the road has useful displays on the Canyon's flora and fauna. There are more some 80 to 100 bighorn sheep in the conservation area.

THE CONSTRUCTION OF THE HOOVER DAM

Hoover Dam sign

More than 1,400 miles (2,250 km) in length, the Colorado River flows through seven states on its journey from the Rocky Mountains to the Gulf of California. A treacherous, unpredictable river, it used to be a raging torrent in spring and a trickle in the heat of summer. As a source of water it was therefore unreliable and, in 1928, the seven states it served signed the Boulder Canyon Project Act to define how much water each state could siphon off. The agreement paved the way for the Hoover Dam, and its construction began in 1931. It was a mammoth task, and more than 5,000 men toiled day and night to build what was, at 726 ft (218 m), the world's tallest dam. Named after Herbert Hoover, the 31st president of the US (1929–33), and an avid supporter of the project, it contains 17 hydroelectric generating units.

View of the Hoover Dam

PRACTICAL INFORMATION

Las Vegas has become one of the world's most popular playgrounds. The Strip at night, in all its blazing glory, is a sight that never seems to tire visitors. Vegas is a city that knows how to cater to its guests, and a wealth of information about hotels, casinos, dining, and entertainment is available. However, with so much to choose from it is a good idea to do some advance planning. Most visitors spend most of their time around the Strip and the Downtown area, but there are many rewarding day trips to be had exploring other nearby sights including Grand Canyon (*see pp 58–63*).

New York New York yellow stretch cab

Façade of the Las Vegas Convention Center

GENERAL INFORMATION

Choosing when to go to Vegas can be tricky if you are looking for a bargain deal. These days the city is a highly popular destination year round, but unless you have prebooked, it is generally best to avoid the major conventions when the hotels can be full. New Year is also an extremely busy time.

Summers are very hot here with an average July temperature of 105°F (40°C). Spring and fall are sunny without such intense heat, and winters can also be warm but with occasional cold winds.

The **Las Vegas Convention and Visitor's Authority (LVCVA)** sends out excellent information packs, and they also have a website, offering information on every aspect of your trip. Once in the city there are numerous free papers such as *What's On*, as well as two daily newspapers, the *Las Vegas Review Journal* and the *Las Vegas Sun*, which contain reviews of the current shows and restaurants.

Although Las Vegas is no longer the low-cost destination it once used to be, hotel prices do vary greatly (*see pp237–40*). As a general rule room rates are usually higher on the weekends than during the week. It is always worth asking for a special rate if you are staying for more than a couple of days. Booking through a travel agent, calling the toll-free numbers, or contacting one of the online reservation agencies (such as **Accommodations Express** and **TripReservations.com**) can also result in a less expensive deal. Each major hotel has its own website with a reservations facility (*see under individual hotel pp237–40*).

TIPPING

Tipping for services rendered is part of life in Las Vegas. Bellhops expect $1 per bag, bartenders $1 a drink, waiters 15 percent of the check, and cab drivers 10–15 percent of the fare. Leave a dollar a day for the chamber maids, and a tip for croupiers, if you are lucky and win.

GETTING AROUND LAS VEGAS

The Las Vegas transit authority, **Citizens Area Transit (CAT)**, runs the Deuce bus, which stops at all the major hotels along the Strip for a flat fare of $3 for one ride, $7 for 24 hours, or $15 for a day pass. Exact change is required; dollar bills are accepted. There is also the **Monorail**, which travels between the MGM Grand and the Sahara ($5 per ride, $13 per day, or $28 for a three-day pass) with stops at Bally's/Paris, the Flamingo/Caesars Palace, Harrah's/Imperial Palace, Las Vegas Convention Center, and the Las Vegas Hilton. A free tram service is available between the Excalibur, the Luxor, and the Mandalay, and a second free tram runs between the Mirage and Treasure Island. These services can save a great deal of pounding up and down the Strip between hotels.

Citizen's Area Transit logo

If used a lot, taxis here can work out to be an expensive way of getting around. They charge $3.30 for the first mile plus $2.40 for each additional mile. A cab from the airport to the south end of the Strip (a five-minute trip) costs around $20, while a trip to the north end can be as much as $30. Cabs can be hailed on the street if their top lights are on, or, more commonly, picked up at one of the hotel lines where you will be expected to tip the doorman at least a dollar. Despite the fact that the majority of your

Monorail linking the Excalibur, Luxor, and Mandalay Bay resorts

time will be spent on one street, the Strip is a very long stretch of road, and while the properties along it appear to be near, this is an optical illusion caused by their vast size. Renting a car in Las Vegas allows you to see everything without getting footsore or spending a fortune on taxis. Parking is easy in Las Vegas; all the large Strip hotels have free parking lots. All the major car rental companies are represented here and cars may be picked up and dropped off at McCarran Airport. Rates can be as low as $30 a day. (For more information about arriving in Las Vegas, see *pp294–5*).

Perhaps the ultimate Las Vegas travel experience is the limousine, particularly the stretch limo. It is possible to rent a wide range of these vehicles, including stretch and superstretch versions that come fitted out with TV, cocktail bar, and even Jacuzzi, for between $50 and $90 an hour. Several companies in the city, such as **Ambassador Limo** and **Las Vegas Limousines**, rent their vehicles by the hour as well as for picking up and dropping off visitors at the airport. **On Demand Sedan & Limousine Service** provides chauffeur-driven vehicles.

SIGHTSEEING TRIPS

For a break from the Strip's attractions, there are a variety of day trips on offer to Las Vegas' surrounding sights. These include the gigantic Hoover Dam and nearby Lake Mead with its extensive opportunities for every kind of water sport (*see p120*). Organized trips by **Gray Line** and **Coach USA** include drives through the scenic Red Rock Canyon National Conservation Area (*see p121*) and cruises aboard the **Desert Princess** on Lake Mead.

One of the most popular excursions from Vegas is to Grand Canyon, which can be visited easily on a day trip. Airplane and helicopter rides can be arranged by various companies, including **Scenic Airlines**. Gray Line also runs flights to Grand Canyon as well as organizing river rafting trips along the Colorado.

City tours, which take in the Stratosphere Tower and Fremont Street Experience, can also be arranged. Perhaps the most exciting city tour is by helicopter at night; **Las Vegas Helicopters** specialize in night flights some 500 ft (150 m) above the Strip, which take in all the major resorts in their amazing settings.

Most hotels have plenty of information on the trips available as well as providing a booking service.

DIRECTORY

USEFUL NUMBERS

Accommodations Express
Tel (800) 444-ROOM (7666).
www.hotels.com

Ambassador Limo
Tel (888) 519-5466.
www.ambassadorlasvegas.com

Citizens Area Transit
Tel (702) CAT RIDE (228-7433).
www.rtcsouthernnevada.com

Coach USA
Tel (800) 634-6579.
www.coachusa.com

Desert Princess
Tel (702) 293-6180.

Gray Line
Tel (800) 634-6579.
www.grayline.com

Las Vegas Convention and Visitors Authority
3150 Paradise Rd.
Tel (800) 332-5333.
www.visitlasvegas.com

Las Vegas Helicopters
Tel (702) 736-0013.
www.lvhelicopters.com

Las Vegas Limousines
Tel (888) 696-4400.
www.lasvegaslimo.com

Las Vegas Monorail
Tel (866) 466-6672.

On Demand Sedan & Limousine Service
Tel (800) 990-0417.
www.odslimo.com

Scenic Airlines
Tel (702) 638-3300.

TripReservations.com
Tel (800) 255-0372.
www.tripres.com

Las Vegas Helicopters' tour vehicles

SHOPPING IN LAS VEGAS

In recent years Las Vegas has consolidated its reputation as a shopper's paradise. Fun and tacky souvenirs are available in small stores along the Strip, whereas jewelry and designer clothes can be found everywhere, from hotel shops to malls. Given the city's hot climate, indoor shopping malls are the norm. All the major resorts have their own covered parades of shops, and some, such as Caesars Palace Forum Shops, are as flamboyant as the hotels themselves. Several malls in Las

Souvenir ornament from Circus Circus

Vegas, such as the Strip's Fashion Show Mall, house upscale department stores such as Saks Fifth Avenue and Neiman Marcus. For bargains in adult and children's clothes and shoes as well as a variety of household items, the two outlet shopping Malls, the Beltz Factory Outlet and Factory Stores of America, are located south of the Strip. Shopping centrally can be expensive, and if you need to pick up everyday items such as shampoo or a toothbrush ordinary malls used by the locals are a short drive away.

Marble floors and a glass ceiling house elegant stores at Via Bellagio

HOTEL SHOPPING

The indoor malls in many of the megaresorts take shopping into a new dimension. Themed styling for the large hotels means that their resort streets are designed to look like Venice, Paris, or ancient Rome.

The **Forum Shops** at Caesars Palace are decorated with columns, arches, statuary, and a *trompe l'oeil* sky, which simulates the changes from dawn to dusk through the day. The statues adorning one ornate fountain spring to life every 90 minutes and move with light and sound depicting the Atlantis myth. Among the 160 stores found here are designer clothes and shoes at Louis Vuitton, DKNY, and Emporio Armani. An enormous moving Trojan

horse sits outside the top American toy store FAO Schwarz. There are specialty candy and chocolate shops, as well as a choice of restaurants including a franchise for renowned Los Angeles chef Wolfgang Puck's Spago.

The beautiful **Grand Canal Shoppes** at the Venetian are set among pretty, winding alleys. A canal, with an amazing replica of St. Mark's Square lies at the center of the mall. Alongside the usual designer apparel, such as Kenneth Cole's shoes and clothes by Cache, there are many specialty stores selling a variety of imported Italian goods, including antiques at Regis Gallery, Murano glass at Ripa De Monti, and a fine collection of Venetian costumes and masks at Il Prato.

Novelty magnets on display in a hotel store

Miracle Mile Shops at Planet Hollywood Resort & Casino has 170 stores and 15 restaurants encircling a huge theatre. Streaming images displayed on an outdoor LED sign welcomes shoppers as they arrive. Hip store H&M stocks European-influenced fashions, while ultra-trendy Urban Outfitters has urban-inspired furniture, and retro and modern clothing. Restaurants range from casual eateries to upscale fine dining establishments. **Le Boulevard** at the Paris hotel is a Francophile's joy, featuring authentic-style Parisian stores selling French goods including children's clothes, cheese, wine, and chocolate. The elegant **Via Bellagio** at the Bellagio hotel offers several upscale boutiques such as Chanel, Prada, and Gucci arranged

Roman statues and a painted sky at Caesars Palace's Forum Shops

Visitors entering the Fashion Show Mall on Las Vegas Boulevard

along a marble-floored walkway with natural sunlight streaming in through an ornate glass ceiling (see p103).

THE MALLS

Right across the street from Treasure Island, the **Fashion Show Mall** houses seven department stores, including Neiman Marcus, Dillard's, Macy's, and Saks Fifth Avenue, as well as the ubiquitous Gap and Abercrombie & Fitch. For everyday items and lower prices head off the Strip to the **Boulevard Mall**, which at 1.2 million square ft (111,500 sq m) is Nevada's largest. The vast range of shops here includes such all-American favorites as Sears and JC Penney as well as book, gift, and jewelry stores. There is also a food court.

If you're searching for real bargains, there are two outlet malls heading south along the Strip past Mandalay Bay (see p102). Outlet malls are proving very popular. They sell branded goods with minor faults or excess stock, often at up to 70 percent discount. The **Las Vegas Outlet Mall** has 130 stores ranging from Levi's denims to Nike goods and Royal Doulton. This mall also has a carousel for children and a food court. Unusual for Las Vegas, **Vegas Point Mall** is an outdoor mall with 40 stores selling everything from clothes to household goods. Five minutes from the Strip, just off the I-15 freeway, is

Las Vegas Premium Outlets with 150 designer and name-brand stores, as well as some unusual independent stores and a large food court.

Façade of Ghirardelli's specialty chocolate shop on the Strip

SOUVENIRS AND SPECIALTY STORES

The Las Vegas of old is often associated with the tacky and kitsch, and souvenirs here can be all those things. All along the Strip stores sell memorabilia; always popular are the Elvis sunglasses, some even have sideburns attached. The largest emporium, the **Bonanza General Store** offers a wide range of gifts, from the cheapest pair of slot machine earrings to luxury sets of poker chips.

1970s retro Elvis sunglasses

The gambling store, **JP Slot Emporium**, offers a wide range of gaming merchandise from the serious to the frivolous. It also stocks an impressive collection of bargain-price one-armed bandits. **Serge's Showgirl Wigs** is one of the largest wig showrooms in the country and is a great place to experiment with different looks.

DIRECTORY

HOTEL SHOPPING

Forum Shops at Caesars
⊙ 10am–11pm Sun–Thu; 10am–midnight Fri–Sat.
Tel (702) 893-4800.
www.forumshops.com

Grand Canal Shoppes
⊙ 10am–11pm Sun–Thu; 10am–midnight Fri–Sat.
Tel (702) 414-4500.

Le Boulevard
⊙ 10am–11pm Sun–Thu; 10am–midnight Fri–Sat.
Tel (702) 946-7000.

Miracle Mile Shops
⊙ 10am–11pm Sun–Thu; 10am–midnight Fri–Sat.
Tel (702) 866-0703.
www.miraclemileshopslv.com

Via Bellagio
⊙ 10am–midnight daily.
Tel (702) 693-7111.

THE MALLS

Boulevard Mall
3528 S. Maryland Pkwy.
⊙ 10am–9pm Mon–Sat; 11am–6pm Sun.
Tel (702) 732-8949.

Fashion Show Mall
3200 Las Vegas Blvd. S.
⊙ 10am–9pm Mon–Sat; 11am–7pm Sun.
Tel (702) 784-7000.

Las Vegas Outlet Mall
7400 Las Vegas Blvd. S.
⊙ 10am–9pm Mon–Sat; 10am–8pm Sun. *Tel (702) 896-5599.*

Las Vegas Premium Outlets
875 S. Grand Central Parkway.
⊙ 10am–9pm Mon–Sat; 10am–8pm Sun. *Tel (702) 474-7500.*

Vegas Point Mall
9155 Las Vegas Blvd. S.
⊙ 10am–7pm Mon–Sat; 10am–5pm Sun. *Tel (702) 897-9090.*

SPECIALTY STORES

Bonanza General Store
2400 Las Vegas Blvd. S.
Tel (702) 384-0005.

JP Slot Emporium
5280 S. Valley View Blvd. Suite C.
Tel (888) 988-SLOT (7568).

Serge's Showgirl Wigs
953 E. Sahara Ave.
Tel (702) 732-1015.

ENTERTAINMENT IN LAS VEGAS

Las Vegas makes a good claim to be the entertainment capital of the world. From free spectaculars such as Treasure Island's pirate battle to lavishly produced theatrical shows, there is a full range of nightlife available. Sinatra and Elvis may be gone but headliners still appear regularly in the city's showrooms, offering a rare chance to see a favorite star in a surprisingly intimate setting. Most of the major venues are concentrated in the hotels along the Strip and Downtown, and range from small lounges to 1,000-seater showrooms. While visitors can still enjoy the kitsch appeal of a Vegas burlesque show such as *Don Arden's Jubilee*, high-quality productions featuring the latest in lighting and special effects are a big draw. Comedy, magic, and music from jazz to salsa are also widely available and often for free or the price of a cocktail.

Cirque du Soleil acrobat

INFORMATION

There is no shortage of information on the entertainment scene in Las Vegas. A variety of free publications lists all the major productions as well as the latest big acts in town. Magazines and free newspapers such as *Las Vegas*, *What's On*, and *Las Vegas Weekly* can usually be picked up in all the major hotels. Even Las Vegas taxis carry free guides to the city, with information on shows and attractions. The **Las Vegas Convention and Visitor's Authority** provides up-to-date showguides, and their website has current listings and reviews *(see p123)*.

BUYING TICKETS

The easiest way to book tickets to the major shows or visiting headliners is to call the venue/hotel directly on their toll-free number. Prices can vary, ranging from around $45 to $150 per ticket. The ticket may also include drinks, a free program, tips, and even dinner. Check in advance if there is preassigned seating, because if there isn't, you can improve your chances of getting a good seat by tipping the maitre d'.

Reservations should always be made in advance, but the length of time varies greatly according to the show's

Las Vegas magazine

popularity. To see the Cirque du Soleil's stunning *Mystère* at Treasure Island you can book up to 90 days in advance, while you can reserve space for most other shows up to 14 days ahead. It is also possible to get tickets on the night of the performance by lining up at the box office an hour or so before showtime. This is especially true at times when there are no major conventions in town and it is not a public holiday. Weekdays are a better bet than weekends, although most shows have one or two days off during the week. For sports events, such as world championship boxing, or the big rock and pop concerts, frequently held at the impressive 15,225-seater MGM Grand Garden, tickets can also be purchased through **Ticketmaster** and other agency outlets. Discounts for

Showgirls from *Don Arden's Jubilee!* at Bally's Hotel

children and senior citizens may be available, and free tickets may be offered to the hotel casino's big winners.

HEADLINERS

Ever since the Strip's early days in the 1940s, Las Vegas resorts have lured some of the world's most famous performers to entertain their

Lavish production number at MGM Grand

Relaxing with a round of golf just minutes from the Strip

gambling guests. Stars such as Frank Sinatra, Dean Martin, Liza Minelli, and Elvis Presley played regularly here, often in relatively small "headliner" showrooms. The 1,400-seat Bally's Celebrity Room has hosted a wide range of performances by some of America's most famous entertainers, from Dean Martin and Liza Minnelli to zany magicians Penn and Teller. Today, such Vegas stalwarts as singers Wayne Newton and Tom Jones can be seen at intimate venues. Rita Rudner, a versatile entertainer, author, and comedian has a headliner show at Harrah's and has risen to superstar status.

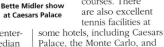

**Bette Midler show
at Caesars Palace**

LOUNGE ACTS

From jazz at Bally's Indigo Lounge to lounge acts at Tropicana's Celebration, there is a variety of music available in the bars along the Strip. The megaresorts generally have at least two venues providing free entertainment throughout the day. Among the liveliest is New York New York's The Bar at Times Square, where requests are played and a lot of boisterous audience participation takes place.

These performances are free except for the price of buying a drink. However, each venue has a minimum drink purchase charge or cover. The wonderful views from the Stratosphere Top of the World Lounge will cost you the additional price of an elevator ticket.

OUTDOOR ACTIVITIES

One of the most popular outdoor activities here is golf. Las Vegas has dozens of superbly designed golf courses, some positioned in the midst of spectacular scenery. As well as private courses there are many public ones, some just a short distance from the Strip itself. The concierge desk in your hotel will advise and book time at one of the many nearby courses. There are also excellent tennis facilities at some hotels, including Caesars Palace, the Monte Carlo, and the Riviera.

Luxurious health spas are a standard element in the big hotels providing services such as weight rooms, personal trainers, and massages.

Hiking is available at the nearby Red Rock Canyon, as is horseback riding at **Mount Charleston** (702 872-5408).

PRODUCTION SHOWS

The first production show to be staged at a Strip resort was the musical revue *Lido de Paris*, at the Stardust, which began in 1958 and ran for 33 years. This prompted other hotels to stage their own productions. Traditionally these shows have long runs – the Tropicana staged the French *Folies Bergère* in 1959, and it ran for almost 50 years. Often performed in built-to-order showrooms, Vegas shows usually have two performances each evening.

GAMBLING IN LAS VEGAS

Despite its growing fame as an all-round adult amusement park, Las Vegas remains famous for its casinos. More than 30 million visitors come to the city every year and, on average, each spends $80 gambling every day. Don't come expecting to make your fortune; with a combined annual income of $7 billion, the casinos appear to have the advantage.

The secret pleasure of gambling is the lure of the unknown – you never know what the next card will be. Casinos know this and aim to keep you playing

Blackjack cards

for as long as possible. Free drinks are sometimes available for gamblers, but it is not a good idea to gamble without a clear head. Before you start, decide on an amount that you can afford to lose and be sure to stick to it.

For a first timer, the casino can seem daunting, but, with a basic understanding of the rules, most of the games are relatively simple to play *(see p130–31)*. Some hotels have gaming guides on their in-house TV channels and Las Vegas' visitor center supplies printed guides. Several large casinos give free lessons at the tables.

Row upon row of "slots" on the gaming floor of New York New York Casino *(see p107)*

GENERAL INFORMATION

Always carry ID if you are young-looking and tend to be carded in bars, because it is illegal to gamble under the age of 21. Children are not welcome on the casino floor, which can make it difficult for families with children in some hotels *(see pp237–40)*.

Be aware that if you are winning it is casino etiquette to tip the dealers. It can also be to your advantage to tip when you first sit down at a table, as it is always a good idea to get the dealer on your side. Dealers can prevent inexperienced gamblers from making silly mistakes and will

usually explain the finer points of the games, if asked. Head for the tables where players are talking and laughing. The chances are that a row of glum faces means that you may be in for an equally dull gambling experience.

SLOT MACHINES

Slots of every kind dominate Las Vegas casinos. The simple one-armed bandit, where pulling a handle spun the reels and a win resulted from a row of cherries or some other icon, has been largely superceded by computerized push-button machines offering a bewildering variety of plays.

There are basically two kinds of slots; flat-top machines and progressive machines. A flat-top machine has a range of fixed payouts depending on different arrangements of winning symbols. There will usually be a choice of stakes, from one to three coins, and if you hit a winning display you will win less for a one-coin stake than if you play the limit. On progressive slots, you give up smaller jackpots in exchange for winning a

A Mirage coin bucket

progressive jackpot. The payout on these machines increases as you play, and the rising jackpot figure is displayed above each machine. The biggest payout is currently

Casino loyalty card

from the Megabucks slots, which operate all across Nevada. A software engineer won $39 million on a machine at the Excalibur Hotel in 2003, the highest payout ever. The majority of machines take quarters, dollars, and $5, but there are a few nickel machines left in the downtown casinos. There are also high-roller slots, which take anything from $10 to $500 for a single play.

Tips

• Usually located together, progressive machines pay out at a certain limit. It is a good idea to ask an attendant what this limit usually is, and when it was last hit. If the jackpot hits at around $10,000 and the machines are displaying $9,000, this could be a good time to start playing.

• Always play the machine limit because if you win, you will be sure to receive the maximum amount.

• Wins on both types of machine allow you to receive coins back or else they rack up credits, which you can use for subsequent bets. Monitoring your display of credits will help keep track of how much you are spending. If your original stake was 10 quarters and you won 30, using credits allows you to decide to walk away when the credit display is down to 20, leaving you 10 quarters up on the game.

• Choose to play at the busier banks of machines where players have buckets full of quarters. Rows of unoccupied machines may mean they are not paying out well.

• Join a slot club. Most casinos have clubs that offer a range of incentives to get you to play

with them; which range from cash back to discounts on hotel rooms. Members are issued with an electronic-strip plastic loyalty card that inserts into the machine; the more money a gambler spends, the greater the rewards.

BLACKJACK

This card game is one of the most popular games on the floor; casino blackjack tables offer minimum bet games from $2 to $500. The aim is to get as close to 21 without going over, and to beat the dealer. Cards are worth their numerical value, with all the face cards worth 10 and an ace worth 1 or 11. Generally the dealer will deal from a "shoe" (a box containing up to six decks of cards). Each player receives two cards face up, while the dealer's second card is face down. Players must not touch the cards and should use hand signals to indicate if they wish to take another card, or "hit" (scratch the table with their forefinger to receive another card) or not take a card, "stand" (wave a flat hand over their cards.)

Traditional slot machine

Once each player has decided to stand or hit the 21 limit, the dealer turns over his second card and plays his hand, hitting 16 or less and standing with 17 or more. This is important because it

is an essential part of "basic strategy" blackjack. The assumption behind basic strategy is that the dealer's second card will be a ten and that the next card in the shoe will also be a ten. This is because there are more tens in the deck than any other card (there are 96 tens in six decks).

Tips

• In basic strategy if the dealer's top card is a "bad" card (from two to six), then the player should stand from 12 up and not risk taking another card. This is because the dealer has to get to 17, so it is most likely that he will go over 21 when he hits his hand.

• If the player has between 12 and 16 and the dealer's first card is seven or higher, the player should gamble on drawing an extra card, as the probability is that the dealer's other card is a ten, which beats a hand of under 17.

• If your first two cards add up to 10 or 11, then you can "double down," or bet the same amount again. If you have a $5 chip on the table then you add another, hoping to get a ten card thereby reaching a winning total of 20 or 21 and doubling your winnings. Be aware that you are only allowed one extra card if you double down.

• Another betting option is to split your hand. If you are dealt two cards of the same value, you can choose to separate them into two hands, placing a second bet by the first on the table. Do this when you have aces and eights.

A winning hand on a blackjack table at Circus Circus (see p117)

Craps

Often the most fun game on the floor, a sense of camaraderie develops in craps because players are betting either with or against the "shooter" (whoever has the dice) on what the next number rolled will

Craps dice

be. The aim of the shooter's first roll, or "coming out," is to make 7 or 11 in any combination (say 3/4, 5/6) to win. A roll of 2, 3, or 12 is craps; everyone loses and the shooter rolls the dice again. If a total of 4, 5, 6, 8, 9, or 10 is

rolled, this becomes the "point" number, and the shooter must roll this number again before rolling a 7 to win. Craps etiquette says that you put your money on the table rather than handing it to the dealer; wooden holders around the table will keep your chips. Always roll with one hand; the dice must hit the end of the table. All betting and laying down of chips must be completed before the next roll.

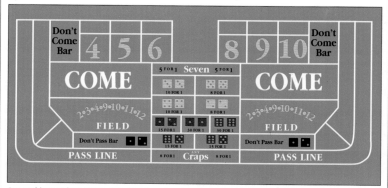

Craps table seen from above, showing the various boxes and areas for the many bets

BETS

Craps can seem confusing as there appears to be a lot going on at any one time; this is largely due to the wide variety of bets it is possible to lay. If you are a beginner the following bets are the best ones to lay.

Laying bets during a craps game at Caesars Palace

The Pass Line Bet

With this one you are basically betting that the shooter will roll a 7/11 on the first roll in order for you to win. The odds at this point are even, so if you do win you get the same amount you laid down. If a point number is rolled, the shooter has to throw the same

number before he rolls another 7. Since there are more ways to roll a 7 than any point number, it pays to take the odds once the shooter has a point, which means placing an additional bet behind your pass line bet. This will pay you the true house odds if the shooter rolls his point. The odds change according to the number, so check with the dealer first.

The Don't Pass Bet

This is the opposite of a pass line bet. The aim here is for the shooter to lose by throwing a 2 or 3 on the first roll, or by rolling a losing 7, which happens before he makes his point number.

The Come Bet

This is an optional bet you can make during the game, when your money comes to the next number that rolls. For example; if the point is 6 you make a come bet, and the shooter rolls an 8. Your come bet "comes" to the 8, and now you have two numbers in play. You can also take odds on a come bet.

The Place Bet

Another way of getting additional numbers is by making a place bet. In this case, you simply pick the number you want and make a place bet on that number. The advantage of place bets is that you pick the number yourself and you can remove your bet at any time. The disadvantage is that the casino charges you from 50 cents to $1 for each $5 bet you place.

POKER

There are several different versions of poker, including video poker, played in Las Vegas casinos. It is important to know the hierarchy of poker hands to play any of these: starting with a pair as the lowest hand, and a royal flush as the highest.

CARIBBEAN STUD POKER

A type of five-card stud poker played on a table with a layout like a blackjack table, where the aim is to beat the dealer. There is a progressive jackpot where winnings increase according to a player's hand. Players win all or part of a progressive jackpot with a Royal Flush, Straight Flush, Four of a Kind, Full House, or Flush.

PAI GOW POKER

Combining the ancient Chinese game of Pai Gow with American poker, this game includes a joker in the standard 52-card pack. The joker is used as an ace or to complete a straight or flush. Each player has to make the best two-card and five-card hand possible to beat the banker's two hands.

TEXAS HOLD 'EM

This is the most popular form of poker played in the poker rooms of Las Vegas casinos. It is also the game of the famous World Series of Poker held each year at Binion's (see p118). Players are dealt two cards and they must make their best hand from five communal cards dealt face up on the table.

ROULETTE

Roulette is quite a simple game but with a great variety of bets. A ball is spun on a wheel containing numbers 1 to 36 divided equally between red and black, plus a single and a double zero, colored green. Each player's chips are a different color so they can be easily identified

A croupier setting up roulette in a private gaming room

Casino poker chips

on the table. The aim is to guess the number that will come up on the spin of the wheel. Bets are placed on the table, which has a grid marked out with the numbers and a choice of betting options. The highest payout odds are 35 to 1 for a straight bet on one number such as 10 black. You can also make a "split bet" on two numbers, which pays 17 to 1 if either number comes up. The most popular bets are the outside bets, which are those placed in the boxes outside the numbered grid. These only pay even money, but allow you to cover more numbers such as Odd or Even, Red or Black, First 18 Numbers or Second 18 Numbers. You can also make a Column Bet covering 12 numbers, which pays 2 to 1.

BACCARAT

A variation of *chemin de fer*, baccarat is played at a leisurely pace with eight decks of cards, the deal rotating from player to player. The object of the game is to guess which hand will be closest to 9: the player's or the banker's. You can bet on either hand.

KENO

One of the easiest games to play, keno is a close relative of bingo. Out of the 80 numbers on a keno ticket, players may choose up to 20. A range of bets is possible and winning depends on your chosen numbers coming up. The prize depends on the amount of numbers matched.

A screen showing a keno game in progress at Circus Circus

RACE AND SPORTS BOOK

Giant video screens adorn these areas of the casino, where you can bet on almost any sport. The race book is for betting on thoroughbred horse racing and features live coverage from racetracks across the US. The sports book covers the main sporting events taking place around the country, as well as the major tournaments staged in Las Vegas itself. Watch the progress of your team on the nearby TVs.

Two cards in each hand of baccarat

The flame-colored hoodoos of Bryce Canyon ▷

SOUTHERN
UTAH

Southern Utah

Southern Utah contains an abundance of stunning natural landscapes, and boasts the highest concentration of national parks in the US. The region, which lies to the north of Grand Canyon and the blue waters of Lake Powell, owes much of its dramatic beauty to the geological wonder of the Grand Staircase, a series of steep terraces of colored rock. Weather and river erosion have sculpted this feature into the fine scenery found at Bryce, Arches, Capitol Reef, Zion, and Canyonlands National Parks. Hiking, boating, and mountain-biking are popular here, with equipment rentals available in such towns as Moab and St. George.

View of the peaks of Zion National Park in spring seen from the nearby visitor center

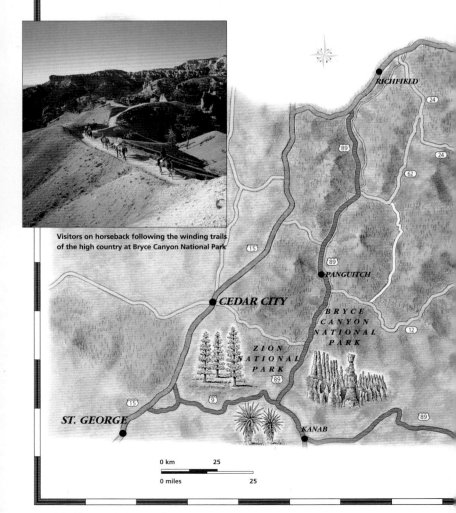

Visitors on horseback following the winding trails of the high country at Bryce Canyon National Park

RICHFIELD

BRYCE CANYON NATIONAL PARK

ZION NATIONAL PARK

PANGUITCH

CEDAR CITY

ST. GEORGE

KANAB

0 km   25

0 miles   25

GETTING AROUND

The best way to explore Southern Utah is by car: every road is a scenic route, and public transportation is limited. One train passes through the region, an Amtrak Superliner, which stops at Thompson, 35 miles (58 km) north of Moab. Greyhound buses travel to some of the region's larger towns. Two Interstate Highways, I-15 and I-70, pass close to Zion and Arches National Parks respectively. Smaller paved highways include Highway 191 via Moab, and the scenic Highway 12, which skirts Grand Staircase-Escalante National Monument. A high-clearance 4WD vehicle is advisable for many of the unpaved roads.

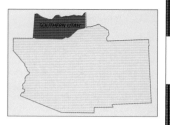

SEE ALSO

- *Where to Stay* pp240–42
- *Where to Eat* pp261–2

KEY

- Interstate
- Major highway
- Highway
- River

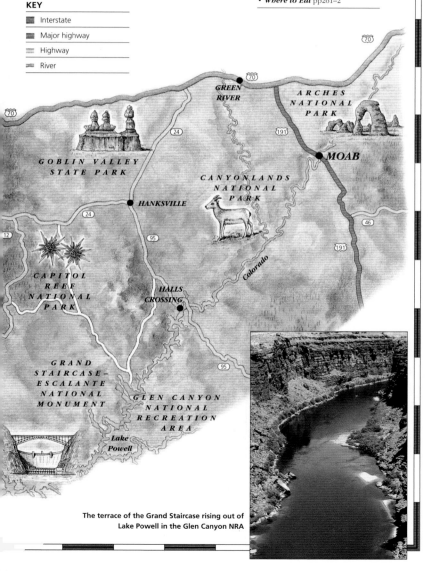

The terrace of the Grand Staircase rising out of Lake Powell in the Glen Canyon NRA

The Mormons

The Church of Jesus Christ of Latter Day Saints was founded by Joseph Smith (1805–44), a farm worker from New York State. In 1820 Smith claimed to have had visions of the Angel Moroni. The angel led him to a set of golden tablets, which he translated and later published as the *Book of Mormon*, leading to the founding of the Mormon church. This new faith grew rapidly but attracted hostility because of its political and economic beliefs, and because it practised polygamy. Seeking refuge, the Mormons moved to Illinois in 1839, where Smith was killed by an angry mob. Leadership passed to Brigham Young (1801–77), who led church members westward. Salt Lake City was founded and Young led his followers to establish farms across Utah's wilderness. Today, 70 percent of Utah's citizens are Mormons.

19th-century depiction *of Joseph Smith's vision. The Angel Moroni is seen delivering the tablets which became the Mormon scriptures.*

On the great trek westward, pilgrims rode or walked for a year, leaving Illinois in 1846 and arriving in Utah in July, 1847.

Mormon pioneers *were intrepid and successful; after they had established themselves in the Salt Lake valley, church members fanned out across the west, establishing agricultural colonies in their wake. One of these colonies was in Las Vegas (see p119), where 30 Mormons, sent here by Brigham Young, built a mission and a small fort.*

Brigham Young and his wives, *nine of whom are seen here, illustrated Mormonism's most controversial practice, polygamy. It was outlawed in 1890 to appease the US Government and pave the way for Statehood in 1896.*

THE GREAT MORMON TREK WEST

In 1847, Brigham Young led a band of Mormons west in the hope of escaping persecution and founding a safe haven in the Salt Lake valley. Young wished to find "a place on Earth that nobody wants." It was an extraordinary enterprise in which the pioneers traveled across bleak prairies and over mountains in primitive wagons, braving the fierce winter and summer weather. Those who could not afford oxen hauled all their possessions in hand carts.

Salt Lake City *was painstakingly laid out in a grid system over the unpromising, and previously unsettled, landscape of Utah's Salt Lake Basin. The grid ensured wide streets, decent-sized houses, and enough land so that each family could be self-sufficient. By 1900, many farms and more than 300 towns had been founded across the West and Southwest.*

BRIGHAM YOUNG

Born in Vermont in 1801 of a Protestant family, Brigham Young, carpenter, painter, and glazier, joined the Mormons in Ohio in 1832. He took charge of the great migration west from Illinois in 1846, arriving in Salt Lake City in 1847. In 1849 he established the territory of Deseret, which encompassed present-

Brigham Young in middle-age

day Utah. "Deseret" means "Honeybee" in the *Book of Mormon* and symbolizes industry. Young's vision and organizational skills helped the settlers turn the desert into fruitful farmland. During his long life, he had several disputes with the federal government, whose authority he both resisted and recognized. Despite being removed from political office in 1857, Young was head of the Mormon church until his death in 1877.

Mormon missionaries *preach their faith throughout the world, placing great emphasis on their social and philosophical concerns. The church enjoys a high rate of conversion, and church membership continues to grow rapidly.*

The St. George Mormon Temple *was constructed under the aegis of Brigham Young. For the eleven million Mormons worldwide, it is a potent symbol of a faith based on work, sobriety, and cooperation, with the emphasis on humanitarian service.*

SOUTHERN UTAH

Wherever you go in southern Utah, it is hard to find a road that does not dazzle the visitor with unforgettable scenery. Winding highways lead through stunning red rock canyons, stark deserts of wind-polished rock, and cool, mountain realms of tall pines and sparkling streams. The five national parks in this region are favorite destinations, such that each is inundated with up to three million visitors a year. Despite this, even in summer there are quiet, undiscovered corners to be found across the region. The Grand Staircase–Escalante National Monument offers visitors a chance to experience this living wilderness by driving such unpaved scenic routes as the Burr Trail *(see p147).*

The first people to live here were Paleo-Indians 12,000 years ago. Later, the Ancestral Puebloan people thrived in southeastern Utah, building cliff dwellings along the San Juan River. The Mormons arrived here in 1847, successfully establishing settlements in this harsh land.

Today, most people come to the area to enjoy the outdoors. Hiking, mountain biking, and 4-wheel driving are all popular activities, as well as riverfloat trips and whitewater adventures.

St. George and Cedar City are the biggest towns in southern Utah. A number of smaller communities, however, such as Springdale and Bluff, offer upscale stores and restaurants. Moab meanwhile offers outdoor activities by day, and entertainment by night.

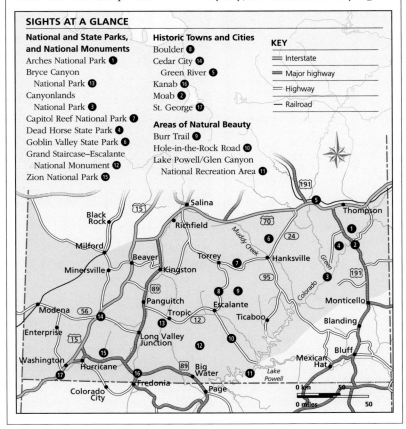

SIGHTS AT A GLANCE

National and State Parks, and National Monuments
Arches National Park **1**
Bryce Canyon National Park **13**
Canyonlands National Park **3**
Capitol Reef National Park **7**
Dead Horse State Park **4**
Goblin Valley State Park **6**
Grand Staircase–Escalante National Monument **12**
Zion National Park **15**

Historic Towns and Cities
Boulder **8**
Cedar City **14**
Green River **5**
Kanab **16**
Moab **2**
St. George **17**

Areas of Natural Beauty
Burr Trail **9**
Hole-in-the-Rock Road **10**
Lake Powell/Glen Canyon National Recreation Area **11**

KEY
═══ Interstate
▬▬ Major highway
═══ Highway
──── Railroad

◁ Relaxing in the rose-colored sandstone of Antelope Canyon, a narrow "slot" canyon in Glen Canyon NRA

Arches National Park ●

Wild flowers in the park

Arches National Park contains the highest number of natural stone arches found anywhere in the world. More than 80 of these natural wonders have formed over millions of years. The park "floats" on a salt bed, which once liquefied under the pressure exerted by the rock above it. About 300 million years ago, this salt layer bulged upward, cracking the sandstone above. Over time the cracks eroded, leaving long "fins" of rock. As these fins eroded, the hard overhead rock formed arches, which range today from the solid looking Turret Arch to the graceful Delicate and Landscape arches.

Devil's Garden
This area contains several of the park's finest arches, including Landscape Arch, a slender curve of sandstone more than 300 ft (91 m) long, thought to be the longest natural arch in the world.

Sunset watch at Delicate Arch
A natural amphitheater surrounds the arch, creating seating from which vistas of the La Sal Mountains are framed.

THE WINDOWS SECTION

In the park's Windows Section, a one-mile loop trail leads to Turret Arch, then the North and South Windows arches, situated side by side. With excellent viewing spots available, many visitors photograph North and South arches framed by the sandstone Turner Arch, as seen here.

EXPLORING THE PARK

The park's highlights can be seen from the many viewpoints dotted along the scenic drive. The drive starts at the visitor center at the park's south end, just off Hwy 191. Several easy trails start from parking lots at the road's viewpoints. The loop at Balanced Rock is a short and easy trail suitable for children, while Delicate Arch Viewpoint Trail has disabled access. The Windows loop is suitable for families.

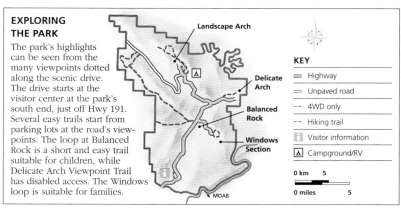

Landscape Arch

Delicate Arch

Balanced Rock

Windows Section

MOAB

KEY

═	Highway
═	Unpaved road
--	4WD only
--	Hiking trail
ℹ	Visitor information
△	Campground/RV

0 km   5

0 miles   5

Delicate Arch
The most celebrated of all the arches here, and a state symbol, Delicate Arch appears on many Utah license plates. It is reached by a moderate 45-minute walk over sandstone.

VISITORS' CHECKLIST

Road map 2C. Arches Visitor Center (435) 719-2299. Apr–Oct: 7:30am–6:30pm daily; Nov–Mar: 8am–4:30pm daily. campground, Park Ave Viewpoint, Delicate Arch Viewpoint Trail, and Balanced Rock Trail. www.nps.gov/arch

Arches are formed through a process that takes millions of years; today's arches continue to erode and will eventually collapse.

Balanced Rock
This precariously balanced boulder atop a sandstone spire is one of the park's landmarks. Good views are available from the trail as well as the scenic road route.

Western-style, timber-clad gift store on Main Street, Moab

Moab ❷

Road map 2C. 6500. Main and Center Sts. (435) 259-8825. 8am–8pm daily spring & summer, 9am–5pm daily fall & winter. www.discovermoab.com

A town of dramatic ups and downs, Moab is once again booming. In 1952 a local prospector discovered the first of several major uranium deposits outside town. Overnight, Moab became one of the wealthiest communities in America. When the uranium market declined in the 1970s, the town was saved by tourism and its proximity to Arches and Canyonlands national parks.

Today, Moab is one of the top destinations for lovers of the outdoors. Mountain bikers come here to experience the famous Slick Rock Trail. They also come for the challenging ride from Moab Rim, reached by Moab Skyway, a scenic tram ride offering panoramic views of the area. There is also a vast choice of hiking and 4WD routes taking in some of this region's fabulous landscapes.

Moab is also a center for whitewater rafting on the Colorado River. **Matheson Wetlands Preserve** off Kane Creek Boulevard has 2 miles (3 km) of hiking trails along a riverside wetland that is home to birds and wildlife. The town is lively and has good facilities.

Matheson Wetlands Preserve
Off Kane Creek Blvd. **Tel** (435) 259-4629. dawn–dusk daily.

Park Avenue and the Courthouse Towers
The large, rock monoliths known as Courthouse Towers bear an uncanny resemblance to city skyscrapers. They can be seen from Park Avenue, an easy, short trail.

Canyonlands National Park ❸

Millions of years ago, the Colorado and Green Rivers cut winding paths deep into rock, creating a labyrinth of rocky canyons that form the heart of this stunning wilderness. At its center, the rivers' confluence divides the park's 527 sq miles (1,365 sq km) into three districts: the Needles, the Maze, and the grassy plateau of the Island in the Sky. Established as a national park in 1964, Canyonlands is growing in popularity. Most wilderness travel, whether on foot or by vehicle, requires a permit.

VISITORS' CHECKLIST

Road map C2. ▌ *Canyonlands National Park, 2282 South West Resource Blvd., Moab (435) 719-2313.* **www**.nps.gov/cany ☐ *Visitor center: 8am–4:30pm (longer during Spring and Fall) daily.* ● *Jan 1, Thanksgiving, Dec 25.* 🎦 & 🗹 🖽 ▣

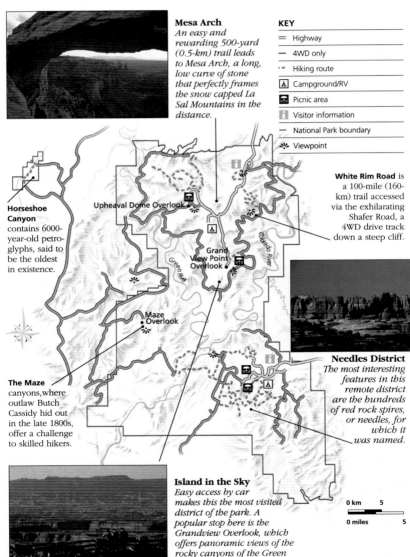

Mesa Arch
An easy and rewarding 500-yard (0.5-km) trail leads to Mesa Arch, a long, low curve of stone that perfectly frames the snow capped La Sal Mountains in the distance.

KEY

=	Highway
—	4WD only
'=	Hiking route
▲	Campground/RV
🏕	Picnic area
▌	Visitor information
—	National Park boundary
☀	Viewpoint

White Rim Road is a 100-mile (160-km) trail accessed via the exhilarating Shafer Road, a 4WD drive track down a steep cliff.

Horseshoe Canyon contains 6000-year-old petroglyphs, said to be the oldest in existence.

Upheaval Dome Overlook

Needles District
The most interesting features in this remote district are the hundreds of red rock spires, or needles, for which it was named.

Grand View Point Overlook

Maze Overlook

The Maze canyons, where outlaw Butch Cassidy hid out in the late 1800s, offer a challenge to skilled hikers.

0 km   5
0 miles   5

Island in the Sky
Easy access by car makes this the most visited district of the park. A popular stop here is the Grandview Overlook, which offers panoramic views of the rocky canyons of the Green and Colorado rivers.

For hotels and restaurants in this region see pp240–42 and pp261–2

The deep crevices of the canyons in the wide valley around Green River

Dead Horse Point State Park ❹

Road map C1. 🚩 *State Route 313* (435) 259-2614. ◯ *6am–10pm daily. Visitor center* ◯ *Apr–Oct: 8am–6pm daily; Nov–Mar: 8am–5pm daily.* 🚻 ♿ **www**.stateparks.utah.gov

The high mesa of Dead Horse Point lies just outside the entry to the Island in the Sky of Canyonlands National Park. Unforgettable views of the Colorado River and the maze of deep canyons are a highpoint here. Legend has it that this park owes its name to the fact that it was once used as a natural corral for wild mustangs. A group of horses not chosen for taming

View of the dramatic cliffs of Dead Horse Point State Park

were once left in this dry site, eventually dying of thirst within sight of the Colorado River far below. The Park also features several short hiking trails that follow the cliff edge, offering variations on the truly amazing view. The drama of this place has not been lost on Hollywood *(see pp30–31)*. Famous as the spot where Thelma and Louise drove off the edge in the 1991 film of the same name, in 2000 these cliffs were scaled by Tom Cruise in *Mission Impossible: 2*.

Green River ❺

Road map C1. 🏠 *1,000.* 🚩 *885 E. Main St (435) 564-3600.* ◯ *Apr–Oct: 8am–8pm; Nov–Mar: 8am–5pm daily.*

Located in a broad, bowl-shaped valley, the town grew around a ford of the wild Green River in the 19th and early 20th centuries. Primarily a service town, it is also a launching spot for those braving the whitewater of the Green and Colorado Rivers.

John Wesley Powell *(see p25)* began his intrepid exploration of the Colorado River and Grand Canyon from here in 1871. Green River has the **John Wesley Powell River History Museum**, with 20,000 sq ft (1,860 sq m) of displays tracing the history of the area's exploration.

🏛 **John Wesley Powell River History Museum**
885 E. Main St. **Tel** (435) 564-3427. ◯ *Apr–Oct: 8am–8pm daily; Nov–Mar: 9am–5pm daily.* ◯ *public hols.* 🚻 🅿

Eroded rock formations of Goblin Valley State Park

Goblin Valley State Park ❻

Road map C1. **Tel** (435) 275-4584. ◯ *6am–10pm daily.* 🚻 🅰 **www**.stateparks.utah.gov

The "Goblins" of Goblin Valley State Park are a group of mushroom-shaped rocks or hoodoos, intricately carved by erosion. Visitors are free to wander among these rocks, which are up to 10 ft (3 m) in height. Two paved and several unpaved trails lead down to the valley floor.

Bathed in the setting sun, the Rainbow Bridge over Lake Powell on a spring evening ▷

Capitol Reef National Park ❼

Around the turn of the 20th century, prospectors coming across the desert were forced to stop at the Waterpocket Fold, a vast 100-mile- (160-km-) long wall of rock that runs north–south through the desert. They likened it to an ocean reef and thought its round white domes looked like the nation's Capitol Building, hence the park's name. Covering 378 square miles (980 sq km), many people pass through the park via Fremont Canyon on Hwy 24. The park is famous for its long record of human habitation; Ancestral Puebloan petroglyphs and a preserved Mormon homestead can still be seen here.

VISITORS' CHECKLIST

Road map 2C. 10 miles E. of Torrey, Hwy 24. 🛈 *Capitol Reef Visitor Center (435) 425-3791.* **www**.nps.gov/care ⬤ *Jun–Sep: 8am–6pm; Oct–May: 8–4:30pm daily.* ⬤ *Dec 25.* 🅿 ♿ 🎥 🅰

Cathedral Valley
The vast rock monoliths that tower over the desert here give the valley its name. An unpaved road crosses this stunning area.

The Fremont Petroglyphs were created by the Ancestral Puebloans between 700 and 1250, and can be seen on a rock wall in the Fremont Canyon.

The Gifford Farmhouse
Visitors can tour the 1908 Gifford home, which is now a cultural center dedicated to the 1880s Mormon settlement that once flourished here.

Capitol Gorge
Capitol Gorge can be reached from the scenic route that extends about 10 miles (16 km) into the heart of the park. Guided walking tours are available during summer, but only experienced hikers should explore the back country here.

Notom-Bullfrog Road is an adventurous drive along a partly-unpaved road for 70 miles (112 km) south to Lake Powell. Cars can negotiate the road in dry weather but extra gas and water are essential.

Waterpocket Fold was formed 65 million years ago as the Earth's crust buckled upward. The multicolored ripples of rock that run the length of the park continue to be shaped by erosion.

KEY

═	Highway
═	Unmade road
▬	4WD only
🚶	Ranger station
🅰	Campground/RV
🍴	Picnic
🛈	Visitor information
☀	Viewpoint

BICKNELL

HANKSVILLE

24

12

WATERPOCKET FOLD

Fremont River

0 km 10

0 miles 10

Boulder ❽

Road map 2C. 🛈 *755 W. Main*
St. Escalante (435) 335-7382.
⬭ *Mar–Nov: 7am–6pm daily.*

The tiny town of Boulder
nestles picturesquely among
the surrounding peaks. The
town is home to the Anasazi
State Park, which offers
restored ruins and a museum
detailing the history of the
Ancestral Puebloans that lived
here between AD 1050 and
1200. Before Hwy 12 was
built, Boulder was virtually
isolated as the last town in
America to receive
its mail by pack mule. Today,
Boulder makes a welcome
rest stop along Hwy 12, which
connects Hwy 89 and Capitol
Reef National Park. This road
boasts what may be the most
spectacular and diverse array
of landscapes found along
any road in the country.

Between Escalante and
Boulder, Hwy 12 winds
through an unforgettable
landscape of vividly colored,
towering rock formations
and twisting canyons. Visitors
can stop at Calf Creek Campground to hike the short trail
along Calf Creek Canyon
ridge to Lower Calf Creek
Falls. The falls are one of the
hidden treasures of the Southwest, a 126-ft (38-m) plume
that drops past lush hanging
gardens into an emerald
green pool. Continuing along
Hwy 12, just before Boulder,
the road offers white-knuckle
excitement as it traverses the
Hogsback, a knife-edge ridge
of rock with guardrails and

steep drops on either side,
and Hell's Backbone Bridge.
Beyond Boulder, Hwy 12
climbs to the 9,400-ft (2,820-m)
summit of Boulder Mountain.

Burr Trail ❾

Road map 2C. 🛈 *755 W. Main St.*
Escalante (435) 826-5499.

The Burr Trail is another
partly paved scenic road,
winding through the Grand
Staircase–Escalante National
Monument. The first 40 miles
(64 km) are paved and follow
Deer Creek, rising through
the winding red-rock maze
of Long Canyon. At the
canyon end, the view opens
out to reveal the pristine
valleys of the Circle Cliffs and
Capitol Reef. The trail crosses
Capitol Reef as an unpaved
road before reaching Bullfrog
Marina at Lake Powell *(see
pp150–51)* and is passable
only by four-wheel drive,
high-clearance vehicles.

Hole-in-the-Rock Road ❿

Road map 2C. 🛈 *755 W. Main St.*
Escalante (435) 826-5499.

In 1879 a determined group
of 230 Mormon settlers
headed out from Panguitch,
hoping to create a new
settlement in southeastern
Utah. Instead they were
brought to a halt by the
yawning 2,000-ft- (600-m-)
deep abyss of Glen Canyon.
Undeterred, they dynamited a

View of Lake Powell from the
end of Hole-in-the-Rock Road

narrow hole through a wall of
rock and constructed a primitive road down the sheer sides
of the canyon. Lowering their
wagons and cattle down the
path by ropes they finally
reached the bottom, only to
repeat the whole process in
reverse to ascend the far side.
They finally founded the town
of Bluff in 1880 *(see p172)*.

Today, their original route,
Hole-in-the-Rock Road, offers
an impressive trip through the
wild interior of the Grand
Staircase–Escalante National
Monument. About 18 miles
(29 km) along the road,
intrepid hikers can explore
Peekaboo and Spooky
canyons, two slot canyons
barely one foot (30 cm) wide
in places. 4WD is necessary
to traverse the last 6 miles
(10 km) to the pioneers' "Hole
in the Rock," a 50-ft (15-m)
slit in the rock which offers a
fine view of Lake Powell.

Hell's Backbone Bridge outside the town of Boulder, with steep mountain drops on either side

Lake Powell ⑪

See pp150–51.

Grand Staircase–Escalante National Monument ⑫

Road map C2. ⑆ *755 W. Main St., Escalante (435) 826-5499.* ⃝ *mid-Mar–mid-Nov: 7:30am–5:30pm daily; mid-Nov–mid-Mar: 8am–4:30pm daily.* **www**.ut.blm.gov/monument

Established by President Clinton in 1996, this national monument encompasses 1.9 million acres (769,000 ha) of pristine rock canyons, mountains, and high desert plateaus. One of the last areas in the US to be explored, the Grand Staircase–Escalante National Park abuts Capitol Reef National Park, Glen Canyon National Recreation Area, and Bryce Canyon National Park. It was named for the four cliff faces, called Vermilion, Grey, White, and Pink, that rise in tiered steps across the Colorado Plateau (*see pp18–19*). Geologically speaking, they are a recent phenomenon, having been raised just 12 million years ago.

This vast area has a special importance, as the Bureau of Land Management intends to preserve its wild and largely pristine state. No new roads, facilities, or campgrounds will be built in the monument, while those roads that already exist will not be improved.

The spectacular beauty of the monument is best explored on scenic drives combined with daylong hikes. Several paved and dirt roads offer access to various parts of the park. Highway 89 follows the southern boundary, in places hugging the base of the towering Vermilion cliffs. Just 10 miles (16 km) east of the town, a road leads north into Johnson Canyon, where there is a mock Western town that has been used for many movies and TV shows (*see p30*).

Information on guided and independent tours in this vast region can be found at the Escalante visitor center.

A few miles east of Bryce Canyon and 9 miles (14 km) south of Hwy 12 stands **Kodachrome Basin State Park**, a distinctive landscape noted for 67 free-standing sand pipes, or rock chimneys, formed millions of years ago as geyser vents.

Vintage wagon outside Cedar City Museum

🌺 **Kodachrome Basin State Park**
⑆ *(435) 679-8562; (800) 322-3770.* ⃝ *6am–10pm daily.* 🅿️ 🄿 🅰️

Bryce Canyon National Park ⑬

See pp152–3.

Stage of the Globe Theatre in Cedar City

Cedar City ⑭

Road map B2. 🏠 *15,750.* ✈️ 🚍 ⑆ *581 N. Main St. (435) 586-5124.* **www**.scenicsouthernutah.com

Founded in 1851 by Mormons, this town developed as a center for mining and smelting iron in the latter part of the 19th century. Today, it offers hotels and restaurants within an hour's drive of the lovely Zion National Park (*see pp154–5*). In town, the Iron Mission State Park and Museum pays tribute to the early Mormons' indomitable pioneering spirit and features an extensive collection of more than 300 wagons and early vehicles, including an original Wells Fargo overland stagecoach. Cedar City's Shakespeare Festival, which runs annually from June to October, is staged in a replica of London's neo-Elizabethan Globe Theatre and attracts large audiences from the area.

Petrified ancient sand pipes rising out of the desert in the Kodachrome Basin State Park

For hotels and restaurants in this region see pp240–42 and pp261–2

An ATV (all-terrain vehicle) rider at the Coral Pink Sand Dunes State Park

Around 20 miles (32 km) east of the town, along Hwy 14, **Cedar Breaks National Monument** features a small but spectacular array of vibrant pink and orange limestone cliffs, topped by deep green forest. Carved by erosion, sculpted columns rise in ranks of color, resembling a smaller, less-visited version of Bryce Canyon *(see pp152–3)*. In winter the monument closes, but the area remains a popular destination for cross-country skiing enthusiasts.

🏕 Cedar Breaks National Monument
Tel (435) 586-9451. ☐ *daily. Visitor center* ☐ *Jun–Labor Day: 8am–6pm daily; Labor Day–mid-Oct: 9am–5:30pm daily.* 🌐 *www.nps.gov/cebr*

Zion National Park ⑮

See pp154–5.

Kanab ⑯

Road map B2. 🏚 *3,900.* ❚ *78 South 100 E. (435) 644-5033.* ☐ *May–Oct: 9am–7pm Mon–Fri, 9am–5pm Sat. Nov–Apr: 9am–5pm Mon–Sat.* **www**.kaneutah.com

This small town was named originally for Fort Kanab, built in 1864 but abandoned two years later because of frequent Indian attacks. Today's Kanab was established in 1874 by Mormon settlers. The town's main occupation these days is offering reasonably priced food and accommodations to vacationers traveling between Grand Canyon, Zion, and Bryce Canyon National Parks. Often referred to as the "gateway to Lake Powell," Kanab is also known as Utah's "Little Hollywood," a reference to the 200 or so movies and TV shows that have been filmed in and around the town since 1963 *(see pp30–31)*. Details of film sets open to the public may be obtained from the **Visitor Center**.

Environs
About 10 miles (16 km) west of Kanab and a few miles from the small town of Mount Carmel Junction, the **Coral Pink Sand Dunes State Park** is a sea of ever-shifting pink dunes that cover more than 3,000 acres (1,200 ha). This distinctive, harsh desert landscape was created when wind eroded the rich red sandstone cliffs surrounding the site, slowly depositing sand in the valley below. Interpretive signs relate the story of the dunes' geological formation. A path leads out into the dunes where you can enjoy the thrill of sliding down their faces. The park is a popular destination for riders of ATVs (all-terrain vehicles) and dune buggies.

🌴 Coral Pink Sand Dunes State Park
Tel (435) 648-2800. ☐ *7am–10pm daily.* 🌐 🚻 **www**.stateparks.utah.gov

St. George ⑰

Road map B2. 🏚 *45,000.* ✕ 🚌 ❚ *97 E. St. George Blvd. (435) 628-1658. Visitor center* ☐ *9am–5pm Mon–Fri; 9am–1pm Sat.*

Established in 1861 by Mormons *(see pp136–7)*, St. George has recently experienced a population boom as retirees from all over the US discover its mild climate and tranquil atmosphere. The towering gold spire that can be seen over the city belongs to Utah's first Mormon Temple, finished in 1877. A beloved project of Mormon leader and visionary Brigham Young (1801–77), it remains a key site. Only Mormons are allowed inside the temple, but the **Visitor Center**, which relates its history, is open to all. St. George's association with Brigham Young began when he decided to build a winter home here in 1871. The elegant and spacious **Brigham Young Winter Home Historic Site** is now a museum and has preserved much of its first owner's original furnishings.

Five miles (8 km) northwest of town on Hwy 18 lies Snow Canyon State Park. The park features hiking trails that lead to volcanic caves and million-year-old-lava flows. A paved bike path leads through the park and back to St. George.

🏛 Brigham Young Winter Home Historic Site
67 West St. N. Tel (435) 673-2517. ☐ *Jun–Sep: 9am–7pm daily; Sep–May: 9am–5pm daily.* 🌐

Façade of Brigham Young's winter home in St. George

Lake Powell and Glen Canyon National Recreation Area ⓫

The Glen Canyon National Recreation Area (NRA) was established in 1972 and covers more than one million acres of dramatic desert and canyon country around the 185-mile- (298-km-) long Lake Powell. The lake was created by damming the Colorado River. The recreation area is "Y"-shaped, following the San Juan River east almost to the town of Mexican Hat and heading north-east toward Canyonlands National Park *(see pp142–3)*. Today, the lake hosts watersports enthusiasts, and after years of drought, the water is once again approaching average levels. It is still a good idea to call ahead for boat launch information. Glen Canyon is also one of the most popular hiking, biking, and 4WD destinations in the US.

Rainbow Bridge National Monument
Rising 309 ft (94 m) above Lake Powell, Rainbow Bridge is the largest natural bridge in North America, only acces-sible by boat from Wahweap or Bullfrog marinas.

General View of Lake Powell
The blue waters of the man-made Lake Powell are encircled by colorful sandstone coves – once Glen Canyon's side canyons – and dramatic buttes and mesas.

Glen Canyon Dam was completed in 1963 and rises 710 ft (213 m) above the bedrock of the Colorado River.

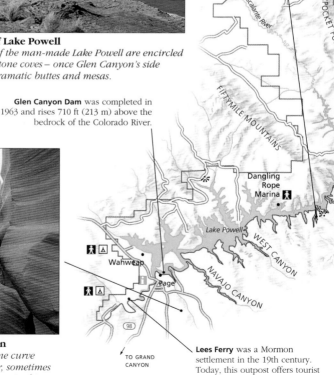

Antelope Canyon
Bands of sandstone curve sinuously together, sometimes just a few feet apart, in this famously deep "slot" canyon.

↙ TO GRAND CANYON

Lees Ferry was a Mormon settlement in the 19th century. Today, this outpost offers tourist facilities, including a ranger station and campground.

For hotels and restaurants in this region see pp240–42 and pp261–2

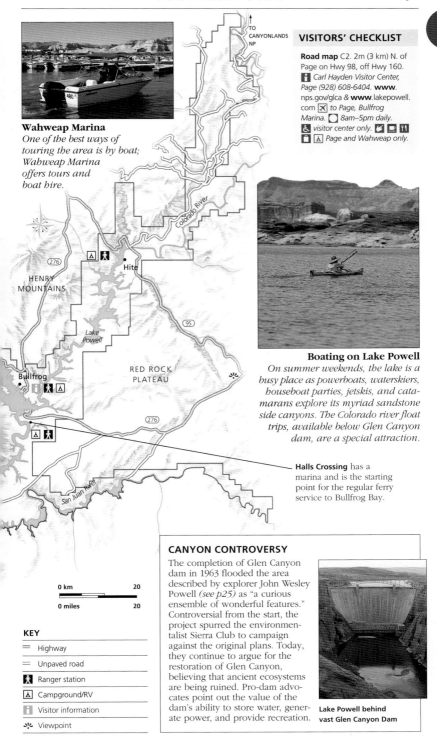

Wahweap Marina
*One of the best ways of
touring the area is by boat;
Wahweap Marina
offers tours and
boat hire.*

Boating on Lake Powell
*On summer weekends, the lake is a
busy place as powerboats, waterskiers,
houseboat parties, jetskis, and cata-
marans explore its myriad sandstone
side canyons. The Colorado river float
trips, available below Glen Canyon
dam, are a special attraction.*

Halls Crossing has a
marina and is the starting
point for the regular ferry
service to Bullfrog Bay.

CANYON CONTROVERSY

The completion of Glen Canyon
dam in 1963 flooded the area
described by explorer John Wesley
Powell *(see p25)* as "a curious
ensemble of wonderful features."
Controversial from the start, the
project spurred the environmen-
talist Sierra Club to campaign
against the original plans. Today,
they continue to argue for the
restoration of Glen Canyon,
believing that ancient ecosystems
are being ruined. Pro-dam advo-
cates point out the value of the
dam's ability to store water, generate power, and provide recreation.

**Lake Powell behind
vast Glen Canyon Dam**

KEY

 Highway

 Unpaved road

 Ranger station

 Campground/RV

 Visitor information

 Viewpoint

0 km   20

0 miles   20

Bryce Canyon National Park ⓭

A series of deep amphitheaters filled with flame-colored rock formations called hoodoos are the hallmark of Bryce Canyon National Park. Bryce is high in altitude, reaching elevations of 8,000–9,000 ft (2,400–2,700 m), with a scenic road traveling for 18 miles (30 km) along the rim of Paunsaugunt Plateau. The highlights here are the views of vast fields of pink, orange, and red spires; the Paiute Indians, once hunters here, described them as "red rocks standing like men in a bowl-shaped recess." The canyon's maze of pillars and channels is best appreciated on foot.

• Shakespear Point

• Mossy Cave

PINK CLIFFS

Fairyland Point

Queen's Garden Trail

Navajo Loop Trail

Sunrise Point

From this lookout it is easy to see why early settler and Mormon farmer Ebenezer Bryce, after whom the park is named, called it "a helluva place to lose a cow."

Thor's Hammer

Carved into the pink cliffs of the highest "step" of the Grand Staircase (see p148), this unusual landscape consists of eroded sandstone. Hoodoos such as Thor's Hammer are formed as rain and wind erode "fins" of harder rock that become columns, then further erode into strangely shaped hoodoos. The high altitude, ice, and wind continue the "carving" process today.

Sunset Point is one of the major lookouts in Bryce Canyon. In spite of its name, it faces east, so while sunrises can be spectacular here, sunsets can be a little anticlimactic.

KEY

═	Highway
▪▪	Hiking route
🚶	Ranger station
Ⓐ	Campground/RV
🏕	Picnic area
ℹ	Visitor information
☄	Viewpoint

Navajo Loop

This 1.4-mile (2-km) round-trip trail zig-zags sharply down the cliff face for 500 ft (150 m) to finish in a slow meander among slot canyons and rock stands. The climb back up the trail is particularly strenuous.

Bryce Amphitheater
This panoramic vista of snow-covered rock spires, is among the most popular views of the park. In both winter and summer the amphitheater is best seen from Inspiration Point.

Natural Bridge
This graceful natural bridge is located a few yards from the park's scenic highway. It frames a picturesque view of the distant valley far below. Officially, it is a natural arch and not a bridge, as it was formed not by a river, but by the same natural forces (of wind, rain, and ice) that created the park's hoodoos.

Agua Canyon
This overlook features some of the most delicate and beautiful of the park's formations, as well as a good view of the layered pink sandstone cliffs typical of the Paunsaugunt Plateau.

Bryce Point

Paria View

PINK CLIFFS

Swamp Canyon Butte

Noon Canyon Butte

Rainbow Point

Ponderosa Canyon

Yovimba Point

PINK CLIFFS

0 km   2
0 miles   2

Utah Prairie Dog
Now threatened, the Utah prairie dog lives only in southern Utah: those living in the park today constitute the largest remaining group.

Zion National Park ⑮

Wild-flowers

Zion Canyon lies at the heart of this beautiful national park and is arguably the most popular of all of Utah's natural wonders. The canyon was carved by the powerful waters of the Virgin River and then widened, sculpted, and reshaped by wind, rain, and ice. The canyon walls rise up to 2,000 ft (600 m) on both sides, and are shaped into jagged peaks and formations in shades of red and white.

The park shuttle is the only way into the canyon from April to November. Shuttles run every few minutes with numerous stops along the way. A number of short walks beginning at the stops follow marked trails to the tough 16-mile (26-km) hike through the canyon. The hike involves wading through the Virgin River.

Horseback and Mule Tours
Half- and full-day mule- and horseback tours follow trails in the park. The Sand Bench Trail leads to a high plateau that offers fine vistas.

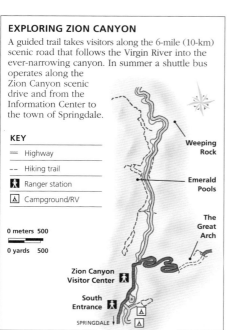

River Walk
At the end of Zion Canyon Scenic Drive lies the park's most popular trail. Involving no climbing, the 1.3-mile- (2-km-) paved River Walk follows the Virgin River to where the canyon walls rise to over 2,000 ft (600 m). The trail offers beautiful views of the river as it winds between red sandstone walls.

EXPLORING ZION CANYON

A guided trail takes visitors along the 6-mile (10-km) scenic road that follows the Virgin River into the ever-narrowing canyon. In summer a shuttle bus operates along the Zion Canyon scenic drive and from the Information Center to the town of Springdale.

KEY

═══	Highway
-- --	Hiking trail
🚶	Ranger station
Ⓐ	Campground/RV

0 meters 500
0 yards 500

Weeping Rock

Emerald Pools

The Great Arch

Zion Canyon Visitor Center 🚶

South Entrance 🚶

SPRINGDALE

ZION CANYON

The lower reaches of the Virgin River meander quietly through the banks of cottonwood, oak, and willow trees that grow beneath the gradually sloping walls at the start of the canyon. The river bank is bordered with wild meadows that, in spring, sport a profusion of wild flowers. However, sudden summer rainstorms may cause floods and areas of the park near the river to be closed. Visitors are advised to check conditions first.

Hiking
Numerous guided walking and hiking tours of Zion's geology and history leave daily from the visitor center. Popular trails are Emerald Pools Trail and Canyon Overlook Trail, which leads to the Great Arch.

Sculpted monoliths of rock rise above the Virgin River as it flows along the canyon.

VISITORS' CHECKLIST

Road map 2B. Hwy 9, near Springdale. 🛈 *Zion Canyon Visitor Center (435) 772-3256.* **www**.nps.gov/zion ◷ *8am–5pm daily (to 8pm Jun–Aug).* 🈂 ♿ *partial.*
📷 💺 🛉 🍴 ⛺

Weeping Rock
An easy, self-guided trail leads to the rock and its hanging gardens, which are full of wildflowers in spring. This spot owes its fertility to the spring and seep-water that flows from the rock.

Luxuriant foliage along the banks of the Virgin River provides shade for the area's abundant wildlife, including birds, mule deer, and bobcats.

The Virgin River seems gentle, but the force of its current is responsible for forming the canyon.

Zion–Mt. Carmel Highway
One of the loveliest routes in the park, the Zion–Mt. Carmel highway leads upward in a set of hairpin switchbacks with splendid views back into the canyon and up to the pastel-colored sandstone of the surrounding peaks.

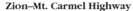

The ancient cliff dwellings of the Ancestral Puebloan people at Mesa Verde ▷

THE FOUR CORNERS

Exploring The Four Corners

The Four Corners region is the only place in the United States where four states meet at a single point. Here, parts of Utah, Colorado, Arizona, and New Mexico make up an area of national monuments and parks, ancient ruins, and dramatic canyonlands, many set on Native American reservations. World-famous vistas include the buttes of Monument Valley, and Colorado's San Juan Skyway, where both the highway and the Durango-Silverton Narrow Gauge Railroad travel through picturesque old alpine towns.

The Keet Seel ruins at the Navajo National Monument in Arizona

One of the distinctive buttes, known as "the Mittens" in Monument Valley

GETTING AROUND

A private car is essential for getting around the Four Corners; a high-clearance 4WD vehicle is recommended for traveling many interesting, unpaved regional roads. Secondary (paved) highways are generally good, while unpaved roads are categorized as follows: Good roads are suitable for all passenger cars; high clearance roads are suitable for 2 or 4WD; 4WD roads should be tackled by only experienced drivers in high-clearance vehicles. Always check on road and weather conditions.

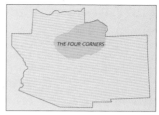

THE FOUR CORNERS

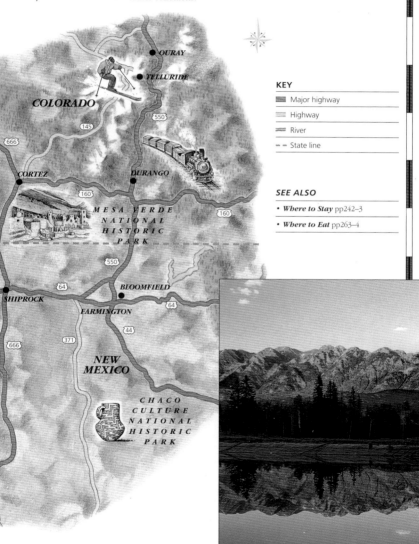

KEY

▰▰▰ Major highway

▰▰▰ Highway

▰▰▰ River

– – State line

SEE ALSO

- *Where to Stay* pp242–3

- *Where to Eat* pp263–4

Mountain view on the San Juan Skyway between Durango and Silverton

The Ancestral Puebloans

The hauntingly beautiful and elaborate ruins left behind by the Ancestral Puebloan people are a key factor in the hold that this prehistoric culture has over the public imagination. Also known as "Anasazi," a name coined by the Navajo meaning "Ancient Enemy Ancestor," today they are more accurately known as the Ancestral Pueblo people, and are seen as the ancestors of today's Pueblo peoples.

The first Ancestral Puebloans *(see p38)* are thought to have settled at Mesa Verde in around AD 550, where they lived in pithouses. By around AD 800 they had developed masonry skills and began building housing complexes using sandstone. From AD 1100 to 1300, impressive levels of craftsmanship were reached in weaving, pottery, jewelry, and tool-making.

Ceramics, *such as this bowl, show the artistry of the Ancestral Puebloans. Pottery is just one of many ancient artifacts on display in Southwestern museums.*

Kivas are round pit-like rooms dug into the ground and roofed with beams and earth.

Jackson Stairway *in Chaco Canyon is evidence of the engineering skills of the Ancestral Puebloans. They also built networks of roads between their communities and extensive irrigation systems.*

Tools *of various types were skillfully shaped from stone, wood, and bone. The Ancestral Puebloans did not work metal, yet they managed to produce such beautiful artifacts as baskets, pottery, and jewelry.*

Bone awl

Needle

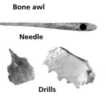

Drills

The blue corn *growing on this Hopi reservation in Arizona today is a similar plant to that grown by Ancestral Puebloans. They were also skilled at utilizing the medicinal properties of plants, including cotton-wood bark, which contains a painkiller.*

The kiva *was the religious and ceremonial center of Ancestral Puebloan life. Still used by modern Pueblo Indians today, a* kiva *usually had no windows and the only access was through a hole in the roof. Small kivas were used by a single family unit, while large* kivas *were designed to accommodate the whole community.*

WHERE TO FIND ANCESTRAL PUEBLOAN RUINS

Canyon de Chelly National Monument *(p168)*; Chaco Culture National Historical Park *(p174)*; Mesa Verde National Park *(p180)*; Navajo National Monument *(p166)*; Hovenweep National Monument *(p172)*; Aztec Ruins National Monument *(p173)*.

Petroglyphs *were often used by Ancestral Puebloans as astronomical markers for the different seasons. This one was found at the Petrified Forest National Park in Arizona* (see p73).

Pueblo Bonito features many examples of the masonry skills used by the Puebloan peoples.

THE PUEBLO PEOPLE

By AD 1300 the Ancestral Puebloans had abandoned many of their cities and migrated to areas where new centers emerged. Theories on why this occurred include a 50-year drought; the strain that a larger population placed on the desert's limited resources; and a lengthy period of social upheaval, perhaps stimulated by increasing trade with tribes as far away as central Mexico. Most archaeologists agree that the Ancestral Puebloans did not disappear but live on today in Puebloan descendants who trace their origins to Mesa Verde, Chaco, and other sacred ancestral sites.

CHACO CANYON'S PUEBLO BONITO

At Chaco Canyon *(see pp174–5)* the largest "great house" ever built was Pueblo Bonito with more than 600 rooms and 40 kivas. One current theory is that these structures did not house populations but were, in fact, public buildings for commerce and ceremonial gatherings. The lives of the Ancestral Puebloans were short, barely 35 years, and as harsh as the environment in which they lived. Their diet was poor, and arthritis and dental problems were common. Women often showed signs of osteoporosis or brittle bones as early as their first childbirth.

Painstaking excavation at an Ancestral Puebloan *kiva* in Chaco Canyon

THE FOUR CORNERS

Dominated by a Navajo reservation the size of Connecticut, and presenting sweeping panoramas of mesas, canyons, and vast expanses of high desert, the Four Corners is the perfect destination for those wanting to experience native culture and the real west.

Although it receives less than 10 in (25 cm) of rainfall per year, this arid land has supported life since the first Paleo-Indians arrived about 12,000 years ago. The Anasazi, today known as the Ancestral Puebloan peoples, lived here from about AD 500 until the 13th century. They are responsible for the many evocative ruins found here, including those at Mesa Verde, Chaco Canyon, and Hovenweep National Monument. Their descendants include the Hopi, whose pueblos are said to be the oldest continually occupied towns in North America. The Navajo arrived here in the 15th century and their spiritual center is Canyon de Chelly with its 1,000-ft (330-m) red rock walls.

Monument Valley's impressive landscape has been used as a backdrop for countless movies and TV shows. The region is also popular for hiking, fishing, and whitewater rafting.

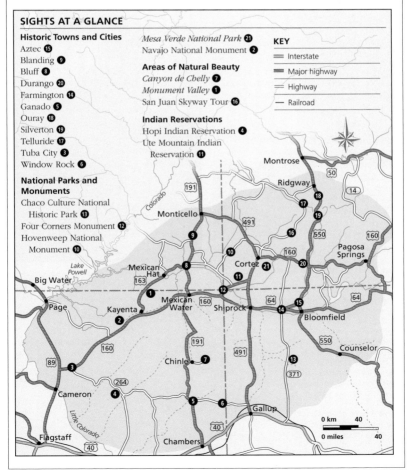

SIGHTS AT A GLANCE

Historic Towns and Cities
Aztec ⑮
Blanding ⑨
Bluff ⑧
Durango ⑳
Farmington ⑭
Ganado ⑤
Ouray ⑱
Silverton ⑲
Telluride ⑰
Tuba City ③
Window Rock ⑥

National Parks and Monuments
Chaco Culture National Historic Park ⑬
Four Corners Monument ⑫
Hovenweep National Monument ⑩

Mesa Verde National Park ㉑
Navajo National Monument ②

Areas of Natural Beauty
Canyon de Chelly ⑦
Monument Valley ①
San Juan Skyway Tour ⑯

Indian Reservations
Hopi Indian Reservation ④
Ute Mountain Indian Reservation ⑪

KEY
━ Interstate
━ Major highway
═ Highway
— Railroad

◁ **Dramatic rock formations known as "the Mittens" in the Navajo Nation's Monument Valley**

Monument Valley ➊

From scenic Highway 163, which crosses the border of Utah and Arizona, it is possible to see the famous towering sandstone buttes and mesas of Monument Valley. These ancient rocks, soaring upward from a seemingly boundless desert, have come to symbolize the American West, largely because Hollywood has used these breathtaking vistas as a backdrop for hundreds of movies, TV shows, and commercials since the 1930s *(see p30)*.

The area's visitor center sits within the boundary of Monument Valley Tribal Park, but many of the valley's spectacular rock formations and other sites are found just outside the park boundary.

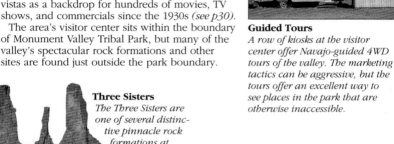

Guided Tours
A row of kiosks at the visitor center offer Navajo-guided 4WD tours of the valley. The marketing tactics can be aggressive, but the tours offer an excellent way to see places in the park that are otherwise inaccessible.

Three Sisters
The Three Sisters are one of several distinctive pinnacle rock formations at Monument Valley. Others include the Totem Pole and the "fingers" of the Mittens. The closest view of the sisters can be seen from John Ford's Point, and is one of the most photographed sights here.

Left Mitten

Art and Ruins
Petroglyphs such as this deer can be seen on Navajo-guided tours of rock art sites, which are dotted around the valley's ancient ruins.

EXPLORING THE VALLEY

The awe-inspiring beauty of Monument Valley's buttes and mesas can be viewed by travelers from Hwy 163. Visitors can also pay a fee to travel on a 17-mile (27-km) self-guided drive along a well-marked dirt road. (Fees are collected at the visitor center.) Alternatively, Navajo guides may be hired for hiking, horseback, or 4WD tours to fascinating and less-visited parts of the valley.

Mitchell Butte
BLANDING
Left Mitten
Merrick Butte
Right Mitten
163
UTAH
ARIZONA
0 km   20
0 miles   20
MONUMENT VALLEY NAVAJO TRIBAL PARK
160
Elephant Butte
Kayenta
SHIPROCK
Gouldings Lodge
John Ford's Point

KEY

▬	Major highway
═	Highway
—	National Park boundary
—	State boundary
🛈	Visitor center

John Ford's Point

The most popular stop along the valley drive is John Ford's Point, which is said to be the film director's favorite view of the valley. Various stands offer a range of Navajo handicrafts. A nearby native hogan *(Navajo dwelling) serves as a gift shop where Navajo weavers demonstrate their craft.*

Right Mitten

Merrick Butte

Navajo Weaver

Navajo women are usually considered to be the finest weavers in the Southwest. One rug can take months to complete and sell for thousands of dollars. Using the natural colors of the land, the weavers often add a "spirit line" to their work to prevent their spirit being "trapped" within the rug.

MONUMENT VALLEY

Monument Valley is not really a valley. The tops of the mesas mark what was once a flat plain. Millions of years ago, this plain was cracked by upheavals within the earth. The cracks widened and eroded, until all that is left today are the formations rising from the desert floor.

Gouldings Lodge

The lodge offers accommodations, a restaurant, and guided bus tours of the valley. The original trading post is now a museum of the valley's cinematic history.

Ancestral Puebloan ruins of Keet Seel at Navajo National Monument

Navajo National Monument ②

Road map C3. **Tel** (928) 672-2700.
◯ 9am–5pm daily (to 6pm end May–mid-Sep). ● Jan 1, Thanksgiving, Dec 25. ☑ △ www.nps.gov/nava

While named because of its location on the Navajo Reservation, this monument is actually known for its Ancestral Puebloan ruins. The most accessible ruin here is the beautifully preserved, 135-room pueblo of Betatakin, which fills a vast, curved niche in the cliffs of Tsegi Canyon. An easy one-mile (1.6-km) trail from the visitor center leads to an overlook where Betatakin is clearly visible on the far side, near the canyon floor. This is a lovely hike through piñon pines and juniper trees. From late May to early September there are daily five-hour hiking tours to Betatakin, which allow a close look at the ruins of these ancient houses.

A much more demanding 17-mile (27-km) round trip hike leads to Keet Seel, a more impressive ruin. Only a limited number of permits to visit the ruin are issued each day. This hike requires overnight camping at a camp site with only the most basic facilities. Keet Seel was a larger and more successful community than Betatakin. Construction began on Keet Seel in about 1250, but the site is thought to have been abandoned by 1300.

These two sites are considered to mark the pinnacle of development of the area's Ancestral Puebloan people.

Tuba City ③

Road map C3. 🏠 17,300. 🚏 Tuba City Trading Post (928) 283-5441.

Named for Tuuvi, a Hopi Indian who converted to the Mormon faith, Tuba City is best known for the 65-million-year-old dinosaur tracks found just off the main highway, 5 miles (8 km) southwest of the town. Beyond that, this is the largest community in the western section of the Navajo Reservation and is a good spot from which to explore both the Navajo National Monument and the Hopi Reservation.

Hopi Indian Reservation ④

Road map C3. 🏠 10,000.
🚏 Highway 264, Second Mesa (928) 734-2401. ◯ May–Sep: 6am–9pm daily; Oct–Apr: 7am–8pm daily. ● Jan 1, Thanksgiving, Dec 25.

Arizona's only Pueblo Indians (see p27), the Hopi, are believed to be direct descendants of the Ancestral Puebloan people, or Anasazi. The Hopi Reservation is surrounded by the lands of the Navajo. The landscape is harsh and barren, yet the Hopi have cultivated the land here for a thousand years. They worship, through the kachina, the living spirits of plants and animals, believed to arrive each year to stay with the tribe during the growing season (see p27). Most of the Hopi villages are located on or near one of three mesas (flat-topped elevations), named First, Second, and Third Mesa. The artisans on each of the mesas specialize in particular crafts: on First Mesa these are carved figures (representing the kachina spirits) and painted pottery; on Second Mesa, silver jewelry and coiled baskets are made; and on Third Mesa, craftspeople fashion wicker baskets and woven rugs.

Walpi, the ancient pueblo on First Mesa, was first inhabited in the 12th century. To reach Walpi, visitors drive up to the Mesa from the Pollaca settlement to the village of Sichomovi. Nearby, the Ponsi

Kachina figure

Historic pueblo town of Walpi on First Mesa at Hopi Indian Reservation

For hotels and restaurants in this region see pp242–3 and pp263–4

A range of merchandise in the general store at Hubbell Trading Post

Visitor Center is the departure point for the one-hour Walpi tours. Walpi was built to be easily defended, and straddles a dramatic knife edge of rock, extending from the tip of First Mesa. In places Walpi is less than 100 ft (33 m) wide with a drop of several hundred feet on both sides. The Walpi tour includes several stops where visitors can purchase *kachina* figurines and distinctive hand-crafted pottery, or sample the Hopi *piki* bread.

Those wishing to shop further can continue on to Second Mesa, where several galleries and stores offer an array of Hopi arts and crafts. The Hopi Cultural Center is home to a restaurant *(see p264)*, the only hotel *(see p243)* for miles around, and a museum that has a collection of photographs depicting scenes of Hopi life.

On Third Mesa, Old Oraibi pueblo, thought to have been founded in the 12th century, is of note only because of claims that it is the oldest continually occupied human settlement in North America.

🏠 Walpi
🛈 *(928) 737-2262. Walking tours available Apr–Sep: 8am–4:30pm daily; Oct–Mar: 9:30am–3:30pm daily.* 🖼

Ganado & Hubbell Trading Post **❺**

Road map D3. 🚶 *4,500.* 🛈 *Hubbell Trading Post, Hwy 264 (928) 755-3254.*

A small, bustling town in the heart of the Navajo Reservation, Ganado's major attraction is the **Hubbell Trading Post National Historic**

Site. Established in the 1870s by John Lorenzo Hubbell, this is the oldest continually operating trading post in the Navajo Nation. Trading posts like this one were once the economic and social centers of the reservations. The Navajo traded sheep, wool, blankets, turquoise, and other items in exchange for tools, household goods, and food. The trading posts were also a resource during times of need. When a smallpox epidemic struck in 1886, John Lorenzo helped care for the sick, using his house as a hospital.

Today, the trading post still hums with traditional trading activities. One room is a working general store, the rafters hung with frying pans and hardware, and shelves stacked with cloth, medicines, and food. Another room is filled with beautiful hand-woven rugs, Hopi *kachina* dolls, and Navajo

Navajo bracelet at Hubbell Trading Post

baskets. Another department has a long row of glass cases displaying an impressive array of silver and turquoise jewelry.

Visitors can tour Hubbell's restored home and view a significant collection of Southwestern art. At the visitor center Navajo women demonstrate rug weaving.

🏠 Hubbell Trading Post National Historic Site
A2264, near Ganado. 🛈 *(928) 755-3475.* ◯ *May 27–Sep 8: 8am–6pm Mon–Sat; Sep 9–May 26: 8am–5pm Mon–Sat.* ⬤ *Jan 1, Thanksgiving, Dec 25.* **www**.nps.gov/hutr

Window Rock **❻**

Road map D3. 🚶 *4,500.* 🚌 🛈 *Highway 264 (928) 871-6436.*

Window Rock is the capital of the Navajo Nation. The town is named for the natural arch found in the sandstone cliffs located about a mile north of the main strip on Hwy 12.

The **Navajo Nation Museum** located here is one of the largest Native American museums in the US. Opened in 1997, the huge hogan-shaped building houses displays that cover the history of the Ancestral Puebloans and the Navajo.

🏛 Navajo Nation Museum
Hwy 264 & Post Office Loop Rd. *(928) 871-7941.* ◯ *8am–5pm Mon, 8am–7pm Tue–Fri, 9am–5pm Sat.*

Eroded sandstone opening of Window Rock, near Highway 12

Canyon de Chelly National Monument ●

Flowering cactus

Few places in North America can boast a longer or more eventful history of human habitation than Canyon de Chelly. Archaeologists have found evidence of four periods of Native culture, starting with the Basketmaker people around AD 300, followed by the Great Pueblo Builders, who created the cliff dwellings in the 12th century. They were succeeded by the Hopi, who lived here seasonally for around 300 years, taking advantage of the canyon's fertile soil. In the 1700s, the Hopi left the area and moved to the mesas, returning to the canyon to farm during the summer months. Today, the canyon is the cultural and geographic heart of the Navajo Nation. Pronounced "d'Shay," de Chelly is a Spanish corruption of the Native name *Tsegi*, meaning Rock Canyon.

Yucca House Ruin
Perched on the mesa top, this ruin of an Ancestral Puebloan house sits in a rock hollow, precariously overhanging a sheer drop to the valley floor.

Mummy Cave Ruin
These two pueblos, separated by a central tower, were built in the 1280s by Ancestral Puebloans who had inhabited the area for more than 1,000 years. An impressive overlook provides a good view of the ruin.

Stone and adobe cliff dwellings were home to the Ancestral Puebloans from the 12th to the 14th century and were built to face south toward the sun, with cooler areas within.

Navajo Fortress
This imposing rock tower was the site of a three-month siege in 1863, when a group of Navajos reached the summit via pole ladders to escape Kit Carson and the Army. The persistence of Carson (see p171) and starvation led them to surrender and they were marched to a camp in New Mexico.

Canyon Landscape
The sandstone cliffs of Canyon de Chelly reach as high as 1,000 ft (300 m), towering above the neighboring meadows and desert landscape in the distance. The canyon floor around the cliffs is fringed with cottonwood bushes, watered by the Chinle Wash.

The pale walls of the White House cliff drop 550 ft (160 m) to the canyon floor.

***Hogan* Interior**
The hogan *is the center of Navajo family life. Made of horizontal logs, a smoke hole in the center provides contact with the sky, while the dirt floor gives contact with the earth. A door faces east to greet the rising sun.*

WHITE HOUSE RUINS
This group of rooms, tucked into a tiny hollow in the cliff, seems barely touched by time. The dwellings were originally situated above a larger pueblo, much of which has now disappeared. It is the only site within the canyon that can be visited without a Navajo guide, and is reached via a steep 2.5-mile (5-km) round-trip trail that winds to the canyon floor and offers magnificent views.

MASSACRE CAVE
The canyon's darkest hour was in 1805, when a Spanish force under Lieutenant Antonio Narbona entered the area. The Spanish wanted to subdue the Navajo, claiming they were raiding their settlements. While some Navajo fled by climbing to the canyon rim, others took refuge in a cave high in the cliffs. The Spanish fired into the cave, and Narbona boasted that he had killed 115 Navajo including 90 warriors. Navajo accounts are different, claiming that most of the warriors were absent (probably hunting) and those killed were mostly women, children, and the elderly. The only Spanish fatality came when a Spaniard attempting to climb into the cave was attacked by a Navajo woman and both plunged over the cliff, gaining the Navajo name "Two Fell Over." The Anglo name is "Massacre Cave."

Pictograph on a canyon wall showing invading Spanish soldiers

Exploring Canyon de Chelly

Navajo ranger

Canyon de Chelly ("de shay") is very different from the sparse desert landscape that spreads from its rim. Weathered red rock walls, just 30-ft- (9-m-) high at the canyon mouth, rise to more than 1,000-ft- (300-m-) high within the canyon, creating a sheltered world. Navajo *hogans* *(see p169)* dot the canyon floor; Navajo women tend herds of sheep and weave rugs at outdoor looms, and everywhere Ancestral Puebloan ruins add to the canyon's appeal. Navajo-led 4WD tours along the scenic North and South rims are a popular way to view the site.

Antelope House Ruin
Named for a pictograph of an antelope painted by Navajo artists in the 1830s, the oldest ruins at Antelope House date from AD 700. They can be seen from the Antelope House Overlook.

Canyon Vegetation
Within the canyon, cottonwood and oak trees line the river washes; the land itself is a fertile oasis of meadows, alfalfa and corn fields, and fruit orchards.

0 km   3

0 miles   3

Chinle

7

Chinle Wash

64

Standing
Co
Rui

Ledge
Ruin
Overlook

Antelope
House
Overlook

White House
Overlook

CANYON DE CHELLY

South Rim Drive

Slidin
Hous
Overlo

Canyon Tour
Half- and full-day tours from Thunderbird Lodge carry passengers in open flatbed or large 6WD army trucks. Of varying length and difficulty, the tours are the best way to see ruins up close.

Tsegi Overlook
This high curve along the South Rim offers good general views of the farm-studded canyon floor and surrounding landscape.

Hiking in the Canyon
Canyon de Chelly is a popular destination for hikers, but only the White House Ruins Trail may be walked without a guide. The visitor center (see p169) offers Navajo-guided hikes on trails of varying lengths.

KEY

=	Highway
▪▪	Hiking route
Ⓐ	Campground/RV
🏕	Picnic area
ℹ	Visitor information
❋	Viewpoint

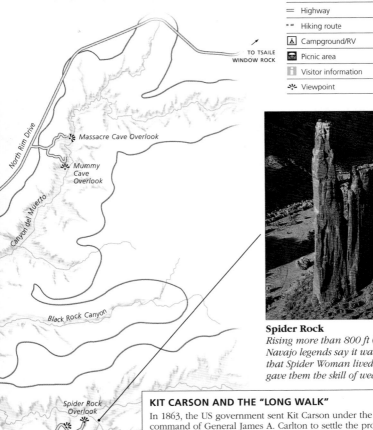

TO TSAILE
WINDOW ROCK

North Rim Drive

❋ *Massacre Cave Overlook*

❋ *Mummy Cave Overlook*

Canyon del Muerto

Black Rock Canyon

Spider Rock Overlook

(7)

Spider Rock
Rising more than 800 ft (245 m), Navajo legends say it was here that Spider Woman lived and gave them the skill of weaving.

KIT CARSON AND THE "LONG WALK"

In 1863, the US government sent Kit Carson under the command of General James A. Carlton to settle the problem of Navajo raids. To avoid outright slaughter Carson led his soldiers through the region, destroying villages and livestock as the Navajo fled ahead of them. In January 1864 Carson entered Canyon de Chelly, capturing the Navajo hiding there. In 1864, they were among 9,000 Navajo who were driven on the "Long Walk," a forced march of 370 miles (595 km) from Fort Defiance to Bosque Redondo in New Mexico. There, in a pitiful reservation, more than 3,000 Navajo died before the US government accepted the resettlement as a failure and allowed them to return to the Four Corners.

Fur trapper and soldier Kit Carson (1809–68)

Dramatic mesas and buttes in the Valley of the Gods near Bluff

Bluff ⓮

Road map D2. ⿻ 300. ⓘ *Blanding
Visitor Center, 12 N Hwy 191. (435)
678-3662.* Ⓐ **www**.bluffutah.org

The charming town of Bluff
was settled in 1880 by the
Mormons of "Hole-in-the-
Rock-Road" fame *(see p147)*.
It is a good base for exploring
Utah's southeast corner. Float
trips along the gentle San
Juan River include stops at
Ancestral Pueblo ruins that
can be reached only by boat.

Environs
About 12 miles (20 km) south
of town, a marked turn leads
onto the 17-mile (27-km)
dirt road through the Valley
of the Gods. Like a smaller
version of Monument Valley
(see pp164–65), this place
features high rock spires,
buttes, and mesas, but none
of the crowds. On a quiet
day visitors may have the
place to themselves and be
able to imagine what it looked
like to the first settlers.

Blanding ⓿

Road map D2. ⿻ 3,800. ⓘ *Edge
of the Cedars State Park Museum,
660 W. 400 N. (435) 678-2238.*
Ⓐ ◯ *9am–5pm Mon–Sat.*
● *Thanksgiving, Dec 25.* ▨
www.stateparks.utah.gov

A tidy Mormon town at the
base of the Abajo Mountains,
Blanding is home to the
Edge of the Cedars State
Park. The park contains
modest Ancestral Puebloan
ruins, including a small *kiva,*

or religious chamber. The
museum has well thoughtout
displays on the history of
these ancient people and
other cultures that have
inhabited the region.

Hovenweep National Monument ⓾

Road map D2. *East of Hwy 191.*
Tel *(970) 562-4282.* ◯ *8am–5pm
daily (6pm Apr–Sep).* ● *Jan 1,
Thanksgiving, Dec 25.* ▨ ▨ Ⓐ
www.nps.gov/hove

One of the most mysterious
Ancestral Puebloan sites in
the Southwest, the ruins at
Hovenweep lie along the rim
of a shallow canyon on a
remote high plateau in the
southwest corner of Colorado.
These well-preserved ruins,
which include unique round,
square, and D-shaped towers,
have neither been restored
nor rebuilt. Indeed, they
look much as they did when
W.D. Huntington, leader of a
Mormon expedition, first came
upon the site in 1854. The site

was named later in 1874,
after an Ute word meaning
"Deserted Valley." The culture
here reached its peak between
1200 and 1275. Little is known
of these people beyond the
clues found in the pottery and
tools that they left behind.
Researchers have speculated
that the towers at Hovenweep
might have been defensive
fortifications, astronomical
observatories, storage silos,
or religious structures.
　The six separate sets of
ruins at Hovenweep can be
visited by walking along
either of the two self-guiding
trails that link them.

Ute Mountain Tribal Park ⓫

Road map D2. ⓘ *Junction of
Highway 160 and Highway 491.
(800) 847-5485.* ◯ *Apr–Oct: 8am–
3:30pm daily; Nov–Mar: 8am–3pm
Wed–Sat.* ▨ ▨ *obligatory.*

The ruins of Ute Mountain
Tribal Park are one of the
better kept secrets of the
Southwest. The Ancestral
Puebloan people first arrived
in this region in
about AD 400.

Ancient brick tower at Hovenweep National Monument

They closely followed the Mesa Verde *(see pp180–81)* pattern of development, eventually creating numerous magnificent cliff dwellings, including the 80-room Lion House. These ruins have few visitors because of their inaccessibility. Visitors can use their own vehicles and join the dusty tours led by local Ute guides, or pay an extra charge to be driven.

Four Corners Monument Navajo Tribal Park ⑫

Road map D2. *Junction of Hwys 160 and 41.* **Tel** *(928) 871-6647.* ◯ *Jun–Sep: 7am–8pm; Oct–May: 8am–5pm.* ● *Thanksgiving, Dec 25.* 🎦 ♿ www.navajonationparks.org

There is something oddly compelling about being able to put one foot and hand in each of four states. It is the whole premise of the Four Corners Monument – the only place in the US where four states meet at one point.

Chaco Culture National Historical Park ⑬

See pp174–75.

Farmington ⑭

Road map D2. 🏘 40,000. ✕ 🚌 🛈 *3041 E. Main St. (505) 326-7602.* www.farmingtonnm.org

A dusty, hard-working ranch town, Farmington is a good base for exploring the surrounding monuments. It is also home to one of the most unusual museums in the Southwest. The vast **Bolack Museum of Fish and Wildlife** houses the largest accumulation of mounted game animals in the world collected over 70 years by oilman and rancher Tom Bolack. It is divided into nine themed game rooms, including African, Asian, European, and Russian. The **Farmington Museum** focuses on the local history

and geology of this area and features a popular children's gallery with several inter-active exhibits.

Environs
About 25 miles (40 km) west of Farmingon is Shiprock, named for the spectacular 1,500-ft (457-m) rock peak that thrusts up from the valley floor about 5 miles (8 km) west of town. To the Navajo, this rock is sacred; to early Anglo-American settlers it was a landmark visible for many miles that reminded them of a ship's prow, hence the name. Now it is only possible for visitors to observe the peak from the roadsides of Hwys 64 or 33.

Eight miles (12 km) south, are the **Salmon Ruins**, which were once an outlying Chaco settlement. These ruins were protected from grave diggers by the Salmon family, who homesteaded here in the 1870s. As a result, a century later archaeologists recovered more than a million artifacts, many of which are on display in the excellent on-site museum. Outside, trails lead to the Salmon homestead and the ruins, which show the exceptional level of skill of these ancient stonemasons.

🏛 Bolack Museum
3901 Bloomfield Hwy. **Tel** *(505) 325-4275.* ◯ *9am–3pm Mon–Sat, appointment only.* 🎦 ♿ 🎥 *obligatory.*

🏛 Farmington Museum
3041 E. Main St. **Tel** *(505) 599-1174.* ◯ *8am–5pm Mon–Sat.* 🎦 ♿ 🎥 www.farmington museum.org

⋔ Salmon Ruins
6131 Hwy 64. **Tel** *(505) 632-2013.* ◯ *8am–5pm Mon–Fri, 9am–5pm Sat, 9am–5pm Sun (from noon Nov–Apr).* ● *Jan 1, Easter, Thanksgiving, Dec 25.* 🎦 ♿ 🎥

Interior of the Great Kiva at Ancestral Puebloan Salmon Ruins

Aztec ⑮

Road map D2. 🏘 6,000. 🛈 *110 North Ash St. (505) 334-9551.*

The small town of Aztec was named for its ruins, which are Ancestral Puebloan and not Aztec as early settlers believed. Preserved as a national monument, the site's 500-room pueblo flourished in the late 1200s. Visitors can look inside a rebuilt *kiva.*

⋔ Aztec Ruins National Monument
North of Hwy 516 on Ruins Rd. **Tel** *(505) 334-6174.* ◯ *8am–5pm daily (6pm in summer).* ● *Jan 1, Thanksgiving, Dec 25.* 🎦 ♿ 🎥 www.nps.gov/azru

The spectacular red peak of Shiprock near Farmington

Chaco Culture National Historical Park ⑬

Arrowhead at Chaco Museum

Chaco Canyon is one of the most impressive cultural sites in the Southwest, reflecting the sophistication of the Ancestral Puebloan civilization that existed here. With its six "great houses" (pueblos containing hundreds of rooms) and many lesser sites, the canyon was once the political, religious, and cultural center for settlements that covered much of the Four Corners. At its peak during the 11th century, Chaco was one of the most impressive pre-Columbian cities in North America. Despite its size, it is thought that Chaco's population was small because the land could not have supported a larger community. Archaeologists believe that the city was mainly used as a ceremonial gathering place, with a year-round population of less than 3,000. Probably the social elite, the inhabitants supported themselves largely by trading.

Architectural Detail
Chaco's skilled builders had only stone tools to work with to create this finely wrought stonework.

The many kivas here were probably used by visitors arriving for religious ceremonies.

PUEBLO BONITO
Pueblo Bonito is an example of a "great house." Begun around AD 850, it was built in stages over the course of 300 years. This reconstruction shows how it might have looked, with its D-shaped four-story structure that contained more than 650 rooms.

Chetro Ketl
A short trail from Pueblo Bonito leads to another great house, Chetro Ketl. Almost as large as Pueblo Bonito, at 3 sq acres (2 ha), Chetro Ketl has more than 500 rooms. The masonry used to build the later portions of this structure is among the most sophisticated found in any Ancestral Puebloan site.

Casa Rinconada
Also known as a great kiva, Casa Rinconada is the largest religious chamber at Chaco, measuring 62 ft (19 m) in diameter. It was used for spiritual gatherings.

For hotels and restaurants in this region see pp242–3 and pp263–4

Pueblo Alto

Pueblo Alto was built atop the mesa at the junction of several ancient Chacoan roads. Reaching the site requires a two-hour hike, but the views over the canyon are well worth it.

VISITORS' CHECKLIST

Road map 3D. 25 miles (40 km)
S.E. of Nageezi off US 550.
🚩 *Chaco Culture Visitor Center*
(505) 786-7014.
www.nps.gov/chcu
⭕ *8am–5pm daily.*
⬤ *public hols.* ♿ 🅿️

This great house was four stories high.

Early Astronomers at Fajada Butte
Measurement of time was vital to the Chacoans for crop planting and the timing of ceremonies. A spiral petroglyph, carved on Fajada Butte, is designed to indicate the changing seasons through the shadows it casts on the rock.

Hundreds of rooms within Pueblo Bonito show little sign of use and are thought to have been kept for storage or for guests arriving to take part in ceremonial events.

EXPLORING CHACO

The site is accessed via a 13-mile (21-km) dirt road that is affected by flash floods in wet weather. Drivers can follow the paved loop road that passes several of Chaco's highlights. There is parking at all major sites. From the visitor center, a trail leads to Una Vida and the petroglyphs.

KEY

═	Highway
═	Unpaved road
--	Hiking route
Ⓐ	Campground/RV
🏕	Picnic area
🚩	Visitor information

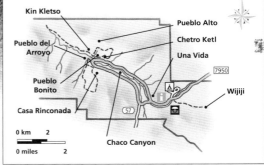

Kin Kletso

Pueblo del Arroyo

Pueblo Bonito

Casa Rinconada

Pueblo Alto

Chetro Ketl

Una Vida

7950

Wijiji

57

Chaco Canyon

0 km 2
0 miles 2

Alta Lake surrounded by pine forests near San Juan in Southern Colorado ▷

San Juan Skyway Tour 🔟

The San Juan Skyway is a 236-mile (380-km) loop through some of America's finest scenery. The route travels three highways (550, 145, and 160) over the San Juan Mountains, past 19th-century mining towns and through forests and canyons. There are 14 peaks above 14,000 ft (4,200 m). Between Silverton and Ouray the road is also known as the Million Dollar Highway, having been named for the gold-rich gravel used in the road's construction or, according to another theory, because the road was expensive to build.

TIPS FOR DRIVERS

Tour Route: *Highway 550 from Durango, then 145 and 160.*
Length: *236 miles (380 km).*
Stopping-off points: *Ridgeway State Park on Hwy 550 offers great views of the San Juan Mountains.*

Telluride ④
Smaller than the ski resorts of Aspen and Vail, Telluride's gentrified Western persona attracts both wealthy jet setters and serious skiers.

Ouray ③
Another very Western mining town with a history similar to Silverton's, Ouray has the added attraction of the Ouray Hot Springs.

Atlas Lake ⑤
One of many lovely alpine lakes to be found along the San Juan Skyway, Atlas Lake lies south of Telluride and just north of the high-mountain Lizard Head Pass.

Dolores ⑥
Two 12th-century Ancestral Pueblos have been preserved here as part of the Anasazi Heritage Center, together with a museum on pueblo life.

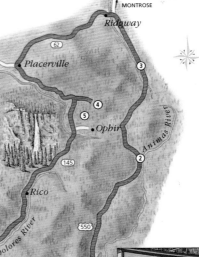

Silverton ②
Silver was discovered here in 1874. Today, this classic frontier town is the scene of daily mock gun-fights along Blair Street.

Durango ①
The start of the Durango and Silverton steam train trip, the town of Durango has a charming Victorian district and hot springs.

KEY

▬ Tour route

⁼ Other roads

0 km   10

0 miles   10

Spectacular views of the Rockies from Telluride's main street

Telluride ⑰

Road map D2. 🏔 *1550.* ✕ 🚌
ℹ *630 W. Colorado Ave. (970) 728-3041; (800) 525-3455.* ◯ *winter: 9am–5pm daily; summer: 9am–8pm daily.* **www**.visittelluride.com

Once a mining town like Silverton, today Telluride is a noted ski resort, as popular with Hollywood celebrities as the equally famous Aspen in northern Colorado. Its late-Victorian center boasts upscale ski shops, boutiques, and restaurants. Yet Telluride retains its authentic charm; it is still possible to imagine the days when the notorious outlaw Butch Cassidy lived here.

The ski resort's exclusive Mountain Village lies across a mountain ridge easily reached by a free 12-minute gondola ride. In winter there is a variety of sports available. In summer there are walks and riding trails, and fishing in the lakes and rivers. The town also hosts an annual international film festival.

Ouray ⑱

Road map D2. 🏔 *800.*
ℹ *1230 North Main St. (970) 325-4746; (800) 228-1876.* ◯ *daily.* **www**.ouraycolorado.com

The wonderfully preserved old mining town of Ouray lies 23 miles (37 km) north of Silverton on Hwy 550. Its stunning setting, amid mountain peaks, has made it a popular base for hikers and 4WD enthusiasts. To the north of town are the Ouray Hot Springs. To the south, a loop road leads to Box Canyon Falls Park. A short trail leads across a swinging bridge to the falls' dramatic cascade.

Silverton ⑲

Road map D2. 🏔 *505.*
ℹ *414 Greene St. (970) 387-5654; (800) 752-4494.* ⛺
www.silvertoncolorado.com

Silverton is set among snow-covered peaks, and is one of the best preserved 19th-century mining towns in the Southwest. The entire town is registered as a National Historic Landmark, and the façades along Blair Street have altered little since the days of the 1880s silver-mining boom that gave the town its name. On Greene Street, most of the buildings date from the late 19th and early 20th centuries, including the 1902 County Jail, which houses the **San Juan County Historical Museum**. Greene Street East leads 13 miles (21 km) north to the ghost town, Animas Forks, abandoned after the mines ran out of silver.

SILVERTON JAIL -1883-

Plaque from Silverton County Jail

🏛 **San Juan County Historical Museum**
1512 Greene St. **Tel** *(970) 387-5838.* ◯ *late May–mid-Oct: 9am–5pm daily.* ● *late Oct–mid-May.* 📷

Durango ⑳

Road map D2. 🏔 *14,700.* ✕ 🚌
ℹ *111 S. Camino del Rio (970) 247-3500; (800) 525-8855.* ◯ *May–Sep: 8am–6pm Mon–Sat, 9am–4pm Sun; Oct–Apr: 8am–5pm Mon–Fri.* **www**.durango.org

Durango is a lovely town with shady tree-lined streets and splendid Victorian architecture. Its attractive setting, on the banks of the Animas River, draws increasing numbers of residents, making the town the largest community in this part of Colorado. It is famous as the starting point of the **Durango and Silverton Narrow Gauge Railroad**, perhaps the most scenic train ride in the US. A 1920s coal-fired steam train ferries more than 200,000 visitors each year along the Animas River valley, up steep gradients through canyons and mountain scenery, to Silverton. Passengers may choose to ride in either Victorian or open-sided "gondola" cars that offer great views. Several stops along the way allow hikers and anglers access to the pristine backcountry of the San Juan National Forest. A good time to make the trip is September when fall colors cover the mountainsides. This is a popular attraction, and booking ahead is recommended.

🚂 **Durango and Silverton Narrow Gauge Railroad**
479 Main Ave. **Tel** *(970) 247-2733; reservations (888) 872-4607.* ◯ *most days year round; call for times.*

Steam train on Durango and Silverton Narrow Gauge Railroad

For hotels and restaurants in this region see pp242–3 and pp263–4

Mesa Verde National Park ㉑

This high, forested mesa overlooking the Montezuma Valley was home to the Ancestral Puebloan people *(see p38)* for more than 700 years. Within canyons that cut through the mesa are some of the best preserved and most elaborate cliff dwellings built by these people. Mesa Verde, meaning "Green Table," was a name given to the area by the Spanish in the 1700s, but the ruins were not widely known until the late 19th century. This site provides a fascinating record of these people from the Basketmaker period, beginning around AD 550, to the complex society that built the many-roomed cliff dwellings between 1000 and 1250. Displays at the Far View Visitor Center and the Chapin Mesa Museum provide a good introduction.

Spruce Tree House
Tucked into a cliff niche, these three-story structures probably housed as many as 100 people.

Guided Tours
Ranger-led tours give visitors a chance to actually enter the ruins and get a feel for the daily lives of these ancient people.

CLIFF PALACE

With 150 rooms, this is the largest Ancestral Puebloan cliff dwelling found anywhere, and is the site that most visitors focus on. The location and symmetry suggest that architecture was important to the builders. Begun around 1200, it was vacated in around 1275.

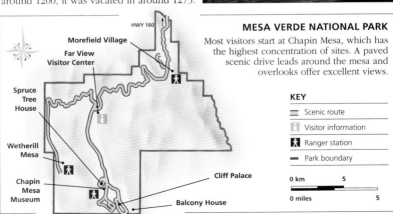

MESA VERDE NATIONAL PARK
Most visitors start at Chapin Mesa, which has the highest concentration of sites. A paved scenic drive leads around the mesa and overlooks offer excellent views.

HWY 160
Morefield Village
Far View Visitor Center
Spruce Tree House
Wetherill Mesa
Chapin Mesa Museum
Cliff Palace
Balcony House

KEY

Scenic route
Visitor information
Ranger station
Park boundary

0 km　5
0 miles　5

Balcony House
Possibly built for defense, Balcony House could not be seen from above. Access was (and still is) difficult. Visitors must climb three ladders high above the canyon floor, then crawl through an access tunnel.

VISITORS' CHECKLIST

Road map D2. 🏠 *PO Box 8, Mesa Verde, CO 81330 (970) 529-4465.* ✈ *Cortez. Far View Visitor Center* ◯ *early Apr–mid-Oct: 8am–5pm daily. Chapin Mesa Archaeological Museum* ◯ *Apr–Sep: 8am–6:30pm daily; Oct–Mar: 8am–5pm daily.*

Towers were probably used for signalling or as lookouts for defense.

Square Tower House
Early cowboys named this ruin for the prominent, tower-like central structure, which was actually a vertical stack of rooms that was once surrounded by other rooms. It may have been used as a dwelling or for ceremonial purposes.

The 23 *kivas* or religious rooms at this site are thought to indicate that at least 23 clans lived here at various times.

Wetherill Mesa Long House
A scenic 12-mile (17-km) drive on a winding mountain road leads to Wetherill Mesa, named for the local rancher, Richard Wetherill, who found Cliff Palace in the 1880s. Two cliff dwellings here, Step and Long houses, are open to visitors.

New Mexican ceramic souvenirs and dried chillies ▷

NEW MEXICO

Introducing New Mexico

New Mexico's scenic beauty, rich cultural heritage, and unique mix of Native American, Hispanic, and Anglo-American people make it a fascinating place to visit. The forested peaks of the Rocky Mountains in the north offer ski resorts in winter and cool retreats in the hot summers. Northern New Mexico is also noted for its quality of light, with stark shadows and soft colors that have attracted generations of artists to the region, especially to the creative centers of Santa Fe and Taos. Albuquerque is the state's centrally located largest city, and, to the south, visitors can explore ancient Native ruins at Gila Cliff Dwellings National Monument, as well as such natural wonders as the gleaming dunes of White Sands National Monument and the cave systems of Carlsbad Caverns.

Adobe in Albuquerque's Old Town (see pp210–11).

KEY

▦ Interstate

▦ Major highway

▭ Highway

= River

SEE ALSO

- *Where to Stay* pp243–7
- *Where to Eat* pp265–9

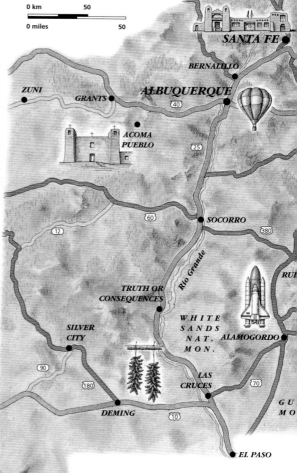

0 km   50

0 miles   50

CHAMA

ESPAÑOLA

SANTA FE

BERNALILLO

ZUNI

GRANTS

ALBUQUERQUE
40

ACOMA
PUEBLO
25

60

SOCORRO
380

12

RUI

TRUTH OR
CONSEQUENCES

Rio Grande

WHITE
SANDS
NAT.
MON.

ALAMOGORDO

SILVER
CITY

90

180

DEMING
10

LAS
CRUCES
70

GU
MO

EL PASO

GETTING AROUND

New Mexico has two major Interstate Highways, I-25 and I-40, which cross each other in Albuquerque. Interstate 25 cuts north into Colorado and south into Mexico. Interstate 40 cuts east to west, into Texas and Arizona respectively. To the south, Interstate 10 connects the city of Las Cruces with Arizona. Albuquerque airport is New Mexico's main hub for both international and domestic flights. Greyhound buses run from Albuquerque to Santa Fe and Taos.

Ancestral Puebloan cliff dwellings at Bandelier National Monument *(see p200)*

Soaptree yucca plant growing among the dunes at White Sands National Monument *(see p223)*

The Atomic Age

During World War II, fears that the Germans were developing an atomic bomb led the US to begin its own nuclear weapons program. In 1942 Britain and the US decided to combine their research efforts; Los Alamos, a remote area of New Mexico, was chosen as the location for the Manhattan Project, which resulted in the world's first nuclear explosion in July 1945. The clear skies, level ground, and sparse population made it an ideal top-secret testing ground.

Today, Los Alamos National Laboratory and Sandia National Laboratory in Albuquerque are the largest nuclear research facilities in the US, and New Mexico's largest employers. Along with White Sands Missile Range, they remain important centers for military research and development. Visitors can find out more about the region's atomic history at museums in Los Alamos *(see p200)* and White Sands *(see p223)*.

Fat Man and Little Boy *were atomic bombs dropped on the Japanese cities of Hiroshima and Nagasaki in August 1945. Reproductions can be seen at the Bradbury Science Museum in Los Alamos (see p200).*

The Nike Ajax *missile at the International Space Hall of Fame in Alamogordo (see p224) was one of the first guided missiles. It was tested at the White Sands Missile Range in 1951. Other rockets from the period are on display in the museum grounds.*

Robert Goddard did not live to see the age of spaceflight. At the time of his death in 1945, he held 214 patents in rocketry.

THE MANHATTAN PROJECT

In 1943 an innocuous former boys' school, the Los Alamos Ranch School set high in New Mexico's remote Pajarito Plateau, was chosen as the research site for the top secret Manhattan Project. Work began immediately under the direction of physicist J. Robert Oppenheimer and General Leslie R. Groves. In just over two years they had developed the first atomic bomb, detonated at the secluded Trinity Test Site, now the White Sands Missile Range, 230 miles (370 km) south of Los Alamos on July 16 1945. The decision to explode the bomb in warfare was highly controversial, and some of the scientists who developed the bomb signed a petition against its use. Displays on the project can be seen at the Bradbury Science Museum and the Los Alamos Historical Museum.

Oppenheimer and Groves at Los Alamos, 1944

Dr. John P. Stapp *testing acceleration in his Sonic Wind I rocket sled in 1954 at Holloman Air Force Base near White Sands Missile Range. His research improved aircraft seatbelt technology.*

Goddard's assistants (left to right) in his workshop were N.T. Ljungquist, A.W. Kisk, and C.W. Mansur.

Ham the space chimp *is helped out of his capsule after becoming the first living creature to be sent into space in 1961.*

ROCKET SCIENCE

Robert Goddard (1882–1945) is often referred to as "the father of modern rocketry," developing rocket science in his workshop in Roswell, New Mexico *(see p227).* He launched his first liquid-fueled rocket in Massachusetts in 1926 and performed 56 flight tests in Roswell in the 1930s. By 1935 he had developed rockets that could carry cameras and record instrument readings. An altitude record was set in 1937 when a Goddard rocket reached 2 miles (3 km) above the earth.

A Goddard rocket without its casing, being studied on an "assembly frame."

The space shuttle *touching down on the Northrup strip at the White Sands Missile Site on March 30, 1982. This was the first time in its three-flight history that the shuttle landed in New Mexico. Today, White Sands is a designated shuttle testing ground and landing site.*

New Mexico *is a major center for astronaut training and selection. Here astronaut Steven Robinson is training in a buoyancy tank to simulate life in space in preparation for his 1998 mission on the* Discovery *shuttle.*

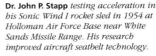

Hispanic Culture in New Mexico

The heart of Hispanic culture in the Southwest is found in New Mexico. Here, the Hispanic population, descendants of the original Spanish colonizers of the 16th century, outnumbers that of the Anglo-Americans. The Spanish introduced sheep and horses to the region, as well as bringing Catholicism with its saints' festivals and colorful church decorations.

Centuries of mixing with both the Southwest's native and Anglo cultures have also influenced every aspect of modern Hispanic society, from language and cooking to festivals and the arts. Contemporary New Mexican residents bear the Hispanic surnames of their ancestors, and speak English with a Spanish accent. Even English speakers use Spanish terms.

Pueblo *pottery traditions go back centuries. Today Hispanic potters use New Mexico's micaceous clay to produce items such as this 1997 jar by Jacobo de la Serna.*

Navajo rugs *are considered a native handicraft, but their designs also show signs of Moorish patterns brought from Spain by the colonizers who first introduced sheep into the New World.*

A Bulto *(carved wooden figure) of St. Joseph sits on the altar of the Morada at El Rancho de las Golondrinas* (see pp198–9). *It is an example of a form of Hispanic folk art, which combined religious beliefs and artistic expression.*

The well was always located in the middle of the main court-yard to be easily accessible.

Hacienda Martínez *was built south of Taos in 1804 by Don Antonio Martínez, an early mayor of the town. It is one of the few Spanish haciendas to be preserved in more or less its original form. Today it is open to visitors who can watch local artisans demonstrating a variety of folk arts.*

Decorations *made from tin originated in Mexico where this metal was a cheap substitute for silver. Shapes were cut out and painted with translucent colors.*

Cockerel

Mexican bird

Bull

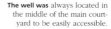

Fiestas are an important element of Hispanic culture, and there are many throughout the year, particularly on saints' days (see pp32–5). Fiestas often combine both indigenous and Spanish influences. Elements of Hispanic celebrations have also been incorporated into events in other cultures; here, young girls perform traditional dances at celebrations for the Fourth of July.

Adobe beehive ovens *(hornos)* were introduced by the Spanish for baking bread. They were originally of Moorish design.

SPANISH INFLUENCE

The restored El Rancho de las Golondrinas *(see pp198–9)* is a living museum showing the way of life – centered on the hacienda – pioneered in the Southwest by the Spanish colonists. In a hacienda, a large number of rooms (approximately 20) would be set around one or two courtyards, reflecting the extended family style of living favored by the Spanish settlers. The Spanish Colonial style is also seen in the layout of many towns, including central Santa Fe *(see pp192–5).*

Chile ristras *are garlands of dried red chiles sold as souvenirs in New Mexico. Chiles were a Native American food, unknown in Europe before Columbus landed in the Americas in 1492. However, they were adopted wholeheartedly by the Spanish.*

Luminarias *fill the square outside San Felipe de Neri church in Albuquerque's Old Town. These Mexican lanterns (also called* farolitos) *consist of a candle set in sand in a paper bag, and are displayed during religious festivals.*

SANTA FE AND NORTHERN NEW MEXICO

The beauty of the landscape and the wealth of cultural attractions make northern New Mexico one of the most popular destinations in the Southwest. Visitors drive through the forests of the San Juan Mountains and the peaks of the Sangre de Cristo Range, part of the southern Rocky Mountains, then through picturesque villages to meet the Rio Grande valley. It was this fertile landscape that probably attracted Ancestral Puebloan people in the 1100s. Their descendents still live today in pueblo villages, and are famous for producing distinctive crafts and pottery. Taos Pueblo is the largest of the pueblos, its fame due both to its adobe architecture and its ceremonial dances performed on feast days. Southward lies the beautiful city of Santa Fe. Founded by Spanish colonists in 1610, Santa Fe is now one of the most visited cities in the United States, renowned for its art galleries and adobe buildings. Today, tourism dominates this historic trading center, with its appealing mix of Hispanic, Native, and Anglo-American cultures.

Many specialty vacations and outdoor activities are available in the area, including archaeological tours, skiing, and white-water rafting.

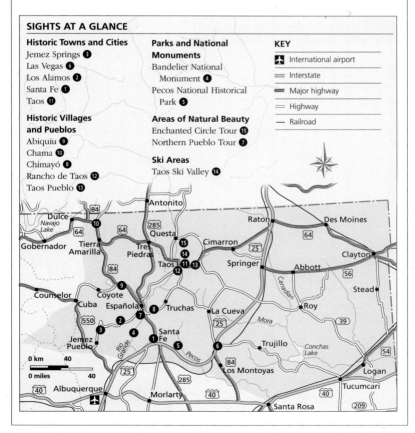

SIGHTS AT A GLANCE

Historic Towns and Cities
Jemez Springs ❸
Las Vegas ❻
Los Alamos ❷
Santa Fe ❶
Taos ⓫

Historic Villages and Pueblos
Abiquiu ❾
Chama ❿
Chimayó ❽
Rancho de Taos ⓬
Taos Pueblo ⓭

Parks and National Monuments
Bandelier National Monument ❹
Pecos National Historical Park ❺

Areas of Natural Beauty
Enchanted Circle Tour ⓯
Northern Pueblo Tour ❼

Ski Areas
Taos Ski Valley ⓮

KEY

✈ International airport
═ Interstate
▬ Major highway
═ Highway
— Railroad

◁ The façade of Taos Pueblo church showing its characteristic stepped roofs and whitewashed adobe walls

Street-by-Street: Santa Fe Plaza ❶

The oldest state capital in North America, Santa Fe was founded by the Spanish conquistador Don Pedro de Peralta, who established a colony here in 1610 *(see p39)*. This colony was abandoned in 1680 following the Pueblo Revolt, but settlers recaptured it in 1692 *(see p40)*. When Mexico gained independence in 1821, Santa Fe was opened up to the wider world and traders and settlers from the US arrived via the Santa Fe Trail *(see p25)*.

The central plaza has been the heart of Santa Fe since its founding, and there is no better place to begin exploring the city. Today, it houses a Native American market under the portal of the Palace of the Governors, and the square is lined with shops, cafés, and galleries.

★ New Mexico Museum of Art
This museum focuses on the paintings and sculpture of Southwestern artists.

The Plaza
The obelisk at the center of this main square commemorates Santa Fe's war veterans. The Plaza is dominated by the Palace of the Governors and lined with old colonial buildings.

LINCOLN

SHERIDAN

AVENUE

PALACE

BURRO ALLEY

W. SAN FRANCISCO STREET

DON GASPAR AVE.

GALISTEO STREET

WATER STREET

0 meters 100
0 yards 100

KEY

– – – Suggested route

STAR SIGHTS

★ Palace of the Governors

★ New Mexico Museum of Art

Original Trading Post
This historic trading post sells Hispanic art, antiques, and Native American crafts.

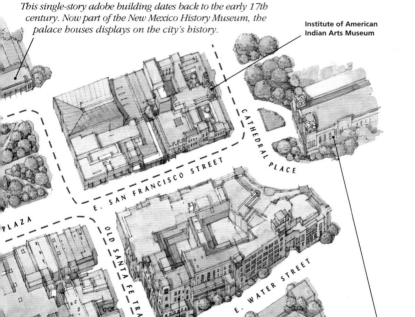

★ **Palace of the Governors**
This single-story adobe building dates back to the early 17th century. Now part of the New Mexico History Museum, the palace houses displays on the city's history.

Institute of American Indian Arts Museum

La Fonda Hotel

VISITORS' CHECKLIST

Road map E3. 65,000.
Santa Fe Municipal Airport, 10 miles (16 km) S.W. of Santa Fe. Lamy, 18 miles S. of city.
858 St. Michael's Dr. 60 E. San Francisco St. (505) 955-6200; (800) 777-2489. Spanish Market (Jul); Santa Fe Opera Season (Jul & Aug); Indian Market (Aug); Fiestas de Santa Fe (Sep). **www**.santafe.org

Loretto Chapel
Built in Gothic style by French architects in the 1870s, the Loretto Chapel was modeled on Ste. Chappelle in Paris. The building and elegant spiral staircase inside were commissioned for the Sisters of Loretto.

Saint Francis Cathedral
This colorful, carved wooden statue of the Virgin stands in a chapel belonging to the original 17th-century church on which the cathedral was built in 1869.

Exploring Central Santa Fe

Santa Fe's rich history and beautiful architecture have made it one of the most popular destinations in the US. Sitting 7,000 ft (2,100 m) up on a high plateau, surrounded by the splendor of the Sangre de Cristo mountains, it basks in clear light and sunshine. The blending of three distinct cultures – Hispanic, Native American, and Anglo – contribute to the city's vibrancy. Santa Fe is an artists' town. About one in six residents work in the arts, and their legacy is everywhere, from the dozens of private galleries along Canyon Road to the fine collections at the New Mexico Museum of Art. Still, Santa Fe has a relaxed atmosphere, and a setting that offers plenty of opportunities for such outdoor activities as hiking or skiing.

Virgin at Palace of the Governors

Exploring Santa Fe

Many of the main attractions in Santa Fe are within easy walking distance of the Plaza (see p192). This is also the city's main shopping district for arts, crafts, and souvenirs, and many popular cafés and restaurants line the nearby streets. Santa Fe is home to the New Mexico Museum of Art's four museums. Visitors are advised to buy the four-day pass that covers all of them.

🛑 Santuario de Guadalupe

100 S. Guadalupe St.
Tel (505) 988-2027. ☐ *daily.*
This 1795 adobe church is dedicated to the Virgin of Guadalupe, the patron saint of both the Mexican and Pueblo peoples. Santuario de Guadalupe marked the end of the old Camino Real (Royal Road), the main trade route from Mexico. A painted altarpiece of the Virgin, dating from 1783, graces the peaceful interior, which is also used as a setting for classical concerts.

🏛 Georgia O'Keeffe Museum

217 Johnson St. *Tel* (505) 946-1000.
☐ *Jun–Oct: 10am–5pm daily; Nov–May: 10am–5pm Sat–Tue & Thu, 10am–8pm Fri.* ● *Wed in winter & public hols. Other closures may occur – check before visiting.* 🅿 *free after 5pm.* 🅰 www.okeeffemuseum.org
Opened in 1997, this museum is dedicated to New Mexico's most famous resident artist, Georgia O'Keeffe (1887–1986; see p203). Some of her best-loved paintings are on display here, including *Jimson Weed* (1932), *Purple Hills II*, and

Jimson Weed (1932), painting at the Georgia O'Keeffe Museum

Ghost Ranch, New Mexico (1934), as well as her sculpture and less well-known works, such as paintings of New York.

🏛 New Mexico Museum of Art

107 W. Palace Ave. *Tel* (505) 476-5072. ☐ *10am–5pm Tue–Sun, 10am–8pm Fri.* ● *Mon, public hols.* 🅿 🅰
Built to showcase New Mexico's growing art scene and completed in 1917, this building is one of the earliest examples of modern Pueblo

Revival-style architecture (see p23). The design owes much to the nearby Pueblo mission churches. Exhibition spaces have square beams, hand-carved decoration, and other traditional features. The collection comprises over 20,000 pieces of Southwestern art from the 19th century onward.

🏛 Palace of the Governors and New Mexico History Museum

105 E. Palace Ave. *Tel* (505) 476-5100. ☐ *10am–5pm Tue–Sun.* ● *Mon, public hols.* 🅿
The Palace of the Governors dominates the north side of the Plaza and is the oldest public building in continuous use in America. Built in 1610, it was the seat of regional government for 300 years. Exhibits here trace the history and culture of New Mexico from 1540 to 1912.

The adjacent New Mexico History Museum presents the stories of the American West through historic artifacts, documents, and interactive exhibits. Native Pueblo peoples, Spanish explorers, artists, and scientists are all included.

🏛 Institute of American Indian Arts

108 Cathedral Pl. *Tel* (505) 983-1777. ☐ *10am–5pm Mon–Sat, noon–5pm Sun.* ● *Nov–May: Tue; public hols.* 🅿 🅰
Housed in a striking Pueblo Revival-style building, this museum contains the National Collection of Contemporary Indian Art. Traditional pottery, textiles, and beadwork are displayed alongside modern paintings and mixed-media works by leading Native American artists.

Sculpture in the courtyard of the New Mexico Museum of Art

The decorative façade of St. Francis Cathedral

St. Francis Cathedral

131 Cathedral Pl. **Tel** (505) 982-5619. ☐ daily. ♿

The Cathedral's French Romanesque-style façade is an anomaly in the heart of this adobe city, yet its honey-colored stone, glowing in the afternoon light, makes it one of its loveliest landmarks. It was built in 1869 under Santa Fe's first Archbishop, Jean Baptiste Lamy. The building replaced most of an earlier adobe church called *La Parroquia*, except for the side chapel of Our Lady of the Rosary. This houses the oldest statue of the Virgin Mary in North America, known as *La Conquistadora*. Carved in Mexico in 1625, the figure was brought to Santa Fe where it gained mythical status as settlers fleeing the Pueblo Revolt in 1680 *(see p40)* claimed to have been saved by the Virgin's protection.

Loretto Chapel

277 Old Santa Fe Trail. **Tel** (505) 982-0092. ☐ Mar–Oct: 9am–6pm Mon–Sat, 10:30am–5pm Sun; Nov–Feb: 9am–5pm Mon–Sat, 10:30am–5pm Sun. 📷 ♿ **www**.lorettochapel.com

This chapel is famous for its staircase, a dramatically curved spiral that winds upward for 21 ft (6 m) with 33 steps that make two complete 360 degree turns. The spiral has no nails or center support – only its perfect craftsmanship keeps it aloft. When the chapel was built it lacked access to the choirloft. A mysterious carpenter appeared, built the spiral, and vanished without payment.

The elegant curves of the spiral staircase at the Loretto Chapel

SANTA FE PLAZA

Canyon Road ⑧
Georgia O'Keeffe Museum ②
Institute of American
   Indian Arts ⑤
Loretto Chapel ⑦

New Mexico Museum
   of Art ③
New Mexico State Capitol ⑩
Palace of the Governors ④
St. Francis Cathedral ⑥

San Miguel Mission ⑨
Santa Fe Southern Railway
   Depot ⑪
Santuario de Guadalupe ①

KEY

▢ Santa Fe Street-by-Street
map *see pp192–3*

Georgia O'Keeffe Museum ②
N GUADALUPE ST
JOHNSON ST
WEST MARCY STREET
Santa Fe Opera,
Santa Fe Ski Arena
New Mexico Museum of Art ③
EAST MARCY STREET
NUSBAUM STREET
WEST PALACE AVENUE
④ Palace of the Governors
WEST SAN FRANCISCO ST
Santa Fe Plaza
Institute of American Indian Arts ⑤
SANDOVAL ST
GALISTEO STREET
Santuario de Guadalupe ①
AGUA FRIA ST
De Vargas Park
WEST ALAMEDA STREET
WEST DE VARGAS STREET
DON GASPAR AVENUE
W WATER ST
La Fonda
St. Francis Cathedral ⑥
CATHEDRAL PLACE
⑦ Loretto Chapel
PASEO DE PERALTA
Santa Fe Southern Railway Depot ⑪
SOUTH GUADALUPE ST
SANDOVAL STREET
GARFIELD STREET
Santa Fe River Park
OLD SANTA FE TRAIL
EAST ALAMEDA STREET
Santa Fe River
CERRILLOS ROAD
READ STREET
GALISTEO STREET
EAST DE VARGAS STREET
El Rancho de las Golondrinas
WEST MANHATTAN AVENUE
Greyhound station 3km (2 miles)
DON GASPAR AVENUE
OLD SANTA FE TRAIL
San Miguel Mission Church ⑨
Canyon Road ⑧
GARCIA STREET
New Mexico State Capitol ⑩
PASEO DE PERALTA
Museum Hill

0 meters   200
0 yards   200

Key to Symbols *see back flap*

Museum of International Folk Art

Mexican jaguar mask

This charming museum houses a stunning collection of folk art from all over the world, including toys, miniature theaters, dolls, and paintings, as well as religious and traditional art. The eastern gallery holds the fine Girard Wing, the largest collection of cross-cultural works in existence. Thousands of objects from more than 100 countries are displayed, including icons and paintings. The highlights are ceramic figures arranged in attractive scenes, ranging from a Polish Christmas to a Mexican baptism. The Hispanic Heritage Wing contains Spanish colonial decorative art, such as rare hide paintings, while the Neutrogena Wing offers textiles from Africa, Asia, and South America.

★ Girard Collection Figures
Created in 1960 in Oaxaca, Mexico, this baptism scene is made up of over 50 painted earthenware villagers.

Neutrogena Wing
Specializing in rugs, textiles, blankets, and costumes, this gallery spans world culture to reveal a depth of craft and detail in each piece, as shown in this former exhibit – a 19th-century dyed Japanese bridal sleeping cover.

The Bartlett Library in the Bartlett Wing is a research facility housing articles, photographs, and audio-visual material on world cultures.

Hispanic Heritage Wing
This hand-carved New-Mexican icon, from 1830–50, represents Mary, Our Lady of Sorrows. It is typical of the Spanish colonial and Hispanic folk art found in this wing.

Library

Entrance

STAR COLLECTION

★ Girard Collection

VISITORS' CHECKLIST

706 Camino Lejo. *Tel (505) 476-1200.* ☐ *10am–5pm Tue–Sun.* ● *public hols.* 🏛 ♿ 🎥 📷

★ **Girard Collection Toy**
This Bangladeshi toy is a 1960s addition to the more than 100,000 artifacts collected by US designer Alexander Girard from 1930 to 1978.

KEY

☐	Girard Wing
☐	Neutrogena Wing
☐	Hispanic Heritage Wing
☐	Bartlett Wing
☐	Non-exhibition space

🚋 Canyon Road

Originally an Indian track between the Rio Grande and Pecos pueblos, Canyon Road was later used by burros (donkeys) hauling firewood down from the mountains. This upscale road is today lined with more than 100 private art galleries, restaurants, and shops, with their premises in historic adobe houses. Canyon Road runs parallel to the river and the former Acequia Madre, or "mother ditch," the city's first irrigation channel, which today is lined with adobe buildings.

🏠 San Miguel Mission

401 Old Santa Fe Trail. *Tel (505) 983-3974.* ☐ *daily.* 🏛 ♿

The chapel of San Miguel is thought to have been built around 1610, making it one of the oldest churches in the US. The original dirt floor and adobe steps are still visible at the front of the altar. It was built by Tlaxcala Indians, who traveled from Mexico with the early Spanish settlers.

This simple church features great roof beams that were restored in 1692, having been burned 12 years earlier in the Pueblo Revolt. A carved wooden *reredos* (altarpiece) frames the centrally placed statue of the patron saint, San Miguel, while the side walls boast paintings of religious scenes on deerskin and buffalo hide.

🏛 Museum Hill

Alongside the Museum of International Folk Art, three other important museums are found on Museum Hill. **The Museum of Indian Arts and Culture** is dedicated to traditional Native American arts and culture. Its main exhibit, *Here, Now & Always,* tells the story of the Southwest's oldest communities in the words of native Pueblo, Navajo, and Apache people.

Ancient male figurine

The Wheelwright Museum of the American Indian, established in 1937 by wealthy philanthropist Mary Cabot Wheelwright of Boston, was built to resemble a Navajo *hogan (see p169).* The museum's focus is on its changing exhibitions of contemporary work by Native American artists. In the basement, the excellent Case Trading Post re-creates the first trading posts established on the Navajo reservation.

The Museum of Spanish Colonial Art holds one of the world's most extensive collections of Spanish Colonial art, with over 3,000 objects including textiles, furniture, religious santos, and ceramics.

🏛 The Museum of Indian Arts and Culture
710 Camino Lejo. *Tel (505) 476-1250.* ☐ *10am–5pm Tue–Sun.* 🏛 ♿

🏛 The Wheelwright Museum of the American Indian
704 Camino Lejo. *Tel (505) 982-4636.* ☐ *daily.* ● *public hols.* ♿ www.wheelwright.org

🏛 The Museum of Spanish Colonial Art
750 Camino Lejo. *Tel (505) 982-2226.* ☐ *10am–5pm Tue–Sun.* 🏛 ♿

Detail of the carved wooden *reredos* at San Miguel Mission

El Rancho de las Golondrinas

Established in the early 1700s, El Rancho de las Golondrinas (Ranch of the Swallows), is a historic stopping place on the Camino Real, the old royal road trading route that ran from Mexico City to Santa Fe. Home to the Baca family for 200 years, the 200-acre (89-ha) ranch was used by settlers and explorers to rest up and water their animals before heading on to the city. Located in a fertile valley just south of Santa Fe, this living history museum, with its restored buildings and historic features, re-creates life on a typical 18th-century Spanish rural hacienda. Authentic historic crops such as squash and corn are grown here, and burros and horses are used to work the fertile land.

Villager Weaving
On weekends, costumed workers demonstrate the hacienda's skills, including weaving.

Sapello Mill and Sierra Village

Lookout Post

★ La Placita
This small central court-yard contains the hornos, or beehive-shaped ovens that were used to bake bread and cookies.

★ Baca House Kitchen
The kitchen, like the rest of the Baca house, dates from the early 1800s. It features a bell-shaped oven and a built-in wall cabinet (alacena) to keep food cool.

★ Chapel
This pretty painted wooden reredos (screen) graces the chapel. Part of the original ranch, a chapel was essential for devout Catholic settlers.

VISITORS' CHECKLIST

334 Los Pinos Rd, 15 miles (24 km) south of Santa Fe off I-25. *Tel* (505) 471-2261. ☐ *Jun–early Oct: 10am–4pm Wed–Sun for self-guided tours; Apr, May, Oct: guided tours only. Call ahead for reservations.* www.golondrinas.org

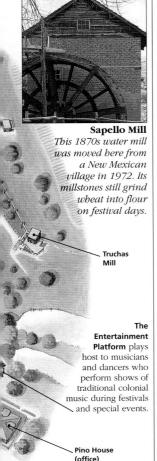

Sapello Mill
This 1870s water mill was moved here from a New Mexican village in 1972. Its millstones still grind wheat into flour on festival days.

Truchas Mill

The Entertainment Platform plays host to musicians and dancers who perform shows of traditional colonial music during festivals and special events.

Pino House (office)

STAR SIGHTS

★ La Placita

★ Chapel

★ Baca House Kitchen

🎭 Santa Fe Opera
5 miles N. of Santa Fe on Hwy 84/285. *Tel* (505) 986-5900; (800) 280-4654. ☐ *Jul–Aug.* www.santafeopera.org

Located just north of Santa Fe near the pueblo villages of Tesuque and Pojoaque, the outdoor auditorium is the setting for one of the finest summer opera companies in the world. It is renowned for innovative productions, which attract international stars. A state-of-the-art electronic system allows the audience to read translations of the libretti on the seats in front of them. Backstage tours are available in July and August. Visitors are advised to come prepared for Santa Fe's changeable weather with warm clothing, umbrellas, rugs, and waterproof gear.

⛷ Santa Fe Ski Area
Hwy 475. *Tel* (505) 982-4429. ☐ *Nov–early Apr: 9am–4pm daily, weather permitting.* www.skisantafe.com

Just a 30-minute drive from central Santa Fe, the ski area sits in a 12,000-ft- (4,000-m-) high basin of the Sangre de Cristo mountains. The resort has 43 trails to suit skiers of every ability, from beginners to experts, and snowboarding runs are also open. A lodge, equipment rentals, ski school, and child care are available, as are a variety of ski packages. From late September to early October, chairlift rides offer splendid views of the fall colors of the golden aspen trees. During the winter, the slopes are open only in safe conditions; always call in advance to check that your preferred runs are open.

The façade of the New Mexico State Capitol with Puebloan sun motif

🏛 New Mexico State Capitol
Old Santa Fe Trail & Paseo de Peralta. *Tel* (505) 986-4589. ☐ *Jun–Aug: 7am–7pm Mon–Fri, 8am–5pm Sat; Sep–May: 7am–6pm Mon–Fri.* www.nmlegis.gov

Built to resemble the sun symbol of the Zia Pueblo people, the circular State Capitol houses works by New Mexican artists from the Capitol Art Collection. Paintings, photographs, sculptures, furniture, and weavings are displayed on four levels.

Buffalo sculpture at State Capitol

A highlight is the sculpture *The Buffalo* (1992), by Holly Hughes, which uses paintbrushes and film for hair.

🏛 Santa Fe Southern Railway
410 S. Guadalupe St. *Tel* (505) 989-8600; (888) 989-8600. www.sfsr.com

Located in the railyard near the corner of Guadalupe Street and Montezuma Avenue, this working freight train offers rides in vintage passenger cars through spectacular desert scenery to the little village of Lamy. The stop for lunch at Lamy is included in the ticket price. The round trip takes between three and four-and-a-half hours. Train schedules change seasonally, so call ahead for times.

The engine car of the Santa Fe freight train

Los Alamos ❷

Road map E3. 🏚 *19,000*. ℹ️ *109*
Central Park Square (505) 662-8105.
www.visit.losalamos.com

The town of Los Alamos is
famous as the location of the
Manhattan Project *(see p186)*,
the US Government's top-
secret research program for
the development of the
atomic bomb during World
War II. Government scientists
took over this remote site in
1943. In 1945 the first atomic
bomb was detonated at the
Trinity test site in the southern New Mexico desert near
Alamogordo *(see p224)*.

Today, the town is home to
scientists from the Los Alamos
National Laboratory, a leading
defense facility. The **Bradbury
Science Museum** showcases
its work, with exhibits on security and technology, and replicas of Little Boy and Fat Man,
the atomic bombs dropped
on Hiroshima and Nagasaki
in 1946. The **Los Alamos
Historical Museum** covers
local geology and history.

🏛 **Bradbury Science
Museum**
15th & Central Ave. **Tel** *(505) 667-
4444.* ◯ *10am–5pm Tue–Sat, 1–
5pm Sun–Mon.* ● *public hols.* ♿

Façade of Bradbury Science Museum in Los Alamos

🏛 **Los Alamos Historical
Museum**
Central & 20th St. **Tel** *(505) 662-
4493.* ◯ *Mon–Sat 10am–4pm
(9:30am–4:30pm in summer);
1–4pm Sun.* ● *public hols.* ♿

Jemez Springs ❸

Road map E3. 🏚 *19,000*.
ℹ️ *Highway 4 (575) 829-3540.*

The small town of Jemez
Springs is located in San
Diego Canyon, by the Jemez
River, on land once occupied
by the Giusewa Pueblo. Its
ruins and those of a 17th-
century mission church are
now part of the **Jemez State
Monument**. Remnants of the
mission walls and a reconstruction of its massive main
gates can be seen here. A few
miles south on Hwy 4, Jemez
Pueblo is open only on feast
days and festivals; call Jemez
Springs visitor center for dates.

The region is famous for
its hot springs. Spence Hot
Springs, 7 miles (11 km) north
of town, has several outdoor
hot pools linked by waterfalls.

♆ **Jemez State Monument**
Off Hwy 4. **Tel** *(575) 829-3530.*
◯ *8:30am–5pm Wed–Mon.* ●
Tue, public hols. 📷 ♿ *partial.*

Mission church of San Jose at Jemez
State Monument

Bandelier National
Monument ❹

Road map E3. Off Hwy 4. **Tel** *(505)
672-3861.* ◯ *sunrise–sunset daily;
visitor center: 9am–4:30pm daily
(8am–6pm Memorial Day to Labor
Day).* ● *Jan 1, Dec 25.* 📷 ♿ *partial.
No pets.* 🅰 **www**.nps.gov/band

Set in the rugged cliffs and
canyons of the Pajarito Plateau,
Bandelier National Monument
shelters over 3,000 archaeological sites that are the remains of
an Ancestral Pueblo culture.
The site is thought to have
been occupied by ancestors
of the Puebloan peoples for

THE RIO GRANDE

One of America's great rivers, the Rio Grande evokes
romantic images of frontier legends, from Billy the Kid to
John Wayne. Its mythic status grew up from movies and TV
westerns, but its historical and geographical importance is no
less fascinating. From its source in Colorado, the fifth-longest
river in the United States flows southeast for 1,885 miles
(3,000 km) to the Gulf of Mexico. It crosses New Mexico,
then forms the entire boundary between Texas and Mexico.
Used for irrigation since ancient times by the pueblos, in the
16th century, Spanish settlers established towns and villages
along the length of the river. Today, crops including cotton,
citrus fruits, and vegetables are grown along its fertile banks.

The dramatic Rio Grande Gorge carved by the river, south of Taos

around 500 years from the 12th to the 16th centuries. During this time successive communities settled here, growing corn and squash, as well as hunting. The earliest occupants are thought to have carved the soft volcanic rock of the towering cliffs to make cave dwellings, while later people built houses and pueblos from rock debris.

One of the most fascinating sights here is the ruin of the 400-room Tyuonyi village. The settlement is laid out with semicircular lines of houses on the floor of Frijoles Canyon.

From the visitor center, also in the canyon, the Main Loop Trail leads past Tyuonyi to some of the cave dwellings and the Long House, multistoried dwellings built into an 800-ft (240-m) stretch of the cliff. Petroglyphs can be spotted above the holes which once held the roof beams. Another short trail leads to the Alcove House, perched 150 ft (45 m) up in the rocks and reached by ladders.

Pecos National Historical Park ❺

Road map E3. Hwy 63. *Tel (505) 757-7200.* ☐ *Jun–Aug: 8am–6pm daily; Sep–May: 8am–5pm daily* ● *Dec 25.* 🅿 ♿ **www**.nps.gov/peco

Located across Hwy 63, around 25 miles (40 km) southeast of Santa Fe, Pecos National Historical Park includes the ruins of the once influential Pecos Pueblo. Situated in a pass through the Sangre de Cristo Mountains, the pueblo dominated trade routes between the Plains Indians and the Pueblo peoples between 1450 and 1550.

The façade of the Plaza Hotel in the main square of Las Vegas

Pecos Puebloans acted as a conduit for such goods as buffalo skins and meat and Puebloan products including pottery, textiles, and turquoise. The village is thought to have been among the largest in the Southwest. It stood up to five stories high, with nearly 700 rooms housing more than 2,000 people, a quarter of them warriors. When the Spanish arrived in the late 16th century, it was a strong regional power. But by 1821 Comanche raids, disease, and migration had taken their toll; the pueblo was almost deserted, and the remaining inhabitants moved to Jemez Pueblo.

The pueblo site can be seen on a 1.25-mile (2-km) trail that winds past them and also the ruined remains of two Spanish mission churches. There are also two reconstructed *kivas* (sacred ceremonial sites) here. The visitor center has exhibits of historic artifacts and crafts, as well as a video covering 1,000 years of Puebloan history in the area.

Las Vegas ❻

Road map E3. 🚶 *17,000.* ☐ 🚍 ℹ *701 Grand Ave. (505) 425-8631; (800) 832-5947.* **www**.lasvegasnewmexico.com

Not to be confused with its Nevada cousin *(see pp94–131)*, Las Vegas, New Mexico has its own high-rolling past. Vegas means "meadows" in Spanish, and the town's old Plaza was established along the lush riverfront by Spanish settlers in 1835. A lucrative trade stop on the Santa Fe Trail, Las Vegas soon became a wild frontier town. Doc Holliday, who briefly owned a saloon here, was among its legendary characters *(see p55).* The coming of the railroad in 1879 brought even greater prosperity, and new building took place around the station.

Grand Victorian architecture still prevails and self-guided tours are available from the visitor center.

Outdoor activities are popular in the area, with golf resorts and the watersports of Storrie Lake just a few miles out of town.

One of the ruined Spanish mission churches in Pecos National Historical Park

Northern Pueblos Tour ❼

Redware pottery

The fertile valley of the Rio Grande between Santa Fe and Taos is home to eight pueblos of the 19 Native American pueblos in New Mexico. Although geographically close, each pueblo has its own government and traditions, and many offer attractions to visitors. Nambe gives stunning views of the surrounding mountains, mesas, and high desert. San Idelfonso is famous for its fine pottery, while other villages produce handcrafted jewelry or rugs.

TIPS FOR DRIVERS

Starting point: *Tesuque Pueblo, north of Santa Fe on Hwy 84.*
Length: *45 miles (70 km). Local roads leading to pueblos are often dirt tracks, so allow extra time.*
Note: *Visitors are welcome, but respect their laws and etiquette (see p286–7).* 🛈 *Indian Pueblo Cultural Center (505) 843-7270.*
www.indianpueblo.org

Santa Clara Pueblo ⑤
This small pueblo is known for its artisans and their work. As in many pueblos, it contains a number of craft shops and small studios, often run by the Native artisans themselves.

Puye Cliff Dwellings ⑥
Now deserted, this site contains over 700 rooms, complete with stone carvings, that were home to Native peoples until 1500.

San Juan Pueblo ⑦
Declared the first capital of New Mexico in 1598, this village is now a center for the visual arts and has an arts cooperative.

San Ildefonso Pueblo ④
Occupied since 1300, this pueblo is best known for its etched black pottery, the proceeds of which saved its people from the Depression of the 1930s.

Nambe Pueblo ③
Set in a beautiful fertile valley, this village is bordered by a lakeside hiking trail with waterfall views and a buffalo ranch.

Pojoaque Pueblo ②
The Peoh Cultural Center and Museum here is an excellent introduction to the pueblo way of life in these small communities.

Tesuque Pueblo ①
The Tewa people here have concentrated on farming and pottery-making for centuries.

KEY

▬▬ Tour route
═ ═ Other roads

0 km   10
0 miles   10

The stone façade of Chimayó Church in the Santa Fe valley

Chimayó ❽

Road map E3. 🏘 *2,800.*
🛈 *(505) 351-4889. Church open:*
9am–5pm daily. 🅰

This village lies 25 miles (40 km) north of Santa Fe in the Rio Grande valley. Chimayó was settled by Spanish colonists in the 1700s on the site of an Indian pueblo famous for having a healing natural spring. The site of the spring is now occupied by the Santuario de Chimayó, built by a local landowner in 1813–16 after he experienced a vision telling him to dig the foundations in earth blessed with healing powers. While digging here he found a cross that once belonged to two martyred priests, and the church became a place of healing pilgrimage. The chapel contains a beautiful *reredos* surrounding the crucifix and a tiny side-room with a pit of "the holy dirt," which visitors are allowed to take away.

Chimayó is also known for its woven blankets and rugs, which have been produced by the Ortega family for generations. Their workshop is just off the junction with Hwy 76, while farther along, Cordova and Truchas villages are also known for their fine craftwork.

Abiquiu ❾

Road map E3. 🏘 *500.* 🛈 *Hwy 84*
(505) 753-2831.

This small adobe village with its sunlit dusty streets was the home of the Southwest's most famous artist, Georgia O'Keeffe, from 1946 until her death in 1986. Her village home and studio can be toured only by reservation and bookings need

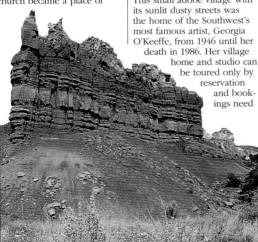

Dramatic red rock landscape near Abiquiu

GEORGIA O'KEEFFE

One of the 20th century's foremost artists, Georgia O'Keeffe (1887–1986) has managed to achieve both critical and popular acclaim for her paintings, which, either as studies of single blooms or sun-washed landscapes of the Southwest, are universally loved. Wisconsin-born and raised, she studied art in Chicago and New York but fell in love with the light of New Mexico when her friend and patron, Mabel Dodge Luhan, invited her to her home in the area. O'Keeffe bought an old adobe in Abiquiu and there created the abstract paintings that brought the beauty of New Mexico to national attention.

Artist Georgia O'Keeffe

to be made in advance on (505) 685-4539. The country around Abiquiu, with its red rocks, mesas, and corrugated slopes, is now known as O'Keeffe Country because it inspired so many of her abstract landscape paintings

A few miles north of town, the fascinating **Ghost Ranch**, a retreat established and now run by Presbyterians, features two small but fascinating museums, which highlight local archaeology and palaeontology. Several hiking trails also start from the ranch.

🏛 **Ghost Ranch**
HC77, Box 11, Abiquiu. **Tel** *(575) 685-4333.* ⬤ *Museums: 9am–5pm Tue–Sat.* 🈺 *donation suggested.*

Chama ❿

Road map E2. 🏘 *1,000.*
🛈 *2372 Hwy 17, (505) 756-2235.*
www.chamavalley.com

Founded during the 1880s silver-mining boom, the main attraction in today's Chama is the **Cumbres and Toltec Scenic Railroad**. This narrow-gauge steam train makes a spectacular 64-mile (102-km) daily trip over the Cumbres Pass and through the Toltec Gorge into Colorado, with views of the San Juan and Sangre de Cristo mountains.

🚂 **Cumbres and Toltec Scenic Railroad**
Hwy 17. **Tel** *(575) 756-2151;*
1 (888) 286-2737. ⬤ *late May to mid-Oct: 10am daily.* 🈺 ♿

Taos ⑪

Gun in the Kit Carson Museum

The small city of Taos is set between the dramatic peaks of the Sangre de Cristo Mountains and the Rio Grande River. Like Santa Fe, it is an important center for the arts but is more bohemian and relaxed in style. Its plaza and the surrounding streets are lined with craft shops, cafés, and galleries, many housed in original adobe buildings.

Taos Indians have lived in the area for around 1,000 years. With the arrival of the Spanish missionaries in 1598, a few settlers followed, but it was not until Don Diego de Vargas resettled the area, after the Pueblo Revolt in 1680, that the town's present foundations were laid *(see p40)*. In 1898, artists Ernest Blumenschein and Bert Phillips stopped in Taos to repair a broken wagon wheel, and never left. In 1915 they established the Taos Society of Artists, which still supports local artists today.

Exploring Taos
There are three parts to Taos: the central historic district, Taos Pueblo to the north, and Rancho de Taos to the south *(see p206)*. Paseo del Pueblo Norte, the main street, leads north then curves west, becoming Hwy 64. It leads to Taos Ski Valley, the Millicent Rogers Museum, and Rio Grande Gorge Bridge.

Furniture displayed in the Blumenschein Museum

🏛 Harwood Museum of Art
238 Ledoux St. *Tel (575) 758-9826.* ◯ *10am–5pm Tue–Sat; noon–5pm Sun.* ● *public hols.* 📷 🎟
www.harwoodmuseum.org
New Mexico's second-oldest museum occupies a 19th-century adobe compound run by the University of New Mexico. It provides a tranquil setting for paintings, sculpture, prints, drawings, and photography. Work by members of the original Taos Society of Artists is displayed alongside that of contemporary local artists. A collection of Hispanic works is also featured.

🏛 Blumenschein Home and Museum
222 Ledoux St. *Tel (575) 758-0505.* ◯ *10am–5pm Mon–Sat, noon–5pm Sun (call for winter hours).* 📷 🎟 *partial.* **www**.taoshistoricmuseums.com
Ernest Blumenschein (1874–1960), along with Bert Phillips and Joseph Henry Sharp, was instrumental in founding the Taos Society of Artists in 1915. The Society promoted their own work and that of other Taos artists. The Museum is located in Blumenschein's former home, sections of which date from the 1790s. Paintings by Blumenschein and his family, as well as representative works produced by the Taos Society of Artists, hang in rooms decorated with Spanish Colonial furniture and European antiques.

🏧 Taos Plaza
Taos Plaza, built by the Spanish and fortified after the Pueblo Revolt of 1680, has been remodeled several times

Shops and cafés line the narrow streets around Taos Plaza

but remains the centerpoint of the town. Its shady trees and benches make it a relaxing spot to sit and people-watch. The copper-topped bandstand was a gift from Mabel Dodge Luhan, New Mexico's leading arts patron in the 1920s. A flag has flown continuously from the flagpole since the Civil War, when Kit Carson and a band of citizens raised the Union Flag to protect Taos from Confederate supporters.

🏛 Kit Carson Home and Museum
113 Kit Carson Rd. *Tel (575) 758-4945.* ◯ *10am–5pm daily (but call to check and for winter opening hours).* 📷 🎟 *partial.* **www**.kitcarsonhome.com
At the age of 17, Christopher "Kit" Carson (1809–68) ran away to join a wagon train and became one of the most famous names in the West. He led a remarkable life, working as a cook and interpreter, a fur-trapping mountain man, a scout for mapping expeditions, an Indian agent, and a military officer *(see p171)*. He purchased this house in Taos in 1843 for his 14-year-old bride, Josefa Jaramillo, and lived here for the rest of his life. Carson's remarkable story, and the unpredictable nature of frontier life, are the focus of the museum exhib-

Cover of a Kit Carson book

its, which feature antique firearms, trapping equipment, photographs, and furniture.

🏛 Taos Art Museum
227 Paseo del Pueblo Norte. *Tel (575) 758-2690.* ◯ *10am–5pm Tue–Sun (call for winter hours).* 📷 🎟 **www**.taosartmuseum.org
Born in Russia in 1881, Nicolai Fechin learned woodcarving from his father. He became a talented artist, producing paintings, drawings, and sculpture. Fechin moved to Taos with his family in 1927 and set about restoring his adobe home with Russian-influenced woodwork including handcrafted doors, windows,

Handcrafted, wooden swing doors in the Fechin Institute

VISITORS' CHECKLIST

Road map E3. 6,000. Greyhound, Taos Bus Center, Hwy 68. 1139 Paseo del Pueblo Sur (575) 758-3873; (800) 732-8267. Taos Spring Arts Celebration (May); Yuletide in Taos (late Nov–New Year).

and furniture. Today his house is the Taos Art Museum, containing examples of his work as well as that of numerous early Taos artists.

🏛 Millicent Rogers Museum

1504 Millicent Rogers Rd. *Tel* (575) 758-2462. Apr–Oct: 10am–5pm daily; Nov–Mar: 10am–5pm Tue–Sun. public hols.

Beautiful heiress and arts patron Millicent Rogers (1902–53) moved to Taos in 1947. Fascinated by the area, she created one of the country's best museums of Southwestern arts and design. Native silver and turquoise jewelry and Navajo weavings form the core of the exhibits. Also featured is the pottery of the famous Puebloan artist Maria Martinez (1887–1980), with its distinctive black-on-black style.

🏛 Governor Bent House and Museum

117a Bent St. *Tel* (575) 758-2376. 10am–5pm daily (Mon–Fri in winter).

Charles Bent became the first Anglo-American governor of New Mexico in 1846. In 1847 he was killed by Hispanic and Indian residents who resented American rule. The hole hacked in the adobe by his family as they attempted to flee can still be seen. Today, exhibits include guns, native artifacts, and animal skins.

🌉 Rio Grande Gorge Bridge

Tel (575) 758-3873.

The dramatic Rio Grande Gorge Bridge, which was built in 1965, is the second-highest suspension bridge in the country. At 650 ft (195 m) above the Rio Grande, its dizzying heights offer awesome views of the gorge and the surrounding stark, sweeping plateau.

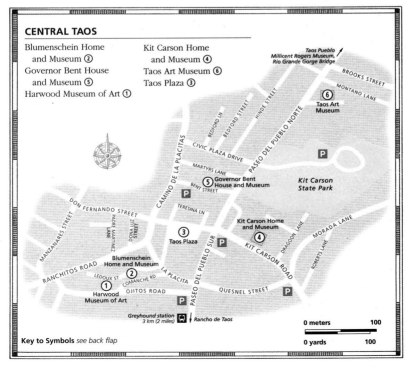

CENTRAL TAOS

Blumenschein Home and Museum ②
Governor Bent House and Museum ⑤
Harwood Museum of Art ①
Kit Carson Home and Museum ④
Taos Art Museum ⑥
Taos Plaza ③

Taos Pueblo
Millicent Rogers Museum,
Rio Grande Gorge Bridge

BROOKS STREET
MONTANO LANE
⑥ Taos Art Museum
BEDFORD LN
BEDFORD STREET
HINDE STREET
PASEO DEL PUEBLO NORTE
CIVIC PLAZA DRIVE
CAMINO DE LA PLACITAS
MARTYRS LANE
⑤ Governor Bent House and Museum
BENT STREET
TERESINA LN
Kit Carson State Park
MORADA LANE
DON FERNANDO STREET
MANZANARES STREET
PADRE MARTINEZ LANE
DONA LUZ STREET
③ Taos Plaza
Kit Carson Home and Museum ④
KIT CARSON ROAD
DRAGON LANE
ROBERTS LANE
RANCHITOS ROAD
LEDOUX ST
② Blumenschein Home and Museum
COMANCHE RD
LA PLACITA
PASEO DEL PUEBLO SUR
QUESNEL STREET
① Harwood Museum of Art
OJITOS ROAD

Greyhound station
3 km (2 miles) Rancho de Taos

0 meters 100
0 yards 100

Key to Symbols *see back flap*

Restored early-19th-century kitchen at the Hacienda Martínez

Rancho de Taos ⑫

Road map E3. 🚶 *Taos Visitor Center, 1139 Paseo de Pueblo Sur, Taos (575) 758-3873.* **www**.*taoschamber.com*

Located 3 miles (5 km) southwest of central Taos, this separate community is centered on a peaceful plaza. Rancho de Taos is also home to the striking adobe church of **San Francisco de Asis**, which was built between 1710 and 1755. The church is one of the best examples of mission architecture in the Southwest and provided inspiration for many artists. It was often painted by Georgia O'Keeffe (*see p203*).

The **Hacienda Martínez** is a Spanish Colonial house built in 1804 and one of the few still in existence (*see p188*). Its adobe walls are 2-ft (60-cm) thick and have heavy *zaguan* (entry) gates. Inside, 21 starkly furnished rooms surround two courtyards. The first owner, Antonio Severino Martinez, prospered through trade with Mexico and later became mayor of Taos. The merchandise he sold is displayed here.

> 🔒 **San Francisco de Asis**
> Hwy 68, Rancho de Taos. **Tel** *(575) 758-2754.* ⏰ *9am–4pm Mon–Fri.* 📷 *1st two weeks Jun.* ♿
>
> 🏛 **Hacienda Martínez**
> 708 Hacienda Rd, Rancho de Taos. **Tel** *(505) 758-1000.* ⏰ *May–Oct: 9am–5pm daily (call for winter hours).* 📷 *public hols.* ♿

Taos Pueblo ⑬

Road map E3. Hwy 150.
🚶 *Taos Pueblo Tourism Office, P.O. Box 1846, Taos (575) 758-1028.* 📷📷 **www**.*taospueblo.com*

This is one of the oldest communities in the US, having been occupied continuously for around 1,000 years. Two multistory adobe communal houses sit on opposite sides of the open central "square". Known as North House and South House, they are the largest pueblo buildings in the country and are thought to date from the early 1700s. More than 100 people live year-round at the pueblo, as their ancestors did, with no electricity, and water supplied only from a stream. Sights include the 1850 St. Jerome Chapel, the ruins of the earlier 1619 San Geronimo Church, and the central plaza, with its corn and chile drying-racks and adobe ovens, or *hornos*. Several ground-floor dwellings are now craft shops. Guided tours are available but there is a fee of $5 for each camera; permission must be granted prior to photographing a resident. No cameras are permitted during ceremonial dances, but several festivals are open to visitors throughout the year.

Downhill view of one of the celebrated ski slopes at Taos

Taos Ski Valley ⑭

Road map E2. 📷 *(575) 776-1413.* ♿ *village only.* **www**.*taosskivalley.com*

A century ago Taos Ski Valley was a bustling mining camp. In 1955, Swiss-born skier Ernie Blake began developing a world-class ski resort on the northern slopes and snow bowls of Wheeler Peak, the 13,161-ft (3,950-m) summit that is the highest in New Mexico. Located 15 miles (24 km) north of Taos, it has 12 lifts and 72 runs for all abilities, but it is particularly known for its challenging expert terrain. The ski season itself generally runs from Thanksgiving to early April depending on the weather. The valley also makes a spectacular summer retreat popular with those seeking relief from the summer heat. Some 100 residents live in the village year-round.

Adobe buildings at the Taos pueblo, inhabited to this day by villagers

For hotels and restaurants in this region see pp243–5 and pp265–7

Enchanted Circle Tour ⑮

The scenery around Taos rises from high desert plateau with its sagebrush and yucca plants to the forested Sangre de Cristo Mountains. The Enchanted Circle tour follows a National Forest Scenic Byway through some of the area's most breathtaking landscapes. Circumnavigating the highest point in New Mexico, Wheeler Peak (13,161 ft/ 3,950 m), it continues through the ruggedly beautiful Carson National Forest. Lakes and hiking trails lie off the tour, which passes through small towns and the home of English novelist D.H. Lawrence.

TIPS FOR DRIVERS

Length: 84 miles (134 km.)
Starting point: North of Taos on Hwy 522, continuing east and south on Hwys 38 & 64.
Getting around: While the main roads offer smooth and rapid driving, bear in mind that many sights are located on dirt tracks and minor roads.

D.H. Lawrence Memorial ①
Known for his innovative, erotic work, the writer's ashes were laid to rest near the farmhouse where he lived in the 1920s.

Questa ②
This hamlet is the gateway to Carson National Forest, with rivers, mountains, and lakes set against a rocky backdrop.

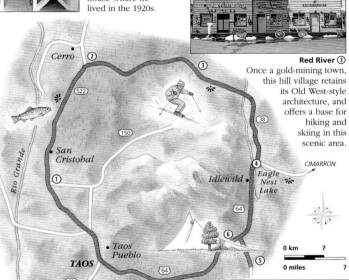

Red River ③
Once a gold-mining town, this hill village retains its Old West-style architecture, and offers a base for hiking and skiing in this scenic area.

DAV Vietnam Veterans Memorial State Park ⑥
Located northeast of Angel Fire, this modern chapel honors all the US troops who lost their lives in Vietnam.

Angel Fire ⑤
Winter sports are foremost here, with sleigh rides, snowmobiling, and horseback trips through the snowy landscape available at this growing resort.

KEY

▨ Tour route

— Other roads

✻ Viewpoint

Eagle Nest ④
Growing in popularity as a base for sports trips, this small town is conveniently located and offers ski and boat rental for the nearby mountains and lakes.

ALBUQUERQUE AND SOUTHERN NEW MEXICO

Southern New Mexico is home to natural wonders such as the Carlsbad Caverns, as well as modern cities thriving on hi-tech research industries. Albuquerque is the state's largest city, with an Old Town plaza and fine museums. West of here is Acoma Pueblo, the oldest continually inhabited settlement in the country. The southern third of the state is dominated by the Chihuahua Desert, which is one of the driest in the region. Despite this, the area was cultivated by Hohokam farmers for centuries. The Gila Cliff Dwellings are the last remnants of the Mogollon people. By the 17th century Apaches occupied much of the region, whose reputation as a "Wild West" outpost stems from the 19th-century exploits of characters such as Billy the Kid.

SIGHTS AT A GLANCE

Historic Towns and Cities
Alamogordo ⑱
Albuquerque ①
Bernalillo ③
Carlsbad ㉓
Cloudcroft ⑲
Deming ⑫
El Paso ⑯
Grants ⑥
Las Cruces ⑭
Lincoln ㉑
Mesilla ⑮
Roswell ㉔
Ruidoso ⑳
Silver City ⑪

Socorro ⑧
Truth or Consequences ⑨

Areas of Natural Beauty
Acoma Pueblo ⑤
Sandia Peak Tramway ②
The Turquoise Trail ④

National Parks and Monuments
Carlsbad Caverns National Park ㉒
El Morro National Monument ⑦

Fort Selden State Monument ⑬
Gila Cliff Dwellings National Monument ⑩
White Sands National Monument ⑰

KEY

✈	International airport
═	Interstate
▬	Major highway
═	Highway
—	Railroad

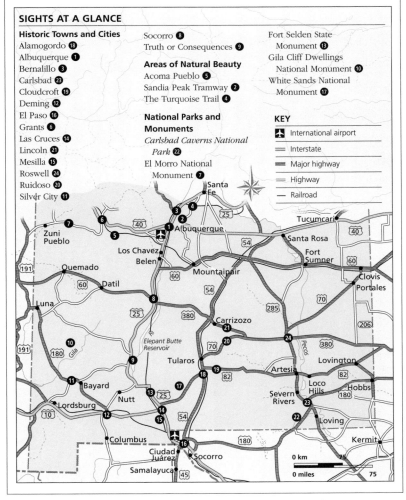

Albuquerque Old Town Street-by-Street ❶

Chile pepper
store sign

Occupied by Native peoples from 1100 to 1300 AD, Albuquerque grew up from a small colonial group of pioneers who first settled by the Rio Grande in the wake of late 16th-century Spanish explorers of the region. In 1706, a band of 18 families won formal approval for their town from the Spanish crown by naming the city after the Spanish Duke of Alburquerque, (the first "r" in the name was later dropped).

Today's Old Town still boasts many original adobe buildings dating from the 1790s. The city's first civic structure, the imposing San Felipe de Neri church was completed in 1793. Despite many renovations, the church retains its original adobe walls. The adjacent plaza forms the heart of the Old Town and is a pleasant open space where both locals and visitors relax on benches, surrounded by the lovely adobe buildings that house craft shops, restaurants, and museums.

Agape Pueblo Pottery
This store features a selection of pueblo pottery such as this hand-crafted pot from Santa Clara Pueblo.

Church Street Café
Said to occupy the oldest house in the city, this café serves excellent New Mexican cuisine and is famous for its spicy chili.

San Felipe de
Neri church

Christmas
shop

CHURCH ST NW

ROMERO NW

RIO GRANDE BOULEVARD NW

NORTH PLAZA

SOUTH PLAZA

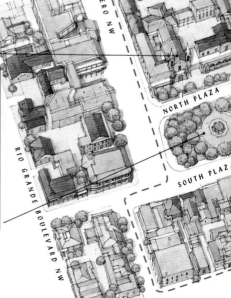

★ Old Town Plaza
The plaza was the center of Albuquerque for over 200 years. Today, this charming square makes a pleasant rest stop for visitors strolling around the nearby streets lined with museums and colorful stores.

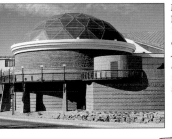

Museum of Natural History

The space-age dome of the LodeStar Astronomy Center houses a planetarium and an observatory (see p212).

VISITORS' CHECKLIST

Road map 3E. 580,000.
Albuquerque International Sunport, 5 miles (8 km) S. of Downtown. Amtrak, 214 1st St. SW. Greyhound, 320 1st St. SW. Albuquerque Convention Center, 401 2nd St. NW, (505) 842-9918; (800) 284-2282. Gathering of Nations Pow-Wow (Apr); New Mexico Arts and Crafts Fair (late Jun); New Mexico State Fair (Sep); Albuquerque International Balloon Fiesta (Oct). www.abqcvb.org

MOUNTAIN ROAD NW

19TH STREET

| 0 meters | 50 |
| 0 yards | 50 |

KEY

– – – – Suggested route

★ Albuquerque Museum of Art and History

This full-scale model of a conquistador on horseback illustrates the kind of Spanish Colonial art and artifacts that dominate this museum's excellent displays. There is also a delightful outdoor sculpture gallery.

SAN FELIPE NW

American International Rattlesnake Museum

This Eastern diamond-back rattlesnake (right) is one of many species of rattler here. There are displays on the snake's role in medicine, history, and Native American culture.

STAR SIGHTS

★ Albuquerque Museum of Art and History

★ Old Town Plaza

Exploring Albuquerque

Albuquerque is New Mexico's largest city, filling the valley that stretches westward from the foothills of the Manzano and Sandia Mountains and across the banks of the Rio Grande. The coming of the railroad during the 1880s brought large numbers of settlers and great prosperity. The city center shifted 2 miles (3 km) east from the Old Town Plaza to what is now the Downtown area. Today, the city has a contemporary buzz with many shops, museums, and high-tech industries concentrated in and around Downtown. At the eastern end of this area lies the University of New Mexico, with its collection of museums and galleries.

Modern sculpture

San Felipe de Neri Church lies at the north end of Old Town Plaza

Exploring Albuquerque

The best way to see the city is by car. The major sights here are all located near highway exits, which are surprisingly close to areas of historic and architectural interest such as the Old Town. Two Interstate highways cross the center of Albuquerque, Highway 25 travels north to south across Downtown, while Highway 40 cuts west to east running just north of Downtown and close by the university campus.

🏊 Albuquerque BioPark

2601 Central Ave. NW. *Tel* (505) 764-6200. ⬜ 9am–5pm daily. ⬤ *Thanksgiving, Dec 25.* 📷 ♿ **www**.cabq.gov/biopark

The park encompasses the Albuquerque Aquarium and the Rio Grande Botanic Garden. The Rio Grande Zoological Park is located nearby. The botanic garden occupies ten acres (4 ha) of woodland along the Rio Grande.

The aquarium focuses on the marine life of the Rio Grande *(see p200)* and features a fascinating walk-through eel cave containing moray eels. There is also an impressive 285,000-gallon (627,000-liter), floor-to-ceiling shark tank.

🏛 Turquoise Museum

2107 Central Ave. NW. *Tel* (505) 247-8650. ⬜ 9:30am–5pm Mon–Sat (to 4pm Sat). ⬤ *Thanksgiving, Dec 25.* 📷 ♿

The entrance to this museum is a replica mine tunnel that leads to the "vault," which contains an unsurpassed collection of rare and varied turquoise specimens from more than fifty mines around the world.

🏛 New Mexico Museum of Natural History and Science

1801 Mountain Rd. NW. *Tel* (505) 841-2800. ⬜ 9am–5pm daily. ⬤ *Jan & Sep: Mon; public hols.* 📷 ♿ **www**.nmnaturalhistory.org

This museum has a series of interactive exhibits. Visitors can stand inside a simulated volcano or explore an ice cave. The "Evolator" is a six-minute ride through 38 million years of the region's evolution using the latest

Glasshouse at Rio Grande Botanic Garden, Albuquerque BioPark

For hotels and restaurants in this region see pp245–7 and pp267–9

video technology. Replica dinosaurs, a state-of-the-art planetarium, and a large-screen film theater are all highly popular with children.

🏛 Albuquerque Museum of Art and History
2000 Mountain Rd. NW.
Tel (505) 242-4600. ⬜ 9am–5pm Tue–Sun. ⬤ public hols. 📷 ♿
www.cabq.gov/museum
This excellent museum depicts four centuries of history in the middle of Rio Grande Valley. The well-chosen Spanish Colonial artifacts (see p39) are expertly arranged and include a reconstructed 18th-century house and chapel. From March to December, walking tours of the Old Town leave from the museum.

🏛 American International Rattlesnake Museum
202 San Felipe Ave. N. **Tel** (505) 242-6569. ⬜ 10am–6pm Mon–Sat (Sep–May: 11:30am–5:30pm), 1–5pm Sun. ⬤ public hols. 📷 ♿
www.rattlesnakes.com
This animal conservation museum explains the life-cycles and ecological importance of some of Earth's most misunderstood creatures. It contains the world's largest collection of live rattlesnakes, including natives of North, Central, and South America.

The snakes are displayed in glass tanks that simulate their natural habitat, and are accompanied by explanatory notices suitable for both adults and children. The museum also features other much-maligned venomous animals, including a Gila monster lizard, tarantulas, and scorpions.

Colorful tiles decorate the Art Deco-style façade of the KiMo Theater

🎭 KiMo Theater
423 Central Ave. NW. **Tel** (505) 768-3544. ⬜ call for program. 📷 ♿ **www**.cabq.gov/kimo
Built in 1927, the KiMo Theater was one of many entertainment venues constructed in the city during the 1920s and 1930s. The theater's design was inspired by that of the nearby Native American pueblos, and created a fusion of Pueblo Revival and Art Deco styles. Today, the KiMo Theater presents an eclectic range of musical and theatrical performances.

🐾 Rio Grande Zoological Park
903 10th St. SW. **Tel** (505) 764-6200. ⬜ 9am–5pm daily (summer: 6pm Sat, Sun). ⬤ Thanksgiving, Dec 25. 📷 ♿
The Rio Grande Zoo forms part of the Albuquerque Bio-Park. The zoo is noted for its imaginative layout with enclosures designed to simulate the animals' natural habitats, including the African savanna. Among the most popular species here are lowland gorillas and white Bengal tigers.

🏛 Explora! Science Center and Children's Museum
1701 Mountain Rd NW. **Tel** (505) 224-8300. ⬜ 10am–6pm Mon–Sat, noon–6pm Sun. ⬤ public hols. 📷 ♿ **www**.explora.mus.nm.us
Explora's kids-oriented science center is enjoyable for adults and children alike with its many interactive exhibits, such as stepping inside a soap bubble. In the Children's Museum, youngsters can look through kaleidoscopes, build wind cars, or practice weaving.

Rio Grande Zoological Park

KEY

▪ Albuquerque Old Town Street-by-Street map see pp210–11

| 0 meters | 500 |
| 0 yards | 500 |

Key to Symbols see back flap

SIGHTS AT A GLANCE

Indian Pueblo Cultural Center

This impressive cultural center is run by the 19 Indian Pueblos that lie along the Rio Grande around Albuquerque and Santa Fe. The complex history and varied culture of the Puebloan peoples is traced here through their oral history and is presented from their viewpoint.

The building is designed to resemble the layout of a pueblo dwelling, and is set around a large central courtyard. The center also contains a restaurant serving Pueblo Indian fusion-cooking, and an excellent group of gift shops offering high-quality pottery, jewelry, and other crafts from each pueblo.

Two female Puebloan dancers in front of a mural in the central courtyard

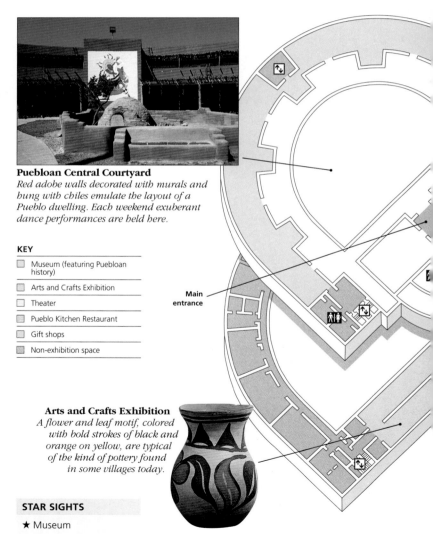

Puebloan Central Courtyard
Red adobe walls decorated with murals and hung with chiles emulate the layout of a Pueblo dwelling. Each weekend exuberant dance performances are held here.

KEY

- Museum (featuring Puebloan history)
- Arts and Crafts Exhibition
- Theater
- Pueblo Kitchen Restaurant
- Gift shops
- Non-exhibition space

Main entrance

Arts and Crafts Exhibition
A flower and leaf motif, colored with bold strokes of black and orange on yellow, are typical of the kind of pottery found in some villages today.

STAR SIGHTS

★ Museum

VISITORS' CHECKLIST

2401 12th St. NW. **Tel** *(505) 843-7270.* 🚌 ⬜ *9am–5pm daily.* ⬤ *major holidays.* 📷 ♿ ✉️ 🍴 🏪 *www.indianpueblo.org*

Courtyard Mural
Painted by Jemez Pueblo artist Jose Rey Toledo in 1979, this mural shows the turtle rain dance.

Museum entrance

★ **Museum**
This wooden baby carrier from Taos Pueblo is one of many artifacts, from ancient to modern, that highlight Puebloan cultural life.

🏛 University of New Mexico

ℹ️ *Welcome Center, Central and Cornell.* **Tel** *(505) 277-1989.* **www**.unm.edu

The campus of New Mexico's largest university is known for its Pueblo Revival-style architecture *(see p23)* and its museums. The **University Art Museum** contains one of the largest fine art collections in the state, including Old Master paintings, sculpture, and other works from the 17th to the 20th centuries.

The **Maxwell Museum of Anthropology** emphasizes the culture of the Southwest, with an important collection of art and artifacts. There are also traveling exhibits on regional and international themes, as well as a permanent exhibition, "Ancestors", which traces human development.

🏛 University Art Museum

Tel *(505) 277-4001.* ⬜ *9am–4pm Tue–Fri, 5–8pm Tue, 1–4pm Sat & Sun.* ⬤ *university holidays.* ♿

🏛 Maxwell Museum of Anthropology

Tel *(505) 277-4405.* ⬜ *10am–4pm Tue–Sat.* ♿

🏛 Anderson-Abruzzo International Balloon Museum

9201 Balloon Museum Dr. NE. **Tel** *(505) 768-6020.* ⬜ *9am–5pm Tue–Sun.* 📷 **www**.cabq.gov/balloon

This museum features soaring gallery spaces that contain the world's most extensive collection of modern and historic balloons, and ballooning memorabilia. Named after two of the city's legendary balloonists, the exhibits tell how balloons have been used in adventurous exploits, warfare, and space exploration, and include artifacts that date from the earliest days of ballooning.

🏛 National Museum of Nuclear Science & History

601 Eubank at Southern Blvd. SE. **Tel** *(505) 245-2137.* ⬜ *9am–5pm daily.* ⬤ *Jan 1, Easter, Thanksgiving, Dec 25.* 📷 **www**.nuclearmuseum.org

This museum presents the stories of nuclear pioneers and the history of nuclear development *(see pp186–7)*. The exhibits explore the many applications of nuclear energy in the past, present, and into the future. Energy Encounter illustrates the amount of wind, solar, or hydro power required to match the output from one nuclear reactor, while Little Albert's Lab introduces children to the concepts of physics. Outdoors, the Heritage Park displays unique military missile systems, rockets, and historic planes including a B-52 bomber.

🏛 Petroglyph National Monument

ℹ️ *4735 Unser Blvd. NW.* **Tel** *(505) 899-0205.* ⬜ *8am–5pm daily.* ⬤ *public hols.* 📷 ♿ *limited.* **www**.nps.gov/petr

This site lies on the western outskirts of Albuquerque. The area was established in 1990 to preserve nearly 20,000 images carved into rock along the 17-mile (27-km) West Mesa escarpment. The earliest petroglyphs date back to 1,000 BC, but the most prolific period is thought to be between 1300 and 1680. The pictures from this time range from human figures such as musicians and dancers to animals, including snakes, birds, and insects. Spirals and other geometric symbols are common, as are hands, feet, and animal tracks. Though the meaning of many petroglyphs has been lost over time, others have great cultural significance to today's Puebloan population.

Hundreds of petroglyphs are accessible along Boca Negra Canyon, 2 miles (3 km) north of the park visitor center, where three self-guided trails wind past them. Do not touch the petroglyphs.

Petroglyphs in Petroglyph National Monument

Sandia Peak tram rising over pine forest and mountains near Albuquerque

Sandia Peak Tramway ❷

10 Tramway Loop N.E.
Tel (505) 856-7325. ☐ 9am–9pm
daily. ⬛ 2 weeks spring & fall for
maintenance. 🖼 ♿
www.sandiapeak.com

The Sandia Peak Tramway is
a breathtaking ride from the
foothills at the northeastern
edge of Albuquerque to
Sandia Peak at 10,378 ft
(3,113 m). The tram was
constructed in the mid-1960s,
and transports tourists from
the outskirts of the city to the
summit's viewing platform.
The ride lasts 15 minutes and
passes through low desert to
ponderosa pine forests and
rugged mountains. The summit offers outstanding panoramic views of Albuquerque
and surrounding countryside.

Bernalillo ❸

🏔 6,000 ℹ (505) 867-8687. Ⓐ
www.sandovalcounty.org

The farming community of
Bernalillo was settled by
Spanish colonists in 1698.
Here, against a striking back-
drop on the banks of the Rio
Grande, is the **Coronado State
Monument**, which encompas-
ses the partially restored ruins
of the Kuaua pueblo. Spanish
explorer Francisco Vasquez de

Coronado is believed to have
been here in 1540 on a quest
to find Cibola, the fabled
seven cities of gold (see p39).
    Nearby Sandia Pueblo is
home to around 300 people.
Their festival on San Antonio's
Day in June features tribal
dancing (see p33).

Environs
Around 16 miles (26 km)
northwest of Bernalillo,
Zia Pueblo is famous for its
redware pottery. Visitors are
welcome to buy the pottery
and watercolors made in this
small community.

⌂ Coronado State Monument
State Highway 550, 1 mile west of
I-25. **Tel** (505) 867-5351. ☐
8:30am–5pm Wed–Mon. ⬛ Jan 1,
Easter, Thanksgiving, Dec 25. 🖼 ♿

The Turquoise Trail ❹

ℹ PO Box 303, Sandia Park 87047
(505) 281-5233.
www.turquoisetrail.org

The scenic Highway 14,
known as the Turquoise Trail,
runs for 52 miles (84 km)
between Albuquerque and
Santa Fe. Passing through the
spectacular countryside of the
Sandia Mountains and Cibola
National Forest, it takes in the
old mining towns of Golden,
Madrid, and Cerillos.
    Golden is the first stop in
a northward direction. It is a
small ghost town with ruined
buildings, and an atmospheric
adobe mission church, which
dates back to 1830. Madrid
was a busy coal-mining town
in the early 20th century. Its

The interior of the Trading Post store at Cerillos

ramshackle houses are now full of artists and New Age entrepreneurs, and there are more than 20 galleries, craft, and antique shops. **The Old Coal Mine Museum** in town displays a variety of old loco-motives, vintage vehicles, buildings, and mining gear, and organizes the staging of Victorian melodramas in the nearby Engine House Theater.

Tiny Cerrillos has a 2,000-year history of mining turquoise, gold, copper, and coal. Today, its sleepy streets attract brows-ing tourists who particularly enjoy the fine **Casa Grande Trading Post** with its turqu-oise mining museum, rock and gift shop, and petting zoo.

⛏ Old Coal Mine Museum
2846 Hwy 14, Madrid. **Tel** (505) 438-3780. ⬜ 9:30am–5:30pm daily (Fri–Sun in winter). 📷 ♿

⛏ Casa Grande Trading Post
Cerrillos. **Tel** (505) 438-3008. 📷 ♿

An old mining cottage in Madrid, midway on the Turquoise Trail

Acoma Pueblo ❺

Rte 23, off I-40. ⬜ year-round.
⬤ some pueblo festivals. 📷
♿ partial. 🎥 obligatory. ℹ
Acoma Tourist Center (505) 552-7860. ⬜ Apr–Oct: 8am–5pm daily; Nov–Mar: 8am–6pm daily.
www.skycitytourism.com

The incredible beauty of Acoma Pueblo's setting on the top of a 357-ft- (107-m-) high mesa, has earned it the sobriquet "Sky City." Looking out over a stunning panorama of distant mountains, mesas, and plains, its high position afforded the Puebloan people natural defense against enem-ies and helped delay submis-sion to Spanish rule. Acoma is

Centuries-old houses at the Acoma Pueblo on a high plateau

one of the oldest continuously inhabited towns in the US, occupied since before the 12th century (see p39). Today, just 30 people live on the 70-acre (40-ha) mesa top year round; 6,000 others from local towns return to their ancestral home for festivals and celebrations.

As well as original pueblo buildings, the village features the 1629 mission church, San Esteben del Rey. There are also seven ceremonial *kivas (see p161)*. Acoma can be visited only on a guided tour, where expert guides explain its rich history.

Grants ❻

🏠 8,600. ℹ 100 N. Iron Street. (800) 748-2142. ▲
www.grants.org

Between the 1950s and the 1980s, Grants was famous as a center for uranium mining. Yellow rocks of the mineral were found by Navajo farmer Paddy Martinez on top of Haystack Mountain, 10 miles (16 km) from town in 1951. The industry has now declined but visitors can relive its heyday at the **New Mexico Mining Museum** – tours go underground to see a re-created mine.

Handcrafted pot from Zuni

Grants is well-placed along Hwy 40/Route 66 for exploring the sights in the area, such as the badlands of El Malpais National Monument.

⛏ New Mexico Mining Museum
100 N. Iron Street. **Tel** (505) 287-4802. ⬜ 9am–4pm Mon–Sat.
⬤ public hols. 📷 ♿

El Morro National Monument ❼

Tel (505) 783-4226. ⬜ Visitor center: Oct–May: 9am–5pm, Jun–Sep: 8am–7pm; Hiking Trail: Oct–Apr: 9am–4pm; May–Sep: 8am–6pm.
⬤ Jan 1, Dec 25. 📷 ♿ 🅿 ▲
www.nps.gov/elmo

Rising dramatically from the surrounding plain, El Morro is a long sandstone cliff that slopes gently upward to a high bluff, where it suddenly drops off. Its centerpiece is the 200-ft- (60-m-) tall Inscrip-tion Rock, which is covered with more than 300 petrogly-phs and pictographs from early pueblo people, as well as some 2,000 inscriptions left by Span-ish and Anglo travelers. For centuries, people were drawn to this remote spot by a pool of fresh water, formed by run-off and snowmelt, beneath the bluff. Here they carved their initials into the rock.

Among the signatures is that of the Spanish colonizer Don Juan de Oñate *(see p39)*, who, in 1605, wrote "pasó por aquí," meaning "passed by here." An easy half-mile (1-km) trail leads past the pool and the inscriptions on the rock.

Environs
The people of the Zuni Pueblo, 32 miles (50 km) west of El Morro, are descendants of the early mesa dwellers of the region. Today, Zuni artists are known for their fine pottery and shell mosaic jewelry. Murals depicting Zuni history can be seen in the pueblo's 17th-century mission church.

Façade of San Miguel Mission in Socorro

Socorro ⑧

Road map E4. 🏘 *10,000.*
ℹ *101 Plaza (505) 835-0424.*
www.socorro-nm.com

Socorro, meaning "aid" in Spanish, was named by explorer Juan de Oñate in 1598 when his party received help from the people of the Pilabo Pueblo, which once stood here. The area was re-settled in the early 1800s, and it was during the silver boom of the 1880s that many of the town's delightful Victorian buildings were constructed, including those surrounding the plaza. Just north of here is the 1821 San Miguel Mission, featuring massive adobe walls, supported by curved arches.

Environs
The **Bosque del Apache National Wildlife Refuge**, a renowned bird-watching area, lies 18 miles (32 km) south of Socorro. It attracts thousands of migrating snow geese and sandhill cranes in winter.

✖ Bosque del Apache National Wildlife Refuge
Hwy 1. **Tel** *(575) 835-1828.* ⬤ *daily.*
⬤ *Jan 1, Thanksgiving, Dec 25.* ♿

Truth or Consequences ⑨

Road map E4. 🏘 *7,000.* ℹ *211 Main St. (575) 894-1968.* Ⓐ

Known by locals as "T-or-C," this town changed its name from Hot Springs to Truth or Consequences for the 10th anniversary of the game show

of the same name, held here in 1950. The original hot springs still exist in the form of bath houses dotted around the town. For centuries the thermal springs had drawn Native Americans to the area, notably the famous Geronimo *(see p42).* The **Geronimo Springs Museum** has displays on local history, including a life-sized statue of the Apache warrior. Hot mineral water from an underground spring flows down the ceramic mountains of an elaborate fountain in the plaza next to the museum. The town is now a mecca for artists and other free spirits.

Truth or Consequences is a popular summer resort, close to both the **Elephant Butte Lake** and the Caballo Lake State Parks. These are famous for a wide range of outdoor

activities, including such water sports as fishing, boating, jetskiing, and windsurfing.

🏛 Geronimo Springs Museum
211 Main St. **Tel** *(575) 894-6600.*
⬤ *9am–5pm Mon–Sat.*
⬤ *Sun, public hols.* ♿

✖ Elephant Butte Lake State Park
Off I-25. **Tel** *(505) 744-5421.*
⬤ *24 hours.* **Visitor center**
⬤ *7:30am–4pm daily.* ♿ Ⓐ

Gila Cliff Dwellings National Monument ⑩

Road map D4.**Tel** *(575) 536-9461.*
⬤ *late May–early Sep: 8am–5pm daily; mid-Sep–mid-May: 8am–4:30pm daily.* ⬤ *Jan 1, Dec 25.*
www.nps.gov/gicl

The Gila (pronounced hee-la) Cliff Dwellings are one of the most remote archaeological sites in the Southwest, situated among the piñon, juniper, and ponderosa evergreens of the Gila National Forest. The dwellings occupy five natural caves in the side of a sandstone bluff high above the Gila River.

Hunter-gatherers and farmers called the Tularosa Mogollon established their 40-room village here in the late 13th century. The Mimbres

CHILE PEPPERS
The chile pepper is a potent symbol of New Mexico. Chiles were first brought to the region by Spanish colonists in 1598, and flourished in the hot, dry climate. Today, some 30,000 acres (12,000 ha) are devoted to growing many varieties of the crop, including the *chipotle, poblano,* New Mexico (or NuMex), and jalapeño peppers. New Mexican cooking is dominated by the chile, either fresh (green) or dried (red). The center of the chile-growing industry is the town of Hatch, which holds a chile festival every September on Labor Day Weekend *(see p34).*

Wreath of red dried chiles

The chile has a reputation as a cure for a range of health problems. In the 18th century, it was used to relieve the toothache. Today, capsaicin, the chemical that gives chile its heat, is added to ointments for muscle and joint pain. The chile's high vitamin C content (a large green chile contains as much as an orange), is believed to help prevent colds and flu.

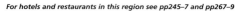

One of the entrances to the Gila Cliff Dwellings, situated high above the Gila River

Mogollon people, famous for their abstract black-and-white pottery designs, also lived in this area *(see p38)*. The ruins are accessed by a one-mile (1.6-km) roundtrip hike from the footbridge crossing the Gila River's West Fork. Allow two hours to drive to the site from Silver City as the road winds and climbs through mountains and canyons.

Silver City ⓫

Road map D5. 🏘 *12,000.* 🚌
🛈 *201 N. Hudson St. (800) 548-9378.* Ⓐ **www**.silvercity.org

As its name suggests, Silver City was a mining town. Located in the foothills of the Pinos Altos Mountains, the town's ornate Victorian architecture dates from its boom period between 1870 and the 1890s. In 1895, a flood washed away the city's main street, and in its place today is Big Ditch Park, an *arroyo* (or waterway) running 50-ft- (15-m-) deep through the town. This area was the site of the cabin where Billy the Kid *(see p225)* spent much of his youth.
Silver City has three defined historic districts – Chihuahua Hill, Gospel Hill, and the old business district – all containing buildings that evoke the town's Wild West boom-town past. The **Silver City Museum** is located in the

beautiful 1881 H.B. Ailman House, and contains frontier-era memorabilia, while the **Western New Mexico University Museum** holds the Southwest's largest collection of Mimbres pottery.
Silver City is a good base for exploring the surrounding region. The nearby forest is home to elk, deer, and bear, and there are several hiking trails and picnic areas.

🏛 **Silver City Museum**
312 W. Broadway. **Tel** *(575) 538-5921.* ◯ *9am–4:30pm Tue–Fri; 10am–4pm Sat & Sun.* ◯ *public hols.* Ⓑ **www**.silvercitymuseum.org

🏛 **Western New Mexico University Museum**
1000 W. College Ave. **Tel** *(575) 538-6386.* ◯ *9am–4:30pm Mon–Fri; 10am–4pm Sat & Sun.* ◯ *public hols.* 🈂 *donation.* ♿

Deming ⓬

Road map D5. 🏘 *14,500.*
🚌 🚉 🛈 *800 E. Pine St. (575) 546-2674; (800) 848-4955.* Ⓐ
www.demingchamber.com

The town of Deming lies 60 miles (96 km) west of Las Cruces. The Deming Luna Mimbres Museum contains excellent pieces of Mimbres pottery, frontier artifacts, and a fine gem and mineral display. Rockhounding (amateur rock and mineral collecting) takes place in **Rockhound State Park** where jasper, agate and other minerals can be found. The town is also known for its Great American Duck Race, run every August *(see p33).*

💒 **Rockhound State Park**
Highway 143. **Tel** *(575) 546 6182.*
◯ *9am–4pm daily.* 🈂 ♿

The H.B. Ailman House, home to the Silver City Museum

Glimmering white dunes of gypsum granules at White Sands National Monument ▷

Remains of the 1865 Fort Selden in Mesilla Valley

Fort Selden State Monument ⓭

Road map E5. **Tel** (575) 526-8911. ◯ 8:30am–5pm Wed–Mon. 🖼 &.

Built in 1865, this adobe fort was erected to protect settlers and railroad construction crews in the Mesilla Valley from attacks by Apaches and outlaws. Its buildings, now in ruins, once housed four companies of the 125th Infantry, a black infantry unit known as the Buffalo Soldiers. Douglas MacArthur, who was to command Allied troops in the Pacific during World War II, lived here for two years as a boy in the 1880s when his father was post commander. The fort was abandoned in 1891. Today, on the second weekend of each month, rangers dressed in period uniforms demonstrate the life of the 19th-century soldier. There are also exhibits on frontier life in the visitor center.

Sentinel statue at Fort Selden

Las Cruces ⓮

Road map E5. 🏔 78,000. ℹ 211 N. Water St. (800) 343-7827. **www**.lascrucescvb.org

Spreading out at the foot of the Organ Mountains, *Las Cruces*, or The Crosses, was named for the graves of early settlers ambushed here by the Apache in 1787 and again in 1830. It has always been a

crossroads – of frontier trails, of the railroads, and now two Interstate Highways (10 and 25). Today, it is New Mexico's second-largest city and a busy manufacturing and farming center, as well as the home of New Mexico State University.

While the town is best used as a base for exploring the region, there are a number of interesting museums here. They include the **Branigan Cultural Complex**, which houses a Cultural Center with a historical museum and fine arts museum. Tours can be arranged here of the nearby Bicentennial Log Cabin, a late 19th-century pioneer house of hand-hewn timber furnished with period antiques and artifacts.

🏛 Branigan Cultural Complex
Downtown Mall, 500 N. Water St. **Tel** (575) 541-2155. ◯ Cultural Center: 10am–4pm Mon–Fri, 9am–1pm Sat; Fine Arts Museum: 10am–2pm Tue–Fri, 9am–1pm Sat. ● public hols. &

Mesilla ⓯

Road map E5. 🏔 2,000. ℹ 211 N. Water St. (800) 343-7827. **www**.oldmesilla.org

This town was established in 1850 by a group of residents who preferred to remain in Mexican territory, when most of New Mexico came under

American rule. However, with the Gadsden Purchase of 1854 *(see p41)*, Mesilla became part of the United States.

Today, Mesilla exudes the atmosphere of a late-19th-century frontier town, especially around the historic plaza. It was here, in Mesilla's former courthouse, that Billy the Kid *(see p225)* was sentenced to hang in 1881. **The Gadsden Museum** contains exhibits on local history and cultures.

🏛 Gadsden Museum
Hwy 28 & Boutz Rd. **Tel** (575) 526-6293. ◯ 9–11am & 1–5pm Mon–Sat, 1–5pm Sun. ● public hols. 🖼 &

Billy the Kid gift shop in the 19th-century town of Mesilla

El Paso ⓰

Road map E5. 🏔 700,000. ✈ 🚊 🚌 ℹ 1 Civic Center Plaza (915) 534-0600; (800) 351-6024. **www**.visitelpaso.com

Large and sprawling, El Paso, Texas, is a key entry point to New Mexico and the Southwest. Facing El Paso on the other side of the Rio Grande is its Mexican sister town of Ciudad Juárez. They share the border, which was established in 1963 after disputes concerning the Rio Grande had been resolved. From the city, Interstate I-10 travels north to Las Cruces and west across southern Arizona. The Amtrak train *Sunset Limited (see p296)* stops at El Paso three times a week.

The Spanish named their early settlement here *El Paso del Norte* (Northern Pass) in

The 1692 Socorro Mission on El Paso's Mission Trail

the late 16th century. It was a stopping place on the famous King's Highway *(Camino Real, see p25)*, which linked Mexico to Spain's northern territories. The city's history as a major hub is reflected today in its typically Southwestern mix of Native American, Hispanic, and European cultures.

El Paso has a series of outstanding mission churches, including the Ysleta and the Socorro, both dating from 1692, while the lovely Chapel San Elizario was built in 1789. **Mission Socorro** combines Native and Spanish styles, with *vigas* (wooden ceiling beams). Major renovations were carried out in 2003.

El Paso's western heritage is further reflected in its links with the famous outlaw Billy the Kid *(see p225)*, who visited the town in 1876 to get his

partner out of jail. Today, El Paso is a center for Western wear, with many stores selling cowboy boots and hats.

🚊 Mission Socorro
Tel (915) 851-8339. ◯ *limited; call in advance.* 🖼 ⅻ ⌗ *obligatory.*

White Sands National Monument ⑰

Road map E4. *Tel (575) 679-2599.* ◯ *Visitor Center: 8am–7pm daily; Dunes Drive: 7am–9pm daily.* ● *Dec 25.* 🖼 ⅻ ⌗ www.nps.gov/whsa

The glistening dunes of the White Sands National Monument rise up from the Tularosa Basin at the northern end of the Chihuahuan Desert. It is the world's largest gypsum

dune field, covering around 300 sq miles (800 sq km). Gypsum is a water soluble mineral, rarely found as sand. But here, with no drainage outlet to the sea, the sediment washed by the rain into the basin becomes trapped. As the rain evaporates dry lakes form, and strong winds blow the gypsum up into the vast fields of rippling dunes.

Visitors can explore White Sands by car on the Dunes Drive, a 16-mile (26-km) loop. Four clearly marked trails lead from points along the way, including the wheelchair-accessible Interdune Boardwalk. Year-round ranger-led walks introduce visitors to the dunes' flora and fauna. Only plants that grow quickly enough not to be buried survive, such as the soaptree yucca. Most of the animals are nocturnal, and include coyotes and porcupines.

The park is surrounded by the White Sands Missile Range. For safety the park and road leading to it (Hwy 70) may shut for up to two hours during testing. **White Sands Missile Range Museum** displays many of the missiles tested here.

🏛 White Sands Missile Range Museum
US 70, 25 m (40 km) E. of Las Cruces. Tel (575) 678-2250. ◯ *8am–4:30pm Mon–Fri, 10am–3pm Sat & Sun.* ● *pub hols.* ⅻ www.wsmr-history.org

Soaptree yucca plants growing at White Sands National Monument

Colorful shops along Ruidoso's attractive main street

Alamogordo ⑱

Road map E4. 🏠 *35,000.* ✈
🛈 *1301 N. White Sands Blvd.*
(575) 437-6120; (800) 826-0294.
www.alamogordo.com

Alamogordo was established
as a railroad town in 1898 by
two New York entrepreneurs,
Charles and John Eddy. Its
wide streets are lined with
cottonwood trees, which reflect
its origins and are at the root
of its name – Alamogordo
means "fat cottonwood" in
Spanish. Located at the foot of
the Sacramento Mountains, the
town was a sleepy backwater
until World War II, when construction of the nearby Holloman Air Force Base sparked
its development as a major
defense research center.

The town is only 15 miles
(21 km) from White Sands
National Monument *(see
p223)* and offers many
opportunities for such outdoor activities as hiking,
biking, and golf, especially
in the Lincoln National
Forest on Alamogordo's
eastern border. In town
the **New Mexico Mu-
seum of Space History** is
a fascinating museum
housed in a golden-
glass, cube-shaped
building. The museum
focuses on the history
of the space race, with
exhibits detailing living
conditions inside
a space station, a
full-size replica of
Sputnik, the first
space satellite, and
a simulated walk in
space to repair the

Hubble Space Telescope.
Another simulator offers the
chance to land the space
shuttle. The Space Hall also
includes the IMAX™ Dome,
a large-screen theater.

**🏛 New Mexico Museum
of Space History**
Scenic Drive. **Tel** *(575) 437-2840;
(877) 333-6589.* ◻ *9am–5pm daily.*
● *Thanksgiving, Dec 25.* 🎟 ♿

Cloudcroft ⑲

Road map E4. 🏠 *750.*
🛈 *Cloudcroft Chamber of
Commerce, Hwy 82 (575) 682-2733.*
Ⓐ **www**.cloudcroft.net

The picturesque mountain
town of Cloudcroft was
established in 1898 as a center
for the lumber trade. Perched
at 8,650 ft (2,600 m) in the
Sacramento Mountains,
the village soon became a
favorite vacation spot for
those escaping the summer
heat of the valley below.
Cloudcroft remains a
popular resort, with its
summer population
more than doubling the
number of year-round
residents. Burro Avenue,
running parallel to the
main highway, looks
much as it did at the turn
of the 20th century with
its rustic timber build-
ings (many are quaint
gift shops). Surrounded
by Lincoln National
Forest, the town
offers many outdoor
sports – mountain
biking, hunting, fish-
ing, skiing, and golf.

**Launch vehicle, Museum
of Space History**

Ruidoso ⑳

Road map E4. 🏠 *7,000.* 🛈 *720
Sudderth Drive (575) 257-7395.* Ⓐ
www.ruidoso.net

Nestled high in the
Sacramento Mountains,
surrounded by cool pine
forest, Ruidoso is one of
New Mexico's fastest growing
resorts. Sudderth Drive is the
long main street lined with
shops, art galleries, cafés, and
restaurants. Here, specialty
shops sell everything from
candles to cowboy boots.

Outdoor activities are the
area's major attraction, with
hiking, horseback riding, and
fishing. There are several golf
courses including the **Links
at Sierra Blanca**, a top-rated
18-hole course. Northwest
of the town is **Ski Apache**.
Owned and operated by the
Mescalero Apache Tribe, it is
famous for its warm-weather
powder snow. The town is
best known for horse racing.
Quarter horse (fast over a quarter of a mile) and thoroughbred racing at **Ruidoso Downs
Racetrack**. The track hosts the
All American Futurity, held
each Labor Day (the first Monday in September). The world's
richest quarter horse race, it
has prize money in excess of
$2 million. The Ruidoso Downs
Racehorse Hall of Fame
exhibits racing memorabilia.
The **Hubbard Museum of the
American West** contains
Western memorabilia, the
heart of which is a collection
of more than 10,000 pieces
assembled by a wealthy New
Jersey horsewoman, Anne
Stradling (1913–92). Formerly

BILLY THE KID

When he died, Billy the Kid was one of the Old West's most notorious outlaws. Born Henry McCarty in 1859, it is believed he changed his name to William Bonney in 1877, when he killed his first victim in Arizona.

Billy fled to Lincoln, where he was hired by John Tunstall and Alexander McSween, who had set up a store competing with one run by Lawrence Murphy and James Dolan. In February 1878, when Dolan's men murdered Tunstall, Billy helped to form the Regulators, who set out to get justice. The Lincoln County War followed, culminating with a violent battle in July. Billy escaped, but was captured by Sheriff Pat Garrett two years later and returned to Lincoln to be hung. Once again, however, he escaped. Billy was eventually shot, by Garrett, at Fort Sumner on July 14, 1881. In spite of his violent life, Billy was a local hero. His story and deeds are memorialized in the little town of Lincoln.

Wild West outlaw, Billy the Kid

One of the historic buildings along Lincoln's main street

Lincoln ㉑

Road map E4. 100. Hwy 380E Lincoln. (575) 653-4025. 8:30am–4:30pm daily. public hols. www.ruidosonow.com

The peacefulness of this small town, surrounded by the beautiful countryside of the Capitan Mountains, belies its violent past. It was the center of the 1878 Lincoln County War, a battle between rival ranchers and merchants involving the legendary Billy the Kid. In those days, Lincoln County covered one-quarter of the state, and Lincoln itself was the county seat.

Lincoln is now a state monument, with 11 buildings kept as they were in the late 1800s. At the Lincoln County Courthouse you can see where Billy the Kid was held, and the bullet hole in the wall from his escape. Tunstall Store has its shelves stocked with original 19th-century merchandise. The Historic Lincoln Visitor Center & Museum has displays on the Apache people, the early Hispanic settlers, and the Buffalo Soldiers all-black regiment from Fort Stanton, as well as the Lincoln County War.

known as the Museum of the Horse, its artifacts range from fine art to horse-drawn carriages. Outside is the fabulous *Free Spirits at Noisy Water* (1995), a monument of seven larger-than-life-sized horses by local artist Dave McGary (b.1958). Every October, the town celebrates life in the Old West with the Lincoln County Cowboy Symposium, which features country music and dancing, celebrity roping, and a chuck wagon cook-off.

Set on a high mesa a few miles north at Alto is the **Spencer Theater for the Performing Arts**, a state-of-the-art venue for theater, music, and dance. Built by Albuquerque architect Antoine Predock in 1997, this sandstone building has a spectacular mountain backdrop.

Links at Sierra Blanca
105 Sierra Blanca Dr. **Tel** (575) 258-5330.

Ski Apache
www.skiapache.com

Ruidoso Downs Racetrack
Hwy 70. **Tel** (575) 378-4431. May–early Sep.

Hubbard Museum of the American West
841 Hwy 70 West. **Tel** (575) 378-4142. 9am–5pm daily. Thanksgiving, Dec 25. www.hubbardmuseum.org

Spencer Theater for the Performing Arts
Airport Rd. **Tel** (575) 336-4800; (888) 818-7872.

The bronze monument, *Free Spirits at Noisy Water* (1995), at the Hubbard Museum of the American West

Carlsbad Caverns National Park ㉒

Located in the remote southeastern corner of New Mexico, Carlsbad Caverns National Park protects one of the world's largest cave systems. Geological forces carved out this complex of chambers, and their decorations began to be formed around 500,000 years ago when dripping water deposited drops of the crystalized mineral calcite. Native pictographs near the Natural Entrance indicate that they had been visited by Native peoples, but it was cowboy Jim White who brought them to national attention, after exploring them in 1901. The caverns were made a national park in 1930, and a United Nations World Heritage Site in 1995, one of 20 in the US.

Underground Lunchroom
A paved section of the cavern is home to a popular underground diner, a kitsch souvenir store, and restrooms.

King's Palace Tour
This tour takes in the deepest cave open to the public, 830 ft (250 m) below ground.

The Boneyard is a complex maze of dissolved limestone rock.

Queens Chamber and Papoose Room

Doll's Theater
This small cave is named for its size. The Doll's Theater resembles a fairy grotto, filled with fine, luminous soda-straw formations.

The Big Room
A self-guided tour takes in the 14-acre (5.6-ha) Big Room and passes features such as the Bottomless Pit.

Visitor Information Center

Natural Entrance

Rock of Ages

Bottomless Pit

VISITORS' CHECKLIST

Road map F5. 3225 National Parks Hwy, Carlsbad. **Tel** (575) 785-2232; (800) 967-2283 (tour reservations). ✈ to Carlsbad. 🚌 to White's City. 🕐 May–Aug: 8:30–5pm daily; Sep–mid-May: 8:30–3:30pm (Natural Entrance) call for last entry times. ● Dec 25. 🅿️ 🚻 partial. 📷 **www**.nps.gov/cave

Bat Cave

Most summer evenings at dusk, clouds of free-tailed bats emerge from the bat cave to cross the desert in search of food.

Doll's Theater

Painted Grotto

0 meters   100

0 yards   100

TOURS

▬ Big Room route

▬ Natural Entrance route

▬ King's Palace tour (Ranger guided only)

Butterfly and lobelia flowers, Living Desert State Park

Carlsbad ㉓

Road map F5. 🏠 25,000. 🅸 302 S. Canal St. (505) 887-6516; (800) 221-1224. Ⓐ **www**.carlsbadchamber.com

The town of Carlsbad is located just 20 miles (32 km) northeast of Carlsbad Caverns National Park. There are plenty of hotels as well as opportunities for outdoor activities. (White's City also has accommodations; *see p247*.) The Pecos River winds through town, there are three lakes, and fishing, boating, and water-skiing are popular pastimes. At the northern edge of town, the Living Desert State Park has exhibits focusing on the ecology of the Chihuahuan Desert *(see p20)*.

Roswell ㉔

Road map F4. 🏠 50,000. 🅸 912 N. Main St. (575) 624-7704. 🕐 8:30am–5:30pm Mon–Fri, 8:30am–4pm Sat, 9am–3pm Sun. **www**.roswellmysteries.com

Once a small ranching town, Roswell is now a byword for aliens and UFOs, due to the Roswell Incident. The **International UFO Museum and Research Center** is devoted to the serious investigation of visitors from outer space and features an extensive collection of newspaper clippings, photographs, and maps of the crash site. A 70-minute film contains over 400 interviews with people connected to the crash.

Roswell's highly respected **Museum and Art Center** houses a collection of 2,000 artifacts on the history of the American West. The fascinating Robert H. Goddard Collection details 11 years of his experiments *(see p187)*.

Roswell's Alien Zone symbol

🏛 **International UFO Museum and Research Center** 114 N. Main St. **Tel** (575) 625-9495. 🕐 daily. 🚻 www.iufomrc.org

🏛 **Roswell Museum and Art Center** 100 W. 11th St. **Tel** (575) 624-6744. 🕐 9am–5pm daily (from 1pm Sun). ● Jan 1, Thanksgiving, Dec 25. 🚻 **www**.roswellmuseum.org

THE ROSWELL INCIDENT

Near midnight on July 4, 1947 an unidentified airborne object crash-landed during a storm in the Capitan Mountains, 75 miles (120 km) northwest of town. Jim Ragsdale was camping nearby and claims to have seen a flash and a craft, 20 ft (6 m) in diameter, hurtling through the trees and the bodies of four "little people," with skin like snakeskin. However, Ragsdale did not tell his story until 1995.

The US Air Force issued a statement that a flying saucer had been recovered, and the story spread around the world. By July 9, however, they said it was just a weather balloon. Witnesses were allegedly sworn to secrecy, fuelling rumors of a cover-up and alien conspiracy theories to this day.

Officers examine "alien" material

TRAVELERS' NEEDS

WHERE TO STAY

The Southwest has a long history of hospitality that is reflected in the wide variety of accommodations on offer to the visitor. Whether luxurious five-star resorts or simple rustic lodges suit your budget, there is a wealth of options. You can choose modern hotels, historic or cozy bed and breakfasts, convenient motels, or fully equipped apartments. For those seeking Western-style adventure, there are dude ranches, many of which are luxurious lodgings with horseback rid-

Weatherford Hotel sign in Flagstaff

ing. Across the range, all are likely to offer private bathrooms and clean, comfortable rooms. Las Vegas hotels are noted for their themes and size and have widely varying prices, depending on occupation and whether you wish to stay mid-week or on weekends. Across the rest of the region prices also tend to vary according to the season. The listings provided on pages 232–47 recommend more than 200 places in all price ranges, each representing the best of their kind.

Traditional adobe architecture of the Hotel Santa Fe façade

HOTEL CLASSIFICATIONS

The tourist industry throughout the Southwest is recognized for its quality lodgings. A guideline to travelers is the diamond rating system of the **American** and **Canadian Automobile Associations** (AAA and CAA). Every accommodation, from the one-diamond motel to the five-diamond resort hotel, is rated for service, cleanliness, and the facilities offered. AAA members also benefit from discounts when they book in advance.

TAXES

Accommodations tax varies across the region as it is charged by both state and city or county governments. Expect to pay between 10 and 14 percent of the room price in tax. Prices given for hotels in this book include taxes.

LUXURY HOTELS

In the Southwest, hotels come in every shape and size, including historic showplaces, such as Grand Canyon's El Tovar *(see p233)*, originally built to impress East Coast investors and prove that the Southwest was an exciting tourist destination. Today, some of the most lavish hotels in the US are located in the region, from the extravagant, themed mega-resorts of Las Vegas *(see pp237–40)* to the Wigwam Resort in Phoenix *(see p235)*, with its three championship 18-hole golf courses, tennis courts, and gourmet dining. The area around Phoenix and southern Arizona is famous for both its luxury health and golf resorts. Small, independently owned

"boutique" hotels offer luxurious facilities combined with an intimate atmosphere and attentive service.

There are also many hotels aimed specifically at corporate travelers, offering weekly rates and computer and fax outlets in the rooms, although these services are now available in a range of hotels.

CHAIN HOTELS AND MOTELS

For the most part, you can count on efficient service, moderate prices, and comfortable (if bland) surroundings at a chain hotel. The most popular chains include **Holiday Inn**, **Comfort Inn**, **Best Western**, **Ramada Inns**, **Econolodge**, and **Super 8**. Particularly good value are suite hotels, such as **Country Inn and Suites** and **Embassy**

A hotel in the Best Western chain

Suites, which offer living rooms and kitchenettes for little more than the cost of a basic hotel room. Chain hotels also offer central reservation systems that can help you find a room at peak times. Motels provide rooms that are usually accessible from the parking area. They are often the only option in remote areas, and can vary from nostalgic Route 66 places *(see pp50–51)* to such bargain lodgings as Motel 6.

Starlight Pines Bed and Breakfast in Flagstaff *(see p232)*

HISTORIC INNS AND BED AND BREAKFASTS

There are many excellent inns and bed and breakfasts across the Southwest. Inns tend to be larger, with more spacious public areas and a dining room. B&Bs are usually noted for their more homey atmosphere. Both inns and B&Bs may be found in restored or reconstructed historic buildings, and many are located in charming Victorian houses in historic towns. These lodgings pride themselves on providing a warm welcome and friendly service. Visual delights often include antiques, art, and gardens. There are Bed and Breakfast and Inn associations in each state that can help you select and make bookings.

WESTERN HOTELS AND DUDE RANCHES

If you want to indulge your "Old West" fantasies, there are plenty of historic hotels in which to do so. Between 1880 and 1920, Western towns gained prestige through the quality and grandeur of their hotels, and many built during this time boast extravagantly ornate decor. Today, many of these places have been carefully restored and offer great settings for a vacation. Durango's Strater Hotel *(see p242)*, for example, is both a historic hotel and a museum.

Dude ranches offer visitors the chance to experience western life. They first appeared in the 1920s – the name "dude" is a colloquialism meaning "a city-dweller unfamiliar with life on the range." Choices range from relaxing vacations that include leisurely horseback rides to working ranches where you participate in such activities as cattle roundups. Meals, accommodations, and horses are usually included in the price. Arizona and Colorado have **Dude Ranch Associations** to help you find the perfect western vacation.

NATIONAL PARK FEES

An entrance fee is charged at many – but not all – state and national parks. The national park fee is usually charged per vehicle and must be paid separately to access hotels and restaurants within national park areas. If you plan to visit several national parks during your trip, consider buying an $80 annual pass. See the National Park Service website (www.nps.gov) for more details. Fees for entry to state parks are not included in national park passes.

CAMPGROUNDS AND RV PARKS

Campgrounds for both tents and RVs (recreational vehicles) are found all over the Southwest and are especially popular in the national parks. The **National Forest Service** provides information on forest campgrounds, which range from extremely basic to those with running water and limited RV hookups.

DIRECTORY

CHAIN HOTELS

Best Western
Tel (800) 528-1234.

Comfort Inn
Tel (800) 221-2222.

Country Inn and Suites
Tel (800) 456-4000.

Econolodge
Tel (800) 424-4777.

Embassy Suites
Tel (800) 362-2779.

Holiday Inn
Tel (800) 465-4329.

Ramada Inns
Tel (800) 272-6232.

Super 8
Tel (800) 800-8000.

HISTORIC INNS AND BED AND BREAKFASTS

Arizona Association of Bed and Breakfast Inns
c/o AABBI President, 3380 E. Lockett Rd., Flagstaff, AZ 86004. *Tel* (800) 752-1912. www. arizona-bed-breakfast.com

Bed and Breakfasts of New Mexico
www.bedandbreakfast.com

New Mexico Bed and Breakfast Association
Tel (800) 661-6649.
www.nmbba.org

DUDE RANCHES

Arizona Dude Ranch Association
P.O. Box 603, Cortaro, AZ 85652. www.azdra.com.

Colorado Dude and Guest Ranch Association
8007 County Rd. 887, Gunnison, CO 81230.
Tel (970) 887-3128.

CAMPGROUNDS AND RV PARKS

National Forest Service
Southwest Regional Office, 333 Broadway SE, Albuquerque, NM 87102. *Tel* (877) 444 6777.
www.reserveusa.com

Choosing a Hotel

The hotels in this guide have been selected for their good value, excellent facilities, or location. Entries are given alphabetically within price category. Prices given are in-season rates, but always enquire about special discounts as rates can vary from week to week and between weekdays and weekends. For restaurant listings, see pages 252–69.

PRICE CATEGORIES IN US DOLLARS ($)
For a standard double room per night, including service charges and any additional taxes.
$ Under $100
$$ $100–$150
$$$ $150–$300
$$$$ $300–$500
$$$$$ Over $500

GRAND CANYON AND NORTHERN ARIZONA

CAMP VERDE Camp Verde Comfort Inn
$
340 N. Goswick Way, AZ, 86322 **Tel** *(928) 567-9000* **Fax** *(928) 567-1828* **Rooms** *85*　　　**Road map** *B4*

A clean chain motel with an outdoor heated pool, the Comfort Inn is located on I-17 in the Verde River Valley, just 3 miles (5 km) from Montezuma Castle and other local sights. It offers a less pricey alternative to hotels in nearby Sedona and Jerome. Try the make-your-own waffles at their complimentary breakfast. **www.choicehotels.com**

COTTONWOOD Best Western Cottonwood Inn
$$
993 S. Main St., AZ, 86326 **Tel** *(928) 634-5575* **Fax** *(928) 634-5576* **Rooms** *78*　　　**Road map** *B3*

At the base of Mingus Mountain, this chain hotel is in the heart of the Verde River Valley, a few miles from Tuzigoot National Monument and the Dead Horse Ranch State Park. Amenities include comfortable rooms (some with fridges), a heated pool most of the year, and a Continental breakfast. **www.bestwesterncottonwoodinn.com**

FLAGSTAFF Hotel Weatherford
$
23 North Leroux St., AZ, 86001 **Tel** *(928) 779-1919* **Fax** *(928) 773-8951* **Rooms** *10*　　　**Road map** *C3*

Located just a block from the Santa Fe Railroad Station, this 1897 sandstone building, with an elegant wraparound veranda, was once a haven for passing politicians, authors, and gunslingers. Reasonably priced, its restored rooms are decorated with antiques but have no telephone or TV. A few have shared baths. **www.weatherfordhotel.com**

FLAGSTAFF Hilton Garden Inn
$$
350 W. Forest Meadows St., AZ, 86001 **Tel** *(928) 226-8888* **Fax** *(928) 556-9059* **Rooms** *90*　　　**Road map** *C3*

Hikers and bikers appreciate the indoor pool, sauna, and whirlpool spa of this hotel, located near downtown and Northern Arizona University. Rooms are equipped with microwaves and refrigerators, two phones, and free Internet. Take advantage of a Stay-Fit Kit – mat, ball, and dumbbells – for an in-room workout. **www.hiltongardeninn.com**

FLAGSTAFF Hotel Monte Vista
$$
100 N. San Francisco St., AZ, 86001 **Tel** *(928) 779-6971* **Fax** *(928) 779-2904* **Rooms** *50*　　　**Road map** *C3*

This 1926 four-story brick hotel boasts an illustrious past. Rooms are named for the celebrities who stayed here, from Bob Hope to John Wayne, and, more recently, rock star Jon Bon Jovi. There's a long list of resident ghosts, too. The Monte Vista is close to the railroad, so you might need to ask for earplugs. **www.hotelmontevista.com**

FLAGSTAFF Little America Hotel
$$$
2515 E. Butler Ave., AZ, 86004 **Tel** *(928) 779-2741* **Fax** *(928) 779-7983* **Rooms** *247*　　　**Road map** *C3*

Head straight for the pool, surrounded by ponderosa pines, at this attractive hotel just minutes from downtown. Save time for a walk along the Coconino Forest Trail, or enjoy family fun time in a game of horseshoe, volleyball, or croquet. Rooms are comfortably decorated with French Provençal furniture. **www.littleamerica.com/flagstaff**

FLAGSTAFF Radisson Woodlands Hotel Flagstaff
$$$
1175 W. Route 66, AZ, 86001 **Tel** *(928) 773-8888* **Fax** *(928) 773-0597* **Rooms** *183*　　　**Road map** *C3*

Take advantage of the treadmill and other machines at this upscale chain hotel located near downtown, off Route 66 and just minutes from Sunset Crater and the Native American ruins at Wupatki. Upgrade to a room with a Sleep Number Bed, which adjusts mattress comfort at the touch of a button. **www.flagstaffwoodlandshotel.com**

FLAGSTAFF Starlight Pines Bed & Breakfast
$$$
3380 E. Lockett Rd., AZ, 86001 **Tel** *(928) 527-1912 or (800) 752-1912* **Rooms** *4*　　　**Road map** *C3*

The Victorian-style Starlight Pines is accessed via a wraparound porch with white wicker furniture. The B&B features a crackling fire and rooms filled with fresh flowers, antiques, and Tiffany lamps. Start the day with a whiff of the pine-scented air mixed with the aroma of the Grand Marnier French toast. **www.starlightpinesbb.com**

GRAND CANYON Phantom Ranch
$
Grand Canyon, AZ, 86023 **Tel** *(303) 297-2757* **Fax** *(303) 297-3175* **Rooms** *40*　　　**Road map** *B3*

Few visitors to the Grand Canyon are given the opportunity to stay in the beautiful Phantom Ranch, far below the Canyon rim. The rustic lodge and timber cabins are reached by rafting the Colorado River, by hiking, or by mule. Segregated accommodation is dormitory-style, in bunk beds. Book very early. **www.grandcanyonlodges.com**

Key to Symbols *see back cover flap*

GRAND CANYON (NORTH RIM) Grand Canyon Lodge

Grand Canyon, AZ, 86052 **Tel** *(480) 337-1320* **Fax** *(303) 297-3175* **Rooms** *205*   **Road map** *B3*

It's a long drive to the Canyon's North Rim, with more convenient access from Utah. Even then, it's a long way to the rim's edge, from where this rustic limestone lodge with motel-style rooms overlooks the Kaibab Plateau. Its log cabins are popular. The lodge is open seasonally, and reservations are a must. **www.grandcanyonlodges.com**

GRAND CANYON (SOUTH RIM) Bright Angel Lodge

Grand Canyon Village, AZ, 86023 **Tel** *(303) 297-2757* **Fax** *(303) 297-3175* **Rooms** *89*   **Road map** *B3*

Make bookings well in advance to get one of the renovated edge-of-the-canyon cabins, priced well below similar lodgings at El Tovar *(see below)*. Designed by Mary Elizabeth Colter in 1935, this historic log-and-stone lodge is very popular. Low-priced motel-like rooms and cabins also got spruced up. **www.grandcanyonlodges.com**

GRAND CANYON (SOUTH RIM) Maswik Lodge

Grand Canyon Village, AZ, 86023 **Tel** *(303) 297-2757* **Fax** *(303) 297-3175* **Rooms** *278*   **Road map** *B3*

This family-friendly lodge, consisting of two buildings sitting among ponderosa pines, is a quarter-mile south of the Canyon rim. The south-facing rooms have all the basics but no air conditioning, while the more spacious north rooms have all mod cons. The rustic cabins can be booked only during the summer. **www.grandcanyonlodges.com**

GRAND CANYON (SOUTH RIM) Thunderbird and Kachina Lodges

Grand Canyon Village, AZ, 86023 **Tel** *(303) 297-2757* **Fax** *(303) 297-3175* **Rooms** *140*   **Road map** *B3*

Right on the Canyon rim, these two lodges have very comfortable family rooms featuring large picture windows and amenities such as a refrigerator, a safe, and full baths. Partial Canyon views can be seen from half the rooms in each lodge, for a slightly higher price. Restaurants are within walking distance. **www.grandcanyonlodges.com**

GRAND CANYON (SOUTH RIM) Yavapai Lodge

Grand Canyon Village, AZ, 86023 **Tel** *(303) 297-2757* **Fax** *(303) 297-3175* **Rooms** *358*   **Road map** *B3*

Those making late reservations will likely find rooms at the Yavapai, near the Market Village, a half-mile from the Canyon rim and the visitors' center, and conveniently located near a general store, bank, and post office. East-facing rooms are air conditioned; west rooms have fans and vaulted ceilings. **www.grandcanyonlodges.com**

GRAND CANYON (SOUTH RIM) El Tovar Hotel

Grand Canyon Village, AZ, 86023 **Tel** *(303) 297-2757* **Fax** *(303) 297-3175* **Rooms** *78*   **Road map** *B3*

Located on the South Rim, this historic landmark lodge celebrated its centennial in 2005. Renowned for luxury in its heyday, when it was visited by the likes of Albert Einstein and Elizabeth Taylor, El Tovar is still the premier lodge in the park. Its distinctive design includes natural stone and Douglas fir. **www.grandcanyonlodges.com**

JEROME Ghost City Inn Bed & Breakfast

541 N. Main St., AZ, 86331 **Tel** *(928) 634-4678 or (888) 634-4678* **Rooms** *6*   **Road map** *B4*

Nestled among Jerome's ghosts and galleries, this 1890s copper miners' boarding house has been made into a tasteful inn. Perched high atop Cleopatra Hill, with views over the Verde River Valley, it has individually decorated rooms. Breakfast is served in the drawing room or on the back patio, next to a waterfall. **www.ghostcityinn.com**

KINGMAN Best Western A Wayfarer's Inn & Suites

2815 E. Andy Devine Ave./Route 66, AZ, 86401 **Tel** *(928) 753-6271* **Fax** *(928) 753-9608* **Rooms** *101* **Road map** *B3*

A comfortable chain hotel with a seasonal outdoor pool and an indoor spa. The Wayfarer's Inn is located a short drive from the Powerhouse Museum, which exhibits Route 66 memorabilia, and the Kingman Army Airfield Museum, displaying World War II airplanes. **www.bestwesternarizona.com**

LAKE HAVASU CITY Hampton Inn

245 London Bridge Rd., AZ, 86403 **Tel** *(928) 855-4071* **Fax** *(928) 855-2379* **Rooms** *162*   **Road map** *A4*

The Hampton Inn has become one of the most popular hotels in town. Just a quarter-mile from the lake, it has many rooms with balconies and lake views. All rooms have refrigerators and microwaves. Guests can try their skill at the horseshoe pit, or take the walking trail to the beach. **www.hamptoninn.com**

LAKE HAVASU CITY Heat

1420 Mcculloch Blvd., AZ, 86403 **Tel** *(888) 898-4328* **Fax** *(928) 854-1130* **Rooms** *17*   **Road map** *A4*

This boutique hotel, with stylish contemporary design and European accents, is a stone's throw from London Bridge and a welcome addition to the town. The plush rooms have views of the bridge and the Bridgewater Channel. The inn places a big emphasis on service. Guests have included Brad Pitt and Angelina Jolie. **www.heathotel.com**

PAGE Best Western at Lake Powell

208 N. Lake Powell Blvd., AZ, 86040 **Tel** *(928) 645-5988* **Fax** *(928) 645-2578* **Rooms** *132*   **Road map** *C2*

In the heart of Page, with views of Glen Canyon Dam and the Vermillion Cliffs, this reliable chain hotel decorated in Southwestern desert colors is within walking distance of shops, restaurants, tour outfitters, and the John Wesley Powell Museum. It has a large outdoor pool and extensive parking facilities. **www.bestwesternarizona.com**

PAGE Courtyard by Marriott

600 Clubhouse Dr., AZ, 86040 **Tel** *(928) 645-5000* **Fax** *(928) 645-5004* **Rooms** *150*   **Road map** *C2*

Surrounded by the lush green fairways of the 18-hole Lake Powell National Championship Golf Course, the Courtyard features upscale rooms in a beautiful Southwestern-style building. Lounge by the pool, book a golf package, see the nearby Glen Canyon Dam, or spend your day on Lake Powell. **www.courtyard.com**

SEDONA Star Motel ⑤
295 Jordan Rd., AZ, 86336 **Tel** *(928) 282-3641* **Rooms** *11* **Road map** C3

Located smack in the center of uptown Sedona, this small, unassuming motel is a real find for budget-minded families. Rooms might be short on romance or atmosphere, but they are spotlessly clean. The Star Motel's main claim to fame is that it's close to everything, and it even has views of Sedona's beautiful red rocks.

SEDONA Amara Resort and Spa ⑤⑤⑤
310 N. Hwy 89A, AZ, 86336 **Tel** *(928) 282-4828* **Fax** *(928) 282-4825* **Rooms** *100* **Road map** C3

This boutique resort, just steps from uptown, has stylish furnishings and vibrant colors. The ambience emphasizes comfort and service. Take a swim in the saltwater pool, or indulge your senses at the Amara Spa. Spend the evening stargazing with a glass of wine, on a comfy cushion next to the fire pit. **www.amararesort.com**

SEDONA Cozy Cactus B&B ⑤⑤⑤
80 Canyon Circle Dr., AZ, 86351 **Tel** *(928) 284-0082* **Fax** *(928) 284-4210* **Rooms** *5* **Road map** C3

The family-friendly Cozy Cactus is attractively furnished with Southwestern accents that complement its stunning view of Bell Rock, Courthouse Butte, and Castle Rock. Relax on the terrace and listen for the call of the coyotes. After breakfast, lace up your boots and hike on unofficial trails, right out the back gate. **www.cozycactus.com**

SEDONA Enchantment Resort ⑤⑤⑤⑤⑤
525 Boynton Canyon Rd., AZ, 86336 **Tel** *(928) 282-2900* **Fax** *(928) 282-9249* **Rooms** *236* **Road map** C3

Hidden among the red rocks of Boynton Canyon, the Enchantment pulls out all the stops for luxury and pampering. Its adobe *casitas* have typically Southwestern interiors. The leisure activities on offer include hiking, biking, croquet, and tennis, plus a full-service spa. Camp Coyote offers a program for children. **www.enchantmentresort.com**

WAHWEAP Lake Powell Resort ⑤⑤
100 Lakeshore Dr., AZ, 86040 **Tel** *(928) 645-2433* **Fax** *(928) 645-1031* **Rooms** *348* **Road map** C2

This resort sits right on the edge of Lake Powell, overlooking Wahweap Marina. Its upscale rooms, each with a balcony or patio, are located in eight two-story buildings. Half of them boast lake views. Activities available at the hotel and at the Glen Canyon National Recreation Area include boat rentals and cruises. **www.lakepowell.com**

WILLIAMS Mountain Side Inn Grand Canyon ⑤
642 E. Route 66, AZ, 86046 **Tel** *(928) 635-4431* **Fax** *(928) 635-2292* **Rooms** *96* **Road map** B3

Tucked away among the tall pines of Kaibab National Forest, the unpretentious Mountain Side Inn is convenient for travelers on their way to the Grand Canyon and is a good base for long walks. Those looking for more action will enjoy the karaoke in the Route 66 Lounge. **www.mountainsideinngrandcanyon.com**

WILLIAMS Grand Canyon Railway Hotel ⑤⑤⑤
235 North Grand Canyon Blvd., AZ, 86046 **Tel** *(928) 635-4010* **Fax** *(928) 635-2180* **Rooms** *297* **Road map** B3

This elegant hotel adjoins the railway terminus that has seen visitors depart by train to the Grand Canyon for a century. The lofty lobby is reminiscent of yesteryear's grand railway hotels. In winter, its fireplace crackles a warm welcome. A nearby pet resort has rooms for dogs and custom condos for cats – no kidding! **www.thetrain.com**

PHOENIX AND SOUTHERN ARIZONA

APACHE JUNCTION Best Western Apache Junction Express Inn ⑤⑤
1101 W. Apache Trail, AZ, 85220 **Tel** *(480) 982-9200* **Fax** *(480) 671-6183* **Rooms** *40* **Road map** C4

East of Phoenix, and convenient to the Apache Trail, this chain hotel has striking views of Superstition Mountain, site of the legendary Lost Dutchman Goldmine. Featuring a Southwestern theme throughout, the small hotel offers comfortable, clean rooms, an outdoor pool, and a deluxe complimentary breakfast. **www.bestwestern.com**

BISBEE Shady Dell ⑤
1 Old Douglas Rd., AZ, 85603 **Tel** *(520) 432-3567* **Rooms** *11* **Road map** C5

High up in the Mule Mountains, close to the Mexican border, the Shady Dell offers a truly unique experience. Step back in time to the 1950s and spend the night in a vintage trailer, such as a sleek aluminum 1949 Airstream or a 1950 Spartanette, while listening to old rhythm-'n'-blues cassette tapes. **www.theshadydell.com**

BISBEE Copper Queen Hotel ⑤⑤⑤
11 Howell Ave., AZ, 85603 **Tel** *(520) 432-2216* **Fax** *(520) 432-3819* **Rooms** *53* **Road map** C5

With its rolltop desk at reception and antique-filled rooms decorated with period wallpaper, the Copper Queen is an early 1900s hotel that welcomed dignitaries in the city's long-gone boomtown days. Today, visitors can cool off in a claw-foot tub (some rooms only) or take a dip in the second-floor pool. **www.copperqueen.com**

DOUGLAS The Gadsden Hotel ⑤
1046 G Ave., AZ, 85607 **Tel** *(520) 364-4481* **Fax** *(520) 364-4005* **Rooms** *160* **Road map** C5

Enter one of the most opulent lobbies in the West at the historic Gadsden, where Eleanor Roosevelt, Lee Marvin, and Shelley Winters once stayed. Prices are reasonable at this hotel with a majestic marble staircase, marble columns topped with gold leaf, and an authentic 42-ft- (13-m-) long Tiffany stained-glass mural. **www.hotelgadsden.com**

DRAGOON Triangle T Guest Ranch

$$$

I-10 exit 318, Dragoon Rd., AZ, 85609 **Tel** *(520) 586-7533* **Fax** *(520) 586-4476* **Rooms** *10* **Road map** *C5*

Situated in the cool Dragoon Mountains in the Texas Canyon, the Triangle T is close to the Kartchner Caverns, Tombstone, and the Amerind Foundation. Its rustic cabins are just steps away from fields of gigantic boulders, popular with birdwatchers, hikers, and artists. Horseback riding is available. **www.triangletguestranch.com**

GREEN VALLEY Best Western Green Valley

$$

111 S. La Cañada Drive, AZ, 85614 **Tel** *(520) 625-2250* **Fax** *(520) 625-0215* **Rooms** *108* **Road map** *C5*

Located mere minutes from the "white dove of the desert," the San Xavier del Bac church, this reliable chain hotel has comfortable rooms and attractive landscaping. Save some time for a swim in the pool after birdwatching at the nearby Madera Canyon, part of a migratory corridor for over 300 bird species. **www.bestwesterngreenvalley.com**

PHOENIX Best Western Central Phoenix Inn & Suites

$$

1100 N. Central Ave., AZ, 85004 **Tel** *(602) 252-2100* **Fax** *(602) 252-2731* **Rooms** *107* **Road map** *B4*

As its name implies, this hotel is indeed centrally located, within walking distance of the city's famous museums and Copper Square. It has an outdoor pool and spa, and a dry sauna in which to chill out after using the fitness center. There are beautiful views of downtown from the rooms on its upper floors. **www.bestwesterncentralphoenix.com**

PHOENIX Quality Inn & Suites

$

202 E. McDowell Rd., AZ, 85004 **Tel** *(602) 955-6600* **Fax** *(602) 258-7259* **Rooms** *48* **Road map** *B4*

A good downtown base for visiting the Phoenix Art Museum, the Quality Inn chain hotel is also only a few blocks from the Heard Museum and offers a free weekday shuttle to Copper Square and the Convention Center. In the summer months, you can escape the hot weather in the outdoor pool. **www.choicehotels.com**

PHOENIX Clarendon Hotel and Suites

$$$

401 W. Clarendon Ave., AZ, 85013 **Tel** *(602) 252-7363* **Fax** *(602) 274-9009* **Rooms** *105* **Road map** *B4*

The trendy Clarendon has an interior reminiscent of Art Deco, and cutting-edge lighting: undulating cobalt-blue and salmon-red lights glow late into the night at its chic French-fusion Camus restaurant. The hotel is located in the business district and offers many perks, including free nationwide calls and free parking. **www.theclarendon.net**

PHOENIX Hotel San Carlos

$$$

202 N. Central Ave., AZ, 85004 **Tel** *(602) 253-4121* **Fax** *(602) 253-6668* **Rooms** *128* **Road map** *B4*

This historic hotel is full of character and charm. Despite some small rooms, it's priced right and filled with nostalgia. Its legendary guest roster includes the likes of Mae West, Clark Gable, and Marilyn Monroe, plus, of course, the obligatory resident ghost. A rooftop pool and a sidewalk café complete the picture. **www.hotelsancarlos.com**

PHOENIX Radisson Hotel Phoenix City Center

$$$

3600 N. 2nd Ave., AZ, 85031 **Tel** *(602) 604-4900* **Fax** *(602) 604-4901* **Rooms** *274* **Road map** *B4*

A breath of fresh air in the city, the upscale Radisson boasts a lovely gazebo garden and two outdoor pools with a massive rock waterfall, plus a rooftop pool, tennis courts, a putting green, and a children's playground. Visitors can also take advantage of the complimentary parking. **www.radisson.com/phoenixaz_citycenter**

PHOENIX Arizona Grand Resort

$$$$

7777 S. Pointe Parkway, AZ, 85044 **Tel** *(602) 438-9000* **Fax** *(602) 431-6535* **Rooms** *640* **Road map** *B4*

This family-friendly resort offers golf, tennis, horseback riding, and a spa. Its pièce de résistance, exclusive to guests, is The Oasis, a waterpark with a slide, a wave pool, and the Zuni River. Each balcony suite has a living room and a wet bar. There are miles of hiking trails in the adjacent South Mountain Preserve. **www.arizonagrandresort.com**

PHOENIX Embassy Suites Phoenix-Biltmore

$$$$

2630 E. Camelback Rd., AZ, 85016 **Tel** *(602) 955-3992* **Fax** *(602) 955-6479* **Rooms** *232* **Road map** *B4*

An exquisite towering atrium filled with tall palms, the sound of waterfalls, and exotic Japanese koi-carp ponds greet visitors at this all-suite hotel. Start the day with a complimentary cooked-to-order breakfast, then visit the exclusive Biltmore Fashion Park adjacent to the hotel. **www.phoenixbiltmore.embassysuites.com**

PHOENIX Ritz-Carlton Hotel

$$$$

2401 E. Camelback Rd., AZ, 85016 **Tel** *(602) 468-0700* **Fax** *(602) 468-0793* **Rooms** *281* **Road map** *B4*

Standing 11 stories tall, the Ritz-Carlton has refined, elegant decor throughout and far-reaching views of the downtown Phoenix skyline, Camelback Mountain, and Squaw Peak. Store your golf bag here, and you will get a complimentary shine for those grassy golf shoes. There are additional fees for valet parking. **www.ritzcarlton.com**

PHOENIX The Wigwam Resort

$$$$

300 E. Wigwam Blvd., Litchfield Pk., AZ, 85251 **Tel** *(623) 935-3811* **Fax** *(623) 935-3737* **Rooms** *331* **Road map** *B4*

This sprawling resort west of downtown was once an Egyptian-cotton plantation in the Sonoran Desert; parts of the agricultural area are now occupied by three magnificent golf courses. Oversized, elegant *casita*-style rooms provide a sense of privacy. Guests can relax at the brand-new Elizabeth Arden Red Door Spa. **www.wigwamresort.com**

PHOENIX Arizona Biltmore Resort & Spa

$$$$$

2400 E. Missouri Ave., AZ, 85016 **Tel** *(602) 955-6600* **Fax** *(602) 381-7600* **Rooms** *738* **Road map** *B4*

This legendary 1930s resort is heralded for its Frank Lloyd Wright-inspired architecture. Enjoy afternoon tea and experience the same luxuries as royalty and statesmen, in the lush surroundings where Irving Berlin penned "White Christmas." Play lawn chess or golf, or order your pet a meal through room service. **www.arizonabiltmore.com**

SCOTTSDALE Hotel Valley Ho
$$$$

6850 E. Main St., AZ, 85251 **Tel** *(480) 248-2000 or (866) 882-4484* **Rooms** *194*   **Road map** *inset map*

A sophisticated playground for the likes of Bogart and Monroe, the Valley Ho became a hip haven when it reopened after major renovations. Retro-chic rooms have glass walls opening onto balcony views to Camelback Mountain. Also available are a yoga-Pilates studio, 24-hour fitness and room service, and tubs for two. **www.HotelValleyHo.com**

SCOTTSDALE Fairmont Scottsdale Princess
$$$$$

7575 E. Princess Dr., AZ, 85255 **Tel** *(480) 585-4848* **Fax** *(480) 585-0091* **Rooms** *651*   **Road map** *inset map*

This relaxed resort features Spanish Colonial architecture, with a tiled roof, arches, pink stucco, and fountains. Rooms are spacious, luxurious, and decorated in earthy accents, with many amenities. The Princess is noted for its two Tournament Players Club golf courses, Willow Stream spa, and kids' club. **www.fairmont.com/scottsdale**

SCOTTSDALE Hyatt Regency Scottsdale Resort and Spa at Gainey Ranch
$$$$$

7500 E. Doubletree Ranch Rd., AZ, 85258 **Tel** *(480) 444-1234* **Fax** *(480) 483-5550* **Rooms** *490*   **Road map** *inset map*

This elegant resort with exquisite modern decor is close to the Old Town. With ten pools, a sandy beach, and tall palms, it's truly a water playground. The spacious rooms, full of deluxe amenities, all have views. Activities include championship golf, a spa, and the fascinating Native American Learning Center. **www.scottsdale.hyatt.com**

SCOTTSDALE The Phoenician
$$$$$

6000 E. Camelback Rd., AZ, 85251 **Tel** *(480) 941-8200* **Fax** *(480) 947-4311* **Rooms** *647*   **Road map** *inset map*

From the art collection to the enchanting cactus garden, or the spa's Meditation Atrium, The Phoenician is a place where lavish opulence mixes with nature's beauty. The graceful rooms have muted tones, marble bathrooms, and selected artworks. Championship golf is also on offer, along with a pampering service. **www.thephoenician.com**

TOMBSTONE Silver Nugget Bed & Breakfast
$

520 E. Allen St., AZ, 85638 **Tel** *(520) 457-9223* **Fax** *(520) 457-3471* **Rooms** *4*   **Road map** *C5*

Sit on the only balcony overlooking dusty Allen Street, and conjure up the 1881 shootout involving Wyatt Earp and Doc Holliday and immortalized in *Gunfight at the OK Corral*. Tombstone was once ruled by cowboys, gunfighters, and gamblers. Did any of them sleep in your bed? **www.tombstone1880.com/silvernugget**

TOMBSTONE Best Western Lookout Lodge
$$

781 N. Hwy 80 W., AZ, 85638 **Tel** *(520) 457-2223* **Fax** *(520) 457-3870* **Rooms** *40*   **Road map** *C5*

Within walking distance of the Boothill Graveyard, where the OK Corral gunslingers were laid to rest, the Lookout Lodge is a good base for seeing the sights of Tombstone, while escaping the hustle and bustle of Allen Street. All rooms have views of the Dragoon Mountains, and the hotel is very pet-friendly. **www.bestwesternarizona.com**

TUCSON El Presidio Bed & Breakfast Inn
$$

297 N. Main Ave., AZ, 85701 **Tel** *(520) 623-6151* **Fax** *(520) 623-3860* **Rooms** *4*   **Road map** *C5*

Close to Old Town Artisans and the Tucson Museum of Art, this Victorian adobe inn, an American Territorial-style home from 1886, is located in a neighborhood of elegant mansions known as Snob Hollow. Filled with antiques, it has a lush and shady courtyard garden and offers fine gourmet breakfasts. **www.bbonline.com/az/elpresidio**

TUCSON Hacienda del Sol Guest Ranch Resort
$$$

5601 N. Hacienda del Sol Rd., AZ, 85718 **Tel** *(520) 299-1501* **Fax** *(520) 299-5554* **Rooms** *30*   **Road map** *C5*

At the foot of the Santa Catalina Mountains, the Hacienda del Sol once housed a school attended by the rich and famous. It is now a relaxing luxury resort with exquisite rooms decorated in warm Southwestern tones and Spanish Colonial design. Go horseback riding, or get a jade-stone massage at the spa. **www.haciendadelsol.com**

TUCSON Royal Elizabeth Bed & Breakfast Inn
$$$

204 S. Scott Ave., AZ, 85701 **Tel** *(520) 670-9022* **Fax** *(928) 833-9974* **Rooms** *6*   **Road map** *C5*

The meticulously restored 1878 Victorian adobe mansion is located in a historic downtown district. Affectionately known as "The Liz," it is richly appointed with original antiques and beautiful woodwork. The list of amenities includes a heated pool, hot tub, garden, and delicious gourmet breakfasts. **www.royalelizabeth.com**

TUCSON Windmill Suites at St. Philip's Plaza
$$$

4250 N. Campbell Ave., AZ, 85718 **Tel** *(520) 577-0007* **Fax** *(520) 577-0045* **Rooms** *122*   **Road map** *C5*

Located on the northern edge of Tucson, at the foot of the Santa Catalina Mountains, the Windmill is part of a pleasant plaza with shops, galleries, and restaurants. It offers spacious accommodation in its two-room suites, guest use of bicycles, a lending library, and a complimentary breakfast. Good value. **www.windmillinns.com**

TUCSON Arizona Inn
$$$$

2200 E. Elm St., AZ, 85719 **Tel** *(520) 325-1541* **Fax** *(520) 881-5830* **Rooms** *95*   **Road map** *C5*

This historic pink-stucco boutique inn is in the heart of Tucson. Individually decorated rooms in *casitas* are spread throughout its lush gardens. Guests feel right at home with complimentary high tea, fireside drinks in the library in winter, and in summertime, ice creams poolside. Clay tennis courts are also available. **www.arizonainn.com**

TUCSON Lodge on the Desert
$$$$

306 N. Alvernon Way, AZ, 85711 **Tel** *(520) 325-3366* **Fax** *(520) 327-5834* **Rooms** *103*   **Road map** *C5*

In operation since 1936, this is an urban oasis near the University of Arizona, with views of the Santa Catalina Mountains. Lodging is in hacienda-style rooms, many with high, wood-beamed ceilings, fireplaces, and tiled patios. Towering palm trees preside over the pool, surrounded by lush desert gardens. **www.lodgeonthedesert.com**

Key to Price Guide *see p232* **Key to Symbols** *see back cover flap*

TUCSON White Stallion Ranch 🖼️🍴🏊🚗🛏️ $$$$

9251 W. Twin Peaks Rd., AZ, 85743 **Tel** *(520) 297-0252* **Fax** *(520) 744-2786* **Rooms** *45* **Road map** *C5*

In the Sonoran Desert, this working ranch allows city slickers to see longhorn cattle and weekly rodeos. Guests can ride Western-style among the saguaro cacti, and take hayrides to cookouts. The Southwestern-style rooms have comfy amenities. Great for families, with outdoor games, a petting zoo, and a pool. **www.wsranch.com**

TUCSON Tanque Verde Guest Ranch 🍴🏊🚗🛏️ $$$$$

14301 E. Speedway Blvd., AZ, 85748 **Tel** *(520) 296-6275* **Fax** *(520) 721-9426* **Rooms** *74* **Road map** *C5*

At the base of the Rincon Mountains, next to Saguaro National Park, this ranch was founded in 1868. With weekly barbecues featuring Western singalongs, cowboy-style breakfasts, and morning horseback rides, it is a great place for families wishing to enjoy nature and outdoor living. Spacious Southwestern-style rooms. **www.tvgr.com**

LAS VEGAS

BOULDER CITY El Rancho Boulder Motel 🏊🛏️ $

725 Nevada Hwy, NV, 89005 **Tel** *(702) 293-1085* **Fax** *(702) 293-3021* **Rooms** *38*

With a wonderful 1950s neon sign outside, this family-run hotel is 20 minutes from the Vegas Strip, and convenient to both Hoover Dam and Lake Mead. The El Rancho prides itself on its caring staff, and offers comfortable, clean rooms at budget prices. Guests can use the poolside BBQ grills. **www.elranchoboulder.com**

DOWNTOWN Binion's Gambling Hall & Hotel 📺🍴🏊🛏️ $

128 E. Fremont St., NV, 89101 **Tel** *(702) 382-1600 or (800) 937-6537* **Fax** *(702) 384-9246* **Rooms** *365*

For 35 years, this hotel was synonymous with the World Series Poker Championship. Binion's neon horseshoe is now gone, and the Poker Series has moved on, but the hotel's Gambling Hall still has its regulars. Affordable rooms are decorated in pink, and the Poker Room Hall of Fame is popular. Guests can relax in the rooftop pool. **www.binions.com**

DOWNTOWN Four Queens Hotel & Casino 📺🍴 $

202 E. Fremont St., NV, 89101 **Tel** *(702) 385-4011 or (800) 634-6045* **Fax** *(702) 385-4011* **Rooms** *690*

One of the most prominent hotels on Fremont Street, the Four Queens occupies an entire downtown block. Renovated rooms have 32-in flat-screen TVs and wireless Internet access. Popular with locals, the hotel is ideal for budget-conscious visitors. Home of Hugo's Cellar restaurant *(see p257)*. **www.fourqueens.com**

DOWNTOWN Main Street Station Casino Brewery & Hotel 📺🍴 $

200 N. Main St., NV, 89101 **Tel** *(702) 387-1896 or (800) 713-8933* **Fax** *(702) 386-4421* **Rooms** *406*

Gas lamps and wrought iron on the facade hint at the treasures inside this hotel. Its casino is a vision straight out of the Old West, with stained-glass windows and tin ceilings. Its collection of antiques – Bill Cody's private railcar, chandeliers from the Figaro Opera House – is priceless. Excellent buffet. A real find. **www.mainstreetcasino.com**

DOWNTOWN Plaza Hotel & Casino 📺🍴🏊🚗🛏️ $

1 Main St., NV, 89101 **Tel** *(702) 386-2110 or (800) 634-6575* **Fax** *(702) 382-8281* **Rooms** *1,037*

Formerly owned by casino legend Jackie Gaughan, the Plaza stands over the Fremont Street Experience, above the old Union Railroad Depot. The comfortable rooms get filled up when NASCAR events are in town. There's a quarter-mile jogging track around a rooftop pool, a fitness center, and four tennis courts. **www.plazahotelcasino.com**

DOWNTOWN El Cortez Hotel & Casino 📺🍴 $$

600 E. Fremont St., NV, 89101 **Tel** *(702) 385-5200 or (800) 634-6703* **Fax** *(702) 474-3626* **Rooms** *300*

The El Cortez has undergone a major renovation – upgraded rooms and a revamped casino – but it still maintains a cool vintage feel. Affordable room rates mean more dollars in your pocket for shows, dining, and tempting Lady Luck. You may even glimpse casino legend Jackie Gaughan at a poker table here. **www.elcortezhotelcasino.com**

DOWNTOWN Fitzgeralds Casino Hotel 📺🍴🏊🛏️ $$$

301 E. Fremont St., NV, 89101 **Tel** *(702) 388-2400 or (800) 274-5825* **Fax** *(702) 388-2183* **Rooms** *638*

The 34-story Fitzgeralds towers over downtown Vegas. Its upper-floor rooms, especially those facing the Strip, have far-reaching views. There is also a pool, which is rare for downtown hotels, and a small balcony facing the Fremont Street Experience. The show *Fitz of Laughter* features Kevin Burke. **www.fitzgeraldslasvegas.com**

DOWNTOWN Golden Nugget Hotel & Casino 📺🍴🏊🚗🛏️ $$$

129 E. Fremont St., NV, 89101 **Tel** *(702) 385-7111 or (800) 896-5336* **Fax** *(702) 386-8362* **Rooms** *1,907*

A favorite with businessmen and families, this is downtown's most luxurious hotel. On display here is the world's largest gold nugget, "Hand of Faith", weighing over 61 lb (30 kg). The sizable rooms have vast marble baths. The hotel's latest addition is The Tank, a 200,000-gallon shark aquarium in the pool. **www.goldennugget.com**

HENDERSON Green Valley Ranch Resort, Spa and Casino 📺🍴🏊🚗🛏️ $$$

2300 Paseo Verde Parkway, NV, 89052 **Tel** *(702) 617-7777 or (866) 782-9487* **Fax** *(702) 617-7778* **Rooms** *490*

The Green Valley Ranch has luxury decor and a hip reputation. It serves the fast-growing eastern neighborhoods of the Las Vegas Valley, as well as celebrities. Its rambling pool with posh pillowed lounges is a big draw, as is the adjacent shopping area, The District. Free shuttle to the Strip. **www.greenvalleyranchresort.com**

OFF STRIP Palms Casino Resort

4321 W. Flamingo Rd., NV, 89103 **Tel** *(702) 942-7777 or (866) 942-7777* **Fax** *(702) 942-7001* **Rooms** *703*

Palms Casino Resort is a hit with the hip crowd, with a fire-spewing nightclub (Rain), the Ghostbar's fabulous views, a 14-screen movie complex, and a popular on-site tattoo studio. The Fantasy Tower features a Playboy Club, the $15,000-a-night Kingpin Suite, with bowling lanes, and the $40,000 Hugh Hefner Suite. **www.palms.com**

OFF STRIP Hard Rock Hotel & Casino

4455 Paradise Rd., NV, 89109 **Tel** *(702) 693-5000 or (800) 473-7625* **Rooms** *645*

On Rehab Sundays at the Hard Rock Hotel, it's all glamor by the pool – this is such a hip hangout, it's got its own website (www.rehablv.com). The hotel rocks inside, too, with musical memorabilia in every corner and a sunken casino. Big-name musicians perform at The Joint. Rooms are equipped with Bose hi-fi systems. **www.hardrockhotel.com**

THE STRIP Riviera Hotel & Casino

2901 Las Vegas Blvd. S., NV, 89109 **Tel** *(702) 734-5110 or (800) 634-3420* **Fax** *(702) 794-9663* **Rooms** *2,100*

One of the Strip's oldest hotels, the Riviera opened in 1955 and features a gargantuan, busy casino. There are nightly shows, ranging from *Ice*, with performers from the Moscow Ice Circus, to comedy and the *Crazy Girls* daring but memorable revue. Rooms are economical but could do with a little refurbishment. **www.rivierahotel.com**

THE STRIP Bally's Las Vegas

3645 Las Vegas Blvd. S., NV, 89109 **Tel** *(702) 967-4111 or (800) 634-3434* **Fax** *(702) 967-4405* **Rooms** *2,814*

A swirl of colorful neon decorates Bally's. Its renovated and sizable rooms are well priced considering the location. A convenient shopping passage leads to Paris Las Vegas *(see p239)*. Try the sumptuous Sunday buffet, or see the long-running showgirl revue *Jubilee!* Tennis courts and an Olympic-size pool complete the picture. **www.ballyslv.com**

THE STRIP Bill's Gamblin' Hall & Saloon

3595 Las Vegas Blvd. S., NV, 89109 **Tel** *(702) 737-2100 or (866) 245-5745* **Fax** *(702) 894-9954* **Rooms** *200*

Formerly known as the Barbary Coast, Bill's Gamblin' Hall sits on a busy (and noisy) corner of the Strip. This tiny hotel has a vintage feel, with its stained glass, oak, and brass accents. Its casino is popular and its rooms are reasonably priced, but be sure to book well in advance. **www.billslasvegas.com**

THE STRIP Circus Circus

2880 Las Vegas Blvd. S., NV, 89109 **Tel** *(702) 734-0410 or (800) 343-9182* **Fax** *(702) 734-5897* **Rooms** *3,773*

Recognizable by its neon clown marquee and vast hot-pink glass dome, this family-friendly hotel houses the Adventure Dome, with its exciting rides. Circus acts take place twice hourly on the mezzanine, and there are trapeze performances over one of the three casinos. Kids love the large video arcade. **www.circuscircus.com**

THE STRIP Excalibur

3850 Las Vegas Blvd. S., NV, 89109 **Tel** *(702) 597-7777 or (877) 750-5464* **Fax** *(702) 597-7009* **Rooms** *3,991*

Bright-blue-and-red castle turrets sit atop this medieval-themed, family-friendly resort, complete with court jesters. The nightly Tournament of Kings dinner show follows the medieval theme. Rooms are reasonably priced, and there is a large casino. The monorail runs to the Luxor *(see below)* and Mandalay Bay *(see p239)*. **www.excalibur.com**

THE STRIP Flamingo Las Vegas Hotel & Casino

3555 Las Vegas Blvd. S., NV, 89109 **Tel** *(702) 733-3111 or (888) 902-9929* **Fax** *(702) 733-3328* **Rooms** *3,642*

Mobster Bugsy Siegel's vision got him killed, but his Flamingo Hotel was the forerunner of today's mega-complexes, with its glittering neon bloom in front and its swank Go Rooms. The place to be is the pool, set in a 15-acre garden with cascading waterfalls. The free Wildlife Habitat houses flamingos and penguins. **www.flamingolv.com**

THE STRIP Harrah's Las Vegas Casino & Hotel

3475 Las Vegas Blvd. S., NV, 89109 **Tel** *(702) 369-5000 or (800) 214-9110* **Fax** *(702) 369-6014* **Rooms** *2,820*

One of the older, moderately priced hotels, Harrah's is in the mid-Strip heartbeat. Rooms are decorated in earth tones and have lots of marble accents. The hotel's spa facility is one of the Strip's best. This one-time haunt of Sammy Davis, Jr. hosts great entertainment and is convenient to the monorail. **www.harrahs.com**

THE STRIP Imperial Palace Hotel & Casino

3535 Las Vegas Blvd. S., NV, 89109 **Tel** *(702) 731-3311 or (800) 351-7400* **Fax** *(702) 735-8328* **Rooms** *2,700*

The tiny, blue-roof pagoda in front is just the tip of this sprawling property. A favorite with tour groups, the resort features Asian-themed rooms and common areas. The highlight here is the Automobile Museum, displaying a selection of classic and collectible cars, all of which are for sale. **www.imperialpalace.com**

THE STRIP Luxor Hotel & Casino

3900 Las Vegas Blvd. S., NV, 89119 **Tel** *(702) 262-4000 or (877) 386-4658* **Fax** *(702) 262-4423* **Rooms** *4,408*

The Luxor's 30-story glistening black-glass pyramid is graced by a ten-story replica Sphinx and Cleopatra's Needle. Inside, Ramses statues tower over the entrance to a large casino. Rooms are decorated in earth tones, with Art Deco accents. Visit the Bodies and the Titanic exhibitions. A fun hotel for the entire family. **www.luxor.com**

THE STRIP MGM Grand Hotel & Casino

3799 Las Vegas Blvd. S., NV, 89109 **Tel** *(702) 891-1111 or (877) 880-0880* **Fax** *(702) 891-3036* **Rooms** *5,044*

The MGM Grand is presided over by a huge bronze lion. The Habitat area inside houses real lions. The Grand Tower rooms are contemporary, while those in the West Wing have a sleek upscale look. Bring walking shoes to get around the vast casino. An arena features concerts and premier sports events. **www.mgmgrand.com**

Key to Price Guide *see p232* **Key to Symbols** *see back cover flap*

THE STRIP Monte Carlo Resort & Casino

3770 Las Vegas Blvd. S., NV, 89109 **Tel** *(702) 730-7777 or (888) 529-4828* **Fax** *(702) 730-7214* **Rooms** *3,002*

This hotel has a subtle Mediterranean flavor, with an elegant fountain and facade, and comfortable rooms in its tall towers. Andre's, a famous downtown French restaurant, also opened here. Master magician Lance Burton amazes the crowds in the Victorian-style theater – watch the chandelier! **www.montecarlo.com**

THE STRIP New York New York Hotel & Casino

3790 Las Vegas Blvd. S., NV, 89109 **Tel** *(702) 740-6969 or (866) 815-4365* **Fax** *(702) 740-6700* **Rooms** *2,023*

Vegas's version of the Big Apple features replicas of New York's famed skyline, a wraparound yellow roller coaster speeding through the complex, and a 150-ft (46-m) Statue of Liberty. The NY theme continues with Greenwich Village, complete with parking meters, and a kid-friendly Coney Island arcade. **www.nynyhotelcasino.com**

THE STRIP Paris Las Vegas

3655 Las Vegas Blvd. S., NV, 89109 **Tel** *(702) 946-7000 or (877) 603-4386* **Fax** *(702) 946-4405* **Rooms** *2,916*

A half-size replica of the Eiffel Tower stands outside this hotel. One of the tower's legs is located right in the middle of the hotel's lovely casino. Exterior facades include beautiful renditions of the Arc de Triomphe and the Paris Opera House. There are great people-watching opportunities from the sidewalk bistro. **www.parislv.com**

THE STRIP Planet Hollywood Resort & Casino

3667 Las Vegas Blvd. S., NV, 89109 **Tel** *(702) 785-5555 or (866) 919-7472* **Fax** *(702) 785-5511* **Rooms** *2,567*

At the heart of the Strip, this resort offers gaming, fine dining restaurants, and an award-winning buffet. Get pampered at the full service spa or take a stroll through the Miracle Mile Mall, home to 170 hip fashion shops, specialty stores, and restaurants. The resort is also home to the hit show *Peepshow*. **www.planethollywood.com**

THE STRIP Sahara Hotel & Casino

2535 Las Vegas Blvd. S., NV, 89109 **Tel** *(702) 737-2654 or (866) 382-8884* **Fax** *(702) 791-2027* **Rooms** *1,720*

With its arched neon dome and Moroccan theme, the Sahara has graced the Strip since 1952. Its Speed roller coaster spins around the NASCAR Café. Rooms are standard, with gemstone colors, but for this location the price is excellent. Close to the Stratosphere *(see below)* and the Convention Center. **www.saharavegas.com**

THE STRIP Stratosphere

2000 Las Vegas Blvd. S., NV, 89104 **Tel** *(702) 380-7777 or (800) 998-6937* **Fax** *(702) 380 7732* **Rooms** *2,400*

Standing 113 stories above Las Vegas Boulevard, the Stratosphere is the place for a classic Strip view. Daredevils can experience the world's highest rides: Insanity, X-Scream, and Big Shot, which catapults riders upward 160 ft (48 m) in 2.5 seconds. Rooms are comfortable, and the pool has Strip views, too. **www.stratospherehotel.com**

THE STRIP Treasure Island

3300 Las Vegas Blvd. S., NV, 89109 **Tel** *(702) 894-7111 or (800) 288-7206* **Fax** *(702) 894-7623* **Rooms** *2,885*

This mid-Strip hotel and casino has undergone a major renovation that has upgraded the guestrooms and added a poker room. The decor is contemporary and the hotel is popular with tourists and business travelers alike. See Cirque du Soleil's spectacular production, *Mystère*, or the hotel's free pirate show, *Sirens of TI*. **www.treasureisland.com**

THE STRIP Bellagio

3600 Las Vegas Blvd. S., NV, 89109 **Tel** *(702) 693-7111 or (888) 987-6667* **Fax** *(702) 693-8585* **Rooms** *3,933*

The east-facing rooms at the Bellagio overlook dancing-to-music fountains, as do several excellent restaurants. This Tuscan-themed hotel is dressed in marble and silk, with mosaic floors and the garden-of-glass lobby ceiling. The Gallery of Fine Art features outstanding exhibitions, including one showing Picasso ceramics. **www.bellagio.com**

THE STRIP Caesars Palace

3570 Las Vegas Blvd. S., NV, 89109 **Tel** *(702) 731-7110 or (866) 227-5938* **Fax** *(702) 866-1700* **Rooms** *3,340*

The ever-expanding Caesars is a Vegas institution. Its Roman-statuary theme carries over to the Forum shops, while the Coliseum arena hosts huge showbiz names, like Cher and Bette Midler. The swanky rooms, all with marble baths, are housed in five separate towers. Great restaurants and a gorgeous pool area. **www.caesarspalace.com**

THE STRIP Mandalay Bay

3950 Las Vegas Blvd. S., NV, 89119 **Tel** *(702) 632-7777 or (877) 632-7800* **Fax** *(702) 632-7108* **Rooms** *3,215*

The Mandalay Bay stands tall on the South Strip, surrounded by a shimmering golden glow. Its luxurious rooms have many amenities and spectacular views. Its elegant lobby has an aquarium – a hint of the Aquarium attraction on site. Everyone loves the vast pool area, with sandy beaches, a wave pool, and a jogging track. **www.mandalaybay.com**

THE STRIP The Mirage

3400 Las Vegas Blvd. S., NV, 89109 **Tel** *(702) 791-7111 or (800) 374-9000* **Fax** *(702) 791-7414* **Rooms** *3,044*

A gamble that paid off, the Mirage is fronted by a booming, fiery volcano exploding over waterfalls. Check in at the lobby's long, tropical aquarium, and walk through a lush garden to the casino. Out back, you can see the famous Secret Garden, filled with exotic lions and tigers, and the Dolphin Habitat. Rooms are pleasant. **www.mirage.com**

THE STRIP The Venetian Resort Hotel Casino

3355 Las Vegas Blvd. S., NV, 89109 **Tel** *(702) 414-1000 or (877) 883-6423* **Fax** *(702) 414-1100* **Rooms** *4,027*

Stop by the canal for a gondola ride and marvel at the exquisite architectural facade replicating Venice's main landmarks (sadly marred by banners promoting inside attractions, like *Phantom of the Opera*). The beautiful rooms have sunken seating areas. Sidewalk cafés surround a replica of St. Mark's Square. **www.venetian.com**

THE STRIP Tropicana Resort & Casino   🏨 🍴 🏊 📶 🅿️ $$$$$
3801 Las Vegas Blvd. S., NV, 89109 **Tel** *(702) 739-2222 or (888) 826-8767* **Fax** *(702) 739-3648* **Rooms** *1,874*

The Tropicana has been on a prime South Strip corner since 1957, and the views are spectacular. Waterfalls in lush gardens spill into lagoon pools famed for summertime swim-up blackjack, and its casino ceiling is beautiful. Bedspreads in the rooms have tropical colors. **www.tropicanalv.com**

THE STRIP Wynn Las Vegas   🏨 🍴 🏊 📶 🅿️ $$$$$
3131 Las Vegas Blvd. S., NV, 89109 **Tel** *(702) 730-7777 or (888) 529-4828* **Fax** *(702) 770-1500* **Rooms** *2,716*

A creation of the hotelier Steve Wynn, this dramatic casino resort is exclusive and refined. The amenities, hotel services, and guest rooms set new standards in Vegas. Features a championship golf course, a Maserati car dealership, and a theater production, *Le Rêve*, created by Franco Dragone **www.wynnlasvegas.com**

SUMMERLIN Red Rock Casino, Resort and Spa   🏨 🍴 🏊 📶 🅿️ $$$
11011 W. Charleston Blvd., Las Vegas, NV, 89135 **Tel** *(702) 797-7777* **Fax** *(702) 797-7053* **Rooms** *816*

Close to Red Rock Canyon, this hotel is filled with crystal chandeliers, rare granite, and artworks, and it attracts a fair share of celebs. Rooms have sleek furnishings, huge plasma TVs, and great views. Day-care facilities, bowling, a movie complex, and nearby world-class golf are other benefits. **www.redrocklasvegas.com**

SOUTHERN UTAH

BOULDER Boulder Mountain Lodge   🏨 🍴 🅿️ $$
20 N. Hwy 12, UT, 84716 **Tel** *(435) 335-7460* **Fax** *(435) 335-7461* **Rooms** *20*   **Road map** *C2*

Leave no carbon footprint at this small Western-style eco-lodge. After a day of hiking in the sandstone canyons, guests can relax in the hot tub, visit the bird sanctuary, or roast marshmallows at the stone fire pit. Next door, the Hell's Backbone grill *(see p261)* is touted as one of Utah's best restaurants. **www.boulder-utah.com**

BRYCE CANYON Best Western Ruby's Inn   🏨 🍴 🏊 $$$
1000 S. Hwy 63, Bryce, UT, 84764 **Tel** *(435) 834-5341* **Fax** *(435) 834-5265* **Rooms** *368*   **Road map** *B2*

This has-it-all complex starts with a grand lobby and offers both rooms in the main building and motel-style accommodation, not to mention restaurants, a general store, gas station, post office, and an art gallery. Several tour desks offer adventure activities. **www.bestwesternutah.com**

BRYCE CANYON Bryce Canyon Lodge   🍴 🅿️ $$$
Bryce Canyon National Park, UT, 84717 **Tel** *(303) 297-2757* **Fax** *(303) 297-3175* **Rooms** *115*   **Road map** *B2*

Built in the 1920s of sandstone and pine, the Bryce Canyon Lodge has a cozy, rustic feel. Decorated with replica hickory furniture, rooms are comfortable, as are the cabins, with gas-log fireplaces. There are no TVs, so guests spend their time walking along nearby trails. Open Apr–Oct. **www.brycecanyonlodge.com**

CEDAR BREAKS NATIONAL MONUMENT Cedar Breaks Lodge & Spa 🏨 🍴 🏊 📶 🅿️ $$
223 Hunter Ridge Rd., Brian Head, UT, 84719 **Tel** *(435) 677-3000* **Fax** *(435) 677-4275* **Rooms** *118*   **Road map** *B2*

This is a popular winter spot for skiers. After a long day on the slopes, they come to soothe their muscles in the fireside Jacuzzi, or to try the hot-stone therapy in the spa. An elegant modern resort, the Cedar Breaks has spacious rooms and storage for skis and bikes, and is a pleasant spot in the summer, too. **www.cedarbreakslodge.com**

CEDAR CITY Crystal Inn Cedar City   🍴 🏊 📶 $$
1575 W. 200 North St., UT, 84720 **Tel** *(435) 586-8888* **Fax** *(435) 586-1010* **Rooms** *100*   **Road map** *B2*

Conveniently located close to a major highway, the Crystal Inn sits at the gateway to several national parks. It offers a shuttle service to the airport and has an outdoor pool, as well as an indoor hot tub and sauna. Those attending the famous Utah Shakespearean Festival should make early reservations. **www.crystalinncedar.com**

ESCALANTE Prospector Inn   🍴 🅿️ $
380 W. Main St., UT, 84726 **Tel** *(435) 826-4653* **Fax** *(435) 826-4285* **Rooms** *50*   **Road map** *C2*

The Grand Staircase–Escalante, a nearly roadless, rugged terrain in remote Utah, is one of America's newest national monuments. Close to it, the Prospector Inn, on scenic Byway 12, is a family-run establishment, with spacious rooms and a restaurant on site. Check out the glass-encased giant bear in the lobby. **www.prospectorinn.com**

KANAB Parry Lodge   🍴 🏊 🅿️ $
89 E. Center St., UT, 84741 **Tel** *(435) 644-2601* **Fax** *(435) 644-2605* **Rooms** *89*   **Road map** *B2*

Steeped in movie history dating back to 1931, the pleasant, original rooms at the Parry Lodge are named for a long list of Hollywood actors. Big names like Ronald Reagan, Frank Sinatra, Gregory Peck, and, of course, the "Duke" – John Wayne – all passed through here while making movies on the Colorado Plateau. **www.parrylodge.com**

KANAB Shilo Inn Suites   🏨 🅿️ $$
296 W. 100 North St., UT, 84741 **Tel** *(435) 644-2562* **Fax** *(435) 644-5333* **Rooms** *117*   **Road map** *B2*

This mini-suite inn just north of the Arizona border is close to several national parks. The comfortable rooms are equipped with refrigerators, microwaves, and coffee-makers. The hotel offers a complimentary shuttle service to the airport, as well as a Continental breakfast and the crisp aroma of freshly made popcorn. **www.shiloinns.com**

Key to Price Guide *see p232* **Key to Symbols** *see back cover flap*

MOAB Kokopelli Lodge

*72 S. 100 East St., UT, 84532 **Tel** (435) 259-7615 **Rooms** 8*   **Road map** *C2*

Built in the 1950s to serve Moab's booming uranium business, the Kokopelli was originally known as the "Atomic Motel." The rooms have been remodeled, and the lodge is pet-friendly, eco-friendly, pro-cyclist, and, best of all, inexpensive. It has a hot tub and is located one block from Main Street. **www.kokopellilodge.com**

MOAB Redstone Inn

*535 S. Main St., UT, 84532 **Tel** (435) 259-3500 **Fax** (435) 259-2717 **Rooms** 52*   **Road map** *C2*

The downtown Redstone caters to adventure travelers, with packages for white-water rafting, four-wheel jeep trips, and other extreme (and not-so-extreme) sports. Cyclists may keep bikes in their rooms, each of which has a kitchen corner. Those returning from places like the Slickrock Bike Trail can relax in the hot tub. **www.moabredstone.com**

MOAB The Gonzo Inn

*100 W. 200 South St., UT, 84532 **Tel** (435) 259-2515 **Fax** (435) 259-6992 **Rooms** 43*   **Road map** *C2*

The Gonzo is a trendy inn with a mix of colorful Southwestern and retro 1970s decor. There's a large outdoor pool and a hot tub, and a Continental breakfast is included in the price. The Espresso Bar offers beverages 24/7. Guests without bikes can arrange rental. Bike storage, wipe-down, and repairs are also available. **www.gonzoinn.com**

MOAB Pack Creek Ranch

*La Sal Mountain Loop Rd., UT, 84532 **Tel** (435) 259-5505 **Fax** (435) 259-8879 **Rooms** 10*   **Road map** *C2*

About 15 miles (24 km) south of Moab, at the base of the La Sal Mountains, is this working ranch with rustic but renovated log cabins, several with rock fireplaces. There are trails for hiking and biking, and beautiful scenery. Bring your own food supplies, and bear in mind that there are no TVs or telephones. **www.packcreekranch.com**

MOAB Sunflower Hill Bed and Breakfast Luxury Inn

*185 N. 300 East St., UT, 84532 **Tel** (435) 259-2974 **Fax** (435) 259-3065 **Rooms** 12*   **Road map** *C2*

The Sunflower Hill offers elegance in a historic, sensitively restored ranch house, just a few blocks from downtown Moab. Each room is individually decorated, many with antiques. There is a seasonal pool and several porches and patios. Included in the price is a breakfast buffet with home-baked pastries. **www.sunflowerhill.com**

MOAB Sorrell River Ranch Resort & Spa

*Hwy 128, Mile 17, UT, 84532 **Tel** (435) 259-4642 **Fax** (435) 259-3016 **Rooms** 55*   **Road map** *C2*

Far from the crowds, in the gorgeous scenery of Castle Valley, the Sorrell River Ranch offers many upscale facilities. Rooms are decorated with log furniture, and each has a kitchenette, sitting area, and porch swing. Relax in the spa, or choose from a wealth of adventure activities, including horseback riding. **www.sorrelriver.com**

PANGUITCH New Western Motel

*180 E. Center St., UT, 84759 **Tel** (435) 676-8876 **Fax** (435) 676-8954 **Rooms** 55*   **Road map** *B2*

The New Western is located in one of the gateway towns to nearby national parks, only a half-hour drive from Bryce Canyon on scenic Byway 12. The motel offers a complimentary Continental breakfast, a seasonal heated pool, and a year-round indoor Jacuzzi. **www.newwesternmotel.com**

SPRINGDALE Best Western Zion Park Inn

*1215 Zion Park Blvd., UT, 84767 **Tel** (435) 772-3200 **Fax** (435) 772-2449 **Rooms** 120*   **Road map** *B2*

Towering red-rock mountains surround this charming wooden lodge, close to Zion's entrance. Visitors can lounge by a roaring fire in the Great Room in winter, or relax poolside or on the porch during warmer months. You can also test your skills on the putting green. The famous Switchback Grille is next door. **www.zionparkinn.com**

SPRINGDALE Majestic View Lodge

*2400 Zion Park Blvd., UT, 84767 **Tel** (435) 772-0665 **Fax** (435) 772-0308 **Rooms** 69*   **Road map** *B2*

This beautiful lodge has unobstructed views of nearby Zion's soaring peaks. The sizable rooms have handmade, rustic furniture and a balcony or patio overlooking the Virgin River and Eagle Crags. The on-site Steakhouse & Saloon has huge picture windows. You can also visit the complimentary Wildlife Museum. **www.majesticviewlodge.com**

ST. GEORGE Howard Johnson Inn

*1040 S. Main St., UT, 84770 **Tel** (435) 628-8000 **Fax** (435) 656-3983 **Rooms** 52*   **Road map** *B2*

The "HoJo," as it is affectionately called, is about a mile from the main Interstate highway. It's a reliable chain hotel, providing clean rooms and mini-suites with kitchenettes at a modest price. Close to businesses and several restaurants, it offers a complimentary Continental breakfast and free Internet access. **www.HowardJohnson.com**

ST. GEORGE Seven Wives Inn

*217 N. 100 West St., UT, 84770 **Tel** (435) 628-3737 **Fax** (435) 628-5646 **Rooms** 13*   **Road map** *B2*

The charming, individually styled rooms of this inn are in two neighboring Victorian houses in a historic district close to Ancestor Square, with its shops and restaurants. The inn is named for a man who hid in the attic when polygamy was outlawed in 1882. He had seven wives. A gourmet breakfast is served. **www.sevenwivesinn.com**

ST. GEORGE Ava House Inn & Spa

*278 N. 100 West St., UT, 84770 **Tel** (435) 673-7755 **Rooms** 5*   **Road map** *B2*

The Ava House is close to Brigham Young's historic home. Each of the uniquely decorated rooms has a private bath and is supplied with luxurious robes. One room, ideal for families, has pocket-twin beds and a claw-foot tub. Guests are served a full gourmet breakfast. The East Wing houses the Massage and Lotus Spa. **www.avahousespa.com**

TORREY Sandstone Inn   ⊞ ⊞ ⊘ $$

875 E. Hwy 24, UT, 84775 **Tel** *(435) 425-3775* **Fax** *(435) 425-3212* **Rooms** *50*   **Road map** *C2*

At the top of the world, close to Capitol Reef National Park, this inn is named for all the surrounding natural desert sandstone – from canyons and mountains, to buttes and monoliths. It has clean, cheerful rooms. The surprise here is a swimming pool completely enclosed by glass, with stunning views. **www.capitolreefwonderland.com**

ZION NATIONAL PARK Zion Lodge   ⊞ ⊘ $$$

Springdale, UT, 84767 **Tel** *(303) 297-2757* **Fax** *(303) 297-3175* **Rooms** *121*   **Road map** *B2*

This lodge is nestled in a wooded area deep inside Zion Canyon, with massive sandstone walls soaring all around, up to 3,800 ft (1,160 m). The rebuilt main lodge has maintained its original appearance, and offers some historic cabins, as well as motel-style rooms. Rates are particularly attractive in the winter months. **www.zionlodge.com**

THE FOUR CORNERS

BLUFF Recapture Lodge   ⊞ ⊘ $

Hwy 191, UT, 84512 **Tel** *(435) 672-2281* **Fax** *(435) 672-2284* **Rooms** *26*   **Road map** *D2*

A favorite place for kayaking and rafting, the Recapture Lodge is on the San Juan River. Shuttles to the rivers can be arranged, and the lodge has regular speakers and slide shows on local geology and archeology. Children can play on the jungle gym with monkey bars and swings. Lodgings are simple but clean. **www.recapturelodge.com**

CAMERON Cameron Trading Post   ⊞ ⊘ $$

Route 89, AZ, 86020 **Tel** *(928) 679-2231* **Fax** *(928) 679-2501* **Rooms** *66*   **Road map** *C3*

Located at a crossroads with routes to Lake Powell, Grand Canyon, and the Four Corners, this Native American hotel and trading post offers reasonable rates and a large Native art gallery. Balconies overlook a desert garden or the Little Colorado River Gorge, with the old 1911 swayback suspension bridge. **www.camerontradingpost.com**

CHINLE Thunderbird Lodge   ⊞ $$

Canyon de Chelly Navajo Route 7, AZ, 86503 **Tel** *(928) 674-5841* **Fax** *(928) 674-5844* **Rooms** *73*   **Road map** *C3*

A century ago, this lovely establishment right at the mouth of Canyon de Chelly was a small trading post with bungalows. Now a pleasant chain motel, it's a pink adobe-style building nestled among mature cottonwoods. Tours by experienced Navajo guides in six-wheel-drive vehicles can be arranged at the lodge. **www.tbirdlodge.com**

CORTEZ Kelly Place Bed & Breakfast   ⊘ $$

14663 Rd. G, CO, 81321 **Tel** *(970) 565-3125* **Fax** *(970) 564-9440* **Rooms** *11*   **Road map** *D2*

Near the Canyons of the Ancients, this family retreat is nestled among the orchards in McElmo Canyon, at the foot of Sleeping Ute Mountain. The estate contains numerous ancient Puebloan sites to explore, including a thousand-year-old *kiva* and pueblo just steps from the lodge. Archeologist-guided hikes are available. **www.kellyplace.com**

DURANGO General Palmer Hotel $$$

567 Main Ave., CO, 81301 **Tel** *(970) 247-4747* **Fax** *(970) 247-1332* **Rooms** *39*   **Road map** *D2*

Victorian elegance with exceptional hospitality is a tradition at this 1898 landmark hotel located in the historic district. Guestrooms are carefully decorated with furnishings from the Victorian era, and a teddy bear placed on each bed. Cookies, tea, and coffee are served in the spacious Victorian lobby. **www.generalpalmer.com**

DURANGO The Rochester Hotel   ⊘ $$$

721 E. Second Ave., CO, 81301 **Tel** *(970) 385-1920 or (800) 664-1929* **Fax** *(970) 385-1967* **Rooms** *15*   **Road map** *D2*

Within walking distance of the major Durango attractions, this beautifully restored 1892 hotel is attractively decorated with Old West and cowboy decor. The spacious guestrooms are comfortable, with 1890s-style furnishings and Western art. Full gourmet breakfast is served in the lobby. **www.rochesterhotel.com**

DURANGO Strater Hotel   ⊡ ⊞ ⊟ $$$

699 Main Ave., CO, 81301 **Tel** *(970) 247-4431* **Fax** *(970) 259-2208* **Rooms** *93*   **Road map** *D2*

Built in 1887, this gorgeous red-and-white gingerbread Victorian building has a rich history and is a prominent landmark in downtown Durango. Richly filled with period antiques, the rooms are all uniquely decorated. Honky-tonk ragtime plays in the Diamond Belle Saloon. **www.strater.com**

FARMINGTON Best Western Inn & Suites   ⊞ ⊞ ⊟ ⊘ $$

700 Scott Ave., NM, 87401 **Tel** *(505) 327-5221* **Fax** *(505) 327-1565* **Rooms** *192*   **Road map** *D2*

Guests can walk or jog along the banks of the Animas River, just behind this dependable chain hotel. A full hot breakfast is included in the price, and an indoor pool is located in a handsome plant-filled atrium. The hotel has a sports bar with billiards, Rookies, and dining at the Riverwalk Patio & Grille. **www.bestwestern.com**

MESA VERDE NATIONAL PARK Far View Motor Lodge   ⊡ ⊞ $$

Mile Marker 15, Mancos, CO, 81328 **Tel** *(602) 331-5210* **Fax** *(970) 564-4311* **Rooms** *150*   **Road map** *D2*

The views from the balconied rooms at this adobe-style lodge stretch clear over the Montezuma Valley. It's a quiet, yet modern retreat near the park's visitors' center, but away from the crowds touring the cliff dwellings. The lodge houses the excellent Metate Room restaurant *(see p264)* and a shop. Closed Dec–Apr. **www.visitmesaverde.com**

Key to Price Guide *see p232* **Key to Symbols** *see back cover flap*

MEXICAN HAT Valley of the Gods Bed and Breakfast

Valley of the Gods Rd., UT, 84531 **Tel** *(970) 749-1164* **Rooms** *4*

Road map C2

Relax on the long porch of this solar- and wind-powered rustic but comfortable home, with a stunning view toward the Valley of the Gods and the Belle's Butte monolith. Staying here is truly a memorable experience. A full breakfast is served daily, but you should bring your own dinner supplies. **www.valleyofthegods.cjb.net**

MONUMENT VALLEY Goulding's Lodge

1000 Main St., off Hwy 163, UT, 84536 **Tel** *(435) 727-3231* **Fax** *(435) 727-3344* **Rooms** *78*

Road map C2

Originally a trading post, Goulding's Lodge is tucked into a mesa just opposite the entrance to Monument Valley. It has a bustling restaurant and superb views of the park buttes from its balconied rooms. The small museum on site displays memorabilia from famed movies by director John Ford. **www.gouldings.com**

MONUMENT VALLEY The View Hotel

Hwy 163 Monument Valley Tribal Park, UT, 84536 **Tel** *(435) 727-5555* **Fax** *(435) 727-4545* **Rooms** *95*

Road map C2

Inside Monument Valley, with amazing views of the monuments, this modern hotel is furnished in contemporary style. The comfortable guestrooms have private balconies with views of the monuments, and the third floor rooms are great for star-gazing. Be sure to watch the sunrise over Monument Valley. **www.monumentvalleyview.com**

SECOND MESA, HOPI RESERVATION Hopi Cultural Center Inn

Route 264, AZ, 86043 **Tel** *(928) 734-2401* **Fax** *(928) 734-6651* **Rooms** *33*

Road map C3

When you get to Second Mesa, you step more than 1,000 years back in time. This adobe, pueblo-style inn, the only one for miles around, has clean, basic rooms, and is an excellent base for touring all three mesas. Expect high-desert windy days in spring, and breathtaking views. Reserve in advance. **www.hopiculturalcenter.com**

TELLURIDE New Sheridan Hotel

231 W. Colorado Ave., CO, 81435 **Tel** *(970) 728-4351* **Fax** *(970) 728-5024* **Rooms** *32*

Road map D2

Built in 1891, the small but historic New Sheridan lacks no luxury. Its rooms are furnished with period antiques, and some come with mountain views. A complimentary breakfast awaits guests in the morning; there is a well-stocked library; and avid skiers can store their equipment securely. On the roof are two hot tubs. **www.newsheridan.com**

TELLURIDE The Victorian Inn

401 W. Pacific Ave., CO, 81435 **Tel** *(970) 728-6601* **Fax** *(970) 728-3233* **Rooms** *33*

Road map D2

The Victorian Inn is just blocks from the historic downtown district of Telluride. In an area where hotels tend to be pricey, this is a supremely affordable option. Ask for a quiet room, and be aware that some lodgings are a bit small. Continental breakfast is served, and the dry sauna is open during the winter months. **www.TheVictorianInn.org**

TELLURIDE The Peaks Resort & Golden Door Spa

136 Country Club Dr., CO, 81435 **Tel** *(970) 728-6800* **Fax** *(970) 728-6175* **Rooms** *174*

Road map D2

If you're looking for luxury and awesome Rocky Mountains views, the place to be is The Peaks Resort in Mountain Village, a gondola ride above Telluride. This is the spot for ski access in winter, golf in summer, and the magnificent Golden Door Spa, open all year round. **www.thepeaksresort.com**

WINDOW ROCK Quality Inn Navajo Nation Capital

48 W. Hwy 264, AZ, 86515 **Tel** *(928) 871-4108* **Fax** *(928) 871-5466* **Rooms** *56*

Road map D3

Close to the governmental center of the Navajo Nation, and next door to the tribal-controlled community college, the Navajo National Museum, and the zoo, this hotel offers rooms with Southwestern decor. As well as a business center, it has an on-site restaurant where a complimentary breakfast is served. **www.qualityinnwindowrock.com**

SANTA FE AND NORTHERN NEW MEXICO

ABIQUIU Casa del Rio Bed & Breakfast

19946 Hwy 84, NM, 87510 **Tel** *(505) 753-2035* **Fax** *(505) 753-2035* **Rooms** *4*

Road map E3

This lovely adobe-style home is in an area known as "Georgia O'Keeffe Country," because it inspired the artist's landscapes. Rooms have Spanish Colonial-style furniture, and some have tiled floors. Relax on the patio, watch for eagles and cranes, or stargaze to the sounds of howling coyotes. **www.casadelrio.net**

CHAMA Branding Iron Motel

1511 W. Main St., NM, 87520 **Tel** *(575) 756-2162* **Rooms** *39*

Road map E2

Close to the Colorado border, high up in the Rocky Mountains of New Mexico, the Branding Iron has pleasant rooms. It's located within walking distance of the depot for America's highest and longest narrow-gauge railroad, the Cumbres and Toltec Scenic Railroad. Closed Nov–Apr. **www.brandingironmotel.com**

CHIMAYÓ Casa Escondida Bed & Breakfast

64 County Rd. 0100, NM, 87522 **Tel** *(505) 351-4805* **Fax** *(505) 351-2575* **Rooms** *8*

Road map E3

In a secluded setting, the Casa Escondida is a great base for exploring the area. Its rooms are creatively decorated with Southwestern antiques and individual accents: a working wood stove, *kiva* fireplaces, a patio. The specialties on the breakfast menu – from green-chile quiche to strawberry pancakes – change daily. **www.casaescondida.com**

CHIMAYÓ Hacienda Rancho de Chimayó

🍴 🅿 **$$**

County Rd. 98, NM, 87522 **Tel** *(505) 351-2222* **Rooms** *7* **Road map** *E3*

This restored hacienda has individually decorated rooms, some with iron or brass beds and beautiful handwoven rugs and draperies. All rooms have their own enclosed courtyard, a sitting area and fireplace, and a private bath. Continental breakfast is included. There is a charming restaurant on site *(see p265)*. **www.ranchodechimayo.com**

CIMARRON St. James Hotel

🍴 🅿 **$$**

17th & Collinson Sts, NM, 87714 **Tel** *(575) 376-2664* **Fax** *(505) 376-2623* **Rooms** *24* **Road map** *E3*

A night at the landmark St. James, dating from the 1880s, could be spent in an antique-filled room where Buffalo Bill, Annie Oakley, or Jessie James slept. Additional rooms are in the newer annex. A restaurant, café, and saloon can also be found on site, but bear in mind that there are no TVs or telephones. **www.stjamescimarron.com**

LAS VEGAS Historic Plaza Hotel

🖥 🍴 **$$**

230 Plaza, NM, 87701 **Tel** *(505) 425-3591* **Fax** *(505) 425-9659* **Rooms** *38* **Road map** *E3*

The restored 1880s Plaza is located in the original Las Vegas (established long before today's casino-filled city). It has Victorian-style rooms but modern amenities, plus, of course, a resident ghost. Famous guests include movie stars, Wild West personalities, and Teddy Roosevelt's Rough Riders. Hot breakfast is included. **www.plazahotel-nm.com**

SANTA FE El Rey Inn

📶 🍴 🅿 **$$**

1862 Cerrillos Rd., NM, 87505 **Tel** *(505) 982-1931* **Fax** *(505) 989-9249* **Rooms** *86* **Road map** *E3*

With a gracious lobby in a white adobe-style building, the El Rey is a mini oasis in Santa Fe. Gardens are filled with chile ristras, fountains, and sculptures; rooms are comfortably decorated with Southwestern accents. One of the best lower-priced hotels in the area, the El Rey is near the Greer Garson Theater. **www.elreyinnsantafe.com**

SANTA FE Don Gaspar Inn

🅿 **$$$**

623 Don Gaspar, NM, 87505 **Tel** *(505) 986-8664* **Fax** *(505) 986-0696* **Rooms** *10* **Road map** *E3*

This gracious bed and breakfast inn is housed in three historic buildings, each with distinct architectural styles – Territorial, Pueblo Revival, and Arts and Crafts. Gardens and courtyards surround the three buildings, and each guestroom has a private entrance and patio. Full gourmet breakfast is served. **www.dongaspar.com**

SANTA FE Hotel Plaza Real

🖥 🅿 **$$$**

125 Washington Ave., NM, 87501 **Tel** *(505) 988-4900* **Fax** *(505) 983-9322* **Rooms** *56* **Road map** *E3*

A boutique hotel with a cozy lobby, the Plaza Real is just steps from the Plaza. Rooms have handcrafted furniture and fireplaces, with balconies or patios looking over the pretty courtyard or the Sangre de Cristo Mountains. Pottery, weavings, and paintings by notable regional artists are scattered throughout. **www.santafehotelplazareal.com**

SANTA FE Hotel Santa Fe

🖥 🍴 📶 🅿 **$$$**

1501 Paseo de Peralta, NM, 87501 **Tel** *(505) 982-1200* **Fax** *(505) 984-2211* **Rooms** *163* **Road map** *E3*

The only Native American hotel in Santa Fe offers spacious rooms in an adobe-style building with many attractive sculptures, totems, and artworks. Check the schedule for tribal dances, flute performances, and storytelling. The Hacienda is an upscale wing filled with artworks from the 19 pueblos. Spa facilities. **www.hotelsantafe.com**

SANTA FE Hotel St. Francis

🖥 🍴 📺 🅿 **$$$**

210 Don Gaspar Ave., NM, 87501 **Tel** *(505) 983-5700* **Fax** *(505) 989-7690* **Rooms** *82* **Road map** *E3*

This elegant landmark hotel built in 1923 has a beautiful arched colonnade. The spacious rooms, each named for its decorative theme, have high ceilings and antique furniture. Afternoon high tea is served in the lobby, which has a massive stone fireplace overlooked by cherubs. The Secreto Bar is on the outdoor patio. **www.hotelstfrancis.com**

SANTA FE Inn of the Turquoise Bear

🅿 **$$$**

342 E. Buena Vista St., NM, 87505 **Tel** *(505) 983-0798* **Fax** *(505) 988-4225* **Rooms** *11* **Road map** *E3*

A historic, rambling adobe villa surrounded by gardens, this elegant inn is a tribute to its owner, Witter Brynner, and his literary and artistic friends. Gracious rooms with *kiva* fireplaces and *viga* ceilings are named for Brynner's visitors, such as Igor Stravinsky, Ansel Adams, and Edna Millay. Delicious breakfasts. **www.turquoisebear.com**

SANTA FE Inn on the Alameda

🖥 🍴 📶 📺 🅿 **$$$**

303 East Alameda, NM, 87501 **Tel** *(505) 984-2121* **Fax** *(505) 986-8325* **Rooms** *71* **Road map** *E3*

Walk through a flower-covered gateway into a pueblo-style boutique hotel where rooms are individually decorated in Southwestern colors. A Continental breakfast and an afternoon wine-and-cheese reception are complimentary. Relax in one of two outdoor whirlpools, or borrow a book from the lobby library. **www.inn-alameda.com**

SANTA FE The Bishop's Lodge

🍴 📶 📺 🅿 **$$$$**

1297 Bishop's Lodge Rd., NM, 87501 **Tel** *(505) 983-6377* **Fax** *(505) 989-8739* **Rooms** *111* **Road map** *E3*

This upscale resort (once an archbishop's private retreat) is housed in adobe-style buildings hidden among the pines of the Sangre de Cristo Mountains, a few minutes from the Plaza. The hotel offers a range of activities, including tennis, horseback riding, hiking, a luxurious spa, and Camp Appaloosa, for the kids. **www.bishopslodge.com**

SANTA FE Inn of the Anasazi

🖥 🍴 📺 🅿 **$$$$**

113 Washington Ave., NM, 87501 **Tel** *(505) 988-3030* **Fax** *(505) 988-3277* **Rooms** *57* **Road map** *E3*

The Anasazi is exquisitely decorated in regional style, with Native American rugs and quilts, four-poster beds, and rustic wood furniture, in an atmosphere that exudes sheer elegance. Note its massive hand-carved doors and sculptured stairways. The inn is also home to the Anasazi Restaurant *(see p267)*. **www.innoftheanasazi.com**

SANTA FE The Inn of the Five Graces

🔲 ⓪   ⑤⑤⑤⑤

150 E. DeVargas, NM, 87501 **Tel** *(505) 992-0957* **Fax** *(505) 955-0549* **Rooms** *22*   **Road map** *E3*

This extraordinary inn combines the taste of an Oriental rug and antiques importer with the talents of a decorator. Every inch is a showcase of remarkable design, especially the bedrooms. The all-suite inn is across the street from the Chapel of San Miguel (the oldest church in America). Delectable breakfasts are included. **www.fivegraces.com**

SANTA FE La Fonda Hotel

🔲 🔲 ≋ 🔲 ⓪   ⑤⑤⑤⑤

100 E. San Francisco St., NM, 87501 **Tel** *(505) 982-5511* **Fax** *(505) 988-2952* **Rooms** *167*   **Road map** *E3*

This grande dame on the Plaza sits on the site of a 1610 adobe inn. Artworks are everywhere: the guest-room headboards, the blanket boxes, and even the light switches have been painted by the hotel's resident artist. Modern amenities include a swimming pool and a state-of-the art fitness center and spa. **www.lafondasantafe.com**

SANTA FE La Posada de Santa Fe

🔲 🔲 ≋ 🔲 ⓪   ⑤⑤⑤⑤

330 E. Palace Ave., NM, 87501 **Tel** *(505) 986-0000* **Fax** *(505) 982-6850* **Rooms** *157*   **Road map** *E3*

This high-end resort was once a summer arts school. Today, it is a romantic retreat filled with artworks. Adobe *casitas*, each decorated with the vibrant colors and warm tones of the Southwest, are dotted around the Posada's fragrant gardens, featuring native plants. Guests can relax in the on-site spa. **www.laposadadesantafe.com**

TAOS American Artists Gallery House Bed & Breakfast

⓪   ⑤⑤

132 Frontier Lane, NM, 87571 **Tel** *(575) 758-4446* **Fax** *(575) 758-0497* **Rooms** *10*   **Road map** *E3*

This B&B with views of Taos Mountain is filled with works by Southwestern artists. Rooms are tastefully decorated with local touches, including *kiva* wood-burning fireplaces and *saltillo* tiles. A few have tubs for two. Breakfast might feature such delicacies as raspberry-flavored stuffed French toast. **www.taosbedandbreakfast.com**

TAOS Don Fernando de Taos

≋ ⓪   ⑤⑤

1005 Paseo del Pueblo Sur, NM, 87571 **Tel** *(575) 758-4444* **Fax** *(575) 758-0055* **Rooms** *124*   **Road map** *E3*

Rooms here are housed in adobe-style buildings around a garden area with courtyards and walkways. They are decorated with hand-carved furniture and artworks. The hotel's glass-enclosed pool and spa is open all year round. Recreation packages, from snowboarding to hot-air ballooning, are available. **www.donfernandodetaos.com**

TAOS Taos Inn

🔲 ⓪   ⑤⑤

125 Paseo del Pueblo Norte, NM, 87571 **Tel** *(575) 758-2233* **Fax** *(575) 758-5776* **Rooms** *44*   **Road map** *E3*

Four buildings beyond the lobby house guest rooms decorated with vibrant colors and artworks; many also have antiques, fireplaces, and wood-beamed ceilings. The on-site Adobe Bar is known as Taos's "living room" and has drawn the likes of Greta Garbo, D.H. Lawrence, and, more recently, Robert Redford. **www.taosinn.com**

TAOS Casa de las Chimeneas Bed & Breakfast Inn

🔲 ⓪   ⑤⑤⑤

405 Cordoba Rd., NM, 87571 **Tel** *(575) 758-4777* **Fax** *(575) 758-3976* **Rooms** *8*   **Road map** *E3*

Filled with artworks, tiled hearths, and wood-beamed ceilings, this inn has gardens with tiered fountains. The name means "House of Chimneys," and all rooms have *kiva* fireplaces. Guests may use the fitness room, sauna, and hot tub, or book a spa treatment. A delicious breakfast and evening buffet dinner are included. **www.visittaos.com**

TAOS SKI VALLEY Salsa del Salto Bed & Breakfast Inn

≋ ⓪   ⑤⑤

543 Hwy 150, Arroyo Seco, NM, 87514 **Tel** *(575) 776-2422* **Fax** *(575) 776-5734* **Rooms** *10*   **Road map** *E3*

This gracious guesthouse is just east of Ski Valley and features beautiful views of the majestic El Salto Mountain and the Truchas Peaks. It has bright, airy rooms with Southwestern touches and handmade furniture. Tennis courts and a swimming pool sit on the spacious grounds. Breakfast includes gourmet omelettes. **www.bandbtaos.com**

ZUNI The Inn at Halona

🔲 🔲 ≋ 🔲 ⓪   ⑤

23B Pia Mesa Rd., NM, 87327 **Tel** *(505) 782-4547* **Fax** *(505) 782-2155* **Rooms** *8*   **Road map** *D3*

This inn offers the unique experience of staying in a genuine Zuni pueblo. Several rooms are on the upper floor of the family residence and have an outside deck; others are in an adjacent pueblo-style building. Rooms are decorated with original Zuni paintings, photographs, and pottery items. A Continental breakfast is served. **www.halona.com**

ALBUQUERQUE AND SOUTHERN NEW MEXICO

ALAMOGORDO Comfort Inn & Suites

🔲 ≋ 🔲 ⓪   ⑤⑤

1020 S. White Sands Blvd., NM, 88310 **Tel** *(575) 434-4200* **Fax** *(575) 437-8872* **Rooms** *91*   **Road map** *E4*

Located near the Flickinger Performing Arts Center, the Comfort Inn is minutes away from White Sands National Monument and the Missile Range. It is a good-value motorlodge, with sizable rooms, business facilities, an outdoor pool, a fitness center, and a picnic area, plus a complimentary Continental breakfast. **www.choicehotels.com**

ALBUQUERQUE MCM Elegante

🔲 🔲 ≋ 🔲 ⓪   ⑤⑤

2020 Menaul Blvd. NE, NM, 87107 **Tel** *(505) 884-2511* **Fax** *(505) 884-5720* **Rooms** *343*   **Road map** *E3*

In downtown Albuquerque, the MCM Elegante offers renovated rooms with contemporary furnishings, some with balconies and views of the Sandia Peak Mountains. The hotel's fitness center has tall glass windows overlooking the pool. Complimentary shuttle to the airport, the malls, and the Old Town. **www.mcmelegantealbuquerque.com**

ALBUQUERQUE Albuquerque Doubletree Hotel $$$

201 Marquette Ave. NW, NM, 87102 **Tel** *(505) 247-3344* **Fax** *(505) 247-7025* **Rooms** *295*   **Road map** *E3*

Close to the Old Town, the Doubletree is accessible from the Convention Center via an underground concourse. Many of its bright, airy rooms have balconies and views of the mountains. Guests can enjoy a cocktail at the Lobby Bar to the tune of a cascading waterfall. Good business facilities. **www.doubletreealbuquerque.com**

ALBUQUERQUE Bottger Mansion of Old Town B&B $$$

110 San Felipe NW, NM, 87104 **Tel** *(505) 243-3639* **Fax** *(505) 243-4378* **Rooms** *8*   **Road map** *E3*

At the Bottger Mansion, the only B&B in the historic district, you can sit under the elms on the patio and admire the spires of the San Felipe de Neri church. Previous guests, famous and infamous, have included the outlaw George "Machine Gun" Kelly, Elvis Presley, and Janis Joplin. Ask for a room with a four-poster bed. **www.bottger.com**

ALBUQUERQUE Casas de Sueños $$$

310 Rio Grande Blvd. SW, NM, 87104 **Tel** *(505) 247-4560* **Fax** *(505) 242-2162* **Rooms** *21*   **Road map** *E3*

The Casa de Sueños (House of Dreams) used to house a 1930s artists' colony. Charming adobe-style *casitas* are hidden among the courtyards and gardens. Each room is uniquely decorated, some with *kiva* fireplaces or *saltillo* tiled floors, others with patios or Jacuzzi tubs. A full American breakfast is served. **www.casasdesuenos.com**

ALBUQUERQUE Hacienda Antigua Inn B&B $$$

6708 Tierra Dr. NW, NM, 87107 **Tel** *(505) 345-5399* **Fax** *(505) 345-3855* **Rooms** *8*   **Road map** *E3*

Originally built as a trading post and stagecoach stop in 1790, this historic North Valley inn offers elegant rooms filled with handsome antiques. Massive gates lead to a courtyard presided over by a cottonwood tree – breakfast is served here on summer days. In winter, you can enjoy a fire in the *kiva* fireplace. **www.haciendantigua.com**

ALBUQUERQUE Hilton Albuquerque $$$

1901 University Blvd. NE, NM, 87102 **Tel** *(505) 884-2500* **Fax** *(505) 880-1196* **Rooms** *263*   **Road map** *E3*

The Hilton is in the midtown district, close to the university, on a sprawling resort-like property. The cabanas are convenient to the pool, whirlpool, fitness center, and sauna. The tower rooms have balconies and splendid views of volcanoes and mountains. Decor is New Mexican throughout, with Indian rugs and pueblo art. **www.hilton.com**

ALBUQUERQUE Mauger Estate B&B Inn $$$

701 Roma Ave. NW, NM, 87102 **Tel** *(505) 242-8755* **Fax** *(505) 842-8835* **Rooms** *10*   **Road map** *E3*

This lovingly restored Queen Anne residence is within walking distance of the Old Town. Snack baskets and fresh flowers add to the charm of the individually styled rooms. The Mauger Estate is the occasional hideaway of stars such as Linda Ronstadt, but all guests are treated like celebrities here. Complimentary breakfast. **www.maugerbb.com**

ALBUQUERQUE Nativo Lodge $$$

6000 Pan American Freeway NE, NM, 87109 **Tel** *(505) 798-4300* **Fax** *(505) 798-4305* **Rooms** *146*   **Road map** *E3*

Native American culture mixed with modern city needs is found at the Nativo Lodge, near the Balloon Fiesta Park. Rooms have modern amenities, Navajo-designed rugs, and balcony views. Take a swim in the indoor-outdoor pool, or relax in the sauna. The lobby is decorated with hand-carved murals. **www.hhandr.com/nativo**

ALBUQUERQUE Sheraton Albuquerque Uptown $$$

2600 Louisiana Blvd. NE, NM, 87110 **Tel** *(505) 881-0000* **Fax** *(505) 881-3736* **Rooms** *296*   **Road map** *E3*

The Sheraton stands eight stories tall over the business district and near the shopping malls and the university. The spacious rooms are tastefully designed and offer views toward the mountains. The indoor heated pool can be used all year round; you can also exercise in the fitness center or relax in the dry spa. **www.sheratonabq.com**

CARLSBAD Holiday Inn Express $$

601 S. Canal St., NM, 88220 **Tel** *(575) 234-1252* **Fax** *(575) 234-1253* **Rooms** *100*   **Road map** *F5*

Located downtown, this full-service Territorial-style hotel offers comfortable rooms decorated with Southwestern fabrics. Amenities include free high-speed internet access and an onsite restaurant serving hot breakfasts. There is a playground area for children and Carlsbad Caverns National Park is a 30-minute drive away. **www.ichotelsgroup.com**

CEDAR CREST Elaine's Bed & Breakfast $$

72 Snowline Rd., NM, 87008 **Tel** *(505) 281-2467* **Fax** *(505) 281-1384* **Rooms** *5*   **Road map** *E3*

This delightful B&B is east of Albuquerque, on New Mexico's Turquoise Trail. Adjacent to Cibola Forest, the log home sits among evergreen trees. Rooms are furnished with European antiques and have Jacuzzi tubs. Breakfast is served by the fireplace or on the patio in summer. A great spot for birdwatching. **www.elainesbnb.com**

CLOUDCROFT The Lodge $$$

1 Corona Place, NM **Tel** *(575) 682-2566* **Fax** *(575) 682-2715* **Rooms** *59*   **Road map** *F5*

Pancho Villa, Judy Garland, Clark Gable, and Rebecca the Ghost, for whom the restaurant *(see p269)* is named, have all enjoyed the casual elegance of The Lodge, built in 1911, and its antique-filled rooms. Above the clouds at 9,000 ft (2,750 m), the hotel's golf course is North America's highest. **www.thelodgeresort.com**

GILA Casitas de Gila Guesthouses $$

50 Casita Flats Rd., NM, 88038 **Tel** *(575) 535-4455* **Fax** *(575) 535-4456* **Rooms** *5*   **Road map** *D4*

A sign reading "Entering Stress-Free Zone" greets guests at this cozy adobe guesthouse complex. Remote enough to allow sightings of the Milky Way at night, the Casitas de Gila is close to Silver City, in Apache country. Try your luck at spotting roadrunners or other wildlife, or relax in the hot tub above Bear Creek. **www.casitasdegila.com**

GRANTS Grants Travelodge

🏨 📶 ⓢ

1608 E. Santa Fe Ave., NM, 87020 **Tel** *(505) 287-7800* **Fax** *(505) 287-7800* **Rooms** *60* **Road map** D3

Located right off I-40, this motorlodge is an economical place to stay if you are en route to Albuquerque or plan to visit the Acoma Pueblo. Its spacious rooms have New Mexican artworks, and there is an indoor pool and a complimentary breakfast. Visit the nearby New Mexico Mining Museum about uranium. **www.travelodge.com**

JEMEZ SPRINGS Cañon del Rio B&B

🏨 🍽 📶 ⓢⓢⓢ

16445 Hwy 4, Jemez Springs, NM, 87025 **Tel** *(575) 829-4377* **Fax** *(575) 829-3138* **Rooms** *7* **Road map** E3

Each of the comfortable rooms surrounding a courtyard with a fountain and pond is named for a Native American tribe and has tribal artifacts. After a delicious Southwest-style breakfast, guests can relax in the Jacuzzi or on a small beach under the cottonwoods at Jemez River, fish, or hike along the riverside trails. **www.canondelrio.com**

LAGUNA Apache Canyon Ranch B&B

🍽 📶 ⓢⓢⓢ

4 Canyon Dr., NM, 87026 **Tel** *(505) 836-7220* **Fax** *(505) 836-2922* **Rooms** *3* **Road map** D3

On a high desert plain near Grants is this lovely adobe home with two luxurious suites and a detached cottage with its own kitchen and jet tub. Guests enjoy a home-cooked Southwestern breakfast, then can walk it off along the nature path or relax in the dry sauna. The ranch is a short drive from the Acoma Pueblo. **www.apachecanyon.net**

LAS CRUCES The Lundeen Inn of the Arts

📶 ⓢ

618 S. Alameda Blvd., NM, 88005 **Tel** *(575) 526-3326* **Fax** *(575) 647-1334* **Rooms** *20* **Road map** E5

An architect and an art dealer have joined forces to restore this early 20th-century Mexican Territorial inn. Two double-story guesthouses flank the magnificent, arched-window Great Room with a tin ceiling and Jacobean-style furniture. Large paintings fill the walls, and guest rooms are named for famous artists. **www.innofthearts.com**

LAS CRUCES Hilltop Hacienda B&B

📶 ⓢⓢ

2600 Westmoreland, NM, 88012 **Tel** *(575) 382-3556* **Fax** *(575) 382-0308* **Rooms** *3* **Road map** E5

Overlooking the Mesilla Valley, the charming B&B is in an arched adobe brick building. The lower-level rooms have private bathrooms and a reading library. Breakfast is served in a dining room with Territorial-style furniture. Try the Dutch Babies (pancakes topped with fresh fruit and nuts) or the green-chile quiche. **www.zianet.com/hilltop**

LINCOLN Ellis Store Country Inn

🍴 📶 ⓢⓢ

Hwy 380, NM, 88338 **Tel** *(575) 653-4609* **Fax** *(575) 653-4610* **Rooms** *8* **Road map** E4

History buffs trailing Billy the Kid inevitably end up at the Ellis Store in Lincoln, one of the sites of the Lincoln County War. Sleep in the room where the Kid stayed while under house arrest. The charming inn has a large covered portal facing a grassy lawn. Make dining reservation at Isaac's Table *(see p269)*. **www.ellisstore.com**

ROSWELL Best Western Sally Port Inn & Suites

🍴 🏨 🍽 ⓢ

2000 N. Main St., NM, 88201 **Tel** *(575) 622-6430* **Fax** *(575) 623-7631* **Rooms** *124* **Road map** F4

With sizable rooms, a large indoor pool, and an adjacent golf course, the comfortable Sally Port is located near the prestigious New Mexico Military Institute, attended by former president Jimmy Carter. Don't leave town without seeing the two museums devoted to the Roswell Incident, a purported UFO crash. **www.bestwestern.com**

RUIDOSO Dan Dee Cabins

📶 ⓢⓢ

310 Main Rd., NM, 88345 **Tel** *(575) 257-2165 or (800) 345-4848* **Rooms** *13* **Road map** E4

Snow-capped peaks surround these comfortable family lodgings in Upper Canyon, in the Rocky Mountains' forests. Cabins are equipped with a wood-burning fireplace, kitchen, and outdoor barbecue with picnic tables. There's also a children's playground, a spa, and what the owners describe as "bear hug" hospitality. **www.dandeecabins.com**

RUIDOSO The Lodge at Sierra Blanca

📺 🏨 🍽 📶 ⓢⓢⓢ

107 Sierra Blanco Dr., NM, 88345 **Tel** *(575) 258-5500* **Fax** *(575) 258-2419* **Rooms** *120* **Road map** E4

Adjacent to the Ruidoso Convention Center, in the heart of Lincoln National Forest, this upscale resort is noted for the links championship golf course that surrounds it. The Lodge has large modern rooms, a pool, fitness center, and complimentary breakfasts. Guests enjoy the slopes at nearby Ski Apache. **www.thelodgeatsierrablanca.com**

SILVER CITY Bear Mountain Lodge

📶 ⓢⓢⓢ

2251 Cottage San Rd., NM, 88061 **Tel** *(575) 538-2538* **Fax** *(575) 534-1827* **Rooms** *11* **Road map** D5

This beautifully restored 1920s hacienda was originally built as a school. Rooms are furnished with handcrafted Mission-style furnishings, and guests are greeted in the mornings with a home-cooked breakfast. Relax by the fire or on the porch, or join a naturalist-guided hike around the property. **www.bearmountainlodge.com**

WHITE'S CITY Cavern Inn

🍴 🏨 📶 ⓢⓢ

6 Carlsbad Caverns Hwy, NM, 88268 **Tel** *(575) 785-2291* **Fax** *(575) 785-2283* **Rooms** *42* **Road map** F5

Conveniently located near the Carlsbad Caverns, where during warm months thousands of cavern bats take flight, this chain hotel is part of the White's City complex and has sizable rooms with Southwestern decor. Guests enjoy free access to the seasonal water park and arcade. Complimentary breakfast. **www.whitescitycaverninn.com**

WHITE'S CITY Walnut Inn

🍴 🏨 📶 ⓢⓢ

17 Carlsbad Caverns Hwy, NM, 88268 **Tel** *(575) 785-2291* **Fax** *(575) 785-2283* **Rooms** *63* **Road map** F5

The second of two hotels located in the White's City complex. Guests enjoy full complimentary access to the seasonal water park, with its long water slides and pirate ship. Rooms are comfortably decorated with handsome Southwestern accents. Take a swim in the pool and enjoy the complimentary breakfast. **www.whitescitywalnutinn.com**

WHERE TO EAT

Pub sign in Flagstaff

As well as offering a top-class regional cuisine, which is rapidly gaining international recognition, the Southwest offers a diverse range of eating experiences, especially in its larger cities. Santa Fe, Phoenix, Albuquerque, Tucson, and Las Vegas rival any city in the country for the quality of ingredients and variety of cuisine available, with ambiences ranging from rustic to romantic. Southwestern cuisine is increasingly served in casual but stylish cafés. Mexican food is often best at local restaurants in New Mexico, Arizona, and Colorado, while Utah favors American fare. Restaurants with a cowboy or Mexican theme are usually inexpensive and can be entertaining. Hotel restaurants often serve the best food in small towns.

The restaurants listed on pages 252–69 have been chosen for their qu ality, variety, and good value. Some typical dishes available in the Southwest are shown on pages 250–51.

Interior of a regional restaurant in Santa Fe

EATING HOURS

As found elsewhere in the US, breakfast is often a banquet: restaurants have extensive breakfast menus to choose from while hotels often have large buffets. Bacon, eggs, hash brown potatoes, pancakes, waffles, cereals, toast, and muffins appear on most menus. Sunday brunch is a feast to be lingered over, with seafood, meat, and poultry dishes served as well. Breakfast times range from 6 or 6:30am to 10:30 or 11am, though "all-day breakfasts" are popular at many cafés. Brunch is frequently served until 2pm.

Lunch is generally served from around 11:30am until 2:30 or 3pm. Many of the pricier restaurants offer scaled-down versions of their evening menu, which can be good value. Evening meals are served from 5:30 or 6pm, and the last seating is seldom later than 9pm. In small towns, many restaurants are closed in the evening. At the other extreme, Las Vegas' 24-hour culture offers a variety of meals at any time of the day or night.

PRICES AND TIPPING

Eating out in the Southwest is very reasonable, and even the most expensive restaurants offer good value. Light meals in cafés and diners usually cost between $10 and $15, while many chain restaurants serve complete dinners such as chicken or steak with potatoes and vegetables or salad for under $15. Mexican restaurants generally offer huge combination plates for $8–$12. At finer restaurants and upscale cafés, dinner entrées range from $15 to over $30, and a three-course meal, excluding wine, can still be found for under $50. In Las Vegas, the casino buffets serve myriad dishes, such as roasts, salads, pasta, and fish, to a high standard at reasonable prices (usually all-you-can-eat for $15–$30).

The standard tip is 15–20 percent of the cost of the meal, after tax. Tipping should be based on service, and if it is outstanding, leave up to 20 percent. Bartenders expect to be tipped accordingly for each round of drinks.

Sales taxes will not be shown on menu prices, but apply to each item of food and drink. Although they vary from state to state and from city to city, these usually add around 5–8 percent to the cost of a meal.

TYPES OF FOOD AND RESTAURANTS

Dining establishments in the Southwest come in a wide variety of shapes and sizes from small and friendly diners offering hearty burgers and snacks to gourmet restaurants serving the latest Southwestern and fusion cuisine, to the lavish dining rooms in some of the area's top resorts, particularly in Phoenix and Las Vegas.

Starting at the lower end of the scale, fast food is a way of life throughout the country, and a string of outlets such as McDonald's, Burger King, Wendy's, and Arby's are found along the main strips of most towns in the region. They serve the usual inexpensive variations on burgers, fries, and soft drinks. Chains such as Applebee's and Denny's offer more variety, with soups, salads, sandwiches, meals, and desserts. These are generally good value, but the quality varies from one establishment to the next. Pizza chains are also ubiquitous in the region.

Mid-range restaurants can include a range of ethnic cuisine, such as Italian, Greek, Chinese, Japanese, and Indian food. Many good restaurants of this type can be found at shopping malls.

Mexican restaurants proliferate in the region, especially in New Mexico and southern Arizona, and vary from roadside stands and snack bars to upscale restaurants where the food is complemented by the architecture. These are often set in adobe buildings with lush interior courtyards that provide a romantic ambience.

"Southwestern" cuisine is a fusion of Native American, Hispanic, and international influences, and is increasingly showcased in the region's finest restaurants. These often feature a renowned resident chef (such as Mark Miller in Santa Fe's Coyote Café, *see p266*). Las Vegas is also home to some of the most elegant restaurants in the country. In the 1990s, several of the city's best hotels recruited celebrity chefs. Now, every hotel has at least one upscale restaurant with a world-class menu and the involvement of such influential names as

Hollywood's Wolfgang Puck of Spago's fame, who owns several restaurants along the Strip including Spago at Caesars Palace *(see p239)*.

Traditional American diner, Lindy's, in Albuquerque

COFFEE HOUSES AND CAFES

Coffee houses are popular throughout Southwest resorts and major cities. Along with specialty coffees, they generally serve pastries, bagels, desserts, and delicatessen fare. Cafés range from simple establishments serving sandwiches to trendy eateries offering Southwestern cuisine.

VEGETARIAN

Southwestern and American cuisine is largely meat based. Vegetarians may not find much variety outside the larger cities and resorts. However, salad bars are big

everywhere, from fine restaurants to fast-food chains. Salads can be a meal in themselves; they usually come with meat and seafood, but vegetarian orders are often accommodated. Many fast food chains also now serve salads, soups, or baked potatoes to cater to the more health-conscious customer.

ALCOHOL

Beer, particularly the *cervezas* imported from Mexico, is the most popular drink in the region, although Las Vegas is renowned for its cocktails. Visitors need to be 21 to buy alcohol. Be sure to carry I.D. as it is often requested before you are served. Utah's licensing laws, influenced by the Mormon community, are stricter, with liquor stores open for shorter hours and never on a Sunday. Alcohol is forbidden on all Native reservations.

DISABLED FACILITIES

Establishments are required to provide wheelchair access and a ground-level restroom by law, but check with older places in advance.

CHILDREN

While Las Vegas is not primarily a family resort, the Southwest is generally child-friendly. Restaurants often serve children's portions and will provide a high chair.

DRESS CODES

Dining is casual throughout the Southwest. Even in upscale restaurants, there is seldom a need for a jacket and tie. In the land of cowboys, jeans are acceptable almost everywhere. In Las Vegas, however, dress smartly for the classier restaurants.

SMOKING

Almost all restaurants have smoking and non-smoking areas, although many ban smoking entirely throughout the establishment, including the bar area.

Colorful Southwestern decor at La Cocina restaurant in Tucson

The Flavors of the Southwest

Southwestern food reflects the region's strong Hispanic and Native cultures. One of the pleasures of a visit to the region is discovering the great variety of dishes available, made with the freshest ingredients, and cooked with expertise. Those with tender tastebuds need not fear the chile pepper, which is at the heart of the cuisine – chiles can pack a powerful bite, but milder varieties add flavor without heat. Most menus in restaurants frequented by tourists provide an explanation of the dishes, and staff are happy to offer advice. The region's other great staple is beef, and there is no shortage of good steaks and burgers in most areas.

Kidney beans

Prime beef steaks on the griddle at a southwestern barbecue

SOUTHWESTERN FOOD

"Red or green?" You'll often hear this question when you order food. This refers to the chile, which is more of a staple than a specialty in much of the region. Many dishes can be served with either green or red chile on top. One is not necessarily hotter than the other. The heat depends on the variety of chile, how many seeds it contains, and on the soil conditions that year. Restaurants used by locals generally serve hotter chiles than those catering to tourists. If you're unsure, many places will serve a little dish of each on the side – this is known as "Christmas". There are more than 100 types of chile available, including jalapeño, poblano, mulato, and chipotle. Very hot varieties include cayenne and habanero.

This is ranching country, so sirloins, T-bones, and other cuts of steak are in plentiful supply, and regional cooking features some great meat dishes. *Carne asada* means roasted or sometimes grilled meat, while *carne seca* is beef that has been dried in the sun before cooking. Poultry also appears in many regional dishes. Fish and seafood are popular, and the quality is high since fresh fish is flown in from California.

Poblano
Dried habanero
Serrano
Dried mulato
Fresh habaneros
Classic New Mexican
Jalapeño

Some of the fresh and dried chiles used in regional dishes

REGIONAL DISHES AND SPECIALTIES

Tortillas are flat pancakes made of wheat or corn. They are the basis of many local dishes, and can be stuffed or rolled, served soft or crispy (fried). Variations on the tortilla include the burrito, or larger burro, a soft, floury pancake, that becomes a crispy chimichanga when deep-fried. Flautas, also fried, are similar but are folded rather than

Avocados

rolled. Salsa is found on almost every table in the region. This cold spicy sauce of tomatoes, onions, chiles, herbs, and spices is served with many dishes. Guacamole is another topping or dip, made from avocados, lime or lemon juice, chile, cilantro (coriander), and spices. Popular desserts include *sopaipilla*, a light pastry that puffs up when fried and is served with honey to drizzle over the top, and *flan*, a firm, creamy, caramel custard.

Enchiladas *are rolled tortillas filled with cheese, chicken, or beef, topped with a red chile sauce and melted cheese.*

Mural on the wall of a café in Tucson's Presidio Historic District

MEXICAN FLAVORS

The main ingredients of Southwestern cuisine are similar to those found in Mexican cooking, including corn, beans, cheese, tomatoes and, of course, chile. But there the similarity ends. New Mexican cuisine has its roots in the Pueblo culture, whose foods and cooking methods were adapted by early settlers. The distinctive taste of many local dishes comes from ingredients such as nuts from the piñon pine which are considered a delicacy; nopales, the fruit of the prickly pear cactus; the chayote (similar to zucchini); and tomatillos, a walnut-sized green berry fruit. Mexican sauces are often tomato-based with chile added as a spice. New Mexican sauces use puréed green or red chile diluted with water; garlic, salt, and sometimes herbs for seasoning, and flour to thicken, are added. Meat may also be added. Mexican food and its Anglo version, Tex-Mex, are found all over the Southwest.

Ice-cold Corona beer, served with a wedge of lime

NATIVE AMERICAN SPECIALITIES

There are few specifically Native American restaurants. Indian fry bread – a flat, fried dough served with honey or other toppings – is often sold at food stands outside tourist attractions or at events. Navajo tacos are made with a base of fry bread rather than tortilla. Hopi piki bread is made from ground corn and boiling water and is cooked in a thin layer over a hot surface. At festivals, special foods may be offered to visitors, such as fried rabbit meat, or Three Sisters Stew made with corn, beans, and squash.

WHAT TO DRINK

Beer is known to cool burning chile mouths, and popular brands include San Miguel, Corona, and Tecate. A margarita, a tequila cocktail served in a salt-rimmed glass, is a typical aperitif. California wines feature on most wine lists, but consider trying some of the little-known regional wines. There are small wineries in southern Arizona and New Mexico. Sonoita Vineyards, near Elgin, Arizona, has received national recognition for its Pinot Noir and Cabernet wines. New Mexico's winemaking tradition stretches back to the first Spanish missionaries. Among its 19 wineries, the Gruet winery is known for its excellent sparkling wines.

Huevos rancheros, *fried eggs on a soft tortilla with chile, cheese, and refried beans, are eaten at breakfast.*

Tacos *are crisp-fried tortillas filled with ground beef, beans, cheese, and salad, and served with guacamole.*

Chile relleno *is a whole green chile stuffed with cheese, meat, or rice, dipped in light batter and then deep-fried.*

Choosing a Restaurant

The restaurants in this guide have been selected across a wide range of price categories for their exceptional food, good value, or interesting location. This chart lists the restaurants under the region chapter headings in the same order as the rest of the guide and in alphabetical order within price category.

PRICE CATEGORIES IN US DOLLARS ($)
For a three-course meal for one, including a glass of house wine (where served), tax, and service.
$ Under $30
$$ $30–$40
$$$ $40–$60
$$$$ $60–$80
$$$$$ Over $80

GRAND CANYON AND NORTHERN ARIZONA

FLAGSTAFF Downtown Diner $

7 E. Aspen Ave., AZ, 86001 **Tel** (928) 774-3492   *Road map C3*

If you are having an early start, join the locals at Downtown Diner, near Heritage Square: It opens at 5:30am and sometimes stays open until 9pm. Have a hearty breakfast, or choose from burgers, sandwiches, or fresh trout from the nearby Oak Creek. Large photos on the walls and booth seating. No alcohol.

FLAGSTAFF San Felipe's Cantina $$

103 N. Leroux St., AZ, 86001 **Tel** (928) 779-6000   *Road map C3*

Just off Route 66, San Felipe's is a Baja-style cantina serving Mexican food "with an attitude." Try the grilled mahi mahi, Mango Tango, or Mango Chicken, each topped with a zesty mango salsa. Sip a margarita or taste the delicious Choco Taco, filled with ice cream. Blues musicians perform here on Sundays, and there's a kid's menu, too.

FLAGSTAFF Black Bart's Steak House $$$

2760 E. Butler Ave., AZ, 86004 **Tel** (928) 779-3142   *Road map C3*

Named for an 1870s stagecoach robber, Black Bart's offers oak-fire-grilled steaks and seafood. Start off with mushrooms – "Bart dips 'em in his secret batter 'n' fries 'em up jest right" – and finish with a Big City Oreo Pie, "so rich, it makes the local banker jealous." A nightly musical review features old standards and Broadway showtunes.

FLAGSTAFF Charly's Pub & Grill $$$

23 N. Leroux St., AZ, 86001 **Tel** (928) 779-1919   *Road map C3*

Popular for people-watching at its sidewalk tables, Charly's serves Navajo tacos, fresh soups, and delicious pies, as well as posole steaks and vegetarian dishes. Late at night, diners can expect varied music acts, from blues to jazz. Located in the Hotel Weatherford (see p232), which offers a selection of bars and restaurants on each floor.

FLAGSTAFF Pasto $$$

19 E. Aspen Ave., AZ, 86001 **Tel** (928) 779-1937   *Road map C3*

A casual, busy downtown restaurant, Pasto serves a range of Italian dishes. Two lifesize female statues carry vases filled with fresh flowers, and the decor is complemented by photos of Italy. Under a painted copper ceiling or, weather permitting, in the garden, you can enjoy Tuscan creamed-bacon crostini, followed by Rabbit Cacciatore.

FLAGSTAFF Cottage Place Restaurant $$$$

126 W. Cottage Ave., AZ, 86001 **Tel** (928) 774-8431   *Road map C3*

Dine in an airy, bungalow-style residence-turned-restaurant with tables dressed in pink linen. The menu offers inspired Continental dishes such as pan-seared tenderloin filet topped with Gorgonzola and served with Port demi-glaze. A good selection of seafood and vegetarian dishes is also available, and there is an extensive wine list. Closed Mon & Tue.

GRAND CANYON Phantom Ranch Canteen $$

Grand Canyon, AZ, 86023 **Tel** (303) 297-2757, (888) 297-2757   *Road map B3*

Adventurers traveling to the canyon bottom – by raft, mule, or on foot – must be early risers. Dinner tends to be an early affair, too. Breakfast and dinner are at specific times here, and reservations are a must; email in advance, along with any lodging requests (see p232). Choose steak, Hiker's Stew, or a vegetarian dish. Sack lunch is also available.

GRAND CANYON (NORTH RIM) Grand Canyon Lodge $$$

Grand Canyon, AZ, 86052 **Tel** (928) 638-2611 ext.160   *Road map B3*

This beautiful, remote restaurant offers astounding views of the Kaibab Plateau through two large windows. Dining is more sophisticated than one would imagine, with delicacies such as crab cakes in a chipotle sauce, or chicken breasts sautéed in Dijon cream sauce. Seasonal reservations can be made a month or two in advance.

GRAND CANYON (SOUTH RIM) Maswik Cafeteria $

Grand Canyon Village, AZ, 86023 **Tel** (928) 638-2631   *Road map B3*

For families on the go, the self-service cafeteria at the Maswik Lodge (see p233) is an excellent choice. Several types of food are sold at various stations – with burgers, traditional meals, and Mexican fare as firm favorites. A well-portioned meal here is both inexpensive and filling.

Key to Symbols *see back cover flap*

GRAND CANYON (SOUTH RIM) Bright Angel Restaurant $$

Grand Canyon Village, AZ, 86023 **Tel** *(928) 638-2631* **Road map** B3

Open all year, the Bright Angel offers family-style casual dining and Southwestern fare named for the people who helped build the lodge. Try the Colter Quesadilla (for the architect who designed the building in 1935) or a Harvey House Steak. Seating is on a first-come, first-served basis, but in high season you can put your name on a waiting list.

GRAND CANYON (SOUTH RIM) El Tovar $$$

Grand Canyon Village, AZ, 86023 **Tel** *(928) 638-2631 ext. 6432* **Road map** B3

Unquestionably, the best dining in the park can be found at El Tovar, where the menu offers a mix of classic and Southwestern flavors. The impressive dining room has a few window tables overlooking the Grand Canyon – meals are pricier in this section, and you must reserve in advance. For views and a light meal, head for the veranda.

JEROME Flatiron Café $

416 N. Main St., AZ, 86331 **Tel** *(928) 634-2733* **Road map** B4

If you travel the tortuous road up to Jerome, a one-time copper boomtown, you can't miss the tiny Flatiron Café, facing downhill where the road splits. Order chicken quesadilla with blue cheese, spinach and homemade cilantro pesto, followed by an exceptionally strong espresso. Be sure not to slip on the café's slanted floors.

JEROME Asylum Restaurant $$$

200 Hill St., AZ, 86331 **Tel** *(928) 639-3197* **Road map** B4

This cozy restaurant is located in the Jerome Grand Hotel and has great views of the Verde Valley. The menu features New American cuisine, including Pacific king salmon with prickly pear barbeque sauce and grilled pork tenderloin with chipotle apricot sauce. The wine list is excellent.

KINGMAN Mr D'z Route 66 $

105 E. Andy Devine Ave., AZ, 86401 **Tel** *(928) 718-0066* **Road map** B3

Decked out in kitsch pink and teal, this gas-station-turned-diner is filled with 50s memorabilia of the Elvis and Marilyn kind. Even Oprah Winfrey stopped by for a burger and onion rings. Try a frothing, homemade root beer or munch on sweet-potato fries while admiring vintage vehicles at the hot-pink picnic tables outside.

LAKE HAVASU CITY Mudshark Brewing Co. $$$

210 Swanson Ave., AZ, 86403 **Tel** *(928) 453-2981* **Road map** A4

Named for a local beach, Mudshark is a popular spot for handcrafted beer on tap. Its varied menu includes burgers, sandwiches, and slow-cooked pork chops. Try the Margarita Shrimp Pizza, with tomato, garlic, and feta cheese, and chase it with a glass of Scorpion Amber Ale. Huge, eye-catching wall murals add to the pleasant ambience.

LAKE HAVASU CITY Shugrue's $$$

1425 McCulloch Blvd., AZ, 86403 **Tel** *(928) 453-1400* **Road map** A4

Shugrue's atrium has open views of London Bridge and the English Village across the boat channel. A second room offers booth seating and a scenic mural. Halibut baked in a Dijon garlic crust with jumbo sea scallops is just one of the many favorites among regular diners. Be there at sunset for unbeatable views.

PAGE Dam Bar and Grille $$$

644 N. Navajo Dr., AZ, 86040 **Tel** *(928) 645-2161* **Road map** C2

Fine dining based on steak, seafood, and pasta is mixed with a lively, contemporary sports-bar atmosphere. An elegant, 30-ft- (9-m-) long etched-glass wall celebrates the nearby Glen Canyon Dam. Diners can sit on the sidewalk patio to watch the sun go down. There's a $5 charge for whining (or so the menu says)!

SEDONA Black Cow Café $

229 N. Hwy 89A, AZ, 86336 **Tel** *(928) 203-9868* **Road map** C3

If there's one word for the homemade ice cream at Black Cow, it's decadence – the Belgian vanilla is to die for. Decorated like an old-time ice-cream parlor, with photos from Sedona in the 1940s and 50s, this café also serves filling sandwiches and pastries, coffee, and smoothies. Located in uptown Sedona.

SEDONA El Rincon Restaurante Mexicano $$$

Tlaquepaque Village, 336 S. Hwy 179, Suite A112, AZ, 86336 **Tel** *(928) 282-4648* **Road map** C3

Arched doorways and Spanish-style furnishings bring the Tlaquepaque charm indoors, or you can dine alfresco on the patio. The Arizona-style Mexican cuisine at El Rincon offers everything from burritos to tamales, always with a touch of Navajo Indian influence. Finish the meal with a fruit-filled dessert chimichanga à la mode.

SEDONA Fournos Restaurant $$$

3000 W. Hwy 89A, AZ, 86336 **Tel** *(928) 282-3331* **Road map** C3

This small, unassuming restaurant with ten tables is decorated in Aegean blue with painted tablecloths. Authentic Greek dishes include handmade dolmades (vine leaves wrapped around rice and meat), flaming shrimp with feta cooked in ouzo, and the signature Cephalonian roast lamb shanks. Two seatings per night. Open Thu–Sat.

SEDONA Oaxaca Restaurante & Rooftop Cantina $$$

321 N. Hwy 89A, AZ, 86336 **Tel** *(928) 282-4179* **Road map** C3

Admire the stunning scenery or a pretty sunset through the archways in the seasonally open rooftop cantina in this lively and long-running restaurant in uptown Sedona. Oaxaca is owned by a dietician, so you can expect to find a heart-healthy menu. The specialty appetizer is marinated and grilled nopalitos cactus in a zesty sauce.

SEDONA Takashi Japanese Restaurant

465 Jordan Rd., AZ, 86336 **Tel** *(928) 282-2334*

Road map *C3*

Take a vacation from Southwestern cuisine and treat your taste buds to sushi and other Japanese dishes at Takashi, near uptown Sedona. Adorned with oriental lanterns and simple wooden furniture, the restaurant offers a broad and enticing menu, with soft-shell crabs, teriyaki, sukiyaki, tempura, and teppanyaki dishes.

SEDONA Dahl & Diluca Ristorante Italiano

2321 W. Hwy 89A, AZ, 86336 **Tel** *(928) 282-5219*

Road map *C3*

Enjoy the romance of old Italy among rich fabrics, warm colors, and tables dressed in white linen, in what seems like a Tuscan villa. A varied menu includes deep-fried cheese-filled olives and linguine with wild mushrooms in a creamy ragout sauce *(linguine con funghi)*. There is also an excellent wine selection to match your fare.

SEDONA The Heartline Café

1610 W. Hwy 89A, AZ, 86336 **Tel** *(928) 282-0785*

Road map *C3*

Colorful blooms from an all-organic garden are used in cooking and decorating at the Heartline Café. Dine in a casual, contemporary atmosphere on a mix of Asian, European, and Mediterranean food. Try the hoisin portobello mushroom tortilla sandwich, or the Game Trio for dinner, with fennel-mustard marinade and garlic mashed potatoes.

SEDONA Shugrue's Hillside Grill

Hillside Courtyard, 671 Hwy 179, AZ, 86336 **Tel** *(928) 282-5300*

Road map *C3*

It's all about the views in Sedona, and Shugrue's lofty floor-to-ceiling windows provide just that. They also have a large outdoor viewing terrace. Considered by many to have great steaks, the restaurant is also known for grilled, sautéed, or blackened seafood, such as blackened shrimp and sambuca sauce with fried saganaki cheese.

WILLIAMS Twisters Soda Fountain & The Route 66

417 E. Route 66, AZ, 86046 **Tel** *(928) 635-0266*

Road map *B3*

With its black-and-white checkerboard floor and red vinyl-topped old-time soda-fountain chairs, Twisters transports you back to the 1950s, aided by its selection of retro music and delectable banana splits. They serve burgers, sandwiches, chile dogs, and more. You can also shop for Route 66, Elvis, and Coca-Cola collectibles while there. Closed Sun.

WILLIAMS Red Raven Restaurant

135 W. Route 66, AZ, 86046 **Tel** *(928) 635-4980*

Road map *B3*

An unexpected gem of a restaurant for this remote area, the casual dining and relaxing environment offer some of the best dining in town. Creative, yet simple, the menu offers a great selection of Southwestern-inspired steaks, salads, soups, and pasta dishes. There is a choice of quality wines and beers, and the desserts are excellent.

WILLIAMS Miss Kitty's Steakhouse & Saloon

Mountainside Inn, 642 E. Route 66, AZ, 86046 **Tel** *(928) 635-4431*

Road map *B3*

Miss Kitty's can be a rollicking place on weekends, and even on weeknights, with country singers or the rhythmic sounds of ragtime bringing the gathered crowds to their feet. Designed like a Wild West saloon, the place offers juicy steaks, prime rib, and barbecue ribs – all at reasonable prices.

WILLIAMS Rod's Steak House

301 E. Route 66, AZ, 86046 **Tel** *(928) 635-2671*

Road map *B3*

Look for a glowing-red neon sign of Domino the Steer, the restaurant's mascot and a landmark for more than 50 years on Route 66 in Williams. Then, once you get to Rod's Steak House, let the slow-cooked prime rib melt in your mouth. The whole joint is a tribute to steer – even the menu is a die-cut of Domino. Closed Sun.

PHOENIX AND SOUTHERN ARIZONA

APACHE JUNCTION Mining Camp Restaurant & Trading Post

6100 E. Mining Camp St., AZ, 85217 **Tel** *(480) 982-3181*

Road map *C4*

Diners sit at long wooden tables, family-style, in this authentic version of an old-time miners' shanty built of rough-sawn ponderosa pine. Heaping platters of roast chicken, oven-baked ham, and barbecue ribs are accompanied by big bowls of coleslaw and baked beans, and Prospector's Cookies for the kids. A long-standing favorite. Closed Jun–Oct.

GLOBE Chalo's Casa Reynoso

902 E. Ash St., AZ, 85501 **Tel** *(928) 425-0515*

Road map *C4*

This local hangout is known for its traditional home cooking and family atmosphere. It is a cozy place where everyone knows each other's name. The interior is sparse, and rumor has it that Chalo's has the prettiest waitresses in the area. Take your choice, spicy or mild, for a large portion of Mexican *sopaipillas* filled with pork and beef.

GLOBE Jerry's Restaurant

699 E. Ash St., AZ, 85501 **Tel** *(928) 425-5282*

Road map *C4*

Locals come to Jerry's for American classics, friendly service, and large portions. The menu features comfort food such as burgers, ham and cheese sandwiches, Reuben sandwiches (corned beef, sauerkraut, Swiss cheese and mayonnaise on rye bread), as well as chicken dishes, steaks, and cornbread.

Key to Price Guide *see p252* **Key to Symbols** *see back cover flap*

NOGALES La Roca Restaurant

Calle Elias 91, Nogales, Mexico **Tel** *(520) 375-5750*

Road map *C5*

For authentic Mexican food, why not cross the border to Nogales? You can dine in a romantic, Spanish Colonial atmosphere on Sonoran cuisine in this century-old hacienda built right into the rocks. Take note of the Mayan and Mexican paintings while eating shrimp ceviche or grilled changarro beef tenderloin. Bring your passport.

PHOENIX Matt's Big Breakfast

801 N. 1st St., AZ, 85004 **Tel** *(602) 254-1074*

Road map *B4*

Matt's uses only grain-fed meats, organic produce, and cage-free eggs. During the week, it's busy with downtown office workers wanting sandwiches and salads; at weekends, people come for a salami scramble, Belgian waffles, and freshly squeezed orange juice. Decorated with 50s dinette tables, a bright-orange counter, and vintage artwork. Closed Mon.

PHOENIX Aunt Chilada's at Squaw Peak

7330 N. Dreamy Draw Dr., AZ, 85020 **Tel** *(602) 944-1286*

Road map *B4*

Casual, rustic, and spilling over with flowers, this out-of-the-way Mexican restaurant offers pleasant alfresco dining on a patio. In the late 19th century, it was a general store serving the local mercury miners. Select the chicken breast mole with sesame seeds, and chase it with a margarita. Colorful murals complement the atmospheric decor.

PHOENIX Pizzeria Bianco

623 E. Adams St., AZ, 85004 **Tel** *(602) 258-8300*

Road map *B4*

Located in a historic brick-faced building with large picture windows, this small eatery offers a simple menu of wood-fired pizzas of coveted award quality – they are rated by locals as the best in town. The toppings on the Wiseguy pizza are wood-roasted onion, fresh house-smoked mozzarella, and fennel sausage – delicious. Closed Mon & Sun.

PHOENIX Cafe at Heard Museum

Heard Museum, 2301 N. Central Ave., AZ, 85004 **Tel** *(602) 252-8848 ext. 5085*

Road map *B4*

Stop here for salads, gourmet sandwiches, and baked tarts, or push the boat out and order the house specialty: *posole* (spicy corn stew) with roasted pork and all the trimmings. Save room for the dark-chocolate ganache. Before or after lunch, see the Heard Museum's extensive collection of Native American cultural and fine artworks.

PHOENIX Rustler's Rooste

Arizona Grand Hotel, 7777 S. Pointe Pkwy. W, AZ, 85044 **Tel** *(602) 431-6474*

Road map *B4*

High on a butte overlooking Pointe South's golf courses and the twinkling lights of Phoenix, Rustler's Rooste is a sawdust-floored, cowboy-themed steakhouse. The fun begins at the mine-like entrance, where guests can opt to ride the slide down to the dining room. Generous portions are served. Try the crispy rattlesnake appetizer.

PHOENIX Sam's Café

2566 E. Camelback Rd., AZ, 85016 **Tel** *(602) 954-7100*

Road map *B4*

Inside Biltmore Fashion Park, Sam's Café provides affordable home-made specialties with a Southwestern twist. A delicious entrée is lightly smoked Atlantic salmon with spicy pecans, served over sautéed spinach and mashed sweet potatoes, and topped with a red papaya-and-cilantro sauce. They're also proud of their margaritas.

PHOENIX Avanti Restaurant

2728 E. Thomas Rd., AZ, 85016 **Tel** *(602) 956-0900*

Road map *B4*

Avanti has been open since the 1980s, serving delicious, classic Italian fare accompanied by a romantic atmosphere. The interior has Art Deco accents, and evening diners can enjoy piano or light jazz from Thursday to Saturday. Try the chicken in a lemon sauce with capers and artichoke hearts. The glitzy bar area serves homemade pasta dishes.

PHOENIX Vincent's on Camelback

3930 E. Camelback Rd., AZ, 85018 **Tel** *(602) 224-0225*

Road map *B4*

For over two decades, Vincent's has set a standard for fine dining, with an inventive menu that blends Southwestern ingredients with a Provençal flair. Start with the corn ravioli with white-truffle oil, followed by poached organic chicken with wild mushrooms, leeks, and thyme broth. Attentive service and an extensive wine list. Closed Sun.

PHOENIX Arizona Kitchen

Wigwam Resort, 300 Wigwam Blvd., Litchfield Pk., AZ, 85340 **Tel** *(623) 935-3811*

Road map *B4*

Arizona cuisine is prepared at a glistening exhibition kitchen with a wood-burning oven at this restaurant. Distinct indigenous flavors make the difference in dishes like the chile-rubbed maple-leaf duck with yellow mole sauce, sweet potato, and roasted corn hash. For dessert, the chile-spiked ice cream is served in a bowl of hardened sugar.

PHOENIX Compass Restaurant

Hyatt Regency, 122 N. 2nd St., AZ, 85004 **Tel** *(602) 440-3166*

Road map *B4*

Two dozen stories above Phoenix, Compass is the city's only revolving restaurant, with predictably splendid views. Decorated with black and red accents, it has a modern feel. On the menu are American regional selections, such as achiote-paste-rubbed pork chop with braised fennel. The restaurant also serves a delicious Sunday brunch.

SCOTTSDALE Frank & Lupe's Restaurant

4121 N. Marshall Way, AZ, 85251 **Tel** *(480) 585-4848*

Road map *inset map*

This small restaurant with minimal decor serves New Mexican favorites, including *mole enchiladas* (meat and vegetable-filled wraps with a cocoa, chili, and tomato sauce), tamales, and tacos, with red or green chile sauce, charro beans, fresh salsa, and crispy home-made chips. Beer and mixed drinks available.

SCOTTSDALE Roaring Fork

4800 N. Scottsdale Rd., Ste 1700, AZ, 85251 Tel (480) 947-0795 $$$
          Road map *inset map*

The creative Southwestern entrées here include filet mignon with green-chile macaroni, fish tacos, and cedar-planked salmon. Bigger appetites will enjoy the Roaring Fork's Big-A burger with roasted green chiles. The wood-fired oven also turns out delicious pizzas.

SCOTTSDALE Cowboy Ciao

7133 E. Stetson Dr., AZ, 85251 Tel (480) 946-3111 $$$$$
          Road map *inset map*

Desserts are listed at the top of the menu (for those who just can't wait) at Cowboy Ciao, on Restaurant Row, in Scottsdale's arts district. Inventive dishes such as Parmesan burritos and calamari chimichanga can be accompanied by a range of unusual global wines. The welcoming decor, defined as "Border Baroque," includes camp cherubs.

SCOTTSDALE Ruth's Chris Steakhouse

7001 N. Scottsdale Rd., AZ, 85253 Tel (480) 991-5988 $$$$$
          Road map *inset map*

Is there anything better than a sizzling, tender steak cooked to perfection? This chain is famed for its corn-fed and aged US prime beef and for its warm hospitality. On the menu, you will also find chicken and seafood dishes. Located in the Seville Shopping Center, the restaurant has pretty mountain views and seasonal patio dining.

SCOTTSDALE Sassi

10455 E. Pinnacle Peak Pkwy., AZ, 85255 Tel (480) 502-9095 $$$$$
          Road map *inset map*

Designed as a southern Italian-style villa, Sassi has an enclosed garden terrace and outdoor patios. Located at the base of Pinnacle Peak, with excellent views, it is a good place to visit with a group of friends, since several specialties are available to share. On the menu are pasta dishes, seafood, and poultry. A tasting menu has five courses.

TOMBSTONE Big Nose Kate's

417 E. Allen St., AZ, 85638 Tel (520) 457-3107 $
          Road map *C5*

Named for Tombstone's first prostitute (allegedly) and Doc Holliday's girlfriend, Big Nose Kate's was built as a hotel in 1881. These days, the bustling saloon is filled with Western memorabilia, steer heads, and stained glass. The Goldie's Over-Stuffed Reuben Sandwich has corned beef, sauerkraut, and Swiss cheese. Live country music daily.

TOMBSTONE OK Café

3rd & Allen Streets, AZ, 85638 Tel (520) 457-3980 $
          Road map *C5*

Locals rub elbows at this tiny café, appropriately located just opposite the famous OK Corral. Enjoy the standard omelette and coffee for breakfast, and great soups for lunch, but bear in mind that this place is billed as the "Home of the Buffalo Burger," and it also serves exotic charbroiled emu and ostrich burgers.

TUCSON Feast

4122 E. Speedway Blvd., AZ, 85712 Tel (520) 326-9363 $$
          Road map *C5*

Definitely a "foodies" restaurant, Feast has a Wine Country feel, with red-brick walls, floor-to-ceiling glass windows facing the Santa Catalina Mountains, and a wine wall filled with boutique labels. The food has a Mediterranean and Eastern influence, and the menu changes monthly. Note that the entire menu is available for takeout. Closed Mon.

TUCSON La Cocina

Old Town Artisans, 201 N. Court Ave., AZ, 85701 Tel (520) 622-0351 $$
          Road map *C5*

La Cocina is situated in the one-time stables of the 18th-century El Presidio. You can dine alfresco – on the patio or in the charming, shaded courtyard – or inside the cantina, surrounded by sculptures and artwork from the Old Town Artisans. Try a chicken enchilada with a green-chile cream sauce. Closed Sun.

TUCSON La Parilla Suiza

5602 E. Speedway Blvd., AZ, 85712 Tel (520) 747-4838 $$
          Road map *C5*

The long-standing La Parilla Suiza is the place for those who want a break from Sonoran cuisine. The family recipes here are firmly rooted in Mexico City. Tacos, meat, and cheese dishes are charcoaled or grilled. The Bistek Tacos consists of diced, charbroiled beef served on two corn tortillas with lettuce, refried beans, and rice.

TUCSON Café Poca Cosa

110 E. Pennington St., AZ, 85701 Tel (520) 622-6400 $$$
          Road map *C5*

This casual-chic bistro serves creative Nuevo Mexican cuisine prepared with fresh ingredients. Your server presents you with a chalkboard menu in English and Spanish; this is changed twice daily. The Plato de Poca Cosa – a chicken, beef, and vegetarian sample of the day's entrées – highlights typically regional flavors.

TUCSON El Charro Café

311 N. Court Ave., AZ, 85701 Tel (520) 622-1922 $$$
          Road map *C5*

The famous El Charro, located in the El Presidio historic district downtown, serves superb Mexican food prepared from ancient family recipes. No one should leave without trying the much sought-after *carne seca* – shredded sundried Angus beef marinated in garlic and lime juice, and grilled with fresh green chile, tomatoes, and onions.

TUCSON El Corral

2201 E. River Rd., AZ, 85718 Tel (520) 299-6092 $$$
          Road map *C5*

An affordable steakhouse located in a historic Territorial ranch house north of downtown, El Corral has a warm ambience with its fireplaces, flagstone floors, and wood-beamed ceilings. Prime rib is the specialty here, but steaks and chicken are also served. Come early, since sometimes there's a line of people waiting for tables.

Key to Price Guide *see p252* **Key to Symbols** *see back cover flap*

TUCSON The Grill

Hacienda del Sol, 5601 N. Hacienda del Sol Rd., AZ, 85718 **Tel** *(520) 529-3500* **Road map** *C5*

Dine in understated elegance at the esteemed Grill restaurant, where fresh ingredients are handpicked from the hacienda's lush gardens. The lobster gazpacho is a popular appetizer, followed by grilled Tasmanian sea trout on a purée of purple Peruvian potatoes. There is also an extensive wine list, and live music Thursdays to Sundays.

TUCSON Janos

Westin La Paloma Resort, 3770 E. Sunrise Dr., AZ, 85718 **Tel** *(520) 615-6100* **Road map** *C5*

At this much-celebrated fine-dining restaurant, Janos Wilder creates Southwestern dishes with a French twist and presents them with imaginative decorative touches. In addition to beautiful views of Tucson and an extensive wine list, there's also a prix-fixe menu with wine pairings. Closed Sun.

TUMACACORI Wisdom's Café

1931 Frontage Rd., AZ, 85640 **Tel** *(520) 398-2397* **Road map** *C5*

Look for two huge roadside white chickens. At the family-run Wisdom Café, recipes have been passed on from one generation to the next, and there are also murals and paintings by aunts and uncles. When a jam-filled tortilla fell into cooking oil, their famous fruit burro was born; it is now served with apples, cherries, peaches, or blueberries.

LAS VEGAS

DOWNTOWN Golden Nugget The Buffet

Golden Nugget, 129 E. Fremont St., NV, 89101 **Tel** *(702) 385-7111*

Simply called The Buffet, this pleasant all-you-can-eat establishment is among the best eateries in downtown Vegas. Lunchtime always sees a happy crowd sitting in comfy booths or at tables. Choose from interesting and varied food platters or the extensive salad bar. At dinner, there's also seafood, and the carving station features roast beef.

DOWNTOWN San Francisco Shrimp Bar & Deli

Golden Gate Hotel, 1 Fremont St., NV, 89101 **Tel** *(702) 385-1906*

Located in Las Vegas's oldest hotel (established in 1906), this claims to be the "home of the original Las Vegas shrimp cocktail." The crustaceans are still served in classic tulip sundae glasses, topped with a mystery sauce, for 99 cents, a rare extant old-school institution in this town. Sandwiches and beer are also available.

DOWNTOWN Firefly

Plaza Hotel & Casino, 1 Main St., NV, 89101 **Tel** *(702) 386-2110*

Dine in style, as Sharon Stone and Robert De Niro did in the film *Casino*, in the glass-domed Firefly, which was a martini-glass-shaped pool in a former life. Feast on an extensive selection of hot and cold Mediterranean small-plates while enjoying a perfect view of the Fremont Street Experience light-and-sound show.

DOWNTOWN Binion's Ranch Steakhouse

Binion's, 128 E. Fremont St., NV, 89101 **Tel** *(702) 382-1600*

If you manage to take your eyes off the Strip view from the 24th floor of Binion's, you'll be able to admire the plush Victorian setting, enhanced by live piano on weekends. Choose a booth and dine on the specialties that made this place popular: lobster bisque, porterhouse steak, and seafood, including the signature Chicken Fried Lobster.

DOWNTOWN Hugo's Cellar

Four Queens, 202 Fremont St., NV, 89101 **Tel** *(702) 385-4011*

At this subterranean, brick-walled restaurant, styled after a European wine cellar, ladies are presented with a rose, setting the mood for romantic dining. Locals come for the classic specialties: Queen's Lobster, rack of lamb, or beef Wellington, followed by Cherries Jubilee (prepared tableside) or chocolate-dipped fruit.

HENDERSON Sushi + Sake

Green Valley Ranch, 2300 Paseo Verde Parkway, NV, 89052 **Tel** *(702) 617-7777*

Stop by for a drink at the bar just to see the ultra-hip creative decor at Sushi + Sake. A 4-ft- (1.2-m-) tall wave wall acts as a light fixture and represents a chef making a sushi roll. The sushi is suitably artistic in presentation. Sashimi and nigiri can be gently washed down with an exotic sake from the restaurant's exclusive collection.

OFF STRIP Capriotti's

322 W. Sahara Ave., NV, 89102 **Tel** *(702) 474-0229*

For a quick foodie fix likely to last all day, stop in at Capriotti's, just steps off the Strip, for a sandwich measuring up to 20 in (50 cm). Special combos come overstuffed: Try the Slaw B Joe, bursting with on-site-roasted beef and coleslaw. There are also vegetarian sandwiches. The decor is sparse, and there is limited booth seating.

OFF STRIP Egg & I

4533 W. Sahara Ave., NV, 89102 **Tel** *(702) 364-9686*

Famished in the morning? Check out Egg & I, a family-friendly place with photos of hens and roosters on the walls. The Egg-Spectations Menu includes a pancake called Flapper Sandwich and the famous eggs Benedict. Egg-ceptional omelettes are served with ranch potatoes and a banana-nut muffin. Burgers, soups, and salads, too.

OFF STRIP Harbor Palace

4275 Spring Mountain Rd., NV, 89102 **Tel** *(702) 253-1688*

Las Vegas's Chinatown offers a vast variety of Pacific Rim restaurants. This Chinese eatery fills up with locals and visitors who share dishes from its lazy-Susan round tables. Dim sum is available daily from 10am to 3pm, and the restaurant also serves fresh seafood from a fish tank and traditional fare. A graveyard menu is served until 5am.

OFF STRIP Pink Taco

Hard Rock, 4455 Paradise Rd., NV, 89109 **Tel** *(702) 693-5525*

A hip spot for yuppies and the Rehab crowd *(see p238)*, this colorful cantina is decorated with a funky assortment of Mexican crafts and has a friendly ambience. On the reasonably priced menu are classic Mexican dishes and *panuchos* – pink tacos filled with chicken, salsa, and avocado. The margarita and tequila list is extensive.

OFF STRIP Nora's Cuisine

6020 W. Flamingo Rd., NV, 89103 **Tel** *(702) 873-8990*

Nora's opened in a tiny room and was immediately a hit for its family recipes with Sicilian accents. Its popularity demanded an expansion, but the quality and taste remain great. The antipasto salad filled with cured meats and mozzarella can't be beat, and the veal marsala is superbly tender. Late-night jazz bands on Fridays and Saturdays.

OFF STRIP Little Buddha

Palms, 4321 W. Flamingo Rd., NV, 89103 **Tel** *(702) 942-7778*

This Parisian favorite, now at the Palms Casino Resort *(see p238)*, serves Asian-fusion dishes with a French twist. A not-so-little Buddha held up by four columns presides over the main dining room. For starters, try the Pacific beef ceviche or Peking duck crêpes, followed by Korean BBQ glazed salmon. Dine at the sushi bar or outside, by the pool.

OFF STRIP Alizé

Palms, 4321 W. Flamingo Rd., NV, 89103 **Tel** *(702) 951-7000*

Sitting sky-high at 56 stories off the ground, with windows on three sides, this restaurant just west of the Strip boasts truly spectacular views. Gourmet cuisine is served in an elegant, romantic environment. Beluga caviar tops the seasonally changing menu. Dine on imported Dover sole or pan-seared Muscovy duck.

OFF STRIP Morton's the Steakhouse

400 E. Flamingo Rd., NV, 89103 **Tel** *(702) 893-0703*

Vying for the accolade of best steakhouse in town, Morton's lets diners select their cut tableside. The dining room has a clubby feel, with dark-wood furniture and photos of famous patrons like Muhammad Ali and Tiger Woods on the walls. A crustacean-filled list of appetizers precedes the steak offerings; there are "slightly smaller" options, too.

OFF STRIP Piero's Italian Cuisine

355 Convention Center Dr., NV, 89109 **Tel** *(702) 369-2305*

An old-time haunt of the rich and famous, starting with the Rat Pack, Piero's has a cozy ambience, as witnessed in Martin Scorsese's film *Casino*. Locals come for the osso buco, a wide selection of veal dishes, and fresh fish. Save room for the signature dessert, the *cassatina al liquore* – ice cream with candied fruit and a splash of liquor.

OFF STRIP Ruth's Chris Steakhouse

3900 Paradise Rd., NV, 89109 **Tel** *(702) 248-7011*

With a reputation for outstanding food, fine wines, and great hospitality, this restaurant has a comfy feel. Creole appetizers come from its New Orleans origins, and steaks arrive on a sizzling hot plate. Dinner is served until 10:30pm. Linger with the bar crowd over a snifter of cognac.

THE STRIP Witchcraft

MGM Grand, 3799 Las Vegas Blvd. S., NV, 89109 **Tel** *(702) 891-1111*

Only a witch could concoct refreshing, inventive sandwiches like those served in this casual spot off Studio Walk, at the MGM Grand *(see p238)*. Order a sublime sandwich like the chicken breast with roasted red pepper, mozzarella, and pesto on country bread. Complete the experience with a glass of wine and a scrumptious dessert.

THE STRIP California Pizza Kitchen

The Mirage, 3400 Las Vegas Blvd. S., NV, 89109 **Tel** *(702) 791-7111*

Popular with families, California Pizza Kitchen offers unique wood-fired pizzas that come out of the hearth with a crisp crust and some unusual toppings. Among its bestsellers are the BBQ Chicken, with smoked cheeses and red onions, and the Portobello, loaded with gourmet mushrooms.

THE STRIP Cravings

The Mirage, 3400 Las Vegas Blvd. S., NV, 89109 **Tel** *(702) 791-7111*

In a totally redesigned, modern, upscale space, Cravings brings new concepts to buffet dining, offering 13 stations where guests can watch food being cooked. It offers a variety of American and ethnic cuisines: barbecued pork ribs, noodles, Japanese sushi, Italian pasta, and pork enchiladas, plus seafood, salad, and dessert bars.

THE STRIP Tamba

Hawaiian Marketplace, 3743 Las Vegas Blvd. S., NV, 89109 **Tel** *(702) 798-7889*

Celebrating India's bold colors and spices, Tamba is decorated in striking reds and yellows, with giant murals and Hindu statuary. Its trademark cuisine comes piping hot out of clay ovens: tandoori prawns, chicken tikka masala in curry sauce, and the popular sandori. Try the Ashoka's Feast, with seven items, or the vegetarian Buddha's Feast.

Key to Price Guide *see p252* **Key to Symbols** *see back cover flap*

THE STRIP The Buffet at Bellagio $$$

Bellagio, 3600 Las Vegas Blvd. S., Nevada, 89109 **Tel** *(702) 693-8111*

Bellagio's upscale Tuscan decor extends to The Buffet, where you will find a wide (and pricey) selection of high-end items: Kobe beef, prime rib, rack of lamb, smoked salmon, Mako shark, and iced crab legs. Ethnic dishes include Chinese dim sum, Japanese sushi, and made-to-order Italian pasta. The Buffet is less expensive during the week.

THE STRIP Grand Lux Café $$$

The Venetian, 3355 Las Vegas Blvd. S., NV, 89109 **Tel** *(702) 414-3888*

In a setting not unlike an upscale Venetian café, this place has a lavish interior and an extensive menu with global influences, from Cajun shrimps to Wiener schnitzels. Meals are freshly prepared in an exhibition-style kitchen, the atmosphere is relaxed, and the doors are open 24/7. A great place to visit after all-night clubbing.

THE STRIP Harley Davidson Café $$$

3725 Las Vegas Blvd. S., NV, 89109 **Tel** *(702) 740-4555*

With its huge Heritage Softail replica bursting out over the entrance, this three-story "hog heaven" is instantly recognizable. The Harley Davidson Café is famous for its BBQ, so be sure to order the Combo Plate, which mixes ribs, chicken, and sausages. Diners can get photographed on the Captain America bike from *Easy Rider*.

THE STRIP Market City Caffe $$$

Monte Carlo, 3770 Las Vegas Blvd. S., NV, 89109 **Tel** *(702) 730-7966*

Market City has a relaxed, low-key atmosphere, a welcome respite from the all-pervading Vegas kitsch. The trattoria prepares solid southern Italian fare – pastas, pizzas, and entrées – from family recipes. A moderately priced antipasto bar includes items such as steamed mussels, calamari pesto salad, and penne pasta with salami.

THE STRIP Rainforest Café $$$

MGM Grand, 3799 Las Vegas Blvd. S., NV, 89109 **Tel** *(702) 891-8580*

The jungle-themed Rainforest Café is a kid-pleaser, with faux gorillas and elephants on the move. While you delve into your sandwich, salad, or pizza of choice, you'll hear thunder rumble and see simulated lightning bolts as a tropical storm sets in overhead. Thankfully, no raindrops will fall. End your meal with the Gorilla Cheesecake.

THE STRIP Spice Market Buffet $$$

Planet Hollywood Resort & Casino, 3667 Las Vegas Blvd. S., NV, 89109 **Tel** *(702) 785-5555*

An amazing variety of international entrées make this the perfect buffet for those times when you can't decide which cuisine to have. It's all here, including Mexican, Italian, Asian, Middle Eastern, and American. Make sure you save room for the delicious desserts.

THE STRIP Emeril's New Orleans Fish House $$$$

MGM Grand, 3799 Las Vegas Blvd. S., NV, 89109 **Tel** *(702) 891-7374*

The famed TV-star chef Emeril brought his delicious Creole and Cajun recipes to Las Vegas. The New Orleans Fish House's modern decor has a casual elegance, and diners here are tempted by the gumbo soup or the signature BBQ shrimp for starters, and tasty roasted Gulf snapper. The extensive wine list is embodied by a 2,200-bottle tower.

THE STRIP Grand Wok & Sushi Bar $$$$

MGM Grand, 3799 Las Vegas Blvd. S., NV, 89109 **Tel** *(702) 891-8670*

In a bright, open kitchen and gleaming sushi bar, chefs prepare Asian cuisine with a cross-section of Chinese, Japanese, Thai, Korean, and Vietnamese dishes. Try the sushi bar, or order a hot dish such as Mongolian Beef or Orange Chicken and enjoy the sounds of the nearby waterfall.

THE STRIP Kristofer's Steak House $$$$

Riviera, 2901 Las Vegas Blvd. S., NV, 89109 **Tel** *(702) 794-9233*

Quiet, airy, and elegant, Kristofer's Steak House serves a choice of excellent dishes including fine cuts of steak, grilled cedar-planked salmon, fresh scallops, and savory chicken. For dessert, try the key-lime pie or Snicker-bar pie. Pleasant Mediterranean setting and friendly staff.

THE STRIP Legends Steak & Seafood $$$$

Tropicana Resort & Casino, 3801 Las Vegas Blvd. S., NV, 89109 **Tel** *(702) 739-3561*

Casually elegant, Legends Steak & Seafood restaurant serves excellent steaks and fresh seafood with entrées of prime rib of beef, New York steak *au bleu*, walnut-crusted sea bass, and a pair of lobster tails. There is also a great wine list and the desserts are totally decadent.

THE STRIP Mon Ami Gabi $$$$

Paris, 3655 Las Vegas Blvd. S., NV, 89109 **Tel** *(702) 944-4224*

Dine alfresco overlooking the Strip, on a sidewalk patio that is perfect for people-watching and, coincidentally, great for viewing the dancing fountains at the Bellagio *(see p239)*. Simple Parisian classics like onion soup au gratin and steak frites, plus several seafood selections, are on the menu. Wines by the glass are served from a rolling cart.

THE STRIP Nero's $$$$

Caesars Palace, 3570 Las Vegas Blvd. S., NV, 89109 **Tel** *(877) 346-4642*

A graceful chandelier suspended from an Art Deco-style ceiling gives Nero's its distinctive elegance. The dining emphasis is on quality ingredients cooked to perfection. Start with roasted bone marrow, then choose an aged beef, such as the rib-eye "lollipop" cut, or fresh wild salmon. Alternatively, splurge on a 2-lb (1-kg) lobster.

THE STRIP Nobhill $$$$

MGM Grand, 3799 Las Vegas Blvd. S., NV, 89109 **Tel** *(702) 891-7337*

Take a trip to a San Francisco neighborhood, minus the fog, at Nobhill. Sleek design includes a floor-to-ceiling wine rack and glass-bordered booths named for SF neighborhood streets. If you are undecided, choose from a tasting menu that includes Kobe steak. The to-die-for masterpiece here is the lobster pot pie in a brandy cream sauce.

THE STRIP Ogden Bradley $$$$

Caesars Palace, 3570 Las Vegas Blvd. S., NV, 89109 **Tel** *(702) 731-7110*

The atmosphere here is calm and peaceful and the innovative, flavorful entrées are well presented. Farm fresh and organic foods are featured when available, presenting American favorites such as pan-roasted Alaskan halibut, Duroc pork loin, and roasted Petaluma free-range chicken.

THE STRIP Pinot Brasserie $$$$

The Venetian, 3355 Las Vegas Blvd. S., NV, 89109 **Tel** *(702) 414-8888*

Wood-paneled walls and maroon-leather banquettes are highlighted with French paintings and antiques in this bustling, Parisian-style brasserie serving Franco-Californian cuisine. An appetizer of roasted beet and prosciutto salad might be followed by braised ginger-and-citrus-glazed pork belly. Save room for the chocolate soufflé.

THE STRIP Tao Asian Bistro $$$$

The Venetian, 3355 Las Vegas Blvd. S., NV, 89109 **Tel** *(702) 388-8338*

A Sin City version of the New York sensation, Tao is part of a multistory entertainment complex. Diners sit under the gaze of a gigantic bronze Buddha in a room filled with antiques, lush velvet, and chandeliers. The menu covers the entire Pacific Rim, with Chinese, Japanese, and Thai cuisines. Specialties include Kobe beef and Peking duck.

THE STRIP Trattoria del Lupo $$$$

Mandalay Bay, 3950 Las Vegas Blvd. S., NV, 89119 **Tel** *(702) 632-7410*

Lofty, arched pillars, soft colors, and wrought-iron fittings give this restaurant a real Italian-trattoria atmosphere. Diners can watch as pizza and pasta dishes are created and crafted. Menu items such as spicy clams have a hint of chile, while the fettuccine is accented with black truffles. Keen people-watchers should reserve a patio table.

THE STRIP Aureole $$$$$

Mandalay Bay, 3950 Las Vegas Blvd. S., NV, 89119 **Tel** *(702) 632-7401*

Come early to Aureole for an aperitif at the bar, just to watch the "wine angels" (wine stewards in harnesses) ascend the four-story glass tower of outstanding wines, then dine in the intimate Swan Court. A prix-fixe menu offers inspired creations – perhaps a cypress-grove goat's-cheese tartine, with an entrée of roasted skate wing?

THE STRIP Fin $$$$$

The Mirage, 3400 Las Vegas Blvd. S., NV, 89109 **Tel** *(702) 791-7111*

Small, yet elegant, and intimate, Fin serves fine Chinese cuisine. Surrounded by emerald-and-gold silk wallpaper and glass baubles, diners can order clay-pot dishes, meat or poultry such as chicken breast macadamia, or select a live fish from Fin's tank. Most items, including the pricey abalone, can be braised, wok-fried, or steamed.

THE STRIP Joe's Seafood, Prime Steak & Stone Crab $$$$$

Forum Shops at Caesars, 3500 Las Vegas Blvd. S., NV, 89109 **Tel** *(702) 792-9222*

With its thick wood ceiling beams and leather booths, Joe's has the same vintage feel of the Miami Beach institution that has been serving unique stone crabs for the past 100 years. Flown in from the Gulf, the crustaceans are prepared tableside with a creamy mustard sauce. The signature dessert is a tangy key-lime pie.

THE STRIP Picasso $$$$$

Bellagio, 3600 Las Vegas Blvd. S., NV, 89109 **Tel** *(702) 693-7111*

Under the watchful eye of original Picasso masterpieces and ceramics, in a flower-filled room, the great Spanish artist is celebrated with award-winning food. Two tasting menus explore French-Mediterranean flavors, with dishes such as sautéed foie gras with honey-roasted figs and walnuts, or roasted pigeon with wild-rice risotto.

THE STRIP Rosewood Grille and Lobster House $$$$$

3763 Las Vegas Blvd.S., NV, 89109 **Tel** *(702) 792-5965*

Nothing much has changed in this long-standing and popular restaurant. You can sip martinis just as the crooners from the Rat Pack did, in an Old Vegas atmosphere. Settle into a comfy leather booth and feast on Maine lobster (sold by the pound). Several cuts of aged beef will please meat lovers, and the wine list is also outstanding.

THE STRIP Stratta $$$$$

Wynn Las Vegas, 3131 Las Vegas Blvd. S., NV, 89109 **Tel** *(702) 770-2040*

Dressed in rich reds and soft lighting, Stratta transports diners to southern Italy, adding a modern touch to traditional Italian fare. Roasted meat or seafood dishes, such as monkfish in parchment, are house specialties. The restaurant is famous for its wood-grilled pizza.

THE STRIP Top of the World $$$$$

Stratosphere Tower, 2000 Las Vegas Blvd. S., NV, 89104 **Tel** *(702) 380-7711*

View Las Vegas as far as the eye can reach – downtown, the Strip, and the surrounding mountains – as this 833-ft-(254-m-) high restaurant slowly revolves around Sin City. The romantic atmosphere might even prompt a proposal in this marrying town. Colorado rack of lamb, crab-stuffed veal, and Chilean sea bass are the house specials.

Key to Price Guide *see p252* **Key to Symbols** *see back cover flap*

SUMMERLIN Hachi $$$
Red Rock Resort, 11011 W. Charleston Blvd., NV, 89135 **Tel** *(702) 797-7777*

This contemporary, upscale restaurant serves a fabulous selection of modern Japanese cuisine. Entrées range from beef tenderloin medallions in a sake and soy sauce to chicken yakisoba. Sushi, sashimi, kushiyaki, and a selection of rolls and dumplings are all available.

SUMMERLIN Terra Rossa Italian Restaurant $$$$
Red Rock Resort, 11011 W. Charleston Blvd., NV, 89135 **Tel** *(702) 797-7576*

Terra Rossa has a Tuscan country feel and cozy elegance, with its elongated lamps and soft beige tones. Select authentic Old World dishes, such as the rarely found *burrata*, a rich, mozzarella-and-ricotta cheese salad with sundried tomatoes. The lasagna is layered with a rich meaty sauce and a delicate béchamel. Seasonal patio dining.

SOUTHERN UTAH

BOULDER Hell's Backbone Grill $$$
20 N. Hwy 12, UT, 82716 **Tel** *(435) 335-7464*   **Road map** *C2*

If you made it across the striking land bridge traversing the Hogsback Ridge, Hell's Backbone will thrill you with its superb regional Southwestern cuisine. Visit the carved stone Buddha that resides in the garden, then feast on jalapeño soup, and grilled chicken soft tacos with rattlesnake beans. The wines come from organic vineyards. Closed Dec–mid-Mar.

BRYCE CANYON Foster's Family Steakhouse $$
1150 Hwy 12, Bryce, UT, 84759 **Tel** *(435) 834-5227*   **Road map** *B2*

Located just on the outskirts of the national park, Foster's is a family place, as the name implies. Hearty meals are served at breakfast, lunch, and dinner. Fresh pastries and bread are baked daily, and slow-roasted prime rib is a popular choice in the evening. Good sandwiches and soup can be enjoyed at lunchtime.

BRYCE CANYON NATIONAL PARK Bryce Canyon Dining Room $$$
Bryce Canyon Lodge, Bryce Canyon National Park, UT, 84717 **Tel** *(435) 834-8760*   **Road map** *B2*

Nestled among ponderosa pines at the canyon, the Dining Room is both rustic and elegant. Its atmosphere is relaxing and very cozy, especially near the large stone fireplaces. Interesting items on the menu include Fairyland Crème Brie and Apple Stuffed Chicken. Be sure to save some room for the fudge lava cake. Reservations are a must. Closed Nov–Mar.

CEDAR CITY Market Grill $
2290 W. 400 North St., UT, 84720 **Tel** *(435) 586-9325*   **Road map** *B2*

The Market Grill started up over three decades ago to feed hungry cattle ranchers at the adjacent livestock auction. It offers good "ole' home cookin'," and you can eat until the cows come home in a Western atmosphere. A firm favorite among locals is the chicken-fried steak, served with mashed potatoes, gravy, and vegetables.

CEDAR CITY Rusty's Ranch House $$$
2275 E. Hwy 14, UT, 84721 **Tel** *(435) 586-3839*   **Road map** *B2*

Travel up Cedar Canyon to Rusty's and enjoy the canyon views through the windows overlooking Cold Creek. The typically Western decor sees mounted heads of moose, deer, and elk all around the dining room. They serve an outstanding filet mignon, tasty coconut shrimp, and honey-glazed ribs. At dinner, you can mingle with the locals.

KANAB Parry Lodge Restaurant $
89 E. Center St., UT, 84741 **Tel** *(435) 644-2601*   **Road map** *B2*

In the heart of Canyon Country, Parry Lodge serves up an affordable daily buffet breakfast, with everything from a Western-style omelette with ham and bell peppers, to French toast. Many movie stars, including Tyrone Power and Lana Turner, have passed through this establishment since way back in 1931, when it first opened. Open Apr–Sep.

MOAB Moab Diner $
189 S. Main St., UT, 84532 **Tel** *(435) 259-4006*   **Road map** *C2*

From its all-day and all-night breakfast (for the disco crowd), through to dinner, this simply decorated diner prices it just right, as confirmed by the numerous cars parked out front. Join the bustle any time for the green-chile cheeseburger, and don't leave without trying an ice-cream sundae or shake: They come in 15 flavors.

MOAB Eddie McStiff's $$$
57 S. Main St., UT, 84532 **Tel** *(435) 259-2337*   **Road map** *C2*

A centrally located, down-to-earth place, Eddie McStiff's pours 14 house microbrews at its 20-seat bar. Its sought-after pizzas are reasonably priced, as are its pasta dishes and steaks. Bite into the gourmet ravioli filled with roasted tomato, goat's cheese, and mozzarella. In addition to the main dining area, there is a covered garden terrace.

MOAB Slickrock Café $$$
5 N. Main St., UT, 84532 **Tel** *(435) 259-8004*   **Road map** *C2*

The Slickrock has an airy, atrium-like feel. It's furnished with bentwood chairs, *saltillo* tiles, and a funky mix of colors. The highlights of its trendy menu are Hell's Revenge, a jalapeño burger with pepper Jack cheese and bacon, and Addied Taylor's Outlaw Meatloaf. Vegetarian dishes are also available.

MOAB Sunset Grill

🚻 📶 🍴 $$$

900 N. Route 191 on Main St., UT, 84532 **Tel** *(435) 259-7146*

Road map *C2*

It's worth hiking uphill to this restaurant, located in what was formerly the home of Charlie Steen, the man who discovered uranium and put Moab on the map. His "discovery boots" are cast in bronze. But the big draws here are the sunset views and the fine dining. Try the filet mignon or the Olivia linguine, tossed with lobster and shrimp.

MOAB Center Café

🚻 📶 🍴 $$$$

60 N. 100 West, UT, 84532 **Tel** *(435) 259-4295*

Road map *C2*

After a day of sporting or touring, stop for a bite to eat at this unassuming restaurant. Dressed in wood, with a stone fireplace and white tablecloths, the Center Café has a friendly, contemporary feel. Specials have global influences and may include an exotic ostrich or bison dish. The Small Bites bistro menu is served 3:30–6pm.

PANGUITCH Cowboy's Smokehouse

🚻 🎵 🍴 $$

95 N. Main St., UT, 84759 **Tel** *(435) 676-8030*

Road map *B2*

The Cowboy's Smokehouse was opened by an amateur rodeo bullrider with a penchant for good food. Steaks and ribs are mesquite-smoked and served with a homemade barbecue sauce, which is also for sale. Decorated with old family and ranch photos and deer and moose heads, the place occasionally features live country music. Beer only.

SPRINGDALE Spotted Dog Restaurant

🚻 📶 🍴 $

Flanigan's Inn, 428 Zion Park Blvd., UT, 84767 **Tel** *(435) 772-0700*

Road map *B2*

Close to Zion's south entrance, the Spotted Dog has alfresco sidewalk dining and great views. The art-filled dining room has a fireplace and tall windows. On the menu are such dishes as goat's-cheese mousse with caper beurre blanc, and braised lamb shank with mint mashed potato. Excellent wine cellar. Open for breakfast and dinner only.

SPRINGDALE Oscar's Café

🚻 📶 🍴 $$

948 Zion Park Blvd., UT, 84767 **Tel** *(435) 772-3232*

Road map *B2*

This adobe-style café has a lovely patio out front for good views of Zion. Inside, diners will find a definite Mexican ambience, with mosaics throughout (created by the owner) and a mix of Mayan masks and plants. Order the famed Murder Burger (with bacon, cheese, and onions), green-chile chimichangas, and great sweet-potato fries.

SPRINGDALE Bit and Spur Saloon

🚻 📶 🍴 $$$

1212 Zion Park Blvd., UT, 84767 **Tel** *(435) 772-3498*

Road map *B2*

Under the watchful eye of Zion's towering West Temple sits this longtime local favorite. The Bit and Spur is a family place first and foremost, and a nightspot second. The simple restaurant, with revolving art exhibits, offers creative Mexican food. Order the Bistek Asado, a chile-rubbed rib eye, and dine on the outdoor patio.

ST. GEORGE Bear Paw Coffee Co.

$

75 North Main St., UT, 84770 **Tel** *(435) 634-0126*

Road map *B2*

Far more than a coffee shop, this friendly restaurant serves breakfast and lunch every day of the year. The extensive menu offers omelets, frittatas, waffles, and much more until 3pm. A lunch menu of sandwiches, soups, and early dinner entrées starts at 11am. Gourmet coffee and tea too.

ST. GEORGE Pancho and Lefty's

🚻 🍴 $

1050 S. Bluff St., UT, 84770 **Tel** *(435) 628-4772*

Road map *B2*

Step through an archway to a traditional Mexican atmosphere with colorful woven blankets and sombreros, where the locals hunger for freshly made tamales and chile. Try the *flautas* or get an enchilada plate, chased by a salted-rim margarita. Grilled steak, chicken, or shrimp fajitas are served with beans, rice, and tortillas.

ST. GEORGE Painted Pony

🚻 📶 🎵 🍴 $$$

Ancestor Square, 2 West St., George Blvd., UT, 84770 **Tel** *(435) 634-1700*

Road map *B2*

The palate-pleasing cuisine found in this romantic restaurant with contemporary decor is an unexpected surprise for a small city. Menus vary seasonally. The sage-smoked quail with a tamarind glaze, and the sesame-crusted *escolar* (snake mackerel) with a sweet ginger sauce are popular items. Local jazz artists occasionally perform. Good wines.

TORREY Capitol Reef Café

🚻 📶 🍴 $$

360 W. Main St., UT, 84775 **Tel** *(435) 425-3271*

Road map *C2*

The locally farmed trout is a specialty at this café that hangs its hat on healthy food. The fish comes grilled, broiled, or smoked, and is served with a ten-vegetable salad. The Capitol Reef is open only during the warmer months, from mid-March to mid-October, and it is located close to its namesake national park.

TORREY Café Diablo

🚻 📶 🍴 $$$

599 W. Main St., UT, 84775 **Tel** *(435) 425-3070*

Road map *C2*

If you order Firecrackers (ladyfingers, cherry bombs, and M-80s) and a Mexican Bridesmaid at Café Diablo, you'll get wrapped shrimp, chicken, and potatoes, with iced tea mixed with lemonade – it will be delicious. In a remote Southern Utah town, this place offers an enticing and whimsical take on Southwestern gastronomy.

ZION NATIONAL PARK Red Rock Grill

🚻 📶 🍴 $$

Zion Lodge, Springdale, UT, 84767 **Tel** *(435) 772-7760*

Road map *B2*

Nestled among the cottonwoods, deep inside the canyon, the rustic Red Rock Grill boasts splendid views. Interesting menu items include the spicy-sweet chipotle tilapia fish and a vegetarian Navajo eggplant with a *tomatillo* cream sauce. Those who have been here before know to save room for the Moose Tracks ice-cream sundae.

Key to Price Guide *see p252* **Key to Symbols** *see back cover flap*

THE FOUR CORNERS

BLUFF Twin Rocks Café   ⑤
913 E. Navajo Twins Dr., UT, 84512 **Tel** *(435) 672-2341*   **Road map** D2

A pair of sandstone pillars stands huddled together high above the cliffs at the Twin Rocks Café. The menu offers a wide variety of moderately priced sandwiches, salads, and dinner entrées, in addition to the unique Navajo pizza, based on fry bread topped with the usual pizza ingredients. Take time to pay a visit to the trading post.

BLUFF Cottonwood Steakhouse   ⑤⑤⑤
Main & 4th West St., Hwy 191, UT, 84512 **Tel** *(435) 672-2282*   **Road map** D2

The cottonwood tree outside this roadside steakhouse is almost bigger than the building and provides nice shade over the picnic tables around the outdoor barbecue pit. Sizable portions of steak, chicken, ribs, shrimp, or even catfish are served with plenty of green salad. Wash them down with beer and malt coolers.

CAMERON Cameron Trading Post   ⑤⑤
Route 89, AZ, 86020 **Tel** *(928) 679-2231*   **Road map** C3

Located at a convenient Four Corners crossroads, the Trading Post *(see also p242)* has windows all the way to the Little Colorado River Gorge. Fine Native American artworks adorn the walls up to the pressed-tin ceiling. The house specialty is the Navajo taco, but a variety of American, Mexican, and Native dishes is also served.

CHINLE Thunderbird Lodge   ⑤
Canyon de Chelly, Navajo Route 7, AZ, 86503 **Tel** *(928) 674-5841*   **Road map** C3

Located on the Navajo reservation at Canyon de Chelly, on the site of an 1896 trading post, this pleasant place serves classic American and Continental dishes, from cafeteria-style breakfast through to dinner. Portions are generous, with different items each day. The Navajo rugs and artworks decorating the walls can be purchased.

CHINLE Garcia's Restaurant   ⑤⑤⑤
Garcia Trading Post at Canyon de Chelly, Navajo Route 7, AZ, 86503 **Tel** *(928) 674-5000*   **Road map** C3

On the site of the old Garcia Trading Post, adjoining the Holiday Inn, is Garcia's Restaurant. Decorated in light colors with white furniture, it serves classic Southwestern dishes, along with Native and Mexican specialties, including fajitas and a marinated sirloin steak. The restaurant keeps limited opening hours in the winter months.

DURANGO Carver Brewing Co.   ⑤⑤
1022 Main Ave., CO, 81301 **Tel** *(970) 259-2545*   **Road map** D2

Considered a Durango institution by the locals, Carver has been brewing beer for two decades, from light lagers to hardy oatmeal stouts. Selections from its diverse menu include Southwest Ravioli, made with ancho chile, and seared sesame ahi stir-fry, served with a ginger-and-peanut sauce. There is a covered beer garden at the back.

DURANGO Ariano's   ⑤⑤⑤⑤
150 E. College Drive, CO, 81301 **Tel** *(970) 247-8146*   **Road map** D2

Dine in an intimate, candlelit atmosphere in a turn-of-the-20th-century building in downtown Durango. Paintings of northern Italy hang on the walls in this split-level restaurant, which is considered one of the best in town. Among the specialties is the *pollo al cartoccio* – chicken with prosciutto and herbs baked in parchment paper.

DURANGO Red Snapper   ⑤⑤⑤⑤
144 E. 9th St., CO, 81301 **Tel** *(970) 259-3417*   **Road map** D2

This haven for seafood lovers is housed in a turn-of-the-20th-century downtown building. Chefs choose fried red snapper in a tamarind sauce, or bake it in tarragon Mornay sauce. Fresh fish is flown in daily. The menu also includes a "landfood" section for meat eaters. The atmosphere is casual, with a huge illuminated aquarium.

FARMINGTON Clancy's Pub   ⑤⑤
2703 E. 20th St., NM, 87402 **Tel** *(505) 325-8176*   **Road map** D2

Housed in an adobe-style building, Clancy's is known as an "Irish cantina" because it is a slice of Ireland in New Mexico. It serves typical Southwestern and Mexican fare but is perhaps better known for its massive burgers. The extraordinary menu also includes a full sushi selection.

GRAY MOUNTAIN Anasazi   ⑤
Hwy 89, Grey Mountain Trading Post, Grey Mountain, AZ, 86016 **Tel** *(928) 679-2203*   **Road map** C3

East of the Grand Canyon's South Rim, on the border of the Navajo Reservation, this convenient roadside restaurant serves up an authentic Navajo fry bread, as well as Mexican and American fare. Its decor probably comes from the adjacent Curio, a shop filled with Navajo arts, crafts, pottery, and trinkets.

KAYENTA Amigo Café   ⑤
Hwy 163, AZ, 86033 **Tel** *(928) 697-8448*   **Road map** C3

Far from the busy city life, on the Navajo Reservation, the Amigo Café is frequented by locals and tourists alike. They serve up a very inexpensive combo plate (#9), which is a kind of taste-of-Mexico platter, with chimichangas, tacos, tamales, tostados, and more. Takeout is also available. Closed Sun.

MESA VERDE NATIONAL PARK Spruce Tree Terrace Café

Mile Marker 15, Mancos, CO, 81328 **Tel** *(970) 529-4444*

Road map D2

Housed in a historic stone building opposite the Chapin Mesa Museum, deep inside the park, the Spruce Tree is open for cafeteria service or takeout. Navajo tacos are a favorite on the expansive menu, and prices are reasonable. Dine inside, or pick a table under a white umbrella on the patio for a cool beer. Open all year round.

MESA VERDE NATIONAL PARK Metate Room

Mile Marker 15, Mancos, CO, 81328 **Tel** *(970) 529-4422*

Road map D2

Extremely remote, Metate Room will delight clients with its adventurous cuisine based on sustainable staples used by the Ancestral Puebloans. From the cactus nopalitos dip or the blue-corn trout, to quail stuffed with fig and chorizo, or the pepper-and-coriander-crusted elk, the menu never fails to surprise. Local wines are on the menu. Closed mid-Oct–Apr.

MONUMENT VALLEY The View Hotel Restaurant

Hwy 163 Monument Valley Tribal Park, UT, 84536 **Tel** *(435) 727-5555*

Road map C2

Dine in a spacious restaurant decorated with Navajo art and with a spectacular view of Monument Valley. The menu features Navajo specialties such as mutton stew with fried bread and American entrées including grilled salmon and steaks. A local flute player often entertains diners.

MONUMENT VALLEY Stagecoach Dining Room

Goulding's Lodge, UT, 84536 **Tel** *(435) 727-3231*

Road map C2

Located high on a hill, the Stagecoach provides a large dining room to cater for the many tourists visiting Monument Valley, just down the road. There's the standard T-bone steak and salad bar, and a more interesting Navajo taco sampler appetizer. Come here for the stunning panorama views from every table.

OURAY Backstreet Bagel & Deli

524 Main St., CO, 81427 **Tel** *(970) 325-0550*

Road map D2

Catering to the climbing community, Backstreet will placate any sweet-tooth needs, as well as any requirement for an energy boost, with its homemade pastries, pies, and phenomenal cheesecake. The three-cheese bagels are popular, as are the sandwiches, soups, and special frozen coffees – try the Bailey's milkshake.

OURAY Bon Ton Restaurant

St. Elmo Hotel, 426 Main St., CO, 81427 **Tel** *(970) 325-4951*

Road map D2

Located in the basement of the historic St. Elmo, Bon Ton offers a cozy atmosphere and upscale Italian fare. The grilled Angus beef wrapped in pastry and the scampi served in a sherry-cream sauce over fettuccine are some of the favorites. For dessert, try the Black Nasty, a decadent chocolate pie. Award-winning wine list and Martini bar.

SECOND MESA, HOPI RESERVATION Hopi Cultural Center Restaurant

Route 264, AZ, 86043 **Tel** *(928) 734-2402*

Road map C3

Steaming mutton stew, fired on a hot stone, with hominy and roasted green chiles, is one of the traditional Hopi dishes served at this restaurant. Piki bread, made of blue corn, is parchment-paper-thin. Mexican and American dishes, and an excellent salad bar, are available at this popular restaurant.

TELLURIDE Maggie's Bakery and Café

217 E. Colorado Ave., CO, 81435 **Tel** *(970) 728-3334*

Road map D2

The aroma of freshly brewed French roast coffee pervades the air of this small café. All the breads and pastries are homemade, from the muffins to the cinnamon rolls. Hearty eggs and pancakes are served for breakfast, and there are vegetarian options and light sandwiches at lunch. Burgers are served on home-baked buns.

TELLURIDE 221 South Oak

221 South Oak, CO, 81435 **Tel** *(970) 728-9507*

Road map D2

This restaurant occupies two rooms in a historic house near the Gondola. There are cushy couches in the entry room, and an overall homey atmosphere, with golden walls, candlelight, and white linen. Among the eclectic dishes are sautéed soft-shell crabs with red-peppercorn sauce. Summertime dining can be enjoyed on the garden patio.

TELLURIDE Excelsior Café

200 W. Colorado Ave., CO, 81435 **Tel** *(970) 728-4250*

Road map D2

Open only for dinner, the Excelsior has a contemporary decor, with large windows and a small sidewalk patio that is great for people-watching. Highlights on the Italian-influenced menu include the tasty wild-mushroom risotto with white-truffle oil, and ruby-red Rocky Mountain trout. Moderately priced and serving mainly Italian wines.

TUBA CITY Hogan Restaurant

Main St. and Moenave Rd., AZ, 86045 **Tel** *(928) 283-5260*

Road map C3

Adjacent to the historic Tuba Trading Post and shaped like a hogan dwelling (hence the name), this restaurant is in the heart of the Navajo tribal lands, near scenic desert landscapes and Grand Canyon. Traditional mutton stew and Navajo tacos can be found on the menu, as well as a variety of Mexican and American dishes.

WINDOW ROCK Diné

Quality Inn, 48 W. Hwy 264, AZ, 86515 **Tel** *(928) 871-4108*

Road map D3

Located near the governmental buildings of the Navajo Nation's capital, Diné is especially busy at lunchtime, when it attracts politicians and businessmen. The restaurant is decorated with Navajo art, and serves traditional mutton stew, Navajo fry bread, and Navajo tacos, in addition to Mexican and American fare.

Key to Price Guide *see p252* **Key to Symbols** *see back cover flap*

SANTA FE AND NORTHERN NEW MEXICO

CHIMAYÓ Restaurante Rancho de Chimayó
$$
County Rd. 98, NM, 87522 **Tel** *(505) 351-4444* **Road map** *E3*

Offering fine Mexican cuisine prepared with local ingredients according to old Spanish recipes, this century-old hacienda is decorated with family photos on its adobe walls. Dine on the terrace in the cool summer breeze, or by a cozy fireplace on winter days. The Bistec Solomillo comes with chile and melted cheese. Beautiful views.

RANCHOS DE TAOS Trading Post Café
$$$$
4179 Hwy 68 (at Hwy 518), NM, 87557 **Tel** *(575) 758-5089* **Road map** *E3*

Located close to the famous San Francisco de Asis church, the historic Trading Post Café is a favorite with locals and celebs, as much for its artworks as for its artistically presented meals. Choose from many daily specials, such as fresh fish or pasta dishes, at this casual place with patio dining. Seafood paella is on the menu at weekends. Closed Mon.

SANTA FE Bumblebee's Baja Grill
$
301 Jefferson St., NM, 87501 **Tel** *(505) 820-2862* **Road map** *E3*

Chargrilled fish tacos served Baja-style with soft corn tortillas top the list of favorites at Bumblebee's "beestro." The Burrito de Tomas house special has grilled asparagus, avocado, and Jack and cheddar cheese. Order at the counter, and the waiter will deliver your meal to the table. Live jazz on Saturdays.

SANTA FE Tomasita's
$
500 S. Guadalupe St., NM, 87501 **Tel** *(505) 983-5721* **Road map** *E3*

Housed in an old brick train station built in 1904, Tomasita's is a firm favorite with the locals, and a no-reservations policy may mean a lengthy wait. Try the blue-corn chicken or the burritos, but go easy on the chile – it's sizzlin' hot. A good place for families, with booth or table seating. Mariachis play on Tuesday nights. Closed Sun.

SANTA FE Blue Corn Café and Brewery
$$
133 Water St., NM, 87501 **Tel** *(505) 984-1800* **Road map** *E3*

The Blue Corn has a modern feel, despite the thick wooden beams overhead. Known for its tap microbrews, it also serves a pale ale, Altitude with an Attitude, for hop-heads, as well as prickly-pear iced tea (yes, it's made with cactus juice). The special is tacos made with blue corn and brimming with beef or chicken.

SANTA FE Cowgirl Bar & Grill
$$
319 S. Guadalupe St., NM, 87501 **Tel** *(505) 982-2565* **Road map** *E3*

Finger-lickin'-good BBQ is served up by cowgirls in this Wild West restaurant, where everything is cooked over a mesquite pit. Photos, art posters, hides, chaps, skulls, and other cowgirl memorabilia cover the walls. Great for families during the day (there is a kids' area), Cowgirl also serves up a variety of live music at night.

SANTA FE Los Potrillos
$$
1947 Cerrillos Rd., NM, 87505 **Tel** *(505) 992-0550* **Road map** *E3*

Los Potrillos ("the colts") serves the kind of authentic dishes Mexicans eat every day, from yummy quesadillas and nopalito cactus leaf, to fish and seafood, such as a stuffed fish filet. Diners sit on carved wooden chairs with a horse relief. Horseshoes hang on the wall, and a colorful horse-themed mural fills the back wall.

SANTA FE Maria's New Mexican Kitchen
$$
555 W. Cordova Rd., NM, 87505 **Tel** *(505) 983-7929* **Road map** *E3*

Start (or end) your meal with a margarita; alternatively, if you are concerned about high-altitude drinking, you can buy the proprietor's book (forward by Robert Redford) and learn about margaritas. Chicken, beef, and vegetarian dishes are served on a sizzling platter with guacamole and *pico de gallo* (tomatoes, onions, and chile sauce).

SANTA FE Santa Fe Bar & Grill
$$
187 Paseo de Peralta, NM, 87501 **Tel** *(505) 982-3033* **Road map** *E3*

Located in the DeVargas Mall, this handsome restaurant has authentic and artistic furnishings, pottery, and vibrant artworks imported from Mexico. Meat lovers should try the garlic-infused, slow-roasted baby back ribs. Satisfy a sweet tooth with the Adobe Mud Pie or the Taos Cow ice cream. Sit at the long bar or on the patio.

SANTA FE The Shed
$$
113½ E. Palace Ave., NM, 87051 **Tel** *(505) 982-9030* **Road map** *E3*

The Shed wants its customers to "downshift a couple of centuries" in its quaint 17th-century adobe hacienda, family-run for four generations. Folk art overlooks diners as they sip a cool red raspberry soup laced with rosé wine, or tuck into a spicy chicken dish or zingy lemon soufflé. Close to the Plaza.

SANTA FE Amaya
$$$
Hotel Santa Fe, 1501 Paseo de Peralta, NM, 87501 **Tel** *(505) 982-1200* **Road map** *E3*

Located in an elegant Native American hotel *(see p244)*, Amaya offers dining by the fireplace or alfresco on the patio. The menu emphasizes regional staples – salmon, game – in dishes such as venison chops marinated in port wine and juniper berries served with purple-potato hash and ancho-chile blackberry sauce. Complimentary parking.

SANTA FE La Boca
72 W. Marcy, NM, 87051 **Tel** (505) 982-3433

Road map E3

A cozy bistro atmosphere pervades the usually packed La Boca ("the mouth"). A favorite Santa Fe chef makes a variety of mouthwatering tapas and entrées, blending Mediterranean and Spanish influences. Among the tapas are pork and fennel sausage with pomegranate, and grilled artichokes with Spanish goat's cheese, orange, and mint.

SANTA FE Mu Du Noodles
1494 Cerrillos Rd., NM, 87505 **Tel** (505) 983-1411

Road map E3

Ask a local where to eat, and they may well suggest Mu Du Noodles, a short drive from downtown. Scant on decor inside, the restaurant has a charming alfresco patio. The house specialty is Beef Jantaboon Stir-Fry, cooked with spicy onions, bok choy, beansprouts, and hot and sweet peppers. A range of dishes covers Asian/Pacific Rim cuisine.

SANTA FE Aqua Santa
451 W. Alameda, NM, 87501 **Tel** (505) 982-6297

Road map E3

Interesting cuisine doesn't require an elegant setting, as proven by this tiny, 12-table storefront restaurant with an open kitchen and informal atmosphere. You'll likely find marinated wild boar or lamb on the ever-changing menu. Quail with risotto and Moroccan spiced squab are prepared with staples bought from local farmers.

SANTA FE Café Paris
31 Burro Alley, NM, 87501 **Tel** (505) 986-9162

Road map E3

Located in the historic Burro Alley, Café Paris serves Santa Fe's most decadent pastries, all concocted by its Parisian chef. Featured French cuisine entrées include chicken Cordon Bleu, beef Bourguignon, and shrimp Provençal, all served with fresh French bread and good wines. Dine indoors or outside on the patio.

SANTA FE Café Pasqual's
121 Don Gaspar Ave., NM, 87501 **Tel** (505) 983-9340, (800) 722-7672

Road map E3

Ready to wait a while for elbow-to-elbow seating? That's what the locals do. Just steps away from the Plaza, in a pueblo-style adobe, this tiny restaurant is lined with whimsical murals and Mexican tiles. Much of the innovative cuisine is organic and natural; try the grilled banana-leaf-wrapped salmon, and squash and red-onion enchiladas.

SANTA FE Coyote Café
132 W. Water St., NM, 87051 **Tel** (505) 983-1615

Road map E3

A short walk from the Plaza, the Coyote Café puts contemporary Southwestern cuisine on the map. In an elegant dining room, creative inventions include Yucatan black-bean soup, and fennel with sherry-pine-nut vinaigrette, not to mention a superb breast of duck with peach *passilla* mole, duck tamale, and cabbage hash.

SANTA FE Dinner for Two
106 N. Guadalupe St., NM, 87051 **Tel** (505) 820-2075

Road map E3

Come to Dinner for Two for romantic dining at its finest. The restaurant offers a great wine list and exceptional American and Continental cuisine simply prepared. The service here is friendly and attentive without being overbearing, and the pricing is just right. Closed Tue.

SANTA FE El Farol
808 Canyon Rd., NM, 87501 **Tel** (505) 983-9912

Road map E3

Located in the Canyon Road arts community, El Farol ("the lantern") has been serving artists and poets since 1835. Giant murals are everywhere. Besides a long list of hot and cold tapas, the restaurant has delicious Spanish cuisine such as paella, and wines. Nightly music gets 'em dancing; the best night is Saturday, featuring flamenco guitars.

SANTA FE La Casa Sena
20 Sena Plaza, 125 E. Palace Ave., NM, 87051 **Tel** (505) 988-9232

Road map E3

Located in an 1860s Territorial-style adobe, this hacienda surrounds a pretty courtyard, beautiful for summertime dining. Tempting the palate is a chorizo-stuffed pork tenderloin with peach-and-prickly-pear purée and pineapple salsa, paired with wines from an outstanding selection. End your meal with the delectable lavender crème brûlée.

SANTA FE Old House Restaurant
309 W. San Francisco St., NM, 87501 **Tel** (505) 988-4455

Road map E3

Frequented by pre-opera diners, the Old House offers fine food and impeccable service. Menus change according to the seasons. The tasting menu might have Dungeness crab bisque or seared Maine diver scallops for appetizers, a roasted duckling entrée, and huckleberry strudel for dessert. A superior wine collection completes the picture.

SANTA FE The Pink Adobe
406 Old Santa Fe Trail, NM, 87501 **Tel** (505) 983-7712

Road map E3

A favorite with celebs and locals, The Pink Adobe was formerly a barracks for conquistadores. It has several candlelit rooms, each with a fireplace, and one with a tree growing through the roof. The superb comfort cuisine includes dishes like grandma used to make; try the Steak Dunigan, with its "mystery" flavor. Boutique-vineyard wines.

SANTA FE SantaCafé
231 Washington Ave., NM, 87501 **Tel** (505) 984-1788

Road map E3

Located in the 150-year-old adobe hacienda of controversial Padre Gallegos, SantaCafé emphasizes flawless service and eclectic cuisine, with a successful blend of Asian and Southwestern ingredients, such as tiger-prawn tempura with red chile. You'll find understated decor, a handful of deer antlers, and a cozy fireplace in each room.

Key to Price Guide see p252 **Key to Symbols** see back cover flap

SANTA FE Anasazi Restaurant
$$$$$

Anasazi Hotel, 113 Washington St., NM, 87501 **Tel** *(505) 988-3236*
Road map *E3*

The large dining of Anasazi has a high, wood-beamed ceiling and rustic furniture. The restaurant's chef is renowned locally for his innovative Southwestern creations. An appetizer of red pepper and lobster bisque with Parmesan might be followed with crispy cashew-crusted yellowfin tuna. Alfresco dining is also available.

SANTA FE Geronimo
$$$$$

724 Canyon Rd., NM, 87501 **Tel** *(505) 982-1500*
Road map *E3*

The Borrego House was built in 1756 by Geronimo Lopez. Here, you can dine in an intimate, candlelit atmosphere, with fireplaces and fresh flowers, and partake in the passion for food and service for which this restaurant is acclaimed. The chef's global fusion-Southwestern creations, like peppery elk, are unparalleled.

TAOS Orlando's New Mexican Café
$$

1114 Don Juan Valdez Lane, NM, 87571 **Tel** *(575) 751-1450*
Road map *E3*

Local chile aficionados choose Orlando's for its regional New Mexican family-friendly fare. Smoky-flavored chile sauce served with pork slices is a favorite, as are the green-chile chicken enchiladas. The café is painted hot pink, tangerine, and lime, and colored umbrellas shade the patio. Have a beer by the fire pit on cool evenings.

TAOS Apple Tree Restaurant
$$$

123 Bent St., NM, 87571 **Tel** *(575) 758-1900*
Road map *E3*

Dine under the old apple tree at this historic adobe building near Taos Plaza. The four rooms inside are cozy and casual. For a light meal, try the signature Apple Tree Salad, made with organic greens, walnuts, and cranberries. Guests rave about the mango and chicken enchiladas served with blue-corn tortillas and paired with chilled sangria.

TAOS Lambert's of Taos
$$$

309 Paseo del Pueblo Sur, NM, 87571 **Tel** *(575) 758-1009*
Road map *E3*

Located three blocks from Taos Plaza, in the Randall Home, Lambert's serves a variety of meat, game, and seafood dishes – from Asian-style shrimp, to the signature pepper-crusted Colorado lamb. The uncompromising fresh-ingredients philosophy results in outstanding cuisine. The ambience is comfortable. Excellent California wines.

TAOS Doc Martin's Restaurant
$$$$

125 Paseo del Pueblo Norte, NM, 87571 **Tel** *(575) 758-1977*
Road map *E3*

Thomas-Paul Martin was the first physician in the county, and he would travel miles to mend bones and birth babies. Named for the famous doctor, this restaurant now heals appetites with superior regional cuisine. Dine à la carte or try the prix-fixe three-course menu, featuring pepper-crusted buffalo steak. Excellent wines.

ALBUQUERQUE AND SOUTHERN NEW MEXICO

ACOMA Huwak'a Restaurant
$

Sky City Casino, I-40 at Exit 102, NM, 87034 **Tel** *(505) 552-6017*
Road map *D3*

Close to the Sky City Cultural Center and the lofty Acoma Pueblo, right off the interstate highway, Huwak'a is a convenient stop, especially because it stays open quite late. The Native American casino features a buffet with Southwestern fare such as green-chile stew, and a taco bar. Seafood is served on Friday nights.

ALAMOGORDO Pepper's Grill
$$$

3200 N. White Sands Blvd., NM, 88310 **Tel** *(575) 437-9717*
Road map *E4*

This family-run restaurant is one of Alamogordo's best. The service here is fast and efficient and the extensive menu offers a good choice of hearty meals. Great steaks off the grill are a favorite, and there are also vegetarian options, pasta dishes, and American comfort food choices.

ALBUQUERQUE Garduño's Restaurant & Cantina
$

2100 Lousiana, NM, 87110 **Tel** *(505) 880-0055*
Road map *E3*

Garduño's is a popular chain serving Mexican dishes that are full of natural flavor. Guacamole is prepared tableside, and enchiladas and burritos come with hatch chile. The place is famous for its handshaken margaritas – sip one slowly on the outdoor patio while contemplating the surrounding mountains. Weekends see strolling mariachis.

ALBUQUERQUE Lindy's Diner
$

500 Central Ave. SW, NM, 87102 **Tel** *(505) 242-2582*
Road map *E3*

This spot on the main drag has been serving huge plates of good basic food since the late 1920s. The breakfast burrito, smothered in green chile and melted cheese, is a perennial favorite. Lunch and dinner feature fresh sandwiches, burgers, and diner staples such as meat loaf. Try the keylime cheesecake and any of the fresh pies.

ALBUQUERQUE 66 Diner
$

1405 Central Ave. NE, NM, 87106 **Tel** *(505) 247-1421*
Road map *E3*

A rim of glowing-red neon beckons travelers to this family-friendly diner from yesteryear. Kids play on a built-in hopscotch game in the hot-pink-and-turquoise environment: a cardboard Betty Boop here, a Marilyn there. Chow down on fried catfish, green-chile fries from the griddle, and thick milkshakes, while the jukebox spins 50s tunes.

ALBUQUERQUE Church Street Café

2111 Church St. NW, NM, 87104 **Tel** *(505) 247-8522*   **Road map** *E3*

Built with 1800s adobe, the Casa de Ruiz has antique Native Indian art and rugs on its walls. Dine inside, by the *kiva* fireplace, or outdoors, among the grapevines. Order the *carne adovada al horno*, a northern New Mexico dish of oven-cooked pork marinated in red chile. Sara, a friendly ghost, may pay a visit while you dine.

ALBUQUERQUE Elephant Bar

2240 Louisiana Blvd. NE, NM, 87110 **Tel** *(505) 884-2355*   **Road map** *E3*

With its jungle statuary, zebra-striped ceilings, and leopard-print carpets, the safari-themed Elephant Bar serves "elephant-sized" portions of Asian cuisine, fiery BBQs, and a wok-fired Shanghai cashew shrimp with pineapple chunks. Try the raspberry or passion-fruit-and-orange Maximo Mojito cocktail.

ALBUQUERQUE La Placita Dining Rooms

208 San Felipe St., NM, 87104 **Tel** *(505) 247-2204*   **Road map** *E3*

One of New Mexico's oldest restaurants, this is housed within the Casa de Armijo, a historic hacienda built in 1706 on Old Town Plaza. La Placita has several rooms, the most notable featuring a cottonwood tree growing in its center. Dine on spicy *sopaipillas*, one with beef, another with chicken, pinto beans, and cheese. Tales of ghosts abound here.

ALBUQUERQUE Pueblo Harvest Café

Indian Pueblo Cultural Center, 2401 12th Street NW, NM, 87104 **Tel** *(505) 724-3510*   **Road map** *E3*

Visitors experience New Mexican Puebloan culture in the museum, enjoy exhibition dances against a backdrop of huge murals, and taste typical Puebloan cuisine in the Harvest Café. The dinner menu also offers native-fusion cuisine, with buffalo tenderloin and grilled salmon.

ALBUQUERQUE St. Clair Winery & Bistro

901 Rio Grande Blvd. NW, NM, 87104 **Tel** *(505) 243-9916 or (888) 870-9916*   **Road map** *E3*

Just steps from Old Town Plaza, the state's largest winery opened a tasting room, as well as a bistro serving French country-style fare paired with its outstanding wine. For starters, try one of the popular cheese dishes or a signature soup. Many entrées are cooked in wine, such as the garlic chicken in Chardonnay or Cabernet-braised pot roast.

ALBUQUERQUE El Pinto

10500 4th St. NW, NM, 87114 **Tel** *(505) 898-1771*   **Road map** *E3*

From the decorative red-chile ristras hanging everywhere, to mariachis strolling among the art-filled dining rooms overflowing with greenery, and a large garden patio, El Pinto offers its guests a pleasant, relaxed ambience. Locals vow that dining here is a real treat – the nachos are great, and the *sopaipillas* to die for.

ALBUQUERQUE High Finance Restaurant and Tavern

40 Tramway Rd. NE, NM, 87122 **Tel** *(505) 243-9742*   **Road map** *E3*

High Finance is situated at the top of the Sandia Peak Tramway. Paintings of financiers decorate its wooden walls: J.P. Morgan, Henry Ford, and William Randolph Hearst, to name a few. But it's the romantic atmosphere and mesmerizing views that delight diners as they enjoy seafood, steaks, poultry, and vegetarian meals.

ALBUQUERQUE High Noon Restaurant and Saloon

425 San Felipe NW, NM, 87104 **Tel** *(505) 765-1455*   **Road map** *E3*

Parts of this rambling restaurant, one of the Old Town's historic treasures, date back to 1785. Many *santos* (icons of saints) stand in small, arched coves, and each room has a theme: Hispanic culture, early pioneers, *kachina* dolls, and Native Indian rugs. The cuisine is typically Southwestern, including bison rib eye and rack of lamb.

ALBUQUERQUE La Hacienda Restaurant

302 San Felipe NW, NM, 87104 **Tel** *(505) 243-3131*   **Road map** *E3*

Housed in the century-old adobe Villa de Albuquerque, this long-standing restaurant attracts hordes of tourists. It has a large mural depicting early settlers, and a colorful interior filled with antiques and Native American artworks. It's famous for its delicious burritos and for *carne adovado* – marinated pork in red chile.

ALBUQUERQUE Landry's Seafood House

5001 Jefferson St. NE, NM, 87109 **Tel** *(505) 875-0101*   **Road map** *E3*

This nationwide chain famous for its movie-marquee entrance started as a small eatery run from the family home. The Albuquerque location features a mural celebrating Native Americans. An extensive menu offers landlubber fare, but their trademark is fresh fish: snapper, halibut, shrimp, and shellfish prepared with special seasoning.

ALBUQUERQUE Seasons Rotisserie & Grill

2031 Mountain Rd., San Felipe Plaza, NM, 87104 **Tel** *(505) 766-5100*   **Road map** *E3*

Sit at the counter for a first-hand view of California-style cuisine being prepared on a wood-burning grill. Dine in a contemporary room warmed by terra-cotta, natural wood, wrought-iron fixtures, and a large floral display, or on the patio, where jazz is played. Order rotisserie chicken or grilled Colorado lamb with goat's cheese. Excellent wines.

ALBUQUERQUE Yanni's

3109 Central Ave. NE, NM, 87106 **Tel** *(505) 268-9250*   **Road map** *E3*

With its traditional Aegean blue-and-white decor, this top-rated local favorite brings Mediterranean delicacies to Nob Hill. Try the saganaki, a type of Greek cheese that is flamed tableside. A combo dinner plate allows you to sample the flavors of Greece. Time your visit for Greek Night, when the place gets hopping with bouzouki music.

Key to Price Guide *see p252* **Key to Symbols** *see back cover flap*

ALBUQUERQUE Zinc Wine Bar & Bistro

3009 Central Ave. NE, NM, 87106 **Tel** *(505) 254-9462* **Road map** *E3*

In Nob Hill, Zinc is dressed in earthy colors, with lofty ceilings, stained glass, and a sophisticated atmosphere. Sit at the zinc bar, watching chefs cook, and start with a classic French onion soup, or smoked trout in truffle vinaigrette. Seasonal entrées include the flank steak and veal. Lighter fare and live music can be found in the Blues Cellar.

ALBUQUERQUE The Artichoke Café

424 Central Ave. SE, NM, 87102 **Tel** *(505) 243-0200* **Road map** *E3*

This stylish downtown restaurant is like an art gallery, with rotating exhibits and a refined, contemporary look. The menu offers excellent French, Italian, and New American items. Tiger prawns served on fettuccini with a vodka and cream sauce come with sugarsnap peas, tomatoes, and artichoke hearts. Good wines.

ALBUQUERQUE Gruet Steakhouse

3201 Central Ave. NE, NM, 87106 **Tel** *(505) 256-9463* **Road map** *E3*

This upscale steakhouse opened in the Monte Vista Fire Station, a historic Pueblo Revival building. It is linked to the local Gruet Winery, whose crest is etched on the restaurant windows. The dining room is decorated with wine bottles. Prime meat is seared to perfection in cast-iron skillets. White-linen service is available on the patio.

ALBUQUERQUE One Up Elevated Lounge

301 Central Ave. NW, NM, 87102 **Tel** *(505) 242-1966* **Road map** *E3*

Sophisticated and hip, this friendly lounge bar and restaurant attracts the business crowd with its relaxed atmosphere and great tapas menu designed for sharing. The menu includes choices such as coconut chicken satay, baby clams, and options for vegetarians. Full bar, lounge, and eleven billiard tables.

CARLSBAD The Flume Room

Stevens Inn, 1829 S. Canal St., NM, 88220 **Tel** *(575) 887-2851* **Road map** *F5*

Named for the famous Pecos River aqueduct, built over a century ago, this restaurant features three large arches and an enormous etched-glass sculpture replicating the river structure. The Cattleman, a 12-oz (340-g) cut of prime rib, is the specialty here, but steaks, chicken, and seafood dishes are all on the menu. Casual and family-friendly.

CLOUDCROFT Rebecca's

The Lodge, 1 Corona Pl., NM, 88317 **Tel** *(575) 682-2566* **Road map** *F5*

In an elegant Victorian room with stained-glass windows and Queen Anne chairs, Rebecca's is named for its resident ghost. Classic fine-dining selections include escargots and Oysters Rockefeller as appetizers, and various cuts of steak, roasted duck, and rainbow trout for the main course. Sunday brunch is elaborate.

LINCOLN Isaac's Table

Mile marker 98, Hwy 380, NM, 88338 **Tel** *(575) 653-4609 or (800) 653-6460* **Road map** *E4*

Isaac's Table serves a gourmet prix-fixe dinner in the historic Ellis Store. The six-course dinner has several seasonal choices, such as fresh asparagus in Asian sauce to start; and rack of antelope or venison, or flounder stuffed with crab as an entrée. The chocolate-whiskey cake is the signature dessert. Reservations are mandatory.

MESILLA La Posta de Mesilla

2410 Calle de San Albino, NM, 88046 **Tel** *(575) 524-3524* **Road map** *E5*

La Posta de Mesilla is housed in a maze of rooms at a historic hitching post – the best one is filled with greenery and lava walls. The staff wear Mexican attire and serve New Mexican fare. Order the signature *tostada compuesta*, a corn tortilla cup with *frijoles* (refried beans), and chili con carne, with cheese and garnish. Delicious margaritas.

MESILLA Double Eagle

2355 Calle de Guadalupe, NM, 88046 **Tel** *(575) 523-6700* **Road map** *E5*

This restaurant is located within the exquisite Imperial Bar and Maximillian Rooms, in a mid-1800s building. Seven-foot- (2-m-) tall Baccarat-crystal chandeliers hang from a gold-overlaid metal ceiling, and there are huge portraits and mirrors on the walls. Order baked brie with pecans and apples to start, then an aged steak, pork, or seafood.

RUIDOSO Café Rio

2547 Sudderth Dr., NM, 88345 **Tel** *(575) 257-7746* **Road map** *E4*

A kaleidoscope of colors greets diners at this family-friendly pizzeria with a funky collection of knickknacks here and there. A more eclectic menu concentrates on deep-dish pizzas, calzones, and Cajun and Greek dishes, plus there is a soda fountain with homemade ice cream. The Portuguese kale soup is delicious.

RUIDOSO Cattle Baron Steak & Seafood Restaurant

657 Sudderth Dr., NM, 88345 **Tel** *(575) 257-9355* **Road map** *E4*

Famous for its steaks and seafood, Cattle Baron, a local chain, also has a legendary salad bar. Its Western-style decor has cowboy saddles, guns, antlers, and photographs of wildlife and Native Americans on horseback. A casual place, it is a good place for families. Prime rib is the house specialty, and it can also be ordered in a combo platter.

SILVER CITY Shevek & Co. Restaurant

602 N. Bullard St., NM, 88061 **Tel** *(575) 534-9168* **Road map** *D5*

This exceptional restaurant offers Mediterranean-inspired food cooked to order. The dining here is relaxed and the staff friendly. Meal sizes are tailored to each guest and there is a choice of tapas and mezze for light dining or full entrées for a more substantial meal. There is also a fine selection of wine and beer.

SHOPPING IN THE SOUTHWEST

With such an exciting range of Native American, Hispanic, and Anglo-American products, shopping in the Southwest is a cultural adventure. Native crafts, including rugs, jewelry, and pottery, top the list of things that people buy. The Southwest is also a center for the fine arts, with Santa Fe *(see pp192–9)* famous for its many galleries, selling everything from Georgia O'Keeffe-inspired landscapes

Chile-shaped pot

and the latest contemporary works, to popular bronze sculptures of cowboys or Indians. Across the region, specialty grocery stores and supermarkets stock a range of Southwestern products, from hot chile sauces to blue-corn tortilla chips. In the major cities there is a choice of glamorous fashion districts, usually situated in air-conditioned, landscaped malls. Las Vegas also ranks shopping among its attractions, with its themed malls *(see pp124–5)*.

SHOPPING HOURS AND PAYMENT

Most major stores are open from 9 or 10am to between 8 and 10pm, seven days a week, although some stores may close just after midday on Sunday or Monday. Most stores take MasterCard, Visa, and ATM cards. Other credit cards and out-of-state checks are often not accepted. Added to the price will be a sales tax of 2.9 percent in Colorado, 4.75 percent in Utah, 5 percent in New Mexico, 5.6 percent in Arizona, and 6.5 percent in Nevada. Local city and county sales taxes may also be added.

SOUTHWESTERN ART AND DECOR

The Southwest has a vibrant artistic heritage, and Santa Fe is the country's second-largest art market after New York. The city's arts district stretches from the downtown Plaza for 2 miles (3 km) along Canyon Road *(see p197)*. More than 200 galleries specialize in locally produced art, with many fine-arts galleries handling leading or up-and-coming Southwestern painters and sculptors. The **Meyer Gallery** specializes in figurative bronze sculpture and features a range of paintings by regional artists. For an evocative souvenir of your time in the area, head to a photographic gallery. The **Andrew Smith Gallery** carries works by Ansel Adams, Edward S. Curtis,

Chimeneas lined up for sale at a local artisan's store in Tubac, Arizona

and other photographers who captured the landscape and people of the Southwest.

Native American and Hispanic artists are also well represented, the latter producing carved *santos* and *bultos* depicting saints and other religious figures. These items can be found at the **Montez Gallery**, which specializes in Hispanic religious art, furniture, and other decorative works.

Other Southwest cities also have dedicated arts districts. The **Tucson Art District** has more than 40 galleries, while **Old Town Artisans** is a collection of shops in a block of 1850s adobe buildings selling Southwestern art, jewelry, clothing, and crafts. Scottsdale *(see p80)* has the Main Street Arts District, where many galleries are open late on Thursdays for the Scottsdale ArtWalk (7–9pm). **Trailside Galleries** specializes in Western art by leading

Mexican Huichol beaded mask

contemporary artists. More than 25 art galleries can also be found in Albuquerque's Old Town, among them the renowned **Weems Gallery**, featuring high-quality works.

The Southwest's bright colors and traditional designs are an inspiration for home decor. Find original crafts and woven rugs designed by Native Americans, at Albuquerque's **Bien Mur Indian Market Center**. A good shop in Santa Fe for Mexican-style decor is **Artesanos**, featuring colorful talavera tiles, punched tin mirrors, furniture, and other items. The entire town of Tubac *(see p90)* is an art colony with dozens of galleries and shops selling fine arts. Other shops sell pottery, textiles, gift items from Mexico, and an array of creative Southwestern-style home decor. Some of the best examples are at **Tubac Ironworks**, opposite the art museum.

NATIVE AMERICAN ARTS AND CRAFTS

Discovering the spiritual beliefs that inspire Native arts and crafts can make shopping for these items a rewarding experience, especially when purchasing directly from Native artists – in their homes, at reservation trading posts, or in pueblo or museum stores. The quality of Native crafts can vary greatly, and it is worth knowing a few guidelines. The term "Indian handmade" means that the item has been made solely by Native Americans, while "Indian crafted" means that they have been involved in the production. Buying directly from the artist ensures authenticity and also gives money to the local Native American community.

Many artists display their work at tourist stops such as those at Canyon de Chelly or on reservations. Trading posts, such as the **Hubbell Trading Post** *(see p167)* on the Navajo Reservation, were established to sell Native products to the region's first tourists in the late 1800s. Other sources of good-quality authentic items include the **Cameron Trading Post** near Flagstaff, which is now a gallery displaying historic and modern rugs, pottery, baskets, and carvings. **Fifth Generation Trading Company** in Farmington and **Sewell's Indian Arts** in Scottsdale also offer a wide choice of goods.

The distinctive pottery of the Pueblo Indian communities is highly prized. Pieces by

famous artists such as Maria Martínez are collector's items with prices to match, but you can also buy affordable works by contemporary artists such as Nancy Youngblood. She is represented by **Andrea Fisher Fine Pottery**. Artists in several of the Pueblo communities north of Santa Fe welcome visitors at their home workshops; look for signs outside. The **Indian Pueblo Cultural Center** *(see pp214–15)* in Albuquerque offers Pueblo Indian art at fair prices.

The **Shiprock Trading Company** specializes in vintage and contemporary Native arts, with branches in Farmington and Santa Fe. You can also buy older pieces of Native American art at Santa Fe's **Morning Star Gallery**, set in a lovely old adobe house on Canyon Road. **Nambé Outlets** features the signature metal bowls and other artworks from the Nambé Pueblo north of the city. At **Chief Dodge Indian Jewelry and Fine Arts** in Scottsdale you can watch Native artists at work.

JEWELRY

Native American artists are known for their fine jewelry, but cheaply manufactured goods abound in tourist areas, and it can be difficult to tell good-quality natural turquoise from cheaper grades or fakes. If you want a special piece, visit Albuquerque's Turquoise Museum *(see p212)* to learn the difference. High-quality Indian-made jewelry can be expensive. Buy from a

Examples of fine turquoise jewelry made by the Navajo tribe

reputable dealer who will give you a written guarantee of authenticity.

The Second Mesa Jewelry Co-operative, on the Hopi Reservation *(see p166)*, is a training facility that offers some of the finest Hopi silverwork. The Native American market under the arcades of the Santa Fe Plaza *(see pp192–3)* is a fun place to buy, with a range of prices and quality. Owned by a Native American artist specializing in turquoise jewelry, **Galeria Zachanee** in the Plaza also sells quality pieces. In Albuquerque, **Native Gold** sells gold jewelry with gem-grade turquoise, coral, and other precious stones.

MUSEUM SHOPS

Wonderful and authentic Native artworks can also be found in the shops of many museums. In Phoenix, the Heard Museum *(see pp78–9)* has a selection of beautiful Native baskets, paintings, sculpture, and *kachina* dolls, as does Flagstaff's Museum of Northern Arizona *(see p68)*. In Santa Fe, the museum shop at the Palace of the Governors *(see p194)* has fine wood carvings and Hispanic art. The re-created trading post at the Wheelwright Museum of the American Indian *(see p197)* specializes in traditional Navajo jewelry and crafts. Top-quality Spanish Colonial arts, furniture, and weavings can be found at markets organized by the **Museum of Spanish Colonial Art** *(see p197)*.

Native American rugs in the Cameron Trading Post

Typical Southwestern wear

MALLS

The searing temperatures of southern Arizona and New Mexico have spawned some of the most stunning malls in the USA. The biggest concentration is in Phoenix, which boasts **Metrocenter**, the largest mall in the Southwest. Large department stores such as Neiman Marcus can be found at the **Scottsdale Fashion Square**. Phoenix's **Biltmore Fashion Park** sells designer clothing and kitchenware, as well as offering great dining options.

Themed malls are also abundant. **Borgata of Scottsdale** is set in a 14th-century-style village with medieval courtyards. The **Arizona Center** in Phoenix is an oasis of restaurants and shops set among gardens, fountains, and a waterfall.

In Tucson, **La Encantada** is a breath of fresh air, with upscale specialty stores, including Tiffany, Anthropologie, and Crate and Barrel, set around an outdoor plaza. New Mexico's largest mall, the **Coronado Center** in Albuquerque, has 150 stores.

Most major Las Vegas hotels feature designer shopping areas *(see pp106–17)*.

FACTORY OUTLET MALLS

If you're looking for bargains, several factory outlet malls offer discounted merchandise and seconds from hundreds of name-brand retailers in apparel, shoes, sportswear, luggage, and homewares. Merchandise is generally of good quality, but check carefully for flaws or damage, and remember that clothing may not be of the current season or latest style.

In the Phoenix suburb of Tempe, **Arizona Mills** has around 175 outlet stores, including the high-end department stores Saks Fifth Avenue and Neiman Marcus. **Outlets at Anthem**, also in Phoenix, has stores selling sporting goods, luggage, and toys. Alongside I-10 between Phoenix and Tucson is **Outlets at Casa Grande**, with shoes, clothing, and Amish furniture stores. In New Mexico, the **Santa Fe Premium Outlets** is located off I-25 and contains around 40 stores.

WESTERN WEAR

Among the most popular souvenirs of the Southwest are hand-tooled cowboy boots, cowboy hats, and decorative leather belts. Western wear is made to high standards throughout the region. Phoenix is famous for cowboy clothes, but El Paso *(see pp222–3)* is also noted for its leather goods. **Az-tex Hats of Phoenix** has the largest selection of cowboy hats in the Southwest, while **Saba's Western Store** has been outfitting customers since 1927. **Bacon's Boots and Saddles**, in the historic mining town of Globe *(see p83)*, is owned by craftsman Ed Bacon, who has been making his wares for more than 50 years. For children's Western wear, try **Sheplers** in Mesa, Arizona.

Vintage Western wear can be found at Santa Fe's **Double Take at the Ranch**, which sells everything from boots and embroidered cowboy shirts to jewelry. At **Back at the Ranch** you can design your own boots or choose from some 1,000 pairs in stock.

FOOD

Southwesterners are proud of their cuisine, and the grocery stores at most malls sell chile sauces, salsa dips, and blue-corn chips. Specialty shops are good places to discover new Southwestern foods. At the **Santa Cruz Chili and Spice Co.**, along the I-19 frontage road at Tumacacori, you can sample some sauces before you buy. In addition to the usual salsas and hot sauces, **The Chile Shop** in Santa Fe sells chile peanut butter and habanero fudge sauce, as well as chile wreaths, cookbooks, and decorative items. Several companies, such as the **Arizona Pepper Products Co.**, have websites where you can order gourmet regional foods. **New Mexico Chili** ships fresh, frozen, and dried chiles from Hatch *(see p218)*, or you can buy them from small shopkeepers in the town.

Farmers' markets are a good source of local produce, but don't overlook the Arizona supermarket chains. **Food City** caters for the Hispanic market, and most large branches of **Fry's** have dedicated Hispanic foods sections.

Visit **The Pecan Store** for fresh pecans grown in Green Valley, south of Tucson.

Colorful fresh vegetables on sale at a farmers' market

DIRECTORY

SOUTHWESTERN ART AND DECOR

Andrew Smith Gallery
122 Grant Ave., Santa Fe, NM 87501.
Tel (505) 984-1234.

Artesanos
1414 Maclovia St., Santa Fe, NM 87505.
Tel (505) 471-8020.

Bien Mur Indian Market Center
I-25 at Tramway Rd., NE, Albuquerque, NM 87113.
Tel (505) 821-5400.

Meyer Gallery
225 Canyon Rd., Santa Fe, NM 87501.
Tel (505) 983-1434.

Montez Gallery
125 E. Palace Ave., Santa Fe, NM 87501.
Tel (505) 982-1828.

Old Town Artisans
201 N. Court Ave., Tucson, AZ 85701.
Tel (520) 623-6024.

Trailside Galleries
7330 Scottsdale Mall, Scottsdale, AZ 85251.
Tel (480) 945-7751.

Tubac Ironworks
217 Plaza Rd., Tubac, AZ 85646.
Tel (520) 398-2163.

Tucson Art District
Congress and Broadway streets; Stone and 4th avenues, Tucson, AZ.
Tel (520) 624-1817.

Weems Gallery
303 Romero St. NW, Albuquerque, NM 87104.
Tel (505) 764-0302.

NATIVE AMERICAN ARTS AND CRAFTS

Andrea Fisher Fine Pottery
100 W. San Francisco St., Santa Fe, NM 87501.
Tel (505) 986-1234.

Cameron Trading Post
Highway 89, Cameron, AZ 86020.
Tel (928) 679-2231.

Chief Dodge Indian Jewelry and Fine Arts
1332 N. Scottsdale Rd., Scottsdale, AZ 85257.
Tel (480) 970-1133.

Fifth Generation Trading Company
232 W. Broadway, Farmington, NM 87401.
Tel (505) 326-3211.

Hubbell Trading Post
Highway 264, Ganado, AZ 86505.
Tel (928) 755-3254.
www.nps.gov/hutr

Indian Pueblo Cultural Center
2401 12th St., Albuquerque, NM 87104.
Tel (505) 843-7270.

Morning Star Gallery
513 Canyon Rd., Santa Fe, NM 87501.
Tel (505) 982-8187.

Nambé Outlets
924 Paseo de Peralta; 104 W. San Francisco St., Santa Fe, NM 87501.
Tel (505) 988-5528/3574.

Sewell's Indian Arts
7087 Fifth Ave., Scottsdale, AZ 85251.
Tel (480) 945-0962.

Shiprock Trading Company
53 Old Santa Fe Trail, Santa Fe, NM 87501.
Tel (505) 982-8478.
For other branches, see
www.shiprocktrading.com

JEWELRY

Galeria Zachanee
66 E. San Francisco St. 16, Santa Fe, NM 87501.
Tel (505) 920-2935.

Native Gold
323 Romero St. NW, Albuquerque, NM 87104.
Tel (505) 247-2242.

MUSEUM SHOPS

Museum of Spanish Colonial Art
750 Camino Lejo, Santa Fe, NM 87505.
Tel (505) 982-2226.

MALLS

Arizona Center
400 E. Van Buren St., Phoenix, AZ 85004.
Tel (602) 271-4000.
www.arizonacenter.com

Biltmore Fashion Park
2502 Camelback Rd., Phoenix, AZ 85253.
www.shopbiltmore.com

Borgata of Scottsdale
6166 N. Scottsdale Rd., Scottsdale, AZ 85253.
www.borgata.com

Coronado Center
6600 Menaul Blvd. NE, Albuquerque, NM 87110.
Tel (505) 881-2700.

La Encantada
2905 E. Skyline Dr., Tucson, AZ 85718.
Tel (520) 615-2561.
www.laencantada shoppingcenter.com

Metrocenter
9617 Metro Parkway, Phoenix, AZ 85051.
Tel (602) 997-2641.
www.metrocentermall. com

Scottsdale Fashion Square
7014 East Camelback Rd., Scottsdale, AZ 85251.
Tel (480) 941-2140.

FACTORY OUTLET MALLS

Arizona Mills
5000 Arizona Mills Circle, Tempe, AZ 85282.
Tel (480) 491-9700.

Outlets at Anthem
4250 W. Anthem Way, Phoenix, AZ 85086.
Tel (623) 465-9500.

Outlets at Casa Grande
2300 E. Tanger Dr., Casa Grande, AZ 85222.
Tel (520) 836-9663.

Santa Fe Premium Outlets
8380 Cerillos Rd. at I-25, Santa Fe, NM 87507.
Tel (505) 474-4000.

WESTERN WEAR

Az-tex Hats of Phoenix
3903 N. Scottsdale Rd., Scottsdale, AZ 85251.
Tel (480) 481-9900.
www.aztexhats.com

Back at the Ranch
209 E. Marcy St., Santa Fe, NM 87501.
Tel (505) 989-8110.

Bacon's Boots and Saddles
290 N. Broad St., Globe, AZ 85501.
Tel (520) 425-2681.

Double Take at the Ranch
319 S. Guadalupe St., Santa Fe, NM 87501.
Tel (505) 820-7775.

Saba's Western Store
www.sabaswesternwear. com

Sheplers
829 N Dobson Rd., Mesa, AZ 85201.
Tel (480) 668-1211.
www.sheplers.com

FOOD

Arizona Pepper Products Co.
P.O. Box 40605, Mesa, AZ 85210.
Tel (480) 844-0302.
www.azgunslinger.com

The Chile Shop
109 E. Water St., Santa Fe, NM 87501.
Tel (505) 983-6080.

Food City
www.myfoodcity.com

Fry's
www.frysfood.com

New Mexico Chili
Tel (888) 336-4228.
www.nmchili.com

The Pecan Store
1625 E. Sahuarita Rd., Sahuarita, AZ 85629.
Tel (520) 791-2062.

Santa Cruz Chili and Spice Co.
1868 East Frontage Rd., Tumacacori, AZ 85640.
Tel (520) 398-2591.

ENTERTAINMENT
IN THE SOUTHWEST

The Southwest's blend of cultures has made the region a thriving center for arts and entertainment. The large cities of Phoenix, Santa Fe, Tucson, and Albuquerque have vibrant artistic communities and offer opera, ballet, classical music, and major theatrical productions. The smaller resort towns of Sedona and Taos are famous for their resident painters and sculptors and

Museum Club sign

regularly host noted touring productions, as well as regional theater, dance, and musical events. And almost every city and major town has a lively nightlife that includes country music, jazz, and rock, as well as dinner theater and standup comedy. Sports fans will be happy here with major league and college football, baseball, and basketball teams playing across the region.

Displaying traditional cowboy skills at one of the region's rodeos

INFORMATION

The best source of events information is in the entertainment guides of local newspapers. Phoenix's *The Arizona Republic*, Tucson's *Daily Star*, the *Santa Fe New Mexican*, and *Albuquerque Journal* are the most useful. Most of these newspapers also have websites. There are several regional magazines that review events and nightlife. Most hotels offer magazines, such as *Where* and *Key*, that feature dining, attractions, and entertainment. You can book tickets for most events through **Ticketmaster** outlets, or at www.ticketmaster.com, their online booking service.

RODEOS AND WILD WEST SHOWS

Since Buffalo Bill's first Wild West shows in the 1880s, the Southwest has been a mecca for Western-style entertainment. Traditional cowboy

skills such as roping steers and breaking wild horses have been transformed into categories of rodeo contest, offering winners substantial money prizes. Rodeos owe their name to the Spanish word for round-up, harking back to the 19th century when herds of cattle crossed New Mexico on their way to California. Today's rodeo circuit is highly competitive and dangerous, attracting full-time professionals whose high pay reflects this risky career. Nevertheless, the allure is comparable with the magic of the circus. Among the largest and most popular rodeos are Tucson's Fiesta de los Vaqueros, Albuquerque's New Mexico State Fair and Rodeo, and Prescott's Frontier Days Rodeo *(see pp32–5)*.

The Southwest offers plenty of opportunities for visitors to sample the atmosphere of the Wild West, either in the many ghost towns or in historic frontier towns such as **Tombstone** *(see p92)*, which stages daily mock-gunfights and tours of its Victorian buildings. There are also Western towns built originally as film studios, such as **Old Tucson Studios** *(see p86)*. Tours of the sets are available. **Rawhide**, north of Scottsdale, has an Old West museum, an old-fashioned ice cream parlor, a famous music venue, and Western theme attractions.

SPORTS

The three most popular spectator sports in the Southwest, as in the rest of the country, are football, baseball, and basketball. The region's largest concentration of major teams is in the Phoenix area. There is only one major league football team in the Southwest, the **Arizona Cardinals** in Phoenix. The Arizona Diamondbacks baseball team joined the majors in 1998 and is based at the $275-million **Chase Field** in Phoenix. Professional basketball is represented by the Phoenix Suns, who share the **US Airways Center** with a football team, the Arizona

Baseball player

Rattlers. While tickets may be hard to obtain for league games, it is easy to gain entrance to the many college games in any sport throughout the region. Phoenix's warm climate also attracts the Cactus League, a series of training games for seven major league baseball teams in February and March.

CLASSICAL MUSIC, BALLET, AND OPERA

In Arizona, the excellent Phoenix Symphony and Arizona Opera both perform at the **Phoenix Symphony Hall** building. The city's $14-million refurbishment of the Spanish Baroque-style **Orpheum Theater** makes it a stunning addition to more than 20 major venues for arts, sports, and entertainment in and around Phoenix. Arizona Theater Company and Actors' Theater occupies the **Herberger Theater Center**, offering a regular program of performances. With more than 20 theater companies in Phoenix, there is an impressive choice of plays, as well as touring Broadway shows and big-name entertainers.

New Mexico's major cultural activities are based in Santa Fe and Albuquerque. Santa Fe has more than 200 art galleries and is also respected for its performing arts. The **Santa Fe Opera** performs both traditional and contemporary operas in its open-air arena during July and August. Santa Fe's Chamber Music Festival, held at venues throughout the city in July and August, is one of the finest in the US. The **New Mexico Symphony Orchestra** is based in

Albuquerque, best known for its classics concerts. The **El Paso Symphony Orchestra** performs throughout the year in the town's historic 1920s Plaza Theater. **New Mexico Jazz Workshops** stage more than 30 concerts each year.

Dancing couple at the Museum Club in Flagstaff, Arizona

NIGHTLIFE

In almost every town there are restaurants, bars, and nightclubs that offer country music and dancing. Among the most famous country music venues is the Western theme town of Rawhide in Scottsdale, where well-known bands play. The **Museum Club** in Flagstaff is a venerable Route 66 (see p51) establishment that hosted such top country music names as Hank Williams in the 1950s and still offers a lively selection of Southwestern bands.

Major cities offer virtually every type of evening entertainment. Jazz bars and cafés are gaining in popularity, and standup comedy and rock music is available in countless venues. Clubs and arenas based in Phoenix, Tucson, Albuquerque, and Santa Fe are regular stops for big stars on US tours. However, the entertainment capital of the region and, some would say, the world, is Las Vegas (see pp126–7). The Las Vegas Strip on a single night hosts as much top talent as all the other cities in the Southwest do in a year: everything from Broadway shows and dazzling homegrown productions to a range of free music in the casinos.

Spectacular outdoor setting of the Santa Fe Opera company

DIRECTORY

SPORTS STADIUMS

Arizona Cardinals
Tel (800) 999-1402.

Chase Field
Tel (602) 462-6000.

US Airways Center
Tel (602) 379-7833.

CLASSICAL MUSIC, BALLET, AND OPERA

El Paso Symphony Orchestra
Tel (915) 532-3776.

Herberger Theater Center
Tel (602) 252-8497.

New Mexico Jazz Workshops
Tel (505) 255-9798.

New Mexico Symphony Orchestra
Tel (505) 881-8999.

Orpheum Theater
Tel (602) 262-7272.

Phoenix Symphony Hall
Tel (602) 495-1999.

Santa Fe Opera
Tel (505) 986-5900.

RODEOS AND WILD WEST SHOWS

Old Tucson Studios
Tel (520) 883-0100.

Rawhide Western Town
Tel (480) 502-5600.

Tombstone Visitor Center
Tel (520) 457-3929.

NIGHTLIFE

The Museum Club
Tel (928) 526-9434.

Rialto Theatre
Tel (520) 740-0071 (Tucson).

TICKETMASTER

For all areas
Tel (800) 745-3000.

SPECIALTY VACATIONS AND ACTIVITIES

With thousands of miles of deep rock canyons, spectacular deserts, and towering, snow-capped mountains, few places in the world offer so many opportunities for outdoor entertainment as the American Southwest. Much of the wilderness here is protected by the Federal Government in national parks, formed during the early 20th century when the region first began to attract tourists. Increasing numbers of visitors are being drawn to the region, and it is now a magnet for climbers,

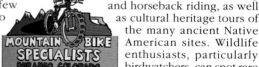

Mountain bike rental sign

mountain bikers, hikers, and 4WD enthusiasts. The range of organized tours includes whitewater rafting and horseback riding, as well as cultural heritage tours of the many ancient Native American sites. Wildlife enthusiasts, particularly birdwatchers, can spot rare species on the spring and fall migration routes that cross the Southwest. The region is also a center for sports activities, especially for golfers and skiers. For information on the main events in the Southwest's sports calendar see pp274–5.

GENERAL INFORMATION

The main centers for outdoor activities in the region are Moab *(see p141)*, Durango *(see p179)*, and Sedona *(see p71)*, with their excellent equipment shops and visitor information centers. Advance planning is advisable for activities such as whitewater rafting along the Colorado River in Grand Canyon, or mule trips into the canyon, as these are often booked up to a year ahead *(see pp58–63)*. Hikers and campers exploring the backcountry will also need permits from the National Park Service as well as detailed maps, which can be obtained from either the Bureau of Land Management, the **U.S.D.A. Forest Service**, or the **US Geological Survey**. Both state and local tourist offices can supply the latest advice on

trails, permits, and weather conditions at most attractions. Anyone exploring desert or canyon country should be aware of the potential for flash floods and should check weather reports daily, especially during the summer months of July and August.

GOLF

With around 275 golf courses in Arizona alone, many of them top-rated, the Southwest is a golfer's paradise. This is particularly true of Southern Arizona with its year-round warm weather. The town of Scottsdale *(see pp80–81)*, is considered by some to be America's premier golf spot and is famous for such resorts as **The Boulders** and the legendary Phoenician, both top-rated championship courses. Tucson is also a well-known golfing area with such

offerings as the Jack Nicklaus-designed golf resort **Westin La Paloma**. New Mexico is also known for its courses and affordable greens fees. Albuquerque's Arroyo del Oso is a challenging municipal course with immaculate fairways. Information on the various courses can be found at **www.golfarizona.com** or **www.golfnewmexico.com**.

Golf course at Phoenix's top-rated Wigwam Resort *(see p235)*

HIKING

Hiking is the single most popular outdoor activity in the Southwest. Day hikes and longer trips draw large numbers of residents and visitors who feel that this is the best way to see the region's stunning scenery. Virtually all of the national parks have excellent well-marked trails as well as fascinating ranger-led hikes that focus on the local flora, fauna, and geology. One of

Whitewater rafting trip on the Colorado River

Mountain biking along one of many red-rock trails near Moab

the most famous, and arduous, hikes in the Southwest is a rim-to-rim hike of Grand Canyon along the Bright Angel and Kaibab trails *(see pp60–63)*. It takes most hikers two to three days to complete. Longer trips into the vast wilderness of Grand Staircase-Escalante National Monument *(see p148)* and the Glen Canyon Recreation Area *(see pp150–51)* are among the highlights of wilderness exploration for hikers. Around the Four Corners region, there are many hikes that explore archaeological sites such as the Ancestral Puebloan ruins at Chaco Canyon where there is an 8-mile (13-km) trail to the pueblo houses at Chetro Ketl *(see pp174–5)*.

Hikers on the trail to Pueblo Alto at Chaco Canyon *(see pp174–5)*

ROCK CLIMBING

Its dry, sunny climate and extensive mountains, canyons, and sheer rock faces make the Southwest a popular climbing spot. Favored sites include the sheer cliffs of Zion National Park *(see pp154–5)*, the rocky landscape around Moab *(see p142)*, and Utah's Canyon-lands National Park *(see p142–3)*. Moab has a good selection of equipment shops, such as **Pagan Mountain-eering**. Red Rock Canyon, 15 miles (24 km) west of Las Vegas, is another favorite area, with guided climbs offered by **Jackson Hole Mountain Guides**.

MOUNTAIN BIKING AND FOUR-WHEEL DRIVING

All of the region's national parks have trails open to mountain biking, but the centers of this activity are Moab and Durango, Colorado *(see p179)*. The state of Utah has declared itself the mountain bike capital of the world, and the Moab area is something of a pilgrimage site for mountain bikers. Named after a well-known bike trail, **Poison Spider Bicycles** sells and repairs bikes as well as housing Nichols Tours, which

4WD at wetlands near Moab

leads groups through wilderness areas. Moab is famous for the Slick Rock Trail, a demanding run across more than 12 miles (19 km) of precipitous rock with stunning views. However, during the summer months the trail can become very crowded.

Around Durango, Colorado, cooler and greener conditions prevail with rides through the pine forests of the Rocky Mountains. Popular bike trails include the level, but scenic, Animas Valley Loop or the more rugged, hilly Animas Mountain Loop. There are also several 4WD trails, leading to remote and beautiful backcountry. Again, Moab is one of the top centers for off-road drivers, with rentals and tours available from **Farabee Jeep Rentals**. Canyonlands National Park and Canyon de Chelly are also popular. Monument Valley in Arizona *(see pp164–5)* is a prime location for 4WD tours to areas not accessible by a regular car, often led by Navajo guides from **Monument Valley Tours**. Also in Arizona, Sedona's red-rock canyons and Coconino National Forest may be toured by 4WD. **Bike Apelli Adventure Tours** and local legend **Pink Jeep Tours** offer a wide variety of tours.

WHITEWATER RAFTING AND KAYAKING

The Green, San Juan, and Colorado rivers make the Southwest one of the world's top destinations for whitewater rafting. These rivers run fast and deep, offering a thrilling ride, often through breathtaking canyons. Trips ranging from beginner to experienced are offered by most outfitters. Tour companies provide rafts, paddles, and lifejackets, and for multi-day trips that involve camping, food and tents may also be provided. Visitors are advised to check a variety of companies to make sure they get the river experience that suits them best. It is also a good idea to check their safety records and expertise.

One of the most exciting rafting trips in the Southwest is the 12–20 day trip along the Colorado River through Grand Canyon. As numbers for some trips may be limited to eight or fewer people, tours can be booked by as much as a year in advance. Many outfitters offer Grand Canyon raft trips: one of the best known is **Canyon Explorations**.

The confluence of the Green and Colorado rivers lies near Moab, Utah. Just beyond their convergence lies Cataract Canyon, one of the most famous whitewater rapids in the world. Shooting these waters should be undertaken only by experienced rafters. One of the best outfitters to take visitors through the canyon is **Sheri Griffith Expeditions**. The company also offers raft tours of varying degrees of difficulty on the smaller rivers in the area. **Canyon Voyages** offers rafting trips ranging from peaceful river journeys to thrilling whitewater adventures. They also offer kayak workshops.

Wild River Expeditions' one-day, gentle drift through the canyons of the Four Corners' San Juan River is led by guides who are also archaeologists and geologists. There are stops at Bluff *(see p172)* and Mexican Hat, as well as at Ancestral Puebloan ruins.

Powerboating near Parker Dam in western Arizona

WATER SPORTS

The dams along the Colorado River have created a chain of artificial lakes starting with Lake Powell *(see pp150–51)* and extending to Lake Mead *(see p120)* and Lake Havasu *(see p70)*. A variety of water sports are available, including powerboating and jetskiing.

Set in the one million-acre (400,000-ha) Glen Canyon Recreation Area, Lake Powell is famous for its houseboat cruises. These offer visitors the chance to experience the many beaches and canyons around the lake. All visitors are shown how to operate the boats and are given an instruction manual. There is also a variety of guided tours available, including cruises to Rainbow Bridge and Antelope Canyon. Gentle raft trips between Glen Canyon Dam and Lees Ferry are offered by **Aramark Inc.**, the main tour concession for the lake. **Lake Powell Resorts and Marinas** rents out both houseboats and powerboats.

On Lake Havasu all kinds of water sports equipment, from waterskis to scuba gear, can be rented from Fun Time Boat Rentals. At Lake Mead numerous shops rent fishing boats and jetskis and offer waterskiing lessons. The **Lake Mead Visitor Center** is a useful source of information.

Boaters on all the lakes are provided with information to make water-based vacations safe and pleasurable. Children aged 12 and under must wear lifejackets, and all boats must be driven at wakeless speed within harbor or beach areas.

FISHING

Lakes Mead, Powell, and Havasu are also noted as popular locations for fishing. The lakes are well stocked with game fish such as striped, largemouth, and smallmouth bass during the fishing season, which runs

Fishing in a lake at Cedar Breaks National Monument, Southern Utah *(see p149)*

Mountain views from the Sandia Peak Tramway near Albuquerque

from March to November. River anglers can also fish for salmon and trout. Each state has different regulations and fishing licenses, although catch and release is the rule in many areas. Information about licenses, tournaments, and tours can be obtained from marinas, outdoor equipment stores, local gas stations, and state **Fish and Game Departments**.

SKIING AND WINTER SPORTS

In general, the ski season in Southwestern resorts runs from November to April. A range of skiing trips is available, from all-inclusive packages to day-trips from nearby towns. There are plenty of equipment rental outlets, although resort packages usually include skis, lift passes, and lessons if necessary. Other winter sports such as snowboarding, snowmobiling, and cross-country skiing are becoming increasingly popular, with runs and equipment now available in most resorts.

Utah hosted the Winter Olympics in 2002 and offers some of the best skiing in the region. The **Telluride Ski Area** is set among the 19th-century towns and mountain scenery of southwestern Colorado. The facilities and runs here, with elevations of more than 11,500 ft (3,450 m), attract many visitors during the season, including many of the country's celebrities. **Purgatory-Durango Ski Resort** is less chic and less pricey, but provides just as much

challenge with vertical drops of over 2,000 ft (600 m). New Mexico's **Taos Ski Valley** includes world-class slopes, and the Arizona Snowbowl near Flagstaff *(see p67)* is particularly popular with cross-country skiers.

HORSEBACK RIDING

Horseback riding is synonymous with the Southwest, and almost every area has stables that rent horses. Some ranches offer guided trail rides as well as the chance to live and work as a cowboy. The range of trips is impressive: from hour-long rides to two-week dude ranch vacations *(see p231)*.

Ranches are dotted across the region, but the best-known are those in southern Arizona, particularly near the town of Wickenburg. The area's pleasant winter climate attracts thousands of visitors, and even large cities such as Phoenix and Tucson have riding stables and offer trails through beautiful desert scenery. Cooler summer locations such as Sedona and Pinetop Lakeside in Arizona are also popular riding centers.

Most of the national parks offer trail-riding tours, but the noted mule trip into Grand Canyon *(see p62)* needs to be booked well in advance. **Xanterra Parks & Resorts** offers adventurous mule rides that last two days from the South Rim, overnighting on the canyon floor at Phantom Ranch *(see p232)*.

AIR TOURS

Air tours are a good option for those time-restricted travelers who wish to see the more remote attractions. Canyonlands National Park is famous for its vast wildernesses: **Redtail** offers one-hour flights over all three districts in Canyonlands, as well as over the stunning Dead Horse Point State Park *(see p143)*. **Slickrock Air Guides of Moab** offer three-hour tours that cover Canyonlands, Lake Powell, Capitol Reef National Park, and the north rim of Grand Canyon. The striking red-rock pinnacles formations of Bryce Canyon *(see pp152–3)* can be seen by both plane and helicopter on tours lasting from 17 minutes to one hour. The most popular air tours are those over Grand Canyon. Several of these are offered from Las Vegas *(see p123)*, and there are ten companies based in Tusayan at the park's southern entrance. However, increasing numbers of airborne tourists are raising the issue of noise pollution as a pressing problem throughout the canyon. Increasing numbers of visitors complain that engine noise diminishes what should be a tranquil experience of the area's beauty.

Horseback riding through the desert near Tuscon, Arizona

International Balloon Fiesta in Albuquerque, New Mexico *(see p34)*

HOT AIR BALLOONING

Cool, still mornings, dependable sunshine, and steady breezes have made the Southwest the top hot air ballooning destination in America. Balloon trips around Albuquerque are a popular excursion, particularly in October, when the International Balloon Fiesta takes place *(see p34)*. Outfitters such as **Discover Balloons** offer a one-hour flight with champagne brunch.

You can also drift over the canyons of Sedona with **Northern Light Balloon Expeditions**, and over the Sonoran Desert with **Hot Air Expeditions**.

BIRDWATCHING

With more than 200 species of bird, including many rare breeds, birdwatching is a popular pastime in the Southwest, particularly in spring, early summer, and fall. These are peak migration seasons for warblers, flycatchers, and shorebirds, while nesting waders and ducks may be seen in New Mexico's **Bosque del Apache Wildlife Refuge**. The refuge also boasts a winter population of more than 17,000 sandhill cranes. Several habitats across the region suit desert birds such as the roadrunner and elf owl, particularly Saguaro National Park in the Sonoran Desert. Capitol Reef *(see p146)* and Bryce Canyon *(see pp152–3)* national parks attract yellow warblers, northern orioles, and black-chinned hummingbirds.

Southern Utah and southern Arizona are noted for their hummingbird population. Tours devoted to the study of these enchanting creatures are run by **Victor**

Broad-billed hummingbird

Emmanuel's Nature Tours. The **Southeastern Arizona Bird Observatory** also offers educational tours in the region.

Many species of hawk may be spotted in the Southwest, and birds of prey such as red-tailed hawks, golden eagles, and peregrine falcons are regular visitors to Bryce Canyon.

LEARNING VACATIONS

In the Southwest, some of the most interesting learning vacations focus on Native cultures and ancient civilizations. Two organizations, **The Crow Canyon Archaeological Center** and **The Four Corners School**, offer a range of vacation courses on geography, flora and fauna, ancient ruins, and Native arts. Archaeology courses often involve working on digs with professional archaeologists; Native culture courses may study both modern and ancient Native groups, their way of life, religious practices, and arts. Most programs last between four and ten days, and visitors are housed either in college campuses or in motels. The **Smithsonian Institute** offers a popular program on past and present arts of the Hopi, Zuni, and Navajo tribes.

The distinctive cuisine of the region has led to an array of courses on Southwestern cooking. The **Santa Fe Cooking School** and the **Santa Fe Photographic Workshops** offer a variety of courses for beginners and professionals. The Workshops also offer photography and painting courses that take advantage of the unique light and landscapes of Santa Fe. In Arizona, Sedona *(see p73)* is a mecca for those interested in New Age philosophy. The Center for the New Age is just one place offering courses in yoga, nutrition, counseling, and aromatherapy. There are also guided tours of the vortexes (points of the Earth's energy) said to be found in the area.

DIRECTORY

INFORMATION

United States Geological Survey (U.S.G.S.)
12201 Sunrise Valley Drive, Reston, VA 20192.
Tel (703) 648-4748.
www.usgs.gov

U.S.D.A Forest Service
333 Broadway SE., Albuquerque, NM 87102.
Tel (505) 842-3898.

GOLF

Boulders Resort
34631 N. Tom Darlington Drive, Carefree AZ 85377.
Tel (480) 488-9028.

Golfarizona.com
www.golfarizona.com

Golf New Mexico
Tel (505) 342-1563.

Westin La Paloma
3800 East Sunrise, Tucson AZ 85718.
Tel (520) 742-6000.

ROCK CLIMBING

Jackson Hole Mountain Guides
8221 West Charleston, Suite 106, Las Vegas, NV 89117.
Tel (702) 254-0885.

Pagan Mountaineering
59 S. Main St, Moab, UT 84532.
Tel (435) 259-1117.

MOUNTAIN BIKING AND 4WD

Bike Apelli Adventure Tours
1695 W. Hwy 89A, Sedona, AZ 86336.
Tel (928) 282-1312.
www.mountainbike heaven.com

Farabee Jeep Rentals
1125 S. Highway 191, Moab, UT 84532.
Tel (435) 259-7734.
www.moabjeeprentals.com

Monument Valley Tours
Highway 163, Goulding, UT 84536.
Tel (435) 727-3231.

Pink Jeep Tours
204 N. Highway 89A, Sedona AZ 86339.
Tel (928) 282-5000; (800) 873-3662.

Poison Spider Bicycles
497 N. Main St., Moab, UT 84532.
Tel (435) 259 7882; (800) 635-1792.

WHITEWATER RAFTING

Canyon Explorations
PO Box 310, Flagstaff, AZ 86002.
Tel (928) 774-4559; (800) 654-0723.

Canyon Voyages
211 N. Main St., Moab UT.
Tel (435) 259-6007; (800) 733-6007.

Sheri Griffith Expeditions
PO Box 1324, Moab, UT 84532.
Tel (435) 259 8229; (800) 332-2439.

WATER SPORTS

Aramark Inc.
50 S. Lake Powell Blvd., Page, AZ 86040.
Tel (888) 896-3829.

Lake Mead Visitor Center
601 Nevada Hwy, Boulder City, NV 89005.
Tel (702) 293-8990.

Lake Powell Resorts and Marinas
PO Box 1597, Page, AZ 86040.
Tel (928) 645-2433, (602) 278-8888; (800) 528-6154.

FISHING

Arizona Game and Fish Department
2222 Greenway Road, Phoenix, AZ 85023.
Tel (602) 942-3000.

Colorado Division of Wildlife
6060 Broadway, Denver, CO 80216.
Tel (303) 291-7533.

New Mexico Department of Game and Fish
Villagra Building, Sante Fe, NM 87503.
Tel (505) 476-8000.

Utah Division of Wildlife Resources
1596 West North Temple, Salt Lake City, UT 84116.
Tel (801) 538-4700.
www.wildlife.utah.gov

SKI RESORTS

Purgatory-Durango Mountain Resort
Route 550 Durango, CO 81301.
Tel (970) 247-9000.

Taos Ski Valley
PO Box 90, Taos Ski Valley, NM 87525.
Tel (575) 776-2291.

Telluride Ski Area
Route 145, Telluride, CO.
Tel (970) 728-6900.

HORSEBACK RIDING

Xanterra Parks & Resorts
Tel (303) 297-2757.

AIR TOURS

Redtail Aviation
Tel (435) 259-7421; (800) 842-9251.

Slickrock Airguides of Moab
Tel (435) 259-6216.

HOT AIR BALLOONING

Discover Balloons
205B San Felipe NW., Albuquerque, NM 87104.
Tel (505) 842-1111.

Hot Air Expeditions
2243 East Rose Garden Loop Suite 1, Phoenix, AZ 85024.
Tel (480) 502-6999; (800) 831-7610.

Northern Light Balloon Expeditions
PO Box 1695, Sedona, AZ 86339.
Tel (928) 282-2274; (800) 230-6222.

BIRDWATCHING

Bosque del Apache Wildlife Refuge
1001 Hwy 1, San Antonio, NM 87832.
Tel (575) 835-1828.

Southeastern Arizona Bird Observatory
PO Box 5521, Bisbee, AZ 85603.
Tel (520) 432-1388.
www.sabo.org

Victor Emmanuel's Nature Tours
2525 Wallingwood Dr., Suite 1003, Austin, TX 78746. *Tel (512) 328-5221; (800) 328-8368.*

LEARNING VACATIONS

The Crow Canyon Archaeological Center
23390 County Road K, Cortez, CO 81321.
Tel (970) 565-8975.

The Four Corners School
Box 1028, Monticello, UT 84535.
Tel (800) 525-4456.
www.fourcorners school. org

The Santa Fe Photographic Workshops
Box 9916, Santa Fe, NM 87504. *Tel (505) 983-1400.* **www**.santafe workshops. com

The Santa Fe School of Cooking
116 W. San Francisco St, Santa Fe, NM 87501.
Tel (505) 983-4511.

The Smithsonian Institute
1000 Jefferson Drive SW, MRC702, Washington DC 20560.
Tel (877) 338-8687.

SURVIVAL
GUIDE

PRACTICAL INFORMATION

The Southwest US is an area of spectacular natural beauty. Arizona, New Mexico, the Four Corners, and Southern Utah are dotted with dramatic rock formations, canyons, ancient archaeological sites, and wild desert scenery that offer visitors a choice of pleasures, including a wide variety of outdoor activities. The cities here are famous for their combination of laid-back Southern culture and sophisticated urban pursuits with excellent museums and great dining. The unique attractions of Las Vegas, Nevada (see pp98–131) also make for

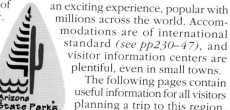

Arizona State Parks sign

an exciting experience, popular with millions across the world. Accommodations are of international standard (see pp230–47), and visitor information centers are plentiful, even in small towns.

The following pages contain useful information for all visitors planning a trip to this region. Personal Security and Health (see pp288–9) recommends a number of precautions, while Banking and Communications (see pp290–93) answers financial and media queries. There is also information on traveling around the country by both public transportation and car.

WHEN TO GO

The Southwest has the advantage of being a year-round destination. Generally speaking, the climate tends to be dictated by the varying elevations in the region. The high-lying areas of northern Arizona and New Mexico, and southern Utah have cold, snowy winters, making them popular destinations for skiing and other winter sports activities. In contrast, the lower elevations of the southern portions of the states are noted for their warm and sunny winter weather, with temperatures averaging a comfortable 70°F (21°C) in the Phoenix area, which receives thousands of winter visitors. Be aware, however, that the summer months of July and August have average temperatures of 100°F (37°C) in Phoenix, making it one of the hottest cities outside the Middle East. Spring and fall are ideal seasons to visit the southwestern United States – there are fewer visitors, and the milder temperatures make outdoor activities, especially hiking, a popular option. However, some services may be closed at these times; the North Rim of Grand Canyon in northern Arizona is open only between May and October, while the mesa tops of the ancient Pueblo site of Mesa Verde in Colorado may

be inaccessible because of snow as late as April or May. Whatever the time of year, this is a region known for having a great deal of sun, with northern areas averaging well over 200 days of sunshine each year, and the southern parts famous for having more than 300 sunny days.

Wet weather warning sign in southern Utah

ENTRY REQUIREMENTS

Citizens from Australia, New Zealand, South Africa, and the UK, and many other European countries can visit the US without the need for a visa if they are planning a stay of 90 days or less. Instead they are required to have a passport that is valid for at

least six months after they leave the country, and must complete the visa waiver application process online through ESTA, the Electronic System for Travel Authorization (https://esta.cbp.dhs.gov). US embassies have the latest information on which countries are participating in the visa waiver program. As a result of tighter security measures US citizens now require a passport for any border crossings into the US. Canadian citizens must also have a passport when crossing the Canada–US border. Check what documentation is needed before traveling as requirements constantly change.

Visitors from countries who do need a visa must apply to a US consulate or embassy well in advance, and may be asked for evidence of financial solvency, as well as for proof that they are intending to return to their country of origin.

Any visitor wishing to extend their stay beyond the 90-day limit should contact the nearest US Immigration and Naturalization Service (I.N.S.) well in advance of the date stamped on their visa waiver form or visa.

TOURIST INFORMATION

Visitor information centers in the US are noted for the quality of their information, offering everything from local maps to hotel and B&B bookings.

◁ **A road running through Monument Valley**

as guided history walks, ranger-led archaeological tours, and wildlife watching can often be arranged through these offices. In addition, all the national and state parks have their own visitor centers, which provide hiking maps, safety advice, and special licenses for wilderness hiking and camping. Some of these areas are managed by special Public Land Management Agencies, which can also be contacted for information.

Each state has a department of tourism, as do all the major towns and cities. Smaller urban centers and sights of special interest have offices that usually provide maps and guides. Information can also be obtained from the network of chambers of commerce throughout the region. If you are planning your trip in advance contact the visitor center of the state you are visiting, and they will be pleased to send you an information pack. Each department of tourism, as well as many individual sights, also have websites, which offer comprehensive information and online booking services for accommodations. Bear in mind that many of the Southwest's attractions, such as the pueblos of New Mexico and the Navajo Nation in the Four Corners, are located on reservation lands

New Mexico tourist sign

and are managed by different Native American tribal councils. For advice on etiquette, opening times, and admission charges to such sights contact the local **Bureau of Indian Affairs** or the **Navajo Tourism Department**.

Ranger on a guided tour at Keet Seel, Navajo National Monument

OPENING HOURS AND ADMISSION CHARGES

Opening times are seasonal. As a rule, most of the major sights are open later through the summer months. Museums and galleries tend to be open through the weekends and closed for one day during the week. Surprisingly, several attractions are open year-round, including many national parks and nearly everything in Las Vegas. In general those places that do close will be shut for such major public holidays as Thanksgiving, Christmas Day, and New Year's Day (see p35).

Most museums, parks, and other attractions in the region charge an admission fee. The amount can vary enormously, and many sights offer discounts for families, children, and senior citizens. Local newspapers may carry discount coupons, while student cards or an I.D. that proves you are over 65 guarantees reduced-cost entry to most major attractions in the Southwest.

TIME ZONES

There are only two time zones that affect the area covered by this book – Mountain Standard Time, which covers Arizona, New Mexico, Colorado, and Utah, and Pacific Time in Nevada. Mountain Standard Time is one hour later than Pacific Time. If it is noon in Las Vegas then it will be 1pm across the rest of the region. However, daylight-saving time runs from late spring to early fall, and the clocks are set forward by one hour, except in Arizona, which does not have daylight-saving.

To confuse matters even more, it is important to also be aware that the Navajo Nation (across Arizona and part of New Mexico) does use daylight-saving time, but the Hopi Indian Reservation (in the middle of the Navajo Reservation), does not.

Water fountains in the courtyard of the Heard Museum in Phoenix

SENIOR TRAVELERS

Although the age when you are considered a senior in the US is 65, a multitude of discounts are also available to people over the age of 50. Reduced rates of up to 50 percent can apply to meals, accommodations, public transportation, and entrance fees, and are often better than those offered to students.

There are several organizations in the US through which discounts can be obtained. The **National Park Service** offers Golden Age Passports that reduce the cost of tours and services in the parks. **Elderhostel** arranges educational trips to various locations for travelers over the age of 55. These include inexpensive accommodations, activities, lectures, and meals. For around $16 senior citizens can join the **American Association of Retired Persons** (AARP), which also offers good travel discounts.

TRAVELING WITH CHILDREN

The Southwest offers a wide range of attractions, theme parks, and museums suitable for families traveling with young children. However, the age at which a child is eligible for discounts varies greatly from four and under, to under 18 years. Most types of accommodations state

National Park Service sign

whether or not they welcome children, and in many hotels a child can share the parent's room at no extra cost. The more expensive hotels also provide babysitting services and children's clubs offering supervised activities. Restaurants in the Southwest are generally child-friendly, providing reasonably priced children's menus and high chairs *(see p249)*.

Although discounted flight tickets are available for children, these can often work out more expensive than an adult Apex fare *(see p295)*. Reduced fares for children on public transportation tend to vary from city to city, and if you are renting a car it is possible to reserve car seats for children in advance.

TRAVELERS WITH DISABILITIES

The US is famous for having excellent facilities for travelers with physical disabilities. Hotels, restaurants, galleries and museums, and other public buildings are legally required to be wheelchair-accessible and to have suitably designed restrooms. Public transportation also comes under this law, and trains, buses, and taxis are designed to accommodate wheelchairs, while road

Wheelchair access

crossings in busy city centers have introduced dropped curbs to enable easier access. Service animals such as guide dogs for the blind are the only animals allowed on public transportation.

Many national parks and major archaeological sights have paved walkways suitable for wheelchairs. The National Park Service offers free Golden Access passes, which grant free entry to all national parks for one year to those who are disabled or blind. **DisabledTravellers. com** and the **Society for Accessible Travel & Hospitality** are two organizations which offer a whole range of advice on traveling for the disabled, from how to rent specially adapted cars to qualifying for parking permits. They also have excellent websites.

STUDENT TRAVELERS

Students from outside the US need to have an identity card, such as the International Student Identity Card (ISIC), to prove their status. This entitles the holder to substantial discounts on admission prices to museums, galleries, and other popular attractions. If you are planning to stay in hostels you will need to join **Hostelling International/American Youth Hostel (HI/AYH)**.

ETIQUETTE AND TIPPING

The Southwest is noted as one of the US's most relaxed regions. Dress tends to be informal, practical, and dependent on the climate. Jeans may be worn even in upscale restaurants or the theater. In general, people are friendly and polite and, as this is a multicultural country, visitors are expected to be aware of and respect the customs of different peoples.

Some of the region's most famous sights, such as Canyon de Chelly *(see pp168–71)*, and Monument Valley *(see pp164–5)*, are located on reservation land. Visitors are welcome but should be

Youngsters enjoying the child-friendly environment of the Southwest

sensitive as to what may cause offense. It is illegal for alcohol to be brought onto reservations – even a bottle visible in a locked car will land you in trouble. Always ask before photographing anything, especially ceremonial dances or Native homes, and take into consideration that a photography fee may be requested. Do not go wandering off marked trails as this is forbidden. Try to dress respectfully – for example, the Hopi people request that people do not wear shorts.

Apart from Las Vegas, most of the Southwest follows the rest of the US in restricting smoking in public places. The majority of hotels are non-smoking, although a few have smoking rooms, or allow customers to smoke in bar areas. However, many restaurants have now banned smoking altogether.

Service is not included on restaurant checks, and you should leave 15 percent of the total as a tip. Hotel bell-hops expect $1–2 per bag, and chamber maids around $1 for each day of your stay.

ELECTRICITY

Throughout the US the electrical current is 110 volts and 60 Hertz. Visitors from abroad will need an adaptor plug for the two-prong sockets and a voltage converter to operate 220-volt appliances, such as hairdryers and rechargers for cell phones and laptop computers.

CONVERSION CHART

Bear in mind that one US pint (0.5 liter) is smaller than one UK pint (0.6 liter).

US Standard to Metric
1 inch = 2.54 centimeters
1 foot = 30 centimeters
1 mile = 1.6 kilometers
1 ounce = 28 grams
1 pound = 454 grams
1 US quart = 0.947 liter
1 US gallon = 3.8 liters

Metric to US Standard
1 centimeter = 0.4 inch
1 meter = 3 feet 3 inches
1 kilometer = 0.6 miles
1 gram = 0.04 ounce
1 kilogram = 2.2 pounds
1 liter = 1.1 US quarts

Relaxing in the informal surroundings of a Southwestern restaurant

DIRECTORY

STATE OFFICES

Arizona Office of Tourism
1110 W. Washington St., Suite 155, Phoenix, AZ 85007.
Tel (602) 364-3700;
(866) 298-3795.
www.arizonaguide.com

Colorado Tourism Office
1625 Broadway, Denver, CO 80202.
Tel (800) 265-6723.
www.colorado.com

Navajo Tourism Department
PO Box 663, Window Rock, AZ 86515.
Tel (928) 871-6436.
www.discovernavajo.com

New Mexico Department of Tourism
491 Old Santa Fe Trail, Santa Fe, NM 87503.
Tel (505) 827-7400;
(800) 733-6396.
www.newmexico.org

Public Lands Information Center
www.publiclands.org

Utah Travel Council
Council Hall, Capitol Hill, Salt Lake City, UT 84114.
Tel (800) 882-4386.
www.utah.com

SENIOR TRAVELERS

American Association of Retired Persons
201 E. Washington St, Suite 1795, Phoenix, AZ 85004. **Tel** (866) 389-5649. **www.**aarp.org

Elderhostel
11 Avenue de Lafayette, Boston, MA 02111.
Tel 1 (877) 426-8056.
www.elderhostel.org

National Park Service
(see also under individual sights)
Intermountain Area, PO Box 25287, Denver, CO 80225. **www.**nps.gov

DISABLED TRAVELERS

DisabledTravelers. com
www.disabledtravelers. com

Society for Accessible Travel & Hospitality (SATH)
347 Fifth Avenue, Suite 605, New York, NY 10016.
Tel (212) 447-7284.
www.sath.org

STUDENT TRAVELERS

Hostelling International/ American Youth Hostel (HI/AYH)
8401 Colesville Rd., Suite 600, Silver Spring, MD 20910.
Tel (301) 495-1240.
www.hiusa.org

US EMBASSIES

England
24/31 Grosvenor Square, London W1A 1AE.
Tel 020 7499-9000.
www.usembassy.org.uk

Canada
1095 W. Pender St., Vancouver, BC VCE2M6.
Tel (604) 685-4311.

Personal Security and Health

Santa Fe police badge

The Southwest is a relatively safe place to visit as long as some general safety precautions are observed. In contrast to other US cities, the urban centers of the Southwest have lower crime rates, but it is wise to be cautious and to find out which parts of town are unsafe at night. When traveling across remote country roads, take a reliable local map and follow the advice of local rangers and visitor information centers. These sources also offer invaluable information on survival in the wilderness for hikers and on the normal safety procedures that should be followed by anyone engaging in any of the outdoor activities available in the region (*see pp276–81*). It is also advisable to check the local media such as newspapers, television, and radio for current weather and safety conditions.

Pedal-pushing policeman on duty in Santa Fe, New Mexico

PERSONAL SAFETY

Most tourist areas in the Southwest are friendly, unthreatening places. However, there is crime here and it is wise to observe a few basic rules. Never carry large amounts of cash, wear obviously expensive jewelry, or keep your wallet in your back pocket, as these are the main temptations for pickpockets. It is also a good idea to wear pocketbooks (handbags) and cameras over one shoulder with the strap across your body. Keep your passport separate from your cash and travelers' checks. Most hotels have safety deposit boxes or safes in which you should store any valuables.

If you are driving, be sure to lock any valuables in the trunk, and to park only in well-lit parking lots. Similarly, when walking at night it is a good idea to stay where there are other people and to be aware of which areas are most likely to be unsafe.

LOST PROPERTY

It is unlikely that small items of lost or stolen property will be retrieved, but it is necessary to report all such incidents to the police in order to make an insurance claim. Telephone the **Police Non-Emergency Line** to report the loss or theft, and they will issue you with a police report so that you can make a claim with your insurance company.

If a credit card is missing, call the credit company's toll-free number immediately. Lost or stolen travelers' checks should also be reported to the issuer. If you have kept a record of the checks' numbers, replacing them should be a painless experience, and new ones are usually issued within 24 hours.

If you lose your passport, contact the nearest embassy or consulate. They will be able to issue a temporary replacement as visitors do not generally need a new full passport if they plan to return directly to their home country. However, if you are traveling on to another destination, you will need a full passport. It is also useful to hold photocopies of your driver's license and birth certificate, as well as notarized passport photographs if you are considering an extended visit or need additional identification.

TRAVEL INSURANCE

The United States has excellent medical services, but they are very expensive. All visitors to the US are strongly advised to make sure they have comprehensive medical and dental coverage for the duration of their stay.

MEDICAL TREATMENT

For serious emergencies requiring assistance from the medical, police, or fire services call 911. The national organization, **Traveler's Aid Society**, may offer help in a variety of emergencies.

City hospitals with emergency rooms can be found in the Blue Pages of the telephone directory, but they are often overcrowded, particularly in larger cities. Private hospitals offer more personal treatment and are listed in the Yellow Pages of the telephone book. You may be required to provide evidence of your ability to pay before a doctor will agree to treat you, hence the importance of adequate medical insurance.

Hotels will usually call a doctor or recommend a local dentist, and nonprescription painkillers and other medicines can be obtained from drugstores, many of which are open 24 hours. Prescription drugs can be dispensed only from a pharmacy. If you

Police car

Paramedics vehicle

Fire engine

EMERGENCY SERVICES

All emergencies
Tel 911 and alert police, fire, or medical services.

Police Non-Emergency Line
Las Vegas
Tel (702) 795-3111.
Phoenix
Tel (602) 262-6151.
Santa Fe
Tel (505) 428-3710.

Traveler's Aid Society
Las Vegas
Tel (702) 369-4357.
Phoenix
Tel (602) 244-1346.
Tucson
Tel (520) 884-5244.

CONSULATES

The consulates closest to the Southwest are found in California.

Australian Consulate
Century Plaza Tower, 31st Floor,
2029 Century Park East,
Los Angeles, CA 90067.
Tel (310) 229-2327.

British Consulate
11766 Wilshire Blvd., Suite 1200,
Los Angeles, CA 90025.
Tel (310) 481-0031.

Canadian Consulate
550 South Hope St., 9th Floor,
Los Angeles, CA 90071-2627.
Tel (213) 346-2700.

New Zealand Consulate
2425 Olympic Blvd., Suite 6006,
Santa Monica, CA 90404.
Tel (310) 566-6555.

are already taking prescribed medication, be sure to carry extra supplies for your trip.

No specific vaccinations are required before entering the US. However, it is always a good idea to have a tetanus booster before setting out, particularly if you are planning to engage in adventurous outdoor activities.

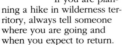

Pharmacy sign

OUTDOOR HAZARDS

The weather in the Southwest can present visitors with a variety of dangerous situations, especially in Southern Utah's canyon country and parts of southern Arizona, where sudden

Park Ranger at the Petrified Forest National Park, Arizona

summer storms can cause flash floods. Visitors may obtain the latest weather information from the ranger stations in the national parks, as well as by listening to the reports on local radio and television channels.

If you are planning a hike in wilderness territory, always tell someone where you are going and when you expect to return.

The dry heat of the region's summers can often be underestimated by visitors, and hikers especially are advised to carry with them at least a gallon (4 liters) of drinking water per person for each day of walking. It is also extremely important for visitors to guard against the risk of forest fires, which can affect the area with devastating results.

At the higher elevations the sun can be surprisingly strong, even on cloudy days. If you are planning on hiking or engaging in other outdoor activities during the summer, an effective sunscreen and a sunhat should always be worn.

While the wilderness of the Southwest is home to certain venomous creatures such as snakes, scorpions, and the Gila monster lizard *(see p21)*, these creatures

Fire Department badge, Sedona

generally avoid humans; it is unlikely you will be bitten if you avoid their habitats. Mostly they hide under rocks and in crevices during the heat of the day. Be careful where you step, and do not turn over rocks. Do not reach up to touch rock ledges with your hands. Insect stings and bites may hurt but are rarely fatal to adults. Always carry a snakebite kit or a first aid kit if you are going into snake or scorpion country. If bitten by a snake or scorpion, seek medical help immediately.

Banking and Currency

Aside from the risk of gambling away all of their money in the Vegas casinos, visitors should encounter no problems with financial transactions in the Southwest. Banks and foreign currency exchanges are plentiful throughout the region, although it is wise to check out opening times. There are a great number of automated teller machines (ATMs) in towns and cities that enable visitors to make cash withdrawals 24 hours a day. Credit cards are a more common form of payment than hard currency, especially at hotels or car rental companies, although they can be used to withdraw cash at ATMs.

The most common international systems are Cirrus and Plus. Ask both your own bank and credit card company which ATM system your card can access, and how much you will be charged for transactions of differing amounts. Withdrawals from ATMs may provide a better foreign currency exchange rate than cash transactions.

Automated teller machine (ATM), open 24 hours a day

BANKS AND FOREIGN CURRENCY EXCHANGES

Bank opening times vary throughout the Southwest, but generally they are open between 9 or 10am and 5 or 6pm. Banks in the larger centers will change foreign currency and traveler's checks, but branches in small towns may not provide this service.

TRAVELER'S CHECKS

Traveler's checks are safer than cash because they can be replaced if lost or stolen. Foreign currency traveler's checks may be cashed at large banks or at major hotels. Airports also have foreign currency exchanges where traveler's checks can be changed, while cities and most large towns have branches of **American Express** and **Thomas Cook**, who will also change them at a slightly higher rate than that offered at a bank. If you buy checks in US dollars they are accepted as cash in many restaurants, hotels, and stores, and you

will not be subject to a transaction fee. A passport is required as identification when using traveler's checks.

CREDIT, CHARGE, AND DEBIT CARDS

Credit and charge cards are practically essential when traveling in the US. The cards are accepted as a guarantee when renting a car *(see p298)*, and are used to book tickets for most forms of entertainment. The most widely used cards are Visa, American Express, Master-Card, and Diner's Club.

All credit, charge, and debit cards can be used to draw money from an ATM. These are usually found at banks, train and bus stations, airports, and convenience stores. Withdrawing cash on a debit card costs less than doing it on a credit or charge card.

American Express charge cards

WIRING MONEY

If you need extra cash, it is possible to have money wired from your bank at home in minutes using an electronic money service. Cash can be wired to major bank branches or to any **Western Union**, **Thomas Cook**, or **American Express Moneygram** outlet.

CURRENCY

American currency, based on the decimal system, has 100 cents to the dollar. Bills are all the same size and color, so check the number before paying. Smaller denominations are preferred in small towns and remote gas stations. Large $500–10,000 bills are no longer printed but are still legal tender, usually found in the hands of collectors. The 25-cent piece is useful for public telephones and Las Vegas slot machines. Always carry cash for tips, public transportation, and taxis.

Bank of Colorado building in the town of Durango

Coins

America's coins (actual size shown) come in 1-dollar, 50-, 25-, 10-, 5-, and 1-cent pieces. The new Golden Dollar, released on January 26, 2000, features the likeness of Sacagawea, an enslaved Shoshone Indian who assisted and guided the Lewis and Clark expedition across the northwest US. On the flip side is a Bald Eagle and 17 stars, indicating the 17 states at the time of this exploration.

**25-cent coin
(a quarter)**

**10-cent coin
(a dime)**

**5-cent coin
(a nickel)**

**1-cent coin
(a penny)**

$1 coin

Bank Notes

The Golden Dollar has not replaced the dollar bill which is still the more widely used form of this unit of currency. Paper bills were first issued in 1862 when coins were in short supply and the Civil War needed financing. The size of the notes, the portraits, and the back designs were decided in 1929; in the 1990s the artwork for most of the bills was re-engraved.

DIRECTORY

American Express

Moneygram US only
Tel (800) 926-9400.
Check replacement
Tel (800) 221-7282.
Stolen credit and charge cards
Tel (800) 992-3404.

Diner's Club

Check replacement and stolen credit cards
Tel (800) 234-6377.

Thomas Cook
(and MasterCard)

Check replacement and stolen credit cards
Tel (800) 307-7309.

VISA

Check replacement
Tel (800) 227-6811.
Stolen credit cards
Tel (800) 336-8472.

Western Union

Wiring money, US
Tel (800) 325-6000.
Wiring money, UK
Tel 0800 833833.

1-dollar bill ($1)

5-dollar bill ($5)

10-dollar bill ($10)

20-dollar bill ($20)

50-dollar bill ($50)

100-dollar bill ($100)

Media and Communications

US mail stamp

The United States has some of the most sophisticated communications systems in the world. Telephone, mail, and Internet services are all readily available, providing fast and efficient services to destinations both local and worldwide. There is a plentiful supply of public pay phones across much of the Southwest region. They can be found in public buildings, cafés, bars, gas stations, hotels, and motels. However, bear in mind that this is a region of remote wildernesses, such as the Four Corners and southern Utah, where mailboxes or pay phones may be hard to find.

AT&T phonecards, available from local stores and vending machines

TELEPHONES

Pay phones are plentiful in the US and are easy to use with the instructions clearly marked on each phone. All numbers within a local area have seven digits.

To dial long-distance, add a one and the three-digit area code in front of the seven-digit number. The cost of a local call within the same area code is usually 35 cents for three minutes. Long-distance calls are to any number outside the area code you are in and cost less when dialed direct and at

off-peak times, generally in the evenings and at weekends. Be aware that if you use your hotel telephone to make calls you may find you are charged at a much higher rate.

International numbers are preceded by 011, then the country code, followed by the city code (dropping the initial 0), and the number. International calls can be made from a pay phone, but you may need a stack of change to dial direct and will be interrupted by the operator for more money when your time runs out. It is easier

to buy a phonecard from one of the major telephone companies such as **AT&T**. These can be obtained from hotels, convenience stores, and vending machines for up to $50 dollars worth of calls. They usually operate by

USING A COIN-OPERATED PHONE

1 Lift the receiver.

3 Press the number.

Coins
Make sure you have the correct coins before you dial.

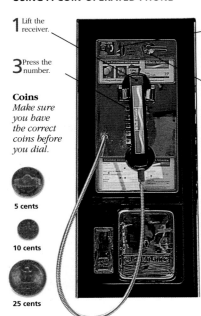

5 cents

10 cents

25 cents

2 Insert the necessary coin or coins. The money drops as soon as you insert it.

4 If you wish to cancel a call before it connects, or if the call does not get through, you can retrieve the coin(s) by pressing the coin release lever.

5 If the call is answered and you talk longer than the allotted three minutes, the operator will interrupt and ask you to deposit more coins. Pay phones do not give change.

USEFUL DIALING CODES

- To make a direct-dial call outside the local area code, but within the US and Canada, dial **1** then the area code: Utah **435** (**801** for the Salt Lake City area); Las Vegas **702**; New Mexico (**505** for Albuquerque & Santa Fe area, **575** for rest of state); Arizona (**520** in the south, **928** in the north, **602**, **623** or **480** for the Phoenix area); Colorado **970**.
- For international direct-dial calls, dial **011** and the appropriate country code. Then dial the area code, omitting the first 0, and the local number.
- To make an international call via the operator, dial **01** and then follow the same procedure above.
- For international operator assistance, dial **01**.
- For local operator assistance, dial **0**.
- For international directory inquiries, dial **00**.
- For local directory inquiries, dial **411**.
- For emergency police, fire, or ambulance services, dial **911**.
- **800**, **877**, and **888** area codes indicate a toll-free number.

giving you a series of code numbers to punch into the phone, which accesses your account and tells you how much call time you have left before you dial. There are clear instructions on how to use them on each card. If you have any difficulty getting through, call the operator and request to be connected as a collect call (in which case the recipient will be liable for the cost of the call).

Toll-free calls have 1-800, 877, or 888 numbers, and are widely-used in the US, offering free calls to a range of businesses and services such as hotels and car rental companies. If you call a toll-free number from outside the US, you will hear a message explaining how you will actually be charged for the call, at the usual toll rate.

US mailbox

CELL PHONES, INTERNET, AND FAX SERVICES

It is possible to rent or purchase a cheap cell (mobile) phone while on vacation, or to have your own phone tuned into local networks. Many hotels provide Wi-Fi and modem outlets in rooms, and there are Internet cafés in cities and larger towns. Shopping malls, university hangouts, and libraries are perhaps the easiest and least expensive place to access the Internet. Faxes can often be sent from the larger hotels, as well as from post offices and copy centers. Charges are based on the time of day, destination, and the number of pages.

MAIL SERVICES

Within the US all mail is first class and generally takes between one and five days to arrive. The correct zip (postal) code usually ensures a swifter delivery.

International mail sent by air can take between five and ten days to arrive, but parcels that are sent at the surface parcel rate may take as long as four to six weeks. There are two special parcel services

run by the federal mail: Priority Mail promises faster delivery than normal first class mail, while the more expensive Express Mail guarantees next day delivery within the US and up to 72 hours delivery for international packages.

Several private international delivery services offer swift, next-day delivery for overseas mail, the best known being **Federal Express**, **UPS**, and **DHL**. All the major cities have a main post office as well as several local offices. In addition, there are post offices in airports, grocery stores, and drugstores. If you have the correct value of postage stamps, both letters and parcels can be mailed in any one of the many mail boxes dotted around every town. These are generally dark blue and have the collection times posted on them. It is also possible to buy postage stamps from convenience stores, vending machines, and in hotels.

NEWSPAPERS, TELEVISION, AND RADIO

The best-selling daily papers country-wide are the *Wall Street Journal, New York Times, USA Today*, and *Los Angeles Times*, which cover the country as a whole. However, there is a wide selection of local newspapers available at even the smallest town in the region, and these are invaluable for local information. Visitor centers also often carry free papers

DIRECTORY

AT&T
Tel (212) 387-5400.

DHL
Tel (800) 225-5345.

Federal Express
Tel (800) 463-3339.

UPS
Tel (800) 742-5877.

detailing local news, events, and weather conditions; they may also contain discount vouchers for local attractions.

Various radio stations offer local news bulletins and weather forecasts. National Public Radio is a good source of commercial-free news and entertainment, and is usually located along the FM band.

The US is famous for having a multitude of TV channels, provided by the four networks – ABC, CBS, FOX, and NBC – as well as many cable channels including magazine programs, sitcoms, cartoons, and special Spanish language channels. Most hotel and motel rooms provide at least the network channels (which all have local services), as well as PBS, the public subscription channel (with no commercials), and Cable News Network (CNN). Other popular cable channels include Home Box Office (HBO), which shows movies and entertainment shows. Most daily newspapers provide network program times, and hotel rooms are often equipped with local television schedules.

Reading the paper over coffee in a southwestern café

TRAVEL INFORMATION

Phoenix, Salt Lake City, and Las Vegas are the main gateways for international visitors arriving in the Southwest by air. There are other major airports at Albuquerque and El Paso, Texas, which serve as entry points to the region. Visitors also arrive by car, long-distance bus or, less frequently, by Amtrak train. However, the US is a nation devoted to driving, and the automobile remains the pre-

United Airlines plane

ferred mode of transport for those touring the Southwest. The highways here are well-maintained, the gas inexpensive, and the cars air-conditioned.

Even in the centers of the major cities here, public transportation tends to be the least-favored option. The only urban train is from Albuquerque to Santa Fe, and there are limited bus networks, offering a minimal service on evenings and weekends.

Las Vegas's McCarran airport with close-up view of the Luxor (see p106)

ARRIVING BY AIR

Unlike many other American destinations, there are few nonstop flights into the Southwest from outside the US. Most visitors will have to connect via one of the country's major hubs such as Los Angeles, San Francisco, Chicago, or Dallas airports. Travelers from Pacific countries generally change at Honolulu, Hawaii. An exception to this is Las Vegas, which has more direct international flights arriving in the city each year, including a

service from London on **Virgin Atlantic** and several flights from Japan and Southeast Asia. Those carriers that fly directly to the Southwest tend to arrive at either Phoenix or Salt Lake City. The few major international airlines that do offer direct flights into the Southwest region include **British Airways**, **Air Canada**, and **Aero Mexico**.

Each state in the Southwest has a major airport as well as some smaller ones, and a

SkyWest Airlines logo

range of airlines here offer connecting flights to and from cities and towns across the country *(see directory box)*. The largest airport in the region is Phoenix's Sky Harbor International, which has three terminals and receives the bulk of domestic arrivals. Phoenix is also a center for major American airlines offering both international and domestic routes, including **American Airlines**, **Continental Airlines**, **Delta Airlines**, **Frontier Airlines**, **Mesa Airlines**, **Scenic Airlines**, **Skywest Airlines**, **Southwest Airlines**, **United Airlines**, and **America West**. From Phoenix, America West flies to Tucson, Sedona, and Yuma. Albuquerque Sunport International airport is a base for **Mesa Air**, which runs services to and from Denver, Dallas (via Roswell), Santa Fe, and other towns across New Mexico. Tucson International Airport in southern Arizona flies to Mexico City, but most travelers to and from abroad have to connect at a larger

AIRPORT	*Tel* INFORMATION	DISTANCE TO CITY CENTER	TRAVEL TIME BY ROAD
Phoenix	(602) 273-3300	4 miles (6.4 km)	15 minutes
Las Vegas	(702) 261-5743	2.5 miles (4 km)	10 minutes
Albuquerque	(505) 244-7700	5 miles (8 km)	20 minutes
El Paso	(915) 772-4271	5 miles (8 km)	20 minutes
Tucson	(928) 556-1234	8 miles (12.8 km)	30 minutes

airport. Although there are immigration and customs here, there are no money changing facilities inside the airport. El Paso airport is a base for several southwestern airlines including America West, and provides links with Tucson, Phoenix, and Albuquerque among other destinations.

Mesa Airlines logo

Visitors rarely choose to travel to southern Utah by air, but there is a small airfield near Moab *(see p141)*. In the Four Corners, the largest airport is the Durango-La Plata County Airport serviced by Frontier Airlines, United Express, and US Airways. The nearest airport to Mesa Verde National Park *(see pp180–81)* is the tiny Cortez-Montezuma Airport, served by Frontier Airlines.

Airport official unloading bags from a tourist flight

INTERNATIONAL ARRIVALS

If you are arriving at one of the major Southwestern airports and you are not a US citizen or resident you must present your passport and visa to the immigration officials before claiming your baggage. If you are catching a connecting flight you will have to pick up your baggage at the first point of entry and check it on to your final destination. Completed customs declaration forms are also given to immigration officials on arrival. Adult non-residents are permitted to bring in a limited amount of

duty free goods. These include 0.2 gallons (1 liter) of alcohol, 200 cigarettes, 50 cigars (but not Cuban), and up to $100 worth of gifts. Cash amounts over $10,000 should be declared, but there is no legal limit on the amount of money brought into the US.

The three major airports offer a good range of services, and several Las Vegas hotels will now check you into your room at the airport. Car rental, shuttle bus, and taxi services are plentiful and most terminals offer facilities for the disabled.

AIR FARES

There is an array of fare types and prices available for travel to and around the Southwest. If you are traveling from outside the US, research the market well in advance, as the least expensive tickets are usually booked early, especially for travel during busy seasons, which are between June and September, as well as around the Christmas and Thanksgiving holidays.

Although there are several websites offering bargains on last minute bookings, such as telme.com, or lastminute.com, direct flights to the Southwest are more likely to be booked in advance through an airline or travel agent. Agents are a good source of information on the latest bargains and ticket restrictions. They may also offer special deals to those booking rental cars, accommodations, and domestic flights in addition to their international ticket. Fly-drive deals, where the cost of the ticket includes car rental, are generally also a lower-priced option.

It is usually less expensive to book an APEX (Advanced Purchase Excursion) fare, which must be bought no less than seven days in advance. However, these tickets impose such restrictions as a minimum (usually seven days) and a maximum (between three and six months) length of stay. It can also be difficult to alter

DIRECTORY

AIRLINE CARRIERS (US CONTACT NUMBERS)

Aero Mexico
Tel (800) 237-6639.

Air Canada
Tel (888) 247-2262.

American Airlines
Tel (800) 433-7300.

British Airways
Tel (800) 247-9297.

Continental Airlines
Tel (800) 525-0280.

Delta Airlines
Tel (800) 221-1212.

Frontier Airlines
Tel (800) 432-1359.

Mesa Airlines
Tel (888) 435-9462 option 4.

Redtail Aviation
Tel (435) 259-7421.

Scenic Airlines
Tel (702) 638-3200.

Skywest Airlines
Tel (435) 634-3000.

Southwest Airlines
Tel (800) 435-9792.

United Airlines
Tel (800) 241-6522.

US Airways/America West
Tel (800) 428-4322.

Virgin Atlantic
Tel (800) 862-8621.

dates of flights after purchase, and you should consider insuring yourself against delays or cancellations.

BAGGAGE RESTRICTIONS

International and domestic passengers are allowed two bags each with an average weight of 50 lb (23 kg), plus one piece of hand luggage. On smaller domestic or sight-seeing flights on light aircraft only one piece of hand luggage is accepted. Size restrictions also apply on some airlines so check before you travel.

Traveling By Train And Bus

Train and bus travel in the Southwest can be slower than the more popular car and plane travel, but it can also be an enjoyable means of exploring the region. Long-distance buses are the least expensive way to travel here, and they also offer the widest choice of destinations. Within the major cities, public transportation is by local bus only. Although these buses tend to focus on daytime services for local commuters, they are also useful to visitors since most routes include centrally placed attractions. Booking a tour can often be the best way of seeing both major city sights and some of the more remote scenery of the Southwest, if you are not driving yourself. Taxis are also an efficient means of traveling around cities.

Amtrak booking desk for train tickets in the Southwest

TRAVELING BY TRAIN

The sad decline of railroad travel in the US has left only a few lines, run by **Amtrak**, which cross the Southwest traveling east and west across the country. Visitors can no longer make the epic, nonstop journey from New York in the east to Los Angeles in the west, but the evocatively named *Southwest Chief* runs daily between Chicago and Los Angeles, stopping at the village of Lamy, near Santa Fe, and at Albuquerque, before heading west, via Navajo and Hopi country at Winslow and Gallup, to Flagstaff. From Flagstaff, Amtrak has a connecting bus service to Grand Canyon, and a bus from Lamy takes passengers into Santa Fe. Two other Amtrak services cross the area covered in this book. The *California Zephyr* begins in Chicago and follows a more northerly route to San Francisco, stopping at Green

River in southern Utah, which lies 40 miles (64 km) northwest of Moab and the attractions of Arches and Canyonlands national parks. The *Sunset Limited* service travels from Miami through Texas and along the southern sections of New Mexico and Arizona. Southwest stops on this service include El Paso, Tucson, (which has a connecting bus service to Phoenix), and Yuma.

All three trains are Amtrak Superliners, which means they have two-tier cars offering a choice of accommodations from luxurious cabins with bathrooms to sleeping recliner chairs. The trains also possess full-length domed windows on the upper level for viewing the spectacular scenery, as well as lounge, restaurant, and snack cars.

SPECIALTY TRIPS

There are three railroad trips on historic rail stock that offer visitors the chance to enjoy some of the region's most delightful scenery. The **Cumbres and Toltec Scenic Railroad**, runs between Chama, New Mexico *(see p203)* and Antonito, Colorado through 64 miles (103 km) of peaks, tunnels, and gorges on a narrow gauge steam locomotive during the summer months. Colorado's **Durango & Silverton Narrow Gauge Railroad** *(see p179)* travels through the foothills of the Rockies past rugged mining country, often including abandoned machinery and wooden shacks, while the **Grand Canyon Railway** offers both diesel and steam rail trips from Williams *(see p70)* to Grand Canyon. The trip takes a little over two hours and offers packages including meals and overnight accommodations at the canyon and features Western entertainments – including a posse of bad guys staging an attack on the train. For rail enthusiasts there is also the

Durango & Silverton Narrow Gauge Railroad train

Santa Fe Southern Railway, which offers a 36-mile (58-km) round trip excursion on a freight train between Santa Fe and the village of Lamy. There are restored vintage cars and special sunset trips with dinner included.

Greyhound bus crossing south-western desert landscape

LONG-DISTANCE BUSES

The major bus company in the US is **Greyhound**. Along with a few affiliated companies, it links all the major and many of the smaller towns and cities across the Southwest region. Greyhound buses also provide essential links with the major airports and Amtrak services. The Amtrak Thruway is a bus service connecting train stops with the major cities. For example, a bus service takes passengers from the *Southwest Chief* train at Flagstaff on to Phoenix.

Some of the most useful bus links operate out of airports. From Albuquerque airport Greyhound provides routes to Durango, Carlsbad, Farming-ton, and Roswell. From Phoe-nix's Sky Harbor airport there are 27 different daily routes throughout Arizona, as well as eight daily trips direct to its second city, Tucson.

Greyhound and a number of other specialist companies also offer package tours, which can provide visitors with a more leisurely way of sightseeing in the area without the need to drive long distances. Everything from national parks such as Grand Canyon to archaeological attractions such as Chaco Canyon can be seen as part of a comfortable tour on luxury, air-conditioned

buses, and the package also includes meals and accommo-dations. **Gray Line Albuquerque** offer daily tours of Acoma Pueblo, Santa Fe, and Albu-querque. Check local papers or the Yellow Pages telephone directory for listings of other bus and coach companies that provide similar services.

TICKETS AND BOOKINGS

In general, both Amtrak and Greyhound tickets should be booked in advance. Not only does this usually mean less expensive fares but you will also be guaranteed a seat. Through Greyhound you can also get Ameripasses, which are discounted tickets valid for varying lengths of time from 7 to 60 days. Discounts are available for children under 12, students, seniors, military families, and veterans.

Reservations are essential on long-distance Amtrak Super-liner services operating in the Southwest, and can be made up to 11 months in advance of the trip. Lower fares are available during off-peak times, between January and mid-May and from mid-September through mid-December.

PUBLIC TRANSPORTATION IN CITIES

With the exceptions of Santa Fe and Flagstaff, which are best explored on foot, the major cities of the Southwest, such as Phoenix and Albuquerque, cover large areas and are increasingly plagued by traffic problems. In these places you might want to consider using some form of public transportation. Albuquerque's metropolitan bus system, **Sun Tran**, covers most parts of the city, including the airport, Old Town, and University District *(see pp210–15)*. New Mexico's

Valley Metro bus in Phoenix

Rail Runner Express connects Albuquerque's Sunport International Airport and Santa Fe. Phoenix and Scottsdale *(see pp76–81)* are covered by the **Valley Metro** bus system, as well as by

Ollie the Trolley, a bus service that runs between Scottsdale's resorts and its many shopping districts. Downtown Phoenix also has the convenient and free **Downtown Dash**, which travels between the State Capitol, Arizona Center, and the Civic Plaza from Monday to Friday.

Traveling By Car and Four-Wheel Drive

Gas pump

When the movie characters Thelma and Louise won a kind of freedom on the open roads of the Southwest, they promoted the pleasures of driving in this visually spectacular region. However, for both residents and visitors, driving is a necessary part of life in the US, particularly in the Southwest, and a car is often the only means of reaching remote country areas. Tours of such picturesque regions as central Arizona *(see p71)*, the Enchanted Circle *(see p207)* in New Mexico, or the San Juan Skyway in Colorado *(see p178)* are best made by car. This is possible because the entire region is served by a network of well-maintained roads, from multilane highways to winding, scenic routes.

Spectacular mountain scenery along the San Juan Highway

RENTING A CAR

Visitors from abroad must have a full driver's license that has been issued for at least a year before the date of travel. International Driving Licenses are not necessary, but they can be helpful if your license is in a script other than Roman. Although it is legal to rent a car to those over the age of 21, some rental companies charge extra to those under 25. It is also essential to have a credit card to pay the rental deposit, as few companies are willing to accept a cash deposit.

There are rental car companies all over the Southwest. Most of the major businesses, such as **Alamo**, **Avis**, and **Hertz**, and some of the budget dealers, such as **Dollar Rent-A-Car**, and **Thrifty Auto**, have outlets at airports and in towns and cities across the region. However, if you are planning to arrive at one of the major hubs such as Las Vegas or Phoenix, the least expensive option is to arrange a fly-drive deal. If you depart from a different airport than the one you arrived at you may be charged a drop-off fee.

Hertz car-rental logo

There is a central computerized booking system for most of the car companies, so use the toll-free number to find the best rates. Bargains can also be had by booking in advance and for travel during off season. Rates vary from state to state, and there may be deals for business travelers, frequent flyers, or members of the **American Automobile Association** (AAA or Triple A.) Currently, discounts are also offered by booking on the Internet. However, the cheapest rates do not always mean the best deal. Check that the price includes unlimited mileage and basic liability insurance, which is a legal requirement and covers any damage to another car. There is also a rental tax of 10 percent. Collision damage waiver saves you from being charged for any visible defects on the car. Return the car with a full tank of gas, and leave plenty of time to complete any formalities.

If you are traveling in summer air conditioning is a necessity. Most rental cars have automatic transmission, although some companies offer a stick shift. Child seats or cars for disabled drivers must be arranged in advance.

RULES OF THE ROAD

The major highways in the US are known popularly as either Freeways or Interstates. Highway speed limits are set by each state. In the Southwest the speed limit on the major highways varies between 55 mph (90 km/h) and 75 mph (120 km/h). The Highway Patrol imposes these rules rigorously, and anyone caught speeding will be fined.

Speed limit (in mph)

Rest area indicated off an Interstate

Wildlife warning

Stop at intersection

Traffic flows in a single direction

Traffic signs
A range of different traffic signs offer warnings and instructions to drivers and should be adhered to.

Gas service station on the legendary Route 66 *(see pp50–51)*

(see pp50–51)

DIRECTORY

CAR RENTAL COMPANIES

Alamo
Tel (800) 354-2322.
www.alamo.com

Avis
Tel (800) 331-1212.
www.avis.com

Budget
Tel (800) 527-0700.
www.budget.com

Dollar Rent-A-Car
Tel (800) 800-4000.
www.dollar.com

Hertz
Tel (800) 654-3131.
www.hertz.com

Thrifty Auto Rental
Tel (800) 847-4389.
www.thrifty.com

USEFUL ORGANIZATIONS

American Automobile Association
742 E. Glendale Ave. #182,
Phoenix 85027.
Tel (602) 285-6241.
www.aaaaz.com

In cities and in small towns especially, watch for signs indicating the speed limit as it can vary from 45 mph (75 km/h) to as little as 15 mph (35 km/h) in school zones. (Note that it is illegal to pass a stationary school bus.) Heed road signs, especially in remote areas where they may issue warnings about local hazards. Heavy penalties are exacted from those who drink and drive, and the alcohol limit is low.

Back Country Byway sign

Get information on US traffic rules from your rental company or the AAA. Some rules may seem strange to foreigners. For example, you can turn right on a red light if there is no oncoming traffic, and the first vehicle to reach a Stop sign junction has the right of way. Americans also drive on the right. The AAA provides maps and may offer help to those affiliated with foreign motoring clubs.

GAS AND SERVICE STATIONS

Despite there being a gasoline tax, gas is cheap in the US, although prices do vary, with service stations in remote areas being more expensive. It is sold by the gallon, rather than the liter as in Europe. Service stations may have a pump attendant or be self-service, in which case it is usual to pay before filling up. If you are planning a long trip, be aware that gas stations can be less common than many visitors expect, so fill your tank before driving across remote areas.

BACKCOUNTRY DRIVING

For any travel in remote parts of the Southwest such as southern Utah's canyon country or the desert regions of Arizona and New Mexico, it is very important to check your route to see if a 4WD vehicle is required. Although some backcountry areas now have roads able to carry conventional cars, a 4WD is essential in some wild and remote areas. Grand Staircase-Escalante National Monument *(see p148)*, for example, intends to maintain its environment by prohibiting further road building. Motoring organizations and tourist centers can provide information to assess your trip properly.

Unimproved road sign in Utah's Kodachrome Basin *(see p148)*

There are basic safety points to be observed on any trip of this kind. Plan your route and carry up-to-date maps. When traveling between remote destinations, inform the police or park wardens of your departure and expected arrival times. Check road conditions before you start, and be aware of seasonal dangers such as flash floods in Utah's canyonlands. Carry plenty of food and water, and a cell (mobile) phone as an added precaution. If you run out of gas or break down, stay with your vehicle since it offers protection from the elements. If you fail to arrive at the expected time, a search party will look for you.

Native flora and fauna must not be removed or damaged. Do not drive off-road, unless in a specially designated area and especially not on reservation land. If driving an RV, you must stop overnight in designated campgrounds.

General Index

Acknowledgments

Dorling Kindersley would like to thank the following people whose contributions and assistance have made the preparation of this book possible.

Main Contributors

Donna Dailey is a writer and photographer who has traveled extensively throughout the Southwest and the Rockies. She has written guidebooks to Denver, Los Angeles, the American West, Kenya, Scotland, and Greece.

Paul Franklin is a travel writer and photographer specializing in the United States and Canada. He is the author of several guide books and magazine articles, and is based in Washington.

Michelle de Larrabeiti is a writer and editor who has traveled widely in the United States, Europe, and Asia. Based in London, she has worked on several Dorling Kindersley travel guides.

Philip Lee is a veteran travel writer and is the author of numerous articles and travel books about countries throughout the world. He has traveled widely, particularly in the United States, Canada, and Europe.

Additional Contributor
Randa Bishop.

For Dorling Kindersley
Senior Revisions Editor Esther Labi
Publishing Manager Jane Ewart
Senior Designer Marisa Renzullo
Director of Publishing Gillian Allan
Revisions Editor Sherry Collins
Production Marie Ingledew
Map Co-ordinators Casper Morris, Dave Pugh

Design and Editorial Assistance
Tessa Bindloss, Mariana Evmolpidou, Sophie Jonathan, Laura Jones, Nancy Mikula, Sonal Modha, Catherine Palmi, Marianne Petrou, Pete Quinlan, Rada Radojicic, Zoë Ross, Sands Publishing Solutions, Brett Steel, Rachel Symons, Ros Walford.

Additional Picture Research
Rachel Barber, Rhiannon Furbear

Additional Photography
Steve Gorton, Dave King, Andrew McKinney, Neil Mersh, Ian O'Leary, Tim Ridley, Clive Streeter.

Cartography
Ben Bowles, Rob Clynes, Sam Johnston, James Macdonald (Colourmap Scanning Ltd).

Fact Checking
Eileen Bailey, Alan Chan, Jessica Hughes, Lynn Kidder, Marshall Trimble, Barney Vinson

Proof Reader
Sam Merrell

Indexer
Helen Peters

Special Assistance
Many thanks for the invaluable help of the following individuals: Margaret Archuleta, Heard Museum; Myram Borders, Las Vegas CVA; Jennifer Franklin; Phoenix CVB; Louann C. Jordan, El Rancho de las Golondrinas; Ken Kraus, Utah Travel Council; Joyce Leonsanders, Albuquerque CVB; Steve Lewis, Santa Fe CVB; Jean McKnight, Tucson CVB; Rekha Parthasarathy, Arizona Office of Tourism; Pat Reck, Indian Pueblo Cultural Center; Gary Romero, New Mexico Department of Tourism; Theresa Valles Jepson, Flagstaff CVB; Charles B. Wahler, Grand Canyon National Park; and all the national park staff in the region.

Photography Permissions
Dorling Kindersley would like to thank all the cathedrals, churches, museums, hotels, restaurants, shops, galleries, national and state parks, and other sights for their assistance and kind permission to photograph at their establishments.

Placement Key - t=top; tl=top left; tlc=top left center; tc=top center; trc=top right center; tr=top right; cla=center left above; ca=center above; cra=center right above; cl=center left; c=center; cr=center right; clb=center left below; cb=center below; crb=center right below; bl=bottom left; b=bottom; bc=bottom center; bcl=bottom center left; br=bottom right; d=detail.

Works of art and images have been produced with the permission of the following copyright holders: Albuquerque Museum of Art and History Museum Purchase, 1993 General Obligation Bond Estella Loretto *Earth Mother, Offerings for a Good Life (No wa Mu Stio)*, 1994 212tl; Capitol Art Foundation, Santa Fe, New Mexico, Capitol Art Collection Holly Hughes *Buffalo* 1992 mixed media sculpture 74" x 50" x 25" 199c; courtesy of Kit Carson Historic Museum 15t, 28c/bl, 204t/cl/cr, 206t; courtesy of the Frank Lloyd Wright Foundation 23b, 81b; Museum of Indian Arts and Cultures/Laboratory of Anthropology, Museum of New Mexico, 44857/12 Ceramic Figurine, Cochiti Pueblo ca. 1885 197tr; University of Arizona Fine Arts Oasis Barbara Grygutis *Front Row Center* 84t.

The publishers would like to thank the following individuals, companies, and picture libraries for their kind permission to reproduce their photographs:

AFP: Spaceimaging.com 13t; ALAMY IMAGES: Danita Delimont/Walter Bibikow 251tl, 270cb; Patrick Eden 105tl; Alan Hanson 270cr; Art Kowalsky 10tbc; pictures-byrob/fc1 250cl; Rollie Rodriguez 10cra; RogerPix 10tc; ARIZONA OFFICE OF TOURISM: Chris Coe 50tl; ARIZONA STATE LIBRARY: Archive+Public Records, Archive Division, Phoenix no.99–0281 36; ARIZONA STATE PARKS: K L Day 93t; ASSOCIATED PRESS: 35b, 96b, Roy Dabner 274t; Louisa Gauerke 51tl; Mickey Krakowski 33b; Julia Malakie 45c; Lennox McLendon 17b; Douglas C. Pizac 31t; Susan Sterner 33t; AURA/NOAO/ NATIONAL SCIENCE FOUNDATION: 91b.

BRIDGEMAN ART LIBRARY: Christie's London Walter Ufer (1876–1936) *The Southwest* 8–9; Private Collection/Index Frederic Remington (1861–1909) *The Conversation or Dubious Company* 1902 54b; Museum of Fine Arts Houston, Texas, USA, Hogg Brothers Collection, Gift of Miss Ima Hogg, Frederic Remington (1861–1909) *Aiding a Comrade* c.1890 54–5; University of Michigan, Museum of Art, USA Charles Ferdinand Wimar (1829–63) *The Attack on the Emigrant Train* 1856 42–3. CAESARS ENTERTAINMENT: 101tr, 103br; CIRQUE

DU SOLEIL: photo Véronique Vial costumes Dominique Lemieux 126t; CORBIS: 25t, 38c, 41c, 43tl, 43b, 45t, 95, 97cbr, 136t, 203tr, 229, James L. Amos 172t; Tom Bean 2–3, 11br, 153b, 161c, 293b; Patrick Bennett 295b; Bettmann 39c/b, 41t, 42c, 42b, 43tr, 44c, 54cb, 96cl, 97t, 103bl, 136b, 171b, 187tr, 225tl, 227b; D. Boone 95–6; Jan Butchofsky-Houser 26c; W. Cody 1; Richard A. Cooke 38t; Raymond Gehman 153t; Aaron Horowitz 219t; H. H. HneyLiz 215br; Hymans 161t; Dewitt Jones 160t; Wolfgang Kaehler 206b; Catherine Karnow 104br; Danny Lehman 189br; Buddy Mays 287; Joe McDonald 87t; David Muench 20cr, 153cb, 160–1; Richard T Nowitz 294c; Pat O'Hara 52bl; Progressive Image/Bob Rowan 26t; Charles E Rotkin 97cla; Phil Schermeister 32b; Baldwin H Ward + Kathyrn C. Ward 186–7; Patrick Ward 137br; Nevada Wier 271tr; Adam Woolfitt 274c.

DIANA DICKER: 27c, 160b; © Mrs. Anna Marie Houser/The Allan Houser Foundation 29t.

EFX: 126b; MARY EVANS PICTURE LIBRARY: 42t, 157.
PAUL FRANKLIN: 63tr.
GETTY IMAGES: Photographer's Choice/Gavin Hellier 11clb; Harald Sund 11tc; GOULDING LODGE: 165b; GRAND CANYON CAVERNS: 50br; GRAND CANYON RAILWAY: 60bc; GRANGER COLLECTION, NEW YORK: 133; RONALD GRANT ARCHIVE: GREENSPUN MEDIA GROUP: 126c; MGM 31br; Paramount Pictures 31cr; Universal Pictures 30br; courtesy GREYHOUND LINES, INC: 297t.

ROBERT HARDING PICTURE LIBRARY: Geoff Renner 134c; Nerda Westwater 33c, 189t; Adam Woolfitt 190; HEARD MUSEUM: 78tr, 79b; 79crb; Fred Harvey Collection 79ca; DAVE G HOUSER: 32c, 223t; Ellen Barone 34; Rankin Harvey 35t; HULTON GETTY COLLECTION: 186b.

IMAGE BANK, LONDON: Archive Photos 97b; IMPACT PHOTOS: Jacqui Spector 50bl; JAMES AGENCY/LIBERACE MUSEUM: 109c; JUBILEE: 126tr.

KIRVAN DOAK COMMUNICATIONS: 102cl; KOBAL COLLECTION, LONDON: Hollywood Pictures/ Cinergi 31clb; MGM Cinerama 30ca; MGM/

PATHE 30cb; Paramount Pictures 55b; RKO 31cla; United Artists 30bl.

LAS VEGAS CONVENTION & VISITORS AUTHORITY: Bob Byre 102tr; LAS VEGAS HILTON: 116br; LAS VEGAS VISITORS' NEWS BUREAU: 96cra, Brian Jones 127c; LONELY PLANET IMAGES: John Hay 272br.

MGM GRAND HOTEL: 108c; MGM MIRAGE: 104ca; MUSEUM OF CHURCH HISTORY AND ART, Salt Lake City: American Publishing Co. 137t; © by Intellectual Reserve, Inc CCA Christensen *Handcart Company* 1900 oil on canvas 136–7; MUSEUM OF INTERNATIONAL FOLK ART, A UNIT OF THE MUSEUM OF NEW MEXICO: Charles D. Carroll Bequest, Photo Blair Clark *Nuestra Señora de los Dolores/Our Lady of Sorrows* (A.78.93–1) Arroyo Hondo Carver, New Mexico 1830–50 196b; Girard Foundation Collection, Photo Michel Monteaux *Baptism* by the Aguilar family, Octolan de Morelos, Oaxaca, Mexico C.1960 196tr, *Jaguar Mask* Mexico C.1960. 196tl, *Toy Horse* Bangladesh, Indian.C.1960. 197tl; Neutrogena Collection, Photo Pat Pollard *Yogi (Bridal Sleeping Cover)* Probably Kyushu Island, Western Japan. 19th century. 196c; courtesy of the MUSEUM OF NEW MEXICO: Fray Orci *Portrait of Don Juan Bautista de Anza* 1774 neg. no. 50828 40br(d); MUSEUM OF SPANISH COLONIAL ART: 1997.10 Jar (Olla), micaceous Clay, 1997, by Jacobo de la Serna, Alcade, New Mexico. 188tr.

NASA: 45br, 187c; NHPA: Stephen Dalton 227tl; Rich Kirchner 280b; Stephen Kraseman 21bl; David Middleton 21bcl; Rod Planck 20bl; Andy Rouse 21tl; John Shaw 14, 21cr/br, 90b; courtesy of the NATIONAL PARK SERVICE, CHACO CULTURE NATIONAL HISTORIC PARK: 161b; Dave Six

160cb, 174tl; PETER NEWARK PICTURES: 24c, 25c/b, 37c, 39t, 40t, 43c, 44t/bl, 54ca, 55t, 136c, 137c; NEW MEXICO TOURISM: 32t. GEORGIA O'KEEFFE MUSEUM: Gift of the Burnett Foundation ©ARS, NY and DACS, London. 2006. Georgia O'Keeffe *Jimson Weed* 1932 194c;

PHOTOLIBRARY: JTB Photo 251c; PHOTOSHOT: Art Foxall 70tr; PRIVATE COLLECTION: 9, 24t, 40c, 47, 183, 283.

BRANSON REYNOLDS: 27b, 290b; RIVIERA HOTEL & CASINO: 105crb, 116tl; JOHN RUNNING: 26b, 27t.

SANTA FE OPERA: Robert Reck 275b; SCOTTSDALE CVB: Tom Johnson 272tl; SCIENCE PHOTO LIBRARY: NASA 187tl/b; STONE: Tom Bean 35c; Paul Chesley 162; Stewart Cohen 97clb; Kerrick James 112–3; Steve Lewis 51tr; Jake Rajs 96crb; Randy Wells 280t. TELEGRAPH COLOUR LIBRARY: F.P.G. (C) T.Yamada 182–3; TUMACACORI NATIONAL HISTORIC PARK: Cal Peters 24b. UNIVERSITY OF NEVADA, LAS VEGAS LIBRARY: Courtesy of Helen J. Stewart Collection 96t. WIGWAM RESORT: 276c. YUMA CONVENTION AND VISITORS BUREAU: ©Robert Herko 1999 90t.

Front endpaper: all special photography except ROBERT HARDING PICTURE LIBRARY: Adam Woolfitt br; STONE: Paul Chesley tr.

JACKET
Front - ALAMY IMAGES: Marek Zuk main image; DK IMAGES: Alan Keohane clb.
Back - DK IMAGES: Demetrio Carrasco bl, cla; Alan Keohane tl.
Spine - ALAMY IMAGES: Marek Zuk t; DK IMAGES: Alan Keohane b.